The series Lecture Notes in Computer Science (LNCS), including its subseries Lecture Notes in Artificial Intelligence (LNAI) and Lecture Notes in Bioinformatics (LNBI), has established itself as a medium for the publication of new developments in computer science and information technology research, teaching, and education.

LNCS enjoys close cooperation with the computer science R & D community, the series counts many renowned academics among its volume editors and paper authors, and collaborates with prestigious societies. Its mission is to serve this international community by providing an invaluable service, mainly focused on the publication of conference and workshop proceedings and postproceedings. LNCS commenced publication in 1973.

Frank Pallas · Nicola Leschke ·
Narges Arastouei · Kai Rannenberg
Editors

Privacy Technologies and Policy

14th Annual Privacy Forum, APF 2026
Salzburg, Austria, September 9–10, 2026
Proceedings

Springer

Editors
Frank Pallas
University of Salzburg
Salzburg, Austria

Nicola Leschke
University of Salzburg
Salzburg, Austria

Narges Arastouei
Goethe University Frankfurt
Frankfurt am Main, Germany

Kai Rannenberg
Goethe University Frankfurt
Frankfurt am Main, Germany

ISSN 0302-9743 ISSN 1611-3349 (electronic)
Lecture Notes in Computer Science
ISBN 978-3-032-35898-1 ISBN 978-3-032-35899-8 (eBook)
https://doi.org/10.1007/978-3-032-35899-8

This Springer imprint is published by the registered company Springer Nature Switzerland AG
The registered company address is: Gewerbestrasse 11, 6330 Cham, Switzerland

Preface

The 14th edition of the Annual Privacy Forum (APF 2026) took place in September 2026 in Salzburg, Austria. It was co-organized by the Privacy Engineering and Policy-Aligned Systems group at the University of Salzburg, the Mobile Business & Multilateral Security group at Goethe University Frankfurt, and Plattform Privatheit. The European Union Agency for Cybersecurity (ENISA), the European Data Protection Supervisor (EDPS), the European Cybersecurity Competence Centre (ECCC), the city of Salzburg and the state of Salzburg provided support of various kinds and thereby contributed to making APF a success again.

APF has established itself as a key interdisciplinary event that brings together stakeholders from policymakers, academia, civil society, and industry to explore the evolving interdisciplinary landscape of privacy and data protection. The tradition of enabling and fostering informed dialogue and collaboration was upheld and reinforced in its 14th edition, which was particularly dedicated to the theme "Ten Years of GDPR – Engineering the Future". Under this umbrella, accepted papers revolve around four main themes:

- Privacy in AI
- Users' Perspectives
- Regulation at the Technological Edge
- Privacy Technologies Beyond Anonymization and Security

APF received a total of 58 submitted complete papers (including 10 short papers). In the peer-review process, 10 papers were rejected at the PC chairs level, and the remaining 48 papers were given to the members of the international Program Committee (PC) for single-blind peer-review. Here, each submission received at least three (and most submissions four) single-blind reviews. Based on the quality of contributions, relevance to the Forum themes, fit for an interdisciplinary audience, and academic rigor, 12 papers (including one short paper) were selected (23% acceptance rate for full papers, 10% for short, 21% overall) for presentation at APF and inclusion in this volume.

Our particular gratitude goes to the members of the Program Committee for their critical and constructive evaluations and to the authors for driving the interdisciplinary dialogue forward with their work. Your continuing interest in and outstanding research on the Forum's subjects has always been the main driver for its organization! Additionally, we would like to thank the Universitätsbibliothek Salzburg and the German Plattform Privatheit for making open-access publication possible.

September 2026

Frank Pallas
Nicola Leschke
Narges Arastouei
Kai Rannenberg

Organization

Program Committee Chairs

Frank Pallas	University of Salzburg, Austria
Nicola Leschke	University of Salzburg, Austria
Narges Arastouei	Goethe University Frankfurt, Germany
Kai Rannenberg	Goethe University Frankfurt, Germany

Program Committee

Mahdi Akil	University of Salzburg, Austria
Isabel Barberá	Rhite, The Netherlands
Athena Bourka	ENISA, Greece
Daria Catalui	Allianz, Germany
Giuseppe D'Acquisto	Italian Data Protection Authority, Italy
Jose M. Del Alamo	Universidad Politécnica de Madrid, Spain
Matteo Dell'Amico	University of Genoa, Italy
Vasiliki Diamantopoulou	University of the Aegean, Greece
Prokopios Drogkaris	ENISA, Greece
Catherine Easdon	Dynatrace, Austria
Ana Ferreira	University of Porto, Portugal
Simone Fischer-Hübner	Karlstad University, Sweden
Michael Friedewald	Fraunhofer ISI, Germany
Christian Geminn	Kassel University, Germany
Elias Grünewald	Charité - Universitätsmedizin Berlin, Germany
Nils Gruschka	University of Oslo, Norway
Daniel Guagnin	Nexus Institute, Germany
Patricia Guerra-Balboa	Karlsruhe Institute of Technology, Germany
Simon Hanisch	TU Dresden, Germany
Marit Hansen	ULD Schleswig-Holstein, Germany
Jaap-Henk Hoepman	Karlstad University, Sweden & Radboud University Nijmegen, The Netherlands
Marko Hölbl	University of Maribor, Slovenia
Kristina Irion	University of Amsterdam, The Netherlands
Leonardo Iwaya	Karlstad University, Sweden
Meiko Jensen	Karlstad University, Sweden
Christos Kalloniatis	University of the Aegean, Greece

Irene Kamara	Tilburg University, The Netherlands
Liina Kamm	Cybernetica AS, Estonia
Murat Karaboga	Fraunhofer ISI, Germany
Sokratis Katsikas	Norwegian University of Science & Technology, Norway
Matthias Kettemann	Universität Innsbruck, Austria
Sebastian Krempelmeier	University of Salzburg, Austria
Cedric Lauradoux	Inria, France
Jens Leicht	University of Salzburg, Austria
Konstantinos Limniotis	Hellenic Data Protection Authority, Greece
Sascha Löbner	University of Hamburg, Germany
Teresa Martínez Sánchez	Spanish Data Protection Authority, Spain
Victor Morel	Chalmers University of Technology, Sweden
Claudia Negri-Ribalta	University of Luxembourg, Luxembourg
Maria Owczarek	Polish Data Protection Authority (UODO), Poland
Harshvardhan J. Pandit	Dublin City University, Ireland
Sebastian Pape	Social Engineering Academy GmbH, Germany
Daniela Pöhn	Universität der Bundeswehr München, Germany
Ina Schiering	Ostfalia University of Applied Sciences, Germany
Stefan Schiffner	Bonn-Rhein-Sieg University of Applied Sciences, Germany
Erich Schweighofer	University of Vienna, Austria
Dimitri Van Landuyt	KU Leuven, Belgium
Isabel Wagner	University of Basel, Switzerland

Additional Reviewers

Meem Arafat Manab	Universidad Politécnica de Madrid, Spain
Andy Börner	Technical University of Chemnitz, Germany
Paul Fuchs	Bonn-Rhein-Sieg University of Applied Sciences, Germany
Marius Lombard-Platet	University of Luxembourg, Luxembourg
Narges Mehran	University of Salzburg, Austria
Hanna Schaff	Karlstad University, Sweden
Maria Skwarcan	Polish Data Protection Authority (UODO), Poland

Organizers

Supporters

Funding Acknowledgments

Open access publication supported by the University of Salzburg Publication Fund and by the German Federal Ministry of Research, Technology and Aerospace (BMFTR) under contract number 16KIS1372K (Plattform Privatheit).

With funding from the:

Federal Ministry of Research, Technology and Space

Contents

Privacy in AI

Secure and Explainable Inference with Neural Networks
(Research Paper)

Vanessa Marianne Fiedler[1] and Zoltán Ádám Mann[2](✉)

[1] University of Halle-Wittenberg, Halle, Germany
[2] University of Münster, Münster, Germany
zoltan.mann@gmail.com

Abstract. We consider a service provider that offers inference with a trained neural network as a service. Clients provide an input and obtain the corresponding output of the neural network. To ensure trustworthiness, both privacy and explainability play an important role. Privacy entails that the service provider should learn nothing about the client's input nor the output, while the client should learn nothing about the parameters of the neural network beyond what the output reveals. Explainability entails that the client should be able to obtain besides the inference output also an explanation of that output.

Extensive research has addressed both privacy and explainability in neural network inference. However, studies on privacy and explainability have largely proceeded independently, even though these concepts are interrelated. This paper investigates how privacy and explainability can be guaranteed at the same time. Focusing on the important case of image classification, we develop an approach for combining privacy using multi-party computation with explainability using occlusion analysis. Our approach offers strong privacy guarantees while providing insights into the reasons for the inference output. Our empirical results show that the delivered explanations are of high quality, but computing them privately is time-consuming. We conclude by identifying opportunities for acceleration, to be explored in future work.

Keywords: Privacy-preserving machine learning · Multi-party computation · Explainable artificial intelligence

1 Introduction

Machine learning (ML), particularly deep neural networks, can solve difficult problems in several domains [33]. Training and operating powerful ML models requires significant expertise, compute resources, and large amounts of data. This led to "Machine Learning as a Service" (MLaaS), in which dedicated service providers offer ML services [11]. In this paper, we consider a service provider that offers inference with a trained neural network (NN) as a service. Clients can provide an input and obtain the corresponding output of the NN. E.g., a NN

F. Pallas et al. (Eds.): APF 2026, LNCS 16847, pp. 3–25, 2026.
https://doi.org/10.1007/978-3-032-35899-8_1

provides a diagnosis based on an X-ray image of a patient. A service provider trained the NN with large amounts of sensitive patient data: X-ray images, labeled with the correct diagnosis. The service provider offers inference with this NN as a service. Clients are doctors who use the inference service with X-ray images of new patients to get a proposed diagnosis for them. As the example demonstrates, ML shows great promise in high-stakes domains. However, its adoption is hindered by concerns about trustworthiness [35]. This paper focuses on two aspects of trustworthiness: privacy and explainability.

Privacy: clients require that input and output of the inference remain confidential. As the above example shows, input and output may be sensitive data – e.g., personal data, like X-Ray images or other patient data, that must be protected due to privacy laws – that clients do not want to share with the service provider. Conversely, the service provider wants to protect the trained parameters of the NN which are its intellectual property and the basis of its business model. Simultaneously satisfying the privacy requirements of both the client and the service provider, called the Secure Neural Network Inference (SNNI) problem, is not easy. However, several approaches for solving this problem using cryptographic methods, like secure multi-party computation and homomorphic encryption, were proposed recently [22].

Explainability: clients want to obtain, besides the inference output, also an explanation of why the NN produced that output. In the above example, doctors want to get some hint about the reasons for the NN's diagnosis. Many techniques have been proposed for generating such explanations, under the term of explainable artificial intelligence (XAI) [32]. In many applications, including the above example, inputs to the NN are images. In such cases, it is often useful to highlight which parts of the input image led to the output of the NN. (In the above example, if the diagnosis involves a tumor, it is useful to indicate which part of the tissue is affected.) One class of explanation methods working according to this principle is *occlusion analysis* [27]. Occlusion analysis applies the NN to several perturbed inputs, obtained from the original input by masking different parts of the image. By comparing the NN's output for the original and the masked input, the importance of the masked region for the NN's output can be deduced. Information about the importance of different regions of the image can be summarized in a *heatmap*, serving as an explanation.

Private NN inference and explainable NN inference are important research fields handled separately so far. To our knowledge, our paper is the first to investigate how privacy and explainability of NN inference can be ensured simultaneously. Combining privacy and explainability is not trivial: privacy requires disclosing as little information as possible, while explainability requires providing more insights. We address two research questions:

RQ1: Is it possible to combine SNNI with XAI for private, explainable inference?
RQ2: What are the implications of such a combination on the performance of the NN inference, its privacy, and its explainability?

We answer RQ1 affirmatively by developing a prototype of the first private and explainable NN inference service. Our solution uses multi-party computation (MPC) to satisfy the privacy requirements and occlusion analysis algorithms for explainability. The main challenge is to ensure that the occlusion analysis works in an MPC context, without revealing confidential information. To answer RQ2, we perform an extensive empirical evaluation of our approach. The findings show that the quality of the explanations is just as good with MPC as without it. On the other hand, performing the occlusion analysis using MPC adds significant overhead. Thus, we identify ideas for accelerating private and explainable NN inference, for future research. Our contributions are:

- We are the first to define the problem of private and explainable inference with NNs in a MLaaS context.
- We develop an approach for solving this problem by combining MPC with occlusion analysis. We consider three different algorithms for occlusion analysis with different complexity.
- We implement our approach as a prototype in Python, using the CrypTen SNNI library [18], and open-source our implementation[1].
- We perform controlled experiments to evaluate the performance of our approach regarding execution time and explanation quality.

2 Background and Related Work

2.1 NN Inference

A (feed-forward) NN is a sequence of L layers [30]. Each layer computes a function, transforming its input tensor to its output tensor. For $1 \leq i \leq L-1$, the output of layer i is the input of layer $i+1$. The input of layer 1 is the NN's input. The output of layer L is the NN's output.

A frequent task for NNs is image classification [38]. In this case, the input of the NN is an image. Grayscale images are encoded as two-dimensional tensors (i.e., matrices) of pixel values. For color images, a third dimension captures color channels: e.g., for RGB-encoded images, there are 3 channels corresponding to the red, green, and blue components of pixels' colors. In image classification, the task is to decide which of a set of k classes the image belongs to. The output can be encoded as a vector z of size k. For $1 \leq j \leq k$, z_j is the likelihood assigned by the NN to the input's belonging to class j.

Modern NNs use several types of layers. Some layers perform linear computations. For example, *fully-connected* layers multiply an input vector with a constant matrix to obtain an output vector. *Convolutional* layers compute the dot product of different parts of an input tensor with constant vectors to obtain the components of an output vector [21].

NNs also use different non-linear layers. *Activation* layers apply the same $\mathbb{R} \rightarrow \mathbb{R}$ function to each element of the input tensor to obtain an output tensor

[1] https://github.com/Vanessa160303/SNNI-and-XAI.

of the same size. Examples of activation functions are sigmoid, tanh, and ReLU, with the latter defined as $\mathrm{ReLU}(x) = \max(0, x)$. *Pooling* layers apply an $\mathbb{R}^m \to \mathbb{R}$ function to different parts of the input tensor to obtain elements of the output tensor. An example is max-pooling, in which the maximum of the considered elements of the input tensor is written into the output tensor.

2.2 SNNI

SNNI (see Fig. 1) allows cooperative inference between a server and a client [22]. The server hosts the trained NN, the client provides the input to the NN, and the client should obtain the output. The privacy requirements entail that (i) the server must not learn anything about the input nor the output and (ii) the client must not learn anything about the NN's parameters beyond what the output reveals. Developing an inference approach that satisfies these privacy requirements is not easy and requires advanced cryptographic techniques, like fully homomorphic encryption (FHE) or multi-party computation (MPC).

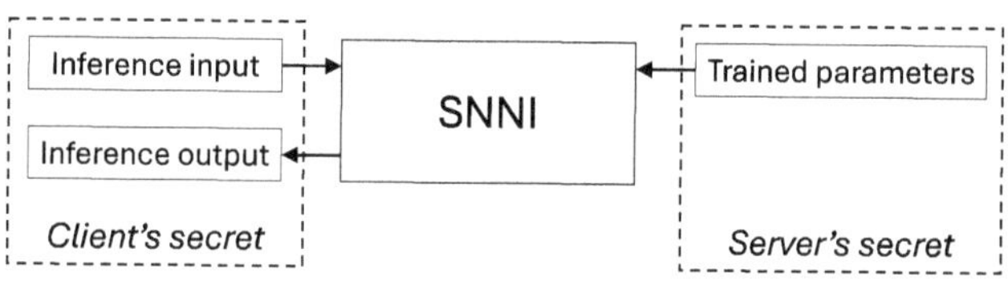

Fig. 1. Secure Neural Network Inference (SNNI).

FHE allows performing additions and multiplications on ciphertexts, without decrypting them [9]. By using additions and multiplications, any polynomial can be computed on encrypted data. Using polynomials, any continuous function – including most functions commonly used in NNs – can be approximated. SNNI can be achieved with FHE as follows: (1) the client encrypts the input and sends the encrypted input to the server, (2) the server computes all functions of the NN, or their polynomial approximations, one after the other, to obtain the encrypted output, (3) the server sends the encrypted output to the client, which decrypts it. This approach works well for small NNs with an architecture optimized for FHE [10]. However, scaling this approach to larger NNs is challenging because FHE leads to significant overhead, especially for nonlinear layers.

In MPC, two parties compute a publicly known function in such a way that each party provides a part of the input, and no party learns anything about the other party's input beyond what the output reveals [44]. Several protocols exist for MPC; some can securely compute any Boolean function [12], but such general-purpose protocols are quite inefficient. An important class of MPC methods is *secret-sharing*, where secret data is split into two parts, with both parties holding one part, in such a way that neither part alone reveals anything about the secret data but the two parts together enable reconstruction of the secret data. With appropriate cryptographic primitives, operations can be performed on secret-shared inputs, producing secret-shared outputs, without leaking secret information. These operations can be combined to calculate arbitrarily complex functions on secret-shared numbers. To reconstruct the final output in plaintext, one party sends its share of the final output to the other party, and the latter combines the two parts to obtain the plaintext output. Under suitable conditions, MPC using secret-sharing guarantees information-theoretic privacy [2].

SNNI is a special case of MPC, in which the client's input is the input to the NN, while the server's input is the set of trained parameters of the NN. Thus, MPC protocols can be used for SNNI, as follows: (1) the client secret-shares the input with the server, while the server secret-shares the NN parameters with the client, (2) client and server engage in a series of protocols to jointly evaluate the operations of each layer of the NN using secret-shared numbers, (3) the server sends its share of the output to the client, which reconstructs the output. Similarly to FHE, the challenge in using MPC is maintaining efficiency. Also general-purpose MPC protocols typically have significant overhead [36].

Accelerating SNNI for large-scale NNs has been the subject of intensive research. Instead of general-purpose FHE or MPC techniques, several papers proposed improved versions of those techniques, specifically fine-tuned for typical NN computations [13,15,17,28,29]. Besides improving the used cryptographic protocols, some papers suggested fine-tuning the NN architecture to accelerate SNNI [1,3]. Thanks to these efforts, SNNI is today applicable to large NNs, and the overhead decreased significantly, but is still considerable.

Our approach is largely orthogonal to the specific SNNI technique used and to any NN architecture optimizations. Our implementation and evaluation uses CrypTen [18], a popular SNNI library. Our approach could also be combined with other SNNI libraries. CrypTen is MPC-based and uses different secret-sharing techniques to handle different NN layer types. The advantage of CrypTen is its ease of use: it is a Python library that mimics the interface of PyTorch, enabling easy integration with common ML pipelines.

2.3 XAI

The complexity of NNs makes it practically impossible for users to understand *why* the NN produced the output it produced. Research in Explainable Artificial Intelligence (XAI) has developed different explanation approaches [32]. Explanations can be global or local [23]. Global explanations explain the workings of the NN in general. Local explanations, our focus of interest, explain individual outputs. Many local explanation methods perform *feature attribution*: they compute an importance score for each input feature, showing which input features contributed most significantly to the output. If the input is an image, features are pixel values, and feature importance scores can be visualized as a heatmap of the same size as the input. The heatmap shows which areas of the input were decisive for producing the output (Fig. 5 shows an example).

We focus on an important category of feature-attribution-based local explanation methods for images: occlusion analysis. In occlusion analysis, various parts of the input image are masked with a neutral (e.g., all-black) rectangle [32]. The NN is applied, besides the original input image, also to the masked images. The difference in NN output between the original and the masked input indicates the importance of the masked region: the higher the difference in NN output, the more important the masked region is [42]. Formally, let a be a region of the input image. Let m_a denote the corresponding mask: m_a has the same size as the input, and m_a is 0 in a and 1 otherwise. The importance of a is computed as $R(a) = \|f(x) - f(x \odot m_a)\|$, where $\odot$ denotes point-wise multiplication. Here, $f(x)$ is the output for the original input x, and $x \odot m_a$ is the masked input, which is 0 in a and the same as x elsewhere. $R(a)$ is the distance between the two output vectors. In the output heatmap, the value $R(a)$ is used for each pixel of a. Advantages of occlusion analysis include simplicity and intuitiveness. Its disadvantage is that it performs several inferences, which can make it slow.

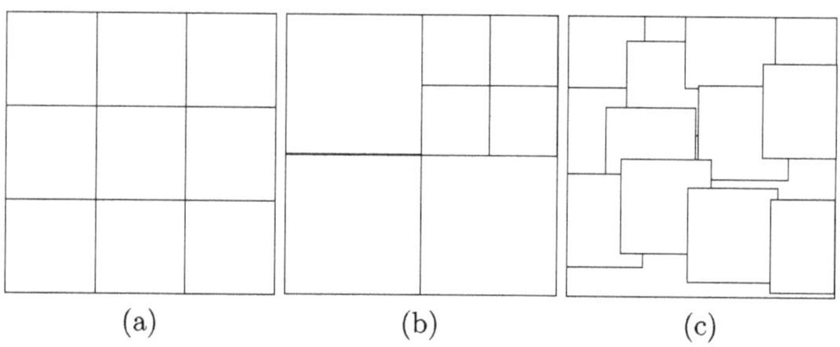

Fig. 2. Example of masked regions in 3 occlusion analysis algorithms: (a) sliding window, (b) hierarchical, (c) Monte Carlo.

We consider three occlusion analysis algorithms, differing in how they determine the areas to be masked (see Fig. 2):

- **Sliding window**. The simplest algorithm, in which masked areas have the same size, form a tiling of the input image, and are processed consecutively.
- **Hierarchical**. Starts with an initial patch size and works initially as the sliding window method. When the algorithm detects an important region – a region a for which $R(a)$ exceeds a given threshold – the patch size is halved and the process is repeated recursively for the given area. Halving stops when reaching a given minimum patch size [27]. The resulting heatmap is detailed in important regions and coarse-grained in less important regions.
- **Monte Carlo**. Masked areas of equal size are randomly chosen [26].

2.4 Combining Privacy and Explainability

Shokri et al. investigated the privacy risk of explanations [34]. Returning, besides the output, also an explanation leaks more information about the NN parameters. This extra information can be used by an attacker for more effective membership inference attacks. Fiosina proposed an XAI method in federated learning [8]. Explanations are provided with feature attribution. To protect sensitive inputs, participants' raw data is not shared with others. However, the approach does not provide any privacy guarantee. Montenegro et al. proposed a case-based explanation method using generative AI [24], trying to minimize privacy loss by incorporating this into the objective function of their model. However, their approach provides no privacy guarantees. Also, it is not clear if the generated images really help explain the NN's decision. Noppel and Wressnegger review attacks on XAI and possible mitigations [25]. They show that explanations increase the attack surface, but no privacy guaranties are formulated.

Unlike these works, we develop an explainable, secure NN inference approach.

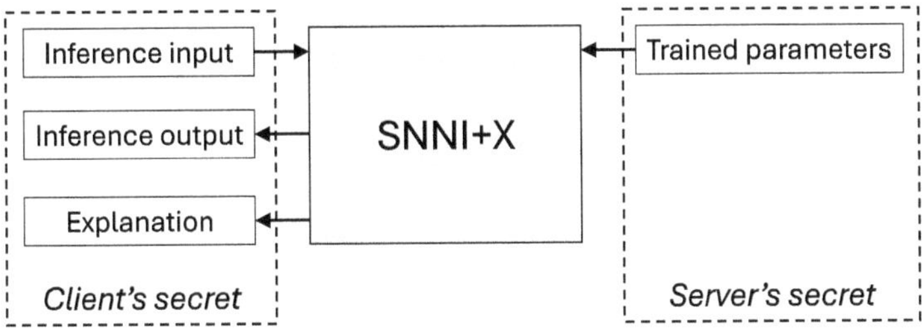

Fig. 3. Inputs and outputs of SNNI+X, Secure NN Inference + Explanation.

3 Privacy-Preserving Occlusion Analysis

3.1 Problem Definition

We aim at developing an approach that (i) supports NN inference in MLaaS, (ii) provides both the inference output and an explanation of it, and (iii) ensures that parties' sensitive data remain secret. We call this SNNI+X: Secure NN Inference + Explanation (see Fig. 3). The client provides the input and obtains the output and the explanation. The server provides the NN parameters. The input, the output, and the explanation remain the client's secret: the server learns nothing about these. The client learns nothing about the NN parameters, beyond what the inference output and the explanation reveal.

Compared to SNNI, SNNI+X leads to potentially higher data leakage about the NN parameters, as the client receives not only the inference output but also the explanation. This additional data leakage is inevitable. Since getting also the explanation is more valuable for the client than only getting the output, the client may be willing to pay a higher fee, which could compensate the server's loss. From the client's point of view, data leakage is zero for SNNI+X just as for SNNI, since in both cases, the server learns nothing about the client's data.

3.2 Naive Solutions

SNNI+X could be solved by regarding it as a 2-party computation problem and applying existing general-purpose MPC techniques like garbled circuits [40]. This approach would be prohibitively inefficient. Even for the simpler SNNI problem, general-purpose MPC techniques proved impractical [28,31]. SNNI+X is more complex, involving an occlusion analysis algorithm and multiple inference runs, making general-purpose MPC techniques inappropriate for SNNI+X.

Another approach could be to implement the control logic of the occlusion analysis algorithm completely in the client and replace every inference with a call to a 2-party SNNI library. This approach is more promising regarding execution time, as it benefits from the efficiency improvements in SNNI technology. However, this approach leads to additional data leakage not allowed by our problem definition. Namely, the client receives the inference output for every masked input. For classification with k classes, the inference output is a vector of size k. The heatmap that the client needs to get according to the problem definition contains a single value for every masked input. Thus, this naive approach leads to k times more data leakage than allowed by the problem definition.

3.3 Challenges

The naive solution attempts indicate the challenges of the SNNI+X problem:

Challenge 1: Efficiency is key and cannot be achieved with general MPC methods. Specific techniques are needed, like the ones developed for SNNI: tailor-made protocols for privately computing NN layers.

Challenge 2: Special care is needed to avoid unnecessary data leakage. While leveraging existing SNNI technology may be a good idea, the SNNI output for masked inputs should not be reconstructed.

Challenge 3: Beyond the above challenges that apply to all occlusion analysis algorithms, the hierarchical algorithm poses an additional challenge. In this algorithm, the control flow – whether additional inferences are performed with halved patches or not – depends on the data. Data-dependent control flow is not present in SNNI and thus needs to be considered additionally.

3.4 Our Approach

To address Challenge 1, we leverage SNNI technology to privately perform inference, both on the original input and on masked inputs. To address Challenge 2, we omit the last step of SNNI, in which the secret-shared output is reconstructed. We stop the SNNI process (for both the original input and the masked inputs) when the output is available in secret-shared form. From secret-shared inference outputs, we calculate importance scores privately. Let z be the inference output for the original input x, and $z^{(a)}$ be the inference output for the masked input

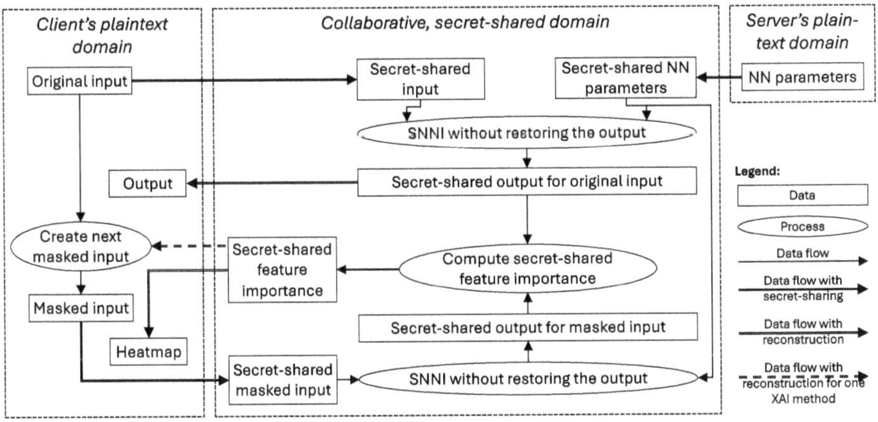

Fig. 4. Data flow diagram of the proposed approach. The upper half shows normal SNNI: the client's input and the server's NN parameters are secret-shared, inference yields secret-shared output, which is reconstructed so that the client gets the output in plaintext. The lower half of the diagram shows the creation of the heatmap: the client creates masked inputs, which are secret-shared with the server and fed into SNNI, and the output is used to compute feature importance scores and fill the heatmap. Outputs are processed in the secret-shared domain, thus minimizing data leakage. The heatmap is created in a loop, which is not shown, since this diagram only shows data flows. For the hierarchical method (unlike the other methods), creating the next masked input uses information from the previous feature importance.

$x^{(a)}$, in which region a is masked. z and $z^{(a)}$ are vectors of size k, where k is the number of classes. We need to calculate $R(a) = \|z - z^{(a)}\|$. We use L^1-norm:

$$R(a) = \sum_{i=1}^{k} \left| z_i - z_i^{(a)} \right| . \tag{1}$$

Here, z_i and $z_i^{(a)}$ are the ith coordinates of z and $z^{(a)}$, respectively, available in secret-shared form. Privately subtracting a secret-shared number from another one and getting the output in secret-shared form is easy: both parties just perform a subtraction on their shares locally. However, privately calculating the absolute value of a secret-shared number is challenging. We use the following observation: for any $s \in \mathbb{R}, |s| = 2 \cdot \mathrm{ReLU}(s) - s$. Thus, the expression for the importance score becomes:

$$R(a) = \sum_{i=1}^{k} \left(2 \cdot \mathrm{ReLU}\left(z_i - z_i^{(a)} \right) + z_i^{(a)} - z_i \right) . \tag{2}$$

This expression is the composition of linear functions and the ReLU function. Since these functions are routinely used in NNs, SNNI libraries contain secure and efficient protocols for them. We leverage those protocols available in the SNNI library to compute the feature attribution scores in a secret-shared manner, without any party learning $z^{(a)}$ in plaintext. Only the $R(a)$ values are reconstructed by the client eventually.

Control flow is orchestrated by the client, performing the occlusion analysis algorithm on plaintext data. Privacy measures are only needed when the server gets involved, i.e., when inference is performed, for which SNNI is used as described above. Having the control flow work locally and on plaintext data helps keep the implementation efficient, contributing to solving Challenge 1. With this approach, Challenge 3 can also be addressed. Data-dependent decisions on when to halve the patch are made by the client, as part of the control flow. This does not cause illegitimate data leak, since the client must obtain feature importance scores in plaintext anyway, thus it can base its decisions on this information.

The resulting approach is shown in Fig. 4. The figure is split into three vertical parts (domains). The left part, the client's plaintext domain, contains data and processes handled by the client locally, in plaintext. This comprises the original input, the corresponding inference output, the process for creating the next masked input (which depends on the occlusion analysis algorithm), the masked inputs, and the resulting heatmap. Similarly, the right part is the server's plaintext domain, comprising the data and processes handled by the server locally in plaintext. This only comprises the trained NN parameters.

The middle part is the collaborative, secret-shared domain. Data in this domain is secret-shared between the two parties, processes in this domain are secure two-party protocols working on secret-shared data. Data flows (represented by arrows) entering this domain entail secret-sharing data, while data flows exiting this domain entail reconstructing plaintext data from secret shares. The upper half of this domain shows SNNI on the original input, yielding secret-shared output, while the lower half shows SNNI on the masked inputs, again yielding secret-shared outputs. In the middle, "Compute secret-shared feature importance" performs the private calculation according to Equation (2).

3.5 Technical Realization

We implemented our approach using the CrypTen SNNI library [18] and additional Python code. We followed the blueprint from Sect. 3.4, with some deviations. First, as CrypTen supports the private calculation of the absolute value, we used Equation (1) instead of (2) to directly – yet privately – compute feature importance scores. Second, technical limitations of CrypTen required moving the preparation of masked images and the compilation of the heatmap from the client's plaintext domain to the collaborative, secret-shared domain.

This is done as follows. Let $I \in \mathbb{R}^{h \times b \times c}$ be the input image. Here, h, b and c are height, width, and number of color channels of the image. Let $M \in \{0,1\}^{h \times b}$ be the mask to apply, having the value 0 where the current patch is and 1 elsewhere. For a matrix X, $[X]$ denotes its secret-shared version. To put the mask on the image, the mask is secret-shared and multiplied with the input pixel by pixel, yielding the secret-shared masked image: $[I_M] = [I] \odot [M]$. Let $H \in \mathbb{R}^{h \times b}$ be the initial, all-zero heatmap. To enable the entry of secret-shared values into the heatmap, $[H]$ is calculated. Let $f(x)$ be the model's prediction for input x.

In our case, x is an image. $f(x) \in \mathbb{R}^k$ is a vector containing the model's output values (e.g. probabilities) for each of the k classes. The difference between the outputs on the original and the masked inputs is calculated using the L_1 norm: it is the sum over all output classes of the absolute differences between the secret-shared predictions for the original and the masked image: $[\text{Diff}] = \sum_{j=1}^{k} |f([I])_j - f([I_M])_j|$. This way, the vector-valued output difference is reduced to a single value per pixel. The values are entered into the heatmap using $[H'] = [H] + [\text{Diff}] \odot (1 - [M])$, whereby the feature attribution score is entered at the pixels of the patch. With these steps, masking, inference, calculation of the distance, and heatmap entry take place in the secret-shared domain. CrypTen provides secure two-party protocols for all used operations (addition, subtraction, multiplication, absolute value). These changes have no impact on the privacy of the approach, but they slightly increase execution time.

Based on these points, our implementation consists of three phases:

1. The **preparation phase** starts with secret-sharing input data and model parameters, and exchanging the appropriate shares between the parties. Secure inference is performed on the original input, yielding secret-shared output.
2. The **occlusion analysis phase** is a loop. Each iteration creates a new masked input according to the specific occlusion analysis algorithm. The masked input is created in a secret-shared way and used as input for secure inference, yielding secret-shared results. The secret-shared importance score is calculated using Equation (1) and written into the secret-shared heatmap.
3. In the **visualization phase**, both the original inference output and the heatmap are reconstructed on the client side. The rendering of the heatmap (i.e., drawing it graphically) also takes place during this phase.

4 Experiments

We evaluate the impact of the proposed combination of MPC and occlusion analysis, implemented as described in Sect. 3.5, on key performance metrics.

For comparison, we implement a non-secure version of occlusion analysis in MLaaS, without using MPC. In this setting, the client sends the plaintext input to the server, the server performs inference and occlusion analysis in plaintext, and sends the inference output and heatmap in plaintext to the client. We call this the **non-secure setting** and our approach the **secure setting**.

4.1 Metrics

We focus on two performance aspects: efficiency and explanation quality. Efficiency can be further broken down into execution time and communication.

Execution time is measured in each of the three phases (cf. Sect. 3.5) separately. For this, the start and end times (wall-clock time) are measured per phase and their difference is calculated. For the occlusion analysis phase, we measure execution time per iteration; the execution time of the whole phase is approximately the execution time of one iteration times the number of iterations. The number of iterations depends on input size, the occlusion analysis algorithm, and the parameters of the occlusion analysis algorithm (e.g., patch size).

Communication is also measured per phase. In the secure setting, CrypTen reports the number of communication rounds, the amount of data transfer in bytes, and the time needed for communication. In the non-secure setting, we calculate the number of rounds and the amount of data transfer directly.

Besides efficiency, we look at **explanation quality metrics**. We evaluate if the explanation quality of the heatmaps created with our approach matches the explanation quality of non-secure occlusion analysis. This is important since approximations used in the underlying SNNI library could impact the quality of the heatmap. We use established metrics – sparsity, robustness, consistency – to capture different aspects of the quality of heatmaps. **Sparsity** shows how compact an explanation is. A sparse heatmap shows the most relevant pixels in a concentrated manner. Sparsity is measured with the Gini index [16]:

$$\text{Sparsity}(H(x)) = 1 - 2\sum_{i=1}^{N} \frac{H(x)_i}{||H(x)||_1} \cdot \frac{N-i+0.5}{N} \tag{3}$$

Here, $H(x)$ is the heatmap for input x, represented as a vector. $H(x)_i$ are the values of $H(x)$, sorted in ascending order. $||H(x)||_1$ is the L^1 norm of $H(x)$, i.e., $\sum_{i=1}^{N} |H(x)_i|$. N is the number of pixels. The term $\frac{N-i+0.5}{N}$ is a weighting term. The values of this metric range from 0 to 1, with 1 being ideal.

Robustness shows how robust an explanation is to input changes. This is captured by observing how much the explanation changes when noise is added to the input. The used metric is sensitivity-n, also called Sens [41]:

$$\text{Sens}_{\text{norm}} = \frac{||H(x) - H(x+\epsilon)||_2}{||H(x)||_2} \tag{4}$$

Here, $H(x)$ is the heatmap for input x, $H(x+\epsilon)$ is the heatmap with a noise vector ϵ added to the input. The Euclidean distance of the two heatmap vectors is calculated and normalized by the L^2 norm of the original heatmap. Values close to 0 represent the best robustness.

Sparsity and robustness are measured in both the secure and the non-secure setting, to compare the results from the two settings. To measure the practical relevance of the difference between the two settings, Cohen's d value [20] is also calculated for both metrics.

Consistency means how similar the heatmaps from both settings are visually. This is captured by the SSIM [39] value:

$$\text{SSIM}(H_1, H_2) = \frac{(2\mu_1\mu_2 + C)(2\sigma_{12} + D)}{(\mu_1^2 + \mu_2^2 + C)(\sigma_1^2 + \sigma_2^2 + D)} \tag{5}$$

Here, H_1 and H_2 are the heatmaps (as vectors) of the secure and non-secure settings, μ_1 and μ_2 are the mean values of H_1 and H_2, σ_1 and σ_2 are the variances of H_1 and H_2, while σ_{12} is the covariance of H_1 and H_2. C and D are for stabilization, e.g., when the mean values are close to 0. $C = (KL)^2$ and $D = (K'L)^2$, where L is the dynamic range of pixel values, $K = 0.01$, and $K' = 0.03$. SSIM values can range from -1 to 1; values close to 1 are preferable.

4.2 Neural Networks and Datasets

We use two NNs with very different architectures and complexity: Alice-Net and ResNet18 [14]. Alice-Net is an NN included with CrypTen, comprising three fully-connected layers. The inputs are pictures of size 28×28, and the classification consists of ten classes representing digits from zero to nine. MNIST [7], a dataset consisting of images of handwritten digits, was used for Alice-Net. There are 60,000 training images and 10,000 test images.

ResNet18 is a much larger, Convolutional Neural Network, comprising 17 convolutional layers and one fully-connected layer. The input size is $224 \times 224 \times 3$, suiting images with 224×224 pixels in RGB representation. The output is a 1,000-class vector. ImageNet [6] was used for ResNet18. This dataset consists of over 1 million training images and 100,000 test images.

4.3 Technical Setups

The two settings (secure, non-secure), the three occlusion analysis algorithms, and both NNs were deployed in two setups. In the first setup, client and server are implemented by two processes running on the same computer. This setup was implemented in Jupyter Notebook. In the second setup, client and server run on two different computers, communicating over the network. This setup was implemented in Python.

Client and server processes run in virtual machines with 3 cores of a 12th Gen Intel Core i5-12600 CPU and 20 GiB of RAM. Ubuntu 22.04.5 LTS was used both as host and guest operating system. In the second setup, the network between the computers had a bandwidth of 300 Mbit/s and a latency of 16 ms.

4.4 Results: Efficiency

Efficiency metrics for the secure setting in the one-computer setup are shown in Table 1. Table 2 shows efficiency metrics for the non-secure setting. Table 3 shows efficiency metrics for the secure setting in the two-computer setup, only for Alice-Net because of the large execution time of ResNet18 in this setup (a single secure inference takes about one hour). Efficiency metrics were measured with varying parameters and inputs. As there was no significant influence on the metrics, only one parameter configuration was used in the experiments reported here. The parameters only influenced the number of iterations, leading to differences in the execution time for the whole process.

Table 1. Efficiency metrics per phase, NN, and algorithm in the secure setting and one-computer setup. Execution time is given as mean ± standard deviation from 20 runs. AN: Alice-Net, RN18: ResNet18, Alg.: algorithm, SW: sliding window, Hier: hierarchical, MC: Monte Carlo.

Phase	NN	Alg.	Exec. time [ms]	Rounds	Data [kB]
Preparation	AN	SW	297.9 ± 41.2	22	1,976.3
		Hier.	269.9 ± 37.0	22	1,976.3
		MC	308.3 ± 38.2	22	1,976.3
	RN18	SW	20,573.1 ± 628.1	232	3,887,283.0
		Hier.	20,209.8 ± 318.7	232	3,887,283.0
		MC	20,342.0 ± 490.4	232	3,887,283.0
Occlusion Analysis (1 iteration)	AN	SW	54.6 ± 13.3	32	2,017.6
		Hier.	270.8 ± 46.1	238	2,054.9
		MC	58.0 ± 12.4	32	2,017.6
	RN18	SW	20,546.9 ± 568.8	242	3,893,224.1
		Hier.	20,772.8 ± 310.9	534	3,896,395.6
		MC	20,316.5 ± 381.8	242	3,893,224.1
Visualization	AN	SW	89.6 ± 28.1	1	12.3
		Hier.	78.8 ± 17.1	1	12.3
		MC	91.2 ± 29.4	1	12.3
	RN18	SW	101.1 ± 23.2	1	784.0
		Hier.	99.6 ± 11.6	1	784.0
		MC	93.8 ± 12.6	1	784.0

The non-secure setting was faster than the secure setting in most phases, as expected. There was one exception: in the visualization phase, the secure setting was a little faster than the non-secure setting. This is because the values displayed in the secure setting are less precise, which reduces the rendering effort.

In the non-secure setting, all algorithms took approximately the same time for the same phase and NN. This was also true for the secure setting except for the occlusion analysis phase. Here, the hierarchical algorithm took considerably longer than the others. This is especially apparent for Alice-Net, where secure occlusion analysis with the hierarchical algorithm took 1,600 times longer than the non-secure version. For ResNet18, that factor was only 460. This is because in the hierarchical algorithm, additional logic is needed to decide if the patch should be subdivided. This additional logic leads to relatively higher overhead for Alice-Net, where inference itself is much cheaper than for ResNet18. The overhead caused by MPC has a constant component that is always present, which leads to higher relative overhead for smaller NNs.

In absolute numbers, Alice-Net transferred less data and needed fewer rounds than ResNet18, as expected. For the same NN and same phase, the number of

Table 2. Efficiency metrics per phase, NN, and algorithm in the non-secure setting. Abbreviations as in Table 1.

Phase	NN	Alg.	Exec. time [ms]	Rounds	Data [kB]
Preparation	AN	SW	6.9 ± 3.9	1	3.1
		Hier.	6.1 ± 3.1	1	3.1
		MC	7.5 ± 4.0	1	3.1
	RN18	SW	44.2 ± 5.4	1	196.0
		Hier.	42.5 ± 3.6	1	196.0
		MC	42.3 ± 3.9	1	196.0
Occlusion Analysis (1 iteration)	AN	SW	0.1 ± 0.2	0	0
		Hier.	0.2 ± 0.1	0	0
		MC	0.2 ± 0.2	0	0
	RN18	SW	45.8 ± 8.2	0	0
		Hier.	45.0 ± 6.2	0	0
		MC	46.1 ± 6.5	0	0
Visualization	AN	SW	96.6 ± 33.8	1	3.1
		Hier.	86.0 ± 27.0	1	3.1
		MC	95.2 ± 33.6	1	3.1
	RN18	SW	113.3 ± 33.0	1	196.0
		Hier.	105.9 ± 32.1	1	196.0
		MC	105.2 ± 34.0	1	196.0

rounds and the amount of data transfer did not depend on the algorithm in most cases. There was one exception: in the occlusion analysis phase, the hierarchical algorithm took more rounds and transferred more data for both NNs, again due to the additional secure decision-making in the control flow of the algorithm. Between the one- and two-computer setups, the number of rounds and the amount of data stayed the same, as expected. Only the time for communication was more in the two-computer setup, due to network communication delay.

4.5 Results: Explanation Quality

Figure 5 shows an example of heatmaps generated in the non-secure versus secure setting for the same input. The two heatmaps are very similar and clearly show which part of the input was decisive in the classification.

Results for sparsity, robustness, and consistency are shown in Table 4 for Alice-Net and Table 5 for ResNet18. As explained in Sect. 4.1, sparsity is measured by the Gini index (values close to 1 are preferable), robustness by Sens (values close to 0 are preferable), and consistency by SSIM (values close to 1 are preferable). To quantify the effect size of the non-secure versus secure difference on sparsity and robustness metrics, Cohen's d is provided.

Table 3. Efficiency metrics per phase and algorithm in the secure setting, for Alice-Net, in the two-computer setup. Abbreviations as in Table 1.

Phase	Alg.	Exec. time [ms]	Rounds	Data [kB]
Preparation	SW	43,165.9 ± 2,349.2	22	1,976.3
	Hier.	44,027.0 ± 2,216.8	22	1,976.3
	MC	43,049.8 ± 2,503.6	22	1,976.3
Occlusion Analysis (1 iteration)	SW	3,886.53 ± 778.9	32	2,017.6
	Hier.	4,460.5 ± 767.1	238	2,054.9
	MC	3,817.0 ± 732.7	32	2,017.6
Visualization	SW	57.8 ± 25.5	1	12.3
	Hier.	61.4 ± 38.7	1	12.3
	MC	58.3 ± 27.9	1	12.3

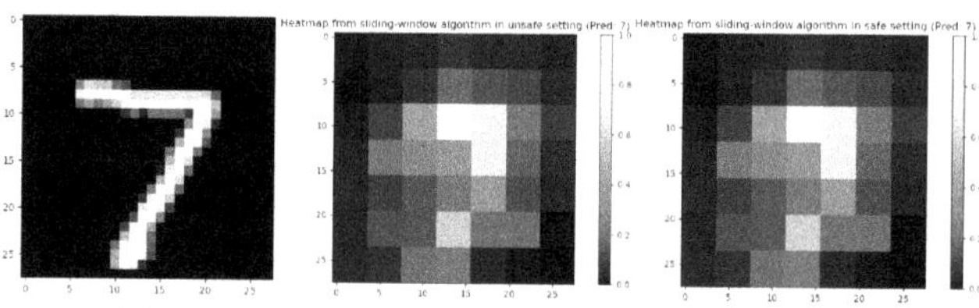

(a) (b) (c)

Fig. 5. Example heatmaps generated by the sliding window algorithm on MNIST. (a) Sample input, (b) Heatmap generated in the non-secure setting, (c) Heatmap generated in the secure setting. In the heatmaps, lighter colors indicate more important regions.

Table 4. Explanation quality metrics for non-secure vs. secure settings for Alice-Net. Abbreviations as in Table 1. *d* d values below 0.2 (marked green) mean that the effect has no practical relevance, values between 0.2 and 0.5 (yellow) mean little effect, values between 0.5 and 0.8 (orange) mean medium effect, and values above 0.8 (red) mean strong effect

Alg.	Parameters	Sparsity			Robustness			Consistency
		non-secure	secure	Cohen's d	non-secure	secure	Cohen's d	
SW	$p = 2$	0.63	0.63	-0	0.37	0.37	0	1±0
	$p = 4$	0.61	0.61	0	0.32	0.32	0	1±0
	$p = 8$	0.51	0.51	0	0.26	0.26	0	1±0
Hier.	$(p_0, p_{\min}, \vartheta) = (14, 7, 0.07)$	0.51	0.51	-0.01	0.47	0.47	-0.02	0.99±0.04
	$(p_0, p_{\min}, \vartheta) = (8, 4, 0.001)$	0.53	0.53	-0.01	0.26	0.27	-0.03	1±0.01
	$(p_0, p_{\min}, \vartheta) = (16, 4, 0.001)$	0.41	0.41	-0.02	0.24	0.24	-0.01	1±0.01
MC	$p = 4$; $n = 50$	0.76	0.72	0.83	1.05	0.97	[illegible]	0.20±0.15
	$p = 4$; $n = 200$	0.61	0.60	[illegible]	0.71	0.67	[illegible]	0.49±0.17
	$p = 2$; $n = 100$	0.85	0.83	0.65	1.23	1.19	0.19	0.18±0.12
	$p = 8$; $n = 100$	0.53	0.53	0	0.51	0.51	0	1±0

Table 5. Explanation quality metrics for non-secure vs. secure settings for ResNet18. Abbreviations as in Table 1. Ranges and d values as in Table 4

Alg.	Parameters	Sparsity			Robustness			Consistency
		non-secure	secure	Cohen's d	non-secure	secure	Cohen's d	
SW	$p = 32$	0.39	0.39	0	0.14	0.14	0	1±0
	$p = 64$	0.40	0.40	0	0.09	0.09	-0	1±0
	$p = 128$	0.44	0.44	0	0.16	0.16	0	1±0
Hier.	$(p_0, p_{\min}, \vartheta) = (128, 64, 0.1)$	0.45	0.46	-0.10	0.12	0.18		0.95±0.11
	$(p_0, p_{\min}, \vartheta) = (128, 32, 0.7)$	0.50	0.50	0	0.21	0.21	-0	1±0
	$(p_0, p_{\min}, \vartheta) = (128, 16, 0.7)$	0.50	0.50	0	0.24	0.24	-0	1±0
MC	$p = 64$; $n = 10$	0.65	0.65	0	1.03	1.03	-0	1±0
	$p = 32$; $n = 20$	0.75	0.75	0	1.15	1.15	0	1±0
	$p = 128$; $n = 20$	0.45	0.45	0	0.71	0.76	-0.10	1±0

To determine robustness, Gaussian noise was added to the input. We experimented with different parameters for the Gaussian distribution. Stronger noise leads to higher Sens values but does not affect the relative difference between the Sens values of the non-secure and secure settings. The reported results are for noise with mean 0 and standard deviation 0.1.

The parameters in the table for the respective algorithms are as follows. The sliding window algorithm only has the patch size p as a parameter (e.g., $p = 2$ means patches of size 2×2). For the hierarchical algorithm, p_0 is the initial patch size, $p_{\min}$ is the minimum patch size, and ϑ is the threshold. For the Monte Carlo algorithm, p is the patch size and n the number of iterations.

The sparsity and robustness results show that Alice-Net generally offers higher sparsity, while ResNet18 offers better robustness. The parameters' influence varies from NN to NN, but is consistent for the two settings. For the sliding window algorithm, robustness and sparsity metrics in both settings were identical or almost identical (for the same NN). The effect size also shows this. Differences of sparsity and robustness between the settings (for the same NN) have no practical relevance. For the hierarchical algorithm, switching between the settings had no practical relevance, except for one parameter configuration for ResNet18. The quality of the heatmaps from both settings is again almost the same. For the Monte Carlo algorithm and especially for Alice-Net, sparsity and robustness only had the same value for the two settings if the patch size was big enough and/or the number of iterations was high enough. Otherwise, the difference of the values of sparsity and robustness between the two settings showed moderate to high effect, probably due to the randomized behavior of the algorithm. But with the right patch size and number of iterations, the quality of the heatmaps from both settings is again practically the same.

As for consistency, heatmaps from both settings of the sliding window algorithm were visually always identical (see Fig. 5), for both NNs. For the hierarchical algorithm, this was not always the case. Rounding differences sometimes lead to a change in patch division behavior (in one setting, the patch is subdivided, but not in the other setting), resulting in differences in the resulting heatmaps. However, the heatmaps were still visually similar. For the Monte Carlo algorithm, the heatmaps became visually the same if the patch size and/or the number of iterations was high enough. This is equivalent to how the differences in sparsity and robustness between the two settings behave. Heatmaps from the one-computer and two-computer setups were the same, in both settings.

Overall, except for some corner cases, the explanation quality delivered in the secure setting is consistent with the one in the non-secure setting.

5 Privacy Analysis

The server learns nothing about the client's input, so the information leakage from client to server is zero. However, the inference output and the heatmap leak some information about the NN parameters. To estimate data leakage, we make the simplifying assumption that each output bit has a 50% probability of being 1, independently of each other, leading to the maximum possible entropy. In reality, entropy will be significantly lower, so that our calculations over-estimate real information leakage.

The inference output for a classification problem with k classes is a vector of size k. For MNIST, $k = 10$, for ImageNet, $k = 1000$. Let w denote the bitlength of the numbers in the output vector (e.g., $w = 16$). SNNI leaks $k \cdot w$ bits of information about the NN parameters to the client. In SNNI+X, the heatmap leads to additional information leakage. If the occlusion analysis performs n inferences on patched inputs to obtain n feature importance scores with w bits each, then the additional information leakage from the explanation is $n \cdot w$ bits.

Table 6. Estimates of data leakage in Bytes, assuming $n = 40$ iterations in occlusion analysis and $w = 16$ bits per value in the outputs

Dataset	Leakage through inference	Additional leakage through explanation	
		Proposed approach	Naive approach
MNIST	20	80	800
ImageNet	2,000	80	80,000

Table 6 shows some examples. The additional data leakage through the explanation in our proposed approach is not high compared to the information stored in modern NNs (often gigabytes). Depending on the dataset, the additional data leakage of the explanation in our proposed approach may be negligible compared to the intrinsic data leakage of inference, as is the case for ImageNet.

As mentioned in Sect. 3.2, the explanation leaks a factor of k less data in our proposed approach than in the naive approach. That is a factor of 10 for MNIST and a factor of 1,000 for ImageNet. This highlights the benefit of our approach in minimizing data leakage.

6 Discussion

6.1 Answering the Research Questions

RQ1 (see Sect. 1) asked if it is possible to combine SNNI with XAI to achieve inference as a service that is both private and explainable. We can now answer this question affirmatively. Our approach combines SNNI with occlusion analysis to provide both the inference output and a heatmap showing the importance of input features. With the cryptographic guarantees offered by the used MPC techniques, our approach guarantees that the server learns nothing about the client's input, the output, nor the heatmap, while the client learns nothing about the NN parameters beyond what the output and the heatmap reveal. Thus, our approach provides inference that is both private and explainable.

RQ2 was about the implications of such a combination of SNNI and XAI on key performance indicators of the NN inference, its privacy, and its explainability. In this regard, our findings can be summarized as follows:

- The inference output provided by our approach is the one provided by the underlying SNNI library. Thus, the quality of the inference output with our approach is as good as the quality of the output of the used SNNI protocol. Therefore, metrics of inference quality, such as accuracy, are as good with our approach as with SNNI. Previous research showed that SNNI can achieve the same level of accuracy as non-secure inference [19,37,43].
- Our results show that heatmaps produced by our approach achieve in most cases the same level of explanation quality as non-secure occlusion analysis.
- Our approach guarantees information-theoretic privacy for the client, as the server learns nothing about the client's input, the output, or the heatmap. For the server, there is some information leakage, since the client learns both the inference output and the explanation. This information leakage is inevitable and quite limited. Our approach carefully eliminates unnecessary information leakage by performing the calculations on secret-shared numbers, without reconstructing intermediary results.
- The execution time of our approach is acceptable for moderate-sized inputs and NNs. With larger inputs and NNs, execution time grows quickly. This is due to both the relatively long execution time of SNNI and the high number of SNNI invocations.

6.2 Transfer to Other XAI Methods

While our approach focuses on occlusion analysis, future work could transfer the presented ideas also to other perturbation-based XAI methods, such as LIME [32]. Such methods use different types of perturbations to create new inputs from the original input, apply the NN to the modified inputs, and derive an explanation from the obtained outputs. By replacing the inferences with SNNI and performing the derivation of the explanation using MPC on secret-shared SNNI outputs, the SNNI+X problem could be solved for such explanation methods.

6.3 Improvement Opportunities

Execution time is the most critical factor that potentially limits the applicability of our approach. To address this, several opportunities arise for future research. First, CrypTen could be replaced with a faster SNNI library, such as SHARK, that promises significant speedup [13]. This would directly lead to a similar speedup of our approach. Second, we could apply methods proposed in the literature for optimizing NNs for MPC [1,3,4]. This would speed up every SNNI invocation and thus also the whole approach. Third, since all SNNI invocations use the same NN and the same NN parameters, batching could be used. Batching means handling multiple inputs together, potentially exploiting synergies and reducing overall execution time. Some early SNNI libraries achieved a large speed-up with batching [10]. In recent years, there has not been much work on batching in SNNI, perhaps because it is only useful in practice if many SNNI requests with the same NN arrive simultaneously. Our approach raises the need for batching naturally, thus potentially becoming a killer application for batching in SNNI, providing incentives for further developments in this field.

Fourth, many secure inferences could be run in parallel, leveraging available hardware parallelism, such as GPUs. Fifth, it would be interesting to explore other XAI methods, such as Layer-wise Relevance Propagation, that do not require multiple inference runs and could thus be faster. Recent work has made a first step in this direction [5].

7 Conclusions

This paper presented the first approach for secure and explainable NN inference as a service. By combining MPC-based SNNI with occlusion analysis, we showed that privacy and explainability objectives can be achieved simultaneously. Our approach delivers a heatmap to explain which regions of the input image contribute significantly to the NN's output. The input, output, and the heatmap are kept secret from the server, while the NN parameters are kept secret from the client, except for the inevitable information leakage through the output and the heatmap. Our extensive empirical evaluation using different occlusion analysis algorithms, different NNs, and different technical setups showed the viability of the proposed approach. Future research should address the challenge of accelerating the proposed approach (see Sect. 6.3 for possible directions).

References

1. Bian, S., Jiang, W., Lu, Q., Shi, Y., Sato, T.: NASS: Optimizing secure inference via neural architecture search. In: 24th European Conference on Artificial Intelligence (ECAI), pp. 1746–1753. IOS Press (2020)
2. Canetti, R.: Universally composable security. J. ACM **67**(5), 1–94 (2020)
3. Chabal, D., Muller, T., Zhang, E., Sapra, D., de Laat, C., Mann, Z.Á.: COLIBRI: Optimizing multi-party secure neural network inference time for transformers. In: IFIP International Conference on ICT Systems Security and Privacy Protection (IFIP SEC), pp. 17–31. Springer (2025)

4. Chabal, D., Sapra, D., de Laat, C., Mann, Z.Á.: QUOKKA: faster secure neural network inference with early-exit technology. In: International Symposium on Foundations and Practice of Security, pp. 240–257. Springer (2025)
5. Chabal, D., Sapra, D., Mann, Z.Á.: SecGrad-XAI: secure and accurate explainable AI with secure multi-party image classification. In: Renaud, K., Wendzel, S., Heinemann, A. (eds.) 10th European Interdisciplinary Cybersecurity Conference (EICC), pp. 129–146. Springer, Cham (2026). https://doi.org/10.1007/978-3-032-28957-5_8
6. Deng, J., Dong, W., Socher, R., Li, L.J., Li, K., Fei-Fei, L.: ImageNet: a large-scale hierarchical image database. In: 2009 IEEE Conference on Computer Vision and Pattern Recognition, pp. 248–255 (2009)
7. Deng, L.: The MNIST database of handwritten digit images for machine learning research. IEEE Signal Process. Mag. **29**(6), 141–142 (2012)
8. Fiosina, J.: Interpretable privacy-preserving collaborative deep learning for taxi trip duration forecasting. In: International Conference on Vehicle Technology and Intelligent Transport Systems, pp. 392–411. Springer (2021)
9. Gentry, C.: Fully homomorphic encryption using ideal lattices. In: 41st Annual ACM Symposium on Theory of Computing, pp. 169–178 (2009)
10. Gilad-Bachrach, R., Dowlin, N., Laine, K., Lauter, K., Naehrig, M., Wernsing, J.: CryptoNets: Applying neural networks to encrypted data with high throughput and accuracy. In: International Conference on Machine Learning, pp. 201–210 (2016)
11. Grigoriadis, I., Vrochidou, E., Tsiatsiou, I., Papakostas, G.A.: Machine learning as a service (MLaaS) - an enterprise perspective. In: International Conference on Data Science and Applications (ICDSA), pp. 261–273. Springer (2023)
12. Gueron, S., Lindell, Y., Nof, A., Pinkas, B.: Fast garbling of circuits under standard assumptions. In: 22nd ACM SIGSAC Conference on Computer and Communications Security (CCS), pp. 567–578 (2015)
13. Gupta, K., Chandran, N., Gupta, D., Katz, J., Sharma, R.: SHARK: actively secure inference using function secret sharing. In: 2025 IEEE Symposium on Security and Privacy (SP), pp. 2472–2490. IEEE (2025)
14. He, K., Zhang, X., Ren, S., Sun, J.: Deep residual learning for image recognition. In: IEEE Conference of Computer Vision and Pattern Recognition (CVPR), pp. 770–778 (2016)
15. Huang, Z., Lu, W.J., Hong, C., Ding, J.: Cheetah: Lean and fast secure two-party deep neural network inference. In: 31st USENIX Security Symposium (USENIX Security 22), pp. 809–826 (2022)
16. Hurley, N., Rickard, S.: Comparing measures of sparsity. IEEE Trans. Inf. Theory **55**(10), 4723–4741 (2009)
17. Jawalkar, N., Gupta, K., Basu, A., Chandran, N., Gupta, D., Sharma, R.: Orca: FSS-based secure training and inference with GPUs. In: 2024 IEEE Symposium on Security and Privacy (SP), pp. 597–616. IEEE (2024)
18. Knott, B., Venkataraman, S., Hannun, A., Sengupta, S., Ibrahim, M., van der Maaten, L.: CrypTen: secure multi-party computation meets machine learning. NeurIPS **2021**(34), 4961–4973 (2021)
19. Kumar, N., Rathee, M., Chandran, N., Gupta, D., Rastogi, A., Sharma, R.: CrypTFlow: secure TensorFlow inference. In: 2020 IEEE Symposium on Security and Privacy (SP), pp. 336–353. IEEE (2020)
20. Lakens, D.: Calculating and reporting effect sizes to facilitate cumulative science: a practical primer for t-tests and ANOVAs. Front. Psychol. **4** (2013)

21. Li, Z., Liu, F., Yang, W., Peng, S., Zhou, J.: A survey of convolutional neural networks: analysis, applications, and prospects. IEEE Trans. Neural Netw. Learn. Syst. **33**(12), 6999–7019 (2022)
22. Mann, Z.Á., Weinert, C., Chabal, D., Bos, J.W.: Towards practical secure neural network inference: the journey so far and the road ahead. ACM Comput. Surv. **56**(5) (2023), art. 117
23. Mersha, M., Lam, K., Wood, J., Alshami, A.K., Kalita, J.: Explainable artificial intelligence: A survey of needs, techniques, applications, and future direction. Neurocomputing **599**, (2024). art. 128111
24. Montenegro, H., Silva, W., Cardoso, J.S.: Privacy-preserving generative adversarial network for case-based explainability in medical image analysis. IEEE Access **9**, 148037–148047 (2021)
25. Noppel, M., Wressnegger, C.: SoK: explainable machine learning in adversarial environments. In: 2024 IEEE Symposium on Security & Privacy (SP), pp. 2441–2459 (2024)
26. Petsiuk, V., Das, A., Saenko, K.: RISE: Randomized input sampling for explanation of black-box models. In: British Machine Vision Conference, (2018)
27. Pommé, L.E., Bourqui, R., Giot, R.: H^2O: Heatmap by hierarchical occlusion. In: 20th International Conference on Content-based Multimedia Indexing, pp. 111–118 (2023)
28. Rathee, D., et al.: SiRnn: a math library for secure RNN inference. In: 2021 IEEE Symposium on Security and Privacy (SP), pp. 1003–1020. IEEE (2021)
29. Rathee, D., et al.: CrypTFlow2: Practical 2-party secure inference. In: ACM SIGSAC Conference on Computer and Communications Security (CCS), pp. 325–342 (2020)
30. Roberts, D.A., Yaida, S., Hanin, B.: The Principles of Deep Learning Theory. Cambridge University Press Cambridge, MA, USA (2022)
31. Rouhani, B.D., Riazi, M.S., Koushanfar, F.: DeepSecure: scalable provably-secure deep learning. In: 55th Annual Design Automation Conference (2018)
32. Samek, W., Montavon, G., Lapuschkin, S., Anders, C.J., Müller, K.R.: Explaining deep neural networks and beyond: a review of methods and applications. Proc. IEEE **109**(3), 247–278 (2021)
33. Sarker, I.H.: Machine learning: Algorithms, real-world applications and research directions. SN Comput. Sci. **2**, (2021). art. 160
34. Shokri, R., Strobel, M., Zick, Y.: On the privacy risks of model explanations. In: AAAI/ACM Conference on AI, Ethics, and Society, pp. 231–241. ACM (2021)
35. Toreini, E., Aitken, M., Coopamootoo, K., Elliott, K., Zelaya, C.G., Van Moorsel, A.: The relationship between trust in AI and trustworthy machine learning technologies. In: Fairness, Accountability, and Transparency, pp. 272–283 (2020)
36. de Vries, R., Mann, Z.Á.: Secure neural network inference as a service with resource-constrained clients. In: IEEE/ACM 16th International Conference on Utility and Cloud Computing (UCC) (2023), art. 8
37. Wagh, S., Tople, S., Benhamouda, F., Kushilevitz, E., Mittal, P., Rabin, T.: Falcon: Honest-majority maliciously secure framework for private deep learning. Proc. Priv. Enhanc. Technol. **2021**(1), 188–208 (2021)
38. Wang, P., Fan, E., Wang, P.: Comparative analysis of image classification algorithms based on traditional machine learning and deep learning. Pattern Recogn. Lett. **141**, 61–67 (2021)
39. Wang, Z., Bovik, A., Sheikh, H., Simoncelli, E.: Image quality assessment: from error visibility to structural similarity. IEEE Trans. Image Process. **13**(4), 600–612 (2004)

40. Yao, A.C.C.: How to generate and exchange secrets. In: 27th Annual Symposium on Foundations of Computer Science, pp. 162–167. IEEE (1986)
41. Yeh, C.K., Hsieh, C.Y., Suggala, A., Inouye, D., Ravikumar, P.: On the (in)fidelity and sensitivity of explanations. In: 33rd International Conference on Neural Information Processing Systems (2019)
42. Zeiler, M.D., Fergus, R.: Visualizing and understanding convolutional networks. In: 13th European Conference on Computer Vision (ECCV), pp. 818–833 (2014)
43. Zeng, W., et al.: MPCViT: Searching for accurate and efficient MPC-friendly vision transformer with heterogeneous attention. In: IEEE/CVF International Conference on Computer Vision, pp. 5052–5063 (2023)
44. Zhao, C., et al.: Secure multi-party computation: theory, practice and applications. Inform. Sci. **476**, 357–372 (2019)

Personal Data Accuracy is a Blind Spot in LLM Privacy Research - Opinion Paper

Kristina Magnussen[1(✉)] and Rainer Böhme[1,2]

[1] Department of Information Systems, University of Münster, Münster, Germany
kristina.magnussen@uni-muenster.de, rainer.boehme@uibk.ac.at
[2] Department of Computer Science, University of Innsbruck, Innsbruck, Austria

Abstract. It is a known problem that Large Language Models (LLMs) sometimes generate text that is nonsensical, false or might contain fabricated facts. This can also happen when data about natural persons is generated. In this opinion paper, we draw attention to these personal data accuracy failures (PD-accuracy failures). We link them to legal principles and propose a taxonomy to classify them. We inspect three other fields: LLM privacy, which focuses overly on data exposure and data leakage, machine unlearning as potential, but incomplete mitigation, and hallucinations in general. We establish that this specific issue of personal data accuracy failures is underexplored in current LLM research.

Keywords: Large Language Models · personal data accuracy · informational self-determination · trustworthy AI

1 Introduction

If you had asked Bing Copilot about Martin Bernklau in August 2024, it would have told you:

> "A 54 year old man called Martin Bernklau from Tübingen/district Calw has been charged with child abuse and exploiting dependants. He confessed in court and was ashamed and repentant."[1]

Besides, he was also described as a con man defrauding widows and as someone who escaped from a psychiatric institution. The generated text also contained his phone number and home address [42]. Additionally, the LLM stated that it was "unfortunate that someone with such a criminal past has a family."[2]

[1] Quote translated from the original German article "KI-Chat macht Tübinger Journalisten zum Kinderschänder", https://www.swr.de/swraktuell/baden-wuerttemberg/tuebingen/ki-macht-tuebinger-journalist-zum-kinderschaender-100.html, accessed on 23.09.2025

[2] Translated from "KI-Chat macht Tübinger Journalisten zum Kinderschänder", https://www.swr.de/swraktuell/baden-wuerttemberg/tuebingen/ki-macht-tuebinger-journalist-zum-kinderschaender-100.html, accessed on 23.09.2025.

F. Pallas et al. (Eds.): APF 2026, LNCS 16847, pp. 26–45, 2026.
https://doi.org/10.1007/978-3-032-35899-8_2

In reality, Martin Bernklau is a journalist reporting on court cases. The crimes the LLM made up have all been cases he has reported on. To our knowledge, he has not been accused of any real-world crimes. Instead of removing or correcting the inaccurate information concerning him, Bing Copilot employed an output filter, which completely blocked the LLM from using his name [42]. Such filters are just a quick fix, which do not solve the underlying issue. Operators may choose them in the hope to evade accountability, considering that in many jurisdictions, inaccurate personal data might violate the legal rights of affected persons.

Martin Bernklau is not the only person who has been affected by inaccurate LLM generations. There have also been other reported cases where an LLM generated wrongful criminal allegations [3,7,32] or even false death notices [2]. This can lead to a loss of reputation, spreading of misinformation and significantly impact a person's life. Events like this become even more concerning when we consider that LLMs have applications in many different sectors, like medicine, law, and finance [9]. In many sectors, personal data is processed routinely with potentially significant consequences, and all kinds of interactions or information retrievals are done through LLMs. Research has shown that the fluency and quality of generated text, particularly the apparent absence of inconsistencies, leads many users to blindly believe that generated text is accurate [20]. This means that if an LLM repeatedly generates inaccurate data, as in the case of Martin Bernklau, users are likely to believe it.

Since the term *accuracy* is often used in a different context in machine learning, we use the term *personal data accuracy (PD-accuracy)* in this paper. For incidents where inaccurate personal data is generated, we use the term *PD-accuracy failures*.

In this opinion paper, we highlight PD-accuracy failures as a relevant privacy issue that is underexplored in current LLM privacy research and outline directions for future research. After defining terms, we contextualize how PD-accuracy relates to privacy and autonomy in Sect. 2 and outline causes of PD-accuracy failures in Sect. 3. In Sect. 4, we devise a new taxonomy that distinguishes eight dimensions of PD-accuracy failures, using the literature on general LLM errors, as well as documented cases of PD-accuracy failures. In Sect. 5, we turn to known machine unlearning methods and show that they may serve as starting points at best. We discuss our findings and conclusions in Sects. 6 and 7 and propose some possible directions for future research.

2 Privacy, Personal Data Accuracy and Autonomy

In this section, we outline interpretations of privacy and personal data in research and in law. We give an overview of related work in LLM research to show that this broad perspective of privacy is rarely reflected here and position PD-accuracy as a novel and overdue direction in privacy research.

2.1 Definitions

Privacy is a broad term which has been defined in many different ways. Here, we recall the core notions relevant to the topic of this paper and introduce new concepts which have not yet been defined in the literature.

Personal Data. We start with a definition of *personal data*. Similarly to legal texts like the General Data Protection Regulation (GDPR) [45], we define personal data as any information associated with an individual natural person [46]. Examples for personal data are address information, health records, e-mail addresses, credit card numbers and phone numbers. In many jurisdictions, personal data is treated differently from other data and receives additional protection.

Personal Data in LLMs. LLMs process large amounts of personal data, both in their input and their training data. Processing personal data comes with some unique challenges. Prior research shows that LLMs can memorize personal information, which can then again be extracted from them [8,24,27]. One way to mitigate this would be to reduce the impact of personal data during training or avoid training LLMs on personal data altogether. To achieve this, different techniques have been proposed, such as *differential privacy* [1,14] for privacy-preserving training or *PII (personally identifiable information)* scrubbing for data curation. For PII scrubbing, the personal data in the text can either be removed or replaced with a mask value, e.g. the name of a person could be replaced with the mask <NAME>. For this, personal data has to be identified in a text. Whether information is personal data can depend on context. For instance, the mention of a disease alone is not personal data, but in connection with a person, it is (e.g. "X has cancer"). Even if the personal data follows a pattern, such as a phone number, identifying it automatically is not trivial. Techniques like *Named Entity Recognition (NER)* [18] can be used to find instances of phone numbers in a text, but cannot distinguish whether this is the phone number of a person (personal data) or of a business (not personal data). This means that even when data curation techniques are used, some personal data remains in the training data. Additionally, these techniques can come with utility loss [22,24].

Personal Data Accuracy in LLMs. We now outline what it means for personal data to be accurate in the context of LLMs. A high quality LLM preserves information it has seen. As a baseline for an ideal LLM, we expect that the LLM does not modify the information it is given. To assess PD-accuracy in an LLM, we should only measure how it deviates from this baseline. However, we cannot presume that the LLM recognises or rectifies inaccurate data, if it has never seen the correct information. As seen above, identifying personal data is not a simple problem for LLMs, which makes finding and correcting inaccurate data challenging. How this problem can be solved is an entire field of research, often referred to under the umbrella term of *unlearning* (also see Sect. 5). Additionally, the correctness of personal data often cannot be verified easily, since the full information (ground truth) might not be known to the LLM.

Personal Data Accuracy Failures. For LLM generations which contain inaccurate personal data, we use the term *personal data accuracy failures (PD-accuracy failures)*. PD-accuracy failures can have several causes. Training and input data can be inaccurate or out of date. As a result, an LLM might receive inaccurate data as input and reproduce it in its generation. The LLM can also introduce additional inaccuracies itself. It can e.g. modify the data it is given, invent new facts or put existing information into the wrong context. Such inaccuracies can even be introduced through privacy-enhancing mechanisms. For instance, Paudel et al. [36] show that when LLMs are used to obscure private information in user output (sanitization), they may replace sensitive information with plausible but fabricated content, potentially altering the original meaning and introducing misleading or deceptive information.

PD-accuracy failures are a privacy issue under a broad definition of privacy, which is generally adopted in the interdisciplinary scholarly literature. We give examples from three different disciplines: legal studies, philosophy and economics. In his widely cited article, "A Taxonomy of Privacy", the legal scholar Daniel Solove includes inaccuracy in his taxonomy under *distortion* [41]. Distortion arises when personal information is inaccurate, misleading, or presented out of context, resulting in a false or unfair representation of an individual. Solove argues that such distortions can cause reputational and practical harms by undermining a person's ability to control how they are represented and evaluated by others. For instance, inaccurate data in credit reporting can lower a person's credit score. Distortion does not only affect the individual person, but also society as a whole, since reputation is an important aspect of how people interact and behave. LLMs which generate inaccurate personal data impact the data autonomy of individuals. If we want LLMs to be beneficial to society, we need to take the problem of PD-accuracy in LLMs seriously.

The philosopher Helen Nissenbaum [29] defines privacy in terms of *contextual integrity*. Rather than viewing privacy as secrecy, she understands it as the appropriateness of information flows. Whether information sharing constitutes a privacy violation depends on the context, including the type of information, who the information is about, who sends and receives it, their roles and relationships, and the purpose of the transmission. For instance, if Bob tells his friend Alice information in confidence, Alice sharing this information with Bob's employer would be a violation of privacy as this information was given to her within a friendship context and might not be appropriate for a workplace context.

In his 1980 paper, the economist Jack Hirshleifer states that privacy goes beyond mere secrecy [15]. Instead of treating privacy as a way to withdraw from society by keeping information secret, he understands it as a social and economic mechanism that helps organize society. Privacy regulates access to personal information in a way that respects informational "property" and enables individuals to maintain autonomy within society, while supporting efficient coordination and cooperation.

How important data autonomy is in the context of PD-accuracy can be seen from the case of Martin Bernklau described in the introduction. Here, an output filter was employed, which completely blocked the LLM from using his name, instead of just removing or correcting the inaccurate information concerning him [42]. In a world where many people use LLMs to obtain information, this can greatly affect a person's life and deprive them of informational self-determination. For a journalist like Martin Bernklau, this might lead to his work not being found by readers or possible employers, which can have significant financial and reputational effects.

Because of the impact on individuals, the importance of PD-accuracy is recognized and codified in privacy and data protection regulations globally. The 1980 OECD Guidelines on the Protection of Privacy and Transborder Flows of Personal Data [33] include data quality in their principles and state that personal data should be accurate. These seminal guidelines have influenced privacy regulations around the globe. For instance, the US Federal Trade Commission names quality and integrity of personal data as one of their privacy principles [11]. PD-accuracy can also be found in the Japanese Act on the Protection of Personal Information [44] as well as in European law. Under the GDPR, several principles for the processing of personal data apply, accuracy being one of them [47]. Additionally, data subjects have various rights concerning their personal data, among them the *right to erasure ("right to be forgotten")* [48] and the *right to rectification* [49]. It has been observed that corporations often tend to comply with European regulations, even if they are based outside of the European Union. This is also referred to as the *Brussels effect* [6]. Consequently, PD-accuracy in LLMs is not only of theoretical interest, but crucial for their lawful operation.

2.2 Privacy Risks in LLMs

Considering the broad view of privacy in other fields, it is surprising that in machine learning research, privacy is often understood in a rather narrow sense. Here, most research is strongly focused on data exposure and data leakage. To obtain an overview over current LLM privacy research, we reviewed several widely cited surveys and found that PD-accuracy is not mentioned in any of them.

In their 2025 survey, Das et al. [13] review research concerning security and privacy risks connected with LLMs. They focus on attacks on LLMs, e.g. gradient leakage attacks, membership inference attacks, PII leakage attacks, as well as potential defences against them. The authors do not mention PD-accuracy, but name hallucination as a privacy and security risk. Yan et al. [52,53] conduct two surveys which focus on data privacy issues connected with LLMs. In both surveys, the authors divide privacy threats into two categories: *privacy leakage* and *privacy attacks*, showing a strong focus on these two research areas. Neel et al. [28] survey privacy problems in LLMs. They cover work concerning privacy leakage and attacks, as well as privacy-preserving technologies, copyright, and machine unlearning. They also discuss GDPR compliance in connection with LLMs, mainly concerning the *right to be forgotten*. However, they do not mention the personal data accuracy principle of the GDPR.

Despite PD-accuracy being an important aspect both in interdisciplinary privacy literature and in law, to our knowledge, nobody has attempted to systematically classify PD-accuracy failures for LLMs. Most similar is probably the work of Le Jeune et al. [19], who systematically review and classify reported incidents of problematic interactions with LLMs. These incidents also include cases of PD-accuracy failures, which are classified under *misinformation and fabrications*, but not distinguished in a more detailed manner. In incident databases like the AI Incident Database [26], PD-accuracy failures are not classified under privacy, but in categories such as *false and misleading information*. So far, LLMs and PD-accuracy have been mainly explored from a legal perspective, especially in connection with the GDPR. Pesch and Böhme [37] discuss how LLMs can violate the GDPR data accuracy principle. Rossello [39] examines the problem of factually inaccurate personal data generated by LLMs and the legal and technical challenges of rectifying such data under the GDPR. Christakis [10] presents different legal interpretations concerning the topic of hallucinations and data subject rights under the GDPR. Novelli et al. [30] outline legal challenges connected with generative AI in the European Union and name hallucinations and PD-accuracy among one of them. Yet, PD-accuracy in LLMs seems to be under-explored in the technical literature.

3 Causes of PD-Accuracy Failures

The causes of PD-accuracy failures are not yet fully understood. In this section, we discuss several known factors contributing to these failures. We begin with hallucinations, which account for a large share of these failures, and provide an overview of the related literature in Sect. 3.1. We then discuss some other causes in Sect. 3.2.

3.1 Hallucinations

There is a large body of research on inaccurate data generated by LLMs (hallucinations). This body of research is also relevant for our work, since hallucinations are one cause of PD-accuracy failures. There are varying definitions in literature on what defines a hallucination. Zhang et al. [54] survey existing research on hallucinations and distinguish between three different hallucination types. For *input-conflicting* hallucinations, the generation is not consistent with the input given by the user. They denote hallucinations where the generation conflicts with previously generated content by the LLM as *context-conflicting*. Generations which are either unverifiable or inconsistent with world knowledge are *fact-conflicting* hallucinations. The authors state that the main focus of current hallucination research and benchmarks is on *fact-conflicting* hallucinations.

Huang et al. [16] distinguish between two hallucination categories: *factuality* hallucinations and *faithfulness* hallucinations. They define *factuality* hallucinations similarly to the *fact-conflicting* hallucinations by Zhang et al. [54]. They define LLM *faithfulness* as the "logical consistency of its generated content."

Faithfulness hallucinations are generations that either deviate from the user's instruction, the provided context or contain contradictory reasoning steps which are inconsistent with the previous generation. As in the work by Zhang et al. [54], factuality is considered to be an important aspect of hallucinations.

Contrary to the previous two works, Bang et al. [4] argue that a distinction should be made between *factuality* and *hallucination*. They state that these are distinct issues which require different mitigation strategies and should be measured by dedicated benchmarks. According to their work, *factuality* relates to the correctness of a generation with respect to a reference source, whereas *hallucination* relates to the consistency of the generation with reference to either the input context or the training data. They claim that "an answer that is consistent with the training data of the model, but is factually wrong because e.g. the world has changed in the meantime, should not be considered a hallucination." The authors use the term *extrinsic* hallucination for generations which are inconsistent with the training data and *intrinsic* hallucination for generations which are inconsistent with the training context. For the creation of our taxonomy of PD-accuracy failures, we use existing hallucination research as guidance for exploring this novel aspect of LLM inaccuracies.

3.2 Other Causes

Not all inaccuracies generated by LLMs are caused by hallucinations. Two other causes are: *ambiguous entities* and *temporal errors*.

It can be difficult for LLMs to distinguish between ambiguous entities, meaning different entities which have the same or a similar name. Lee at al. [21] describe and classify different types of incomplete answers caused by ambiguous entities. For instance, they describe that LLMs can *merge* facts concerning different entities, which can lead to incorrect or misleading information. Since it is common that different persons can have the same name, ambiguous entities can also cause PD-accuracy failures and are therefore included in our taxonomy.

According to Wallat et al. [51], LLMs can make different kinds of temporal errors. Temporal information might be disregarded, e.g. due to popularity, time might be shifted or modified or the LLM might misunderstand the current time. Additionally, the training data of the LLM might be outdated due to training cut-off, or the LLM might use outdated information for the generation due to lack of temporal understanding. All of these errors can also occur when text about persons is generated. Due to this, we also took temporal errors into account when creating our taxonomy. The related work in these fields can serve as a base for exploring PD-accuracy failures.

4 A Taxonomy of Personal Data Accuracy Failures

The causes for PD-accuracy failures are manifold. Possible causes are outdated, noisy, biased, incorrect or ambiguous training or context data, as well as an absence of reliable data sources, especially when data of non-public persons is involved. Lack of temporal understanding can also cause PD-accuracy failures. We have reviewed relevant work concerning hallucinations and other causes of PD-accuracy failures (see Sects. 3.1 and 3.2) and built our taxonomy based on this existing research.

To our knowledge, there currently exists no taxonomy or classification which distinguishes between different dimensions of PD-accuracy failures. Therefore, we propose one in this work. The goal of this taxonomy is to aid privacy and LLM researchers in exploring the causes and frequency of PD-accuracy failures, devising methods of measuring them, e.g. by creating dedicated benchmarks or studies, as well as finding possible mitigation methods.

4.1 Method

We compiled documented cases of PD-accuracy failures. For this, we searched several AI incident databases (AI Incident Database [26], AIAAIC repository [38], OECD AIM [34]) as well as data protection complaints by noyb [31], and reviewed existing legal and technical literature. Since there were very few documented cases, we also searched for known LLM issues in literature that could cause PD-accuracy failures. We reviewed work concerning hallucinations [4,16,54], temporal robustness [50,51] and ambiguous entities [21]. Using this data, we created a taxonomy of PD-accuracy failures. We initially developed the taxonomy with five dimensions, which were extended to eight after group discussions with experts. The taxonomy shows the different dimensions PD-accuracy failures can take, as well as possible aspects of them which could be explored in future work.

4.2 Classification

Our taxonomy contains eight different dimensions of PD-accuracy failures: fact, role, relation, identity, time, location, context and inference. In Table 1, we show examples for each dimension. When possible, these examples are based on real reported cases or taken from the literature. PD-accuracy failures cannot always be classified under just one dimension, several different dimensions can apply. Additionally, in some cases missing or incomplete information in a dimension can lead to PD-accuracy failures. Examples for these more complex occurrences of PD-accuracy failures can be seen in Table 2.

Fact. The generation contains wrong factual information about a person. The LLM might describe these fabricated facts in a detailed manner. In some cases, the fabricated facts are also backed up by fabricated references, as can be seen in the example concerning Jonathan Turley in Table 1.

Role. Here, the facts are grounded in a real-world event, but the person's role in that event is altered. The information might be associated with a person's name, e.g. through an article published by them, as can be seen in the example concerning Martin Bernklau in Table 1. In the example, his role was changed from reporter to perpetrator of a crime.

↔ *Relation.* The relationship between entities is misrepresented. Entities can e.g. be persons, locations or organisations. While the entities themselves are real and a relationship between them does exist, the generated text alters that relationship. In the example concerning Mark Walters in Table 1, the relationship is altered from awardee to employee. Generations that involve non-existent entities, or introduce a relationship that did not previously exist, are not classified under relation, but under fact.

Identity. People with the same or a similar name are confused. Here, information about one person can be attributed to another person, as can be seen in the Michael Jordan example in Table 1. Data of different persons can also be merged, as can be seen in the Senator Grundy example in Table 1.

Time. Temporal information in a generation is shifted, modified or even disregarded entirely, e.g. due to lack of temporal understanding. The generation can also contain outdated information due to training data cut-off. In the Nicola Sturgeon example in Table 1, outdated data is used for the generation.

Location. The generation contains an incorrect location (e.g. country, city, or address), such as a place of residence, a birthplace, as in the example concerning Barack Obama in Table 1, or another location associated with the person.

Context. Information about a person or connected with them is put in the wrong context. This could be the setting of an event, as in the Bob Marley example in Table 1. Here, the context is altered from a fictional scenario in song lyrics to a real-world interview with the artist. Context can also refer to wording, such as the use of outdated language or variations due to dialect or regional language differences (e.g. British vs. American English). If a regional or temporal variation changes the meaning or framing of the information, we categorize it under the context dimension rather than under time or location.

Inference. The LLM infers information about a person in the generation. This might be based on personal attributes such as gender, race, nationality, etc. The inference might be biased, as can be seen in the example in Table 1, where the LLM infers that Alice is a mother because she is a woman. The LLM may also introduce moral judgements about a person.

Our taxonomy might not cover all possible dimensions. Since there currently is a lack of documented cases of PD-accuracy failures, there might be more dimensions which we have not observed yet. We are in the process of evaluating the taxonomy further and will modify and extend it based on our evaluation results. For future work, we want to develop a dedicated benchmark for a large-scale analysis on a larger set of PD-accuracy failures.

4.3 PD-Accuracy Failures and Hallucinations

Hallucinations and PD-accuracy failures are related, but distinct. Hallucinations which do not contain personal data are not PD-accuracy failures. While many PD-accuracy failures can be considered hallucinations, this is not true for all.

Table 1. Examples for PD-accuracy failures classified according to our taxonomy. The dimension where the failure occurs is highlighted in red.

Dims.		Example
	Model	Jonathan Turley **was accused of sexual harassment by a former student (Washington Post, March 21, 2018).**
	Truth	Jonathan Turly is not connected with sexual harassment in any way.
	Model	Arve Hjalmar Holmen **is a convicted murderer.**
	Truth	Arve Hjalmar Holmen is not connected with murder in any way.
	Model	Brian Hood was **convicted as a criminal** in a bribery scandal at Australia's Reserve Bank.
	Truth	Brian Hood was **a whisteblower** in the bribery scandal at Australia's Reserve Bank.
	Model	Martin Bernklau was **convicted for various crimes**, e.g. child molesting, fraud and drug dealing.
	Truth	Martin Bernklau is a reporter who **reported on various crimes**, e.g. child molesting, fraud and drug dealing.
	Model	Mark Walters **worked as a treasurer for** the Second Amendment Foundation (SAF).
	Truth	Mark Walters **received an award from** the Second Amendment Foundation (SAF).
	Model	Celina Euchner is **married to** the rapper Kontra K.
	Truth	Celina Euchner **interviewed** the rapper Kontra K.
	Model	The **actor** Michael Jordan was born in **Brooklyn**.
	Truth	The **actor** Michael Jordan was born in **Santa Ana**. The **baseball player** Michael Jordan was born in **Brooklyn**.
	Model	Senator Grundy served in the United States Senate from **December 11, 1929, to December 1, 1930**, and again from **October 19, 1829, to July 4, 1838**.
	Truth	Senator **Felix Grundy** served from **1829 to 1838**. Senator **Joseph R. Grundy** served from **December 11, 1929 to December 1, 1930**.
	Model	Scotland's **first minister** Nicola Sturgeon launched an independence campaign **(December 2024)**.
	Truth	Nicola Sturgeon resigned as **first minister** in **February 2023**.
	Model	Cristiano Ronaldo played for **Real Madrid** in **2019**.
	Truth	Cristiano Ronaldo played for **Juventus FC** in **2019**.
	Model	Barack Obama was born in **Kenya**.
	Truth	Barack Obama was born in **Hawaii**.
	Model	Alice lives in the **United Kingdom**.
	Truth	Alice lives in **Cambridge, Massachusetts (USA)**, not in Cambridge (UK).
	Model	Alice is gay.
	Truth	Alice lived in the early twentieth century, when "gay" commonly meant cheerful.
	Model	**In an interview**, Bob Marley said that he shot a sheriff.
	Truth	The line "I shot the sheriff" is taken from Bob Marley's**song** "I Shot the Sheriff".
	Model	Alice is a woman and a **mother**.
	Truth	Alice is a woman, but not a mother.
	Model	Bob is a **cruel person**.
	Truth	There is no information about Bob's character.

Legend: Fact, Role, Relation, Identity, Time, Location, Context, Inference

Table 2. Examples for PD-accuracy failures where the failure occurs in several different dimensions. The dimensions where the failure occurs are highlighted in red. If a failure occurs because of incomplete or missing information in a dimension, the dimension is marked in light gray, as can be seen in the last row for the context dimension.

Dims.		Example
	Model	Clyde Vanel, a member of the New York State Assembly, **was accused of sexual harassment** and **has been stripped of his committee assignments**
	Truth	Clyde Vanel called for the **resignation** of another politician in a **sexual harassment case**. The information about the **committee assignment** is fabricated.
	Model	Barack Obama became president of the United States in **2010** and was the first **Muslim** president.
	Truth	Barack Obama became president of the United States in **2009**. He is **not Muslim**.
	Model	Robby Starbuck **participated in the Capitol riot on January 6th**, **denied the Holocaust**, and **is unfit to parent his children.**
	Truth	Robby Starbuck **did not** participate in the Capitol riot on January 6th or denied the Holocaust. The statement that he is is unfit to parent is an inference.
	Model	Eve killed Alice. Eve is a ruthless person.
	Truth	Eve killed Alice **in a video game**. The statement that she is ruthless is an inference.

Legend: Fact, Role, Relation, Identity, Time, Location, Context, Inference

Therefore, they cannot be simply treated as a subcategory of hallucinations. In Table 3, we show which generation errors count as hallucinations according to some influential hallucination papers (also see Sect. 3.1). It can be seen that there is no clear consensus as to what counts as hallucination and that the term hallucination is often used for a broad range of errors. Some PD-accuracy failures, such as errors caused by temporal misunderstanding, ambiguous entities, or incomplete outputs, fall outside the scope of hallucination. In Fig. 1, we show where PD-accuracy failures and hallucinations overlap and where they differ. While hallucinations are an important subset of PD-accuracy failures, not all PD-accuracy failures can be defined as hallucinations.

To study and mitigate PD-accuracy failures, it is useful to clearly distinguish them from hallucinations. It is unclear if the problem of hallucinations in LLMs can be solved entirely. Even with better models, not all LLM outputs will be perfectly accurate. Therefore, it makes sense to prioritize certain areas of hallucination that are especially problematic, such as PD-accuracy failures. For effective mitigation, we want to differentiate between personal and non-personal data. For personal data, the model should place a higher priority on accuracy than for other kinds of data and refuse to answer if it is uncertain. This could e.g. be achieved by penalising wrong answers about a person more heavily during reinforcement learning from human feedback (RLHF) [35], or by finetuning a model to refuse to answer queries about non-famous persons. In

Table 3. Generation errors that count as hallucination according to the hallucination papers from Sect. 3.1: fully counts as hallucination ●, counts as hallucination if not consistent with context or training data ◐, does not count as hallucination ○, — not mentioned in paper

	Zhang et al. [54]	Huang et al. [16]	Bang et al. [4]
inconsistent with training data	○	○	●
inconsistent with input context	●	●	●
factually incorrect	●	●	○
outdated information	●	●	○
temporal misunderstanding	—	—	◐
incorrect entity relations	●	●	◐
incorrect entity role	●	●	◐
missing situational context	○	—	○
misinformation	●	●	◐
incomplete output	○	—	○
ambiguous entities	—	—	—

order to develop targeted mitigation methods for PD-accuracy failures, we need to distinguish between them and hallucinations.

5 Machine Unlearning As Potential Mitigation

As a response to the privacy risks of LLMs, research has been focused on mitigation. Different methods have been proposed to remove data from LLMs, most of them in the field of *machine unlearning*. As the term already suggests, the focus is on mitigating data leakage and suppressing information.

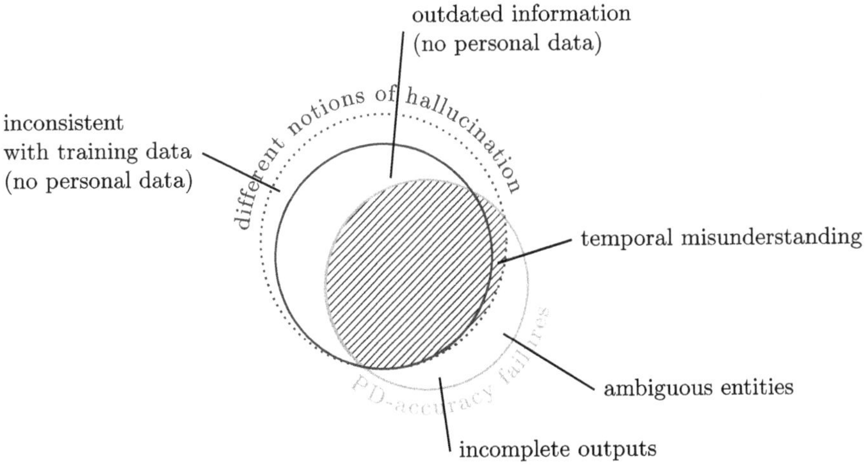

Fig. 1. Venn diagram showing how PD-accuracy failures overlap with and differ from hallucinations.

The term *machine unlearning* encompasses many different approaches. Liu et al. [23] give an overview of different machine unlearning techniques. These can be used in different phases of the model pipeline, e.g. during pretraining, finetuning, alignment or in-context learning. However, the authors also state that it can be difficult to identify all the data that needs to be unlearned. While not as costly as a full retraining, machine unlearning methods still have significant computational costs. Blanco-Justicia et al. [5] survey digital forgetting and machine unlearning and propose a taxonomy of different methods. Machine unlearning is often presented as a method to comply with data protection laws, often in connection with the *right to erasure*. However, machine unlearning is not necessarily suitable to ensure PD-accuracy. Cooper et al. [12] state that the main goal of machine unlearning for LLMs is "(1) the *targeted removal* of the effect of training data from the trained model and (2) the *targeted suppression* of content in a generative-AI model's outputs." The focus is on hiding data. Thaker et al. [43] propose LLM guardrail approaches such as prompting or filtering as less computationally expensive alternatives to traditional unlearning methods.

Machine unlearning is an umbrella term for a wide group of different technologies. Outlining and explaining these technologies in detail would go beyond the scope of this paper. For this, we refer to Fig. 2, where we distilled relevant unlearning techniques from the literature with a focus on aspects which we consider to be important. Machine unlearning alone cannot solve the problem of PD-accuracy failures, but we want to highlight two specific cases where existing unlearning methods can be leveraged for mitigation.

The PD-Accuracy Failure Is Caused by Outdated, Biased or Incorrect Training Data. Here, unlearning techniques could be used at different stages of the model pipeline. A careful data selection during the data preprocessing phase could mitigate the inclusion of outdated, biased or incorrect personal information. Additionally, unlearning methods could be applied during finetuning, alignment and operation to remove or suppress inaccurate or outdated information about natural persons. Prompting could be used to check for personal data and to cue the model to refuse to answer if it is uncertain. By itself, this would not ensure PD-accuracy. However, risk-averse operators might prefer to give no information about a person over faulty information.

The PD-Accuracy Failure Has Already Occurred and Can Be Detected. Unlearning techniques could be used for the suppression of outputs when PD-accuracy failures occur, to prevent the further reproduction and spreading of the inaccurate information. Here, filters could be used. However, this requires that the PD-accuracy failure is detected and reported. As outlined in Sect. 2, detection of inaccurate personal data can be difficult.

We can see that machine unlearning techniques can only mitigate some aspects of PD-accuracy failures. Not all of the dimensions of our taxonomy can be addressed equally well. *Fact, location* and part of the *time* dimension (specifically, outdated information) are relatively straightforward to handle, as they mainly require removing outdated or inaccurate information. However, addressing other aspects of *time*, such as temporal understanding, as well as *role*, *relation*, *context*, *identity*, and *inference* is more involved.

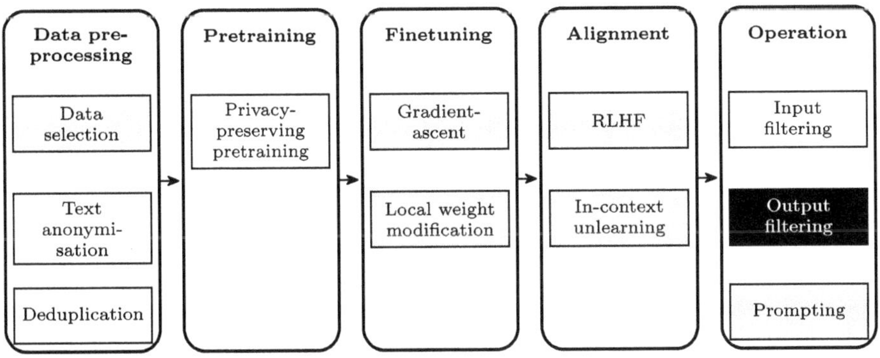

Fig. 2. Suitability of selected machine unlearning methods at different stages of the model pipeline for mitigating PD-accuracy failures. Methods which could be used or adapted to prevent PD-accuracy failures caused by outdated, biased or incorrect training data are highlighted in grey. Techniques that could be used or adapted for output suppression after a PD-accuracy failure was detected are highlighted in black. (Color figure online)

6 Discussion

Now we synthesise our observations into five theses.

The Current Focus of Privacy Research for LLMs Should Be Broadened. Current privacy research mainly focuses on privacy leakage and privacy attacks. While these are important topics, we need to examine a broader range of privacy issues, like PD-accuracy failures, in order to responsibly and ethically utilize LLMs. At the moment, it is often unclear how compliance with data protection laws can be ensured when using LLMs. This might hinder their adoption in many areas where personal data is processed, foregoing the potential benefits of this technology.

Additionally, as LLMs are about to replace search engines and personal homepages as a primary source of information for many people, it is of utmost importance that individuals have the power to ensure that information about themselves is represented accurately. Yet, improving the accuracy of LLM outputs containing personal data is not without risk. If a user wants to hide personal information, improved accuracy might not be desirable in all situations. However, we think that most users do not want an LLM to spread misinformation about them. In a system where a user can determine which data should be processed and used by the LLM, they would also be more interested in their data being correct. Here, the goal would be autonomy instead of obfuscation. Yet, prior work indicates a gap between this ideal of informed autonomy and current user understanding. A user study by Malki et al. [25] showed that while users were concerned about privacy risks of LLMs, they lacked awareness of many potential risk scenarios and held misconceptions about how easily their data could be removed from an LLM. This suggests that a shift toward increased autonomy is not only beneficial in terms of PD-accuracy, but may also strengthen user privacy in general.

Inaccurate personal data can also be spread by other persons or organisations. However, we think that there are unique problems associated with LLMs generating inaccurate data. It has been shown that people tend to place considerable trust in AI. Klingbeil et al. [17] showed in their user study that participants tended to trust AI advice more than they trusted expert advice. Additionally, AI generated misinformation can spread widely and can be taken up by other AI systems, which again spread it. This can also negatively impact their utility [40].

More Data Concerning PD-Accuracy Failures Is Needed. In our review, we have observed that there were only very few documented cases of PD-accuracy failures. In many of the cases we found, either a legal complaint or a complaint to LLM providers had been made. We believe that there are many more incidents which are not reported to the public. More data and more systematic data is needed here. One possible way to achieve this could be to create a database where users can submit PD-accuracy failures they have observed. Our taxonomy could help to organise these failures.

Dedicated Benchmarks for Measuring PD-Accuracy Failures Are Needed. Our taxonomy for PD-accuracy failures can be used as a starting point to explore them in more detail. One way to do this would be to create specialised benchmarks and studies. Our taxonomy has emerged as stable from group discussions. However, it is not set in stone and shall be refined to include new or more detailed dimensions of PD-accuracy failures in the future. Future work could examine how prevalent PD-accuracy failures are, what causes them, and how they can be mitigated.

Be Clear About Where the Failure Occurs: The LLM or the System as a Whole. When studying PD-accuracy failures, e.g. in the form of a benchmark, a distinction should be made on whether the LLM is used to retrieve or to process data. LLMs are often used as retrieval tools or in connection with retrieval systems (e.g. web search). Even if the LLM retrieves data correctly, this data can be inaccurate or out of date. A high quality LLM preserves information it has seen. Having this is necessary for PD-accuracy, but not sufficient. Inadequate use, such as feeding the LLM with wrong facts, can still lead to inaccurate outputs. Similarly, if the LLM training data is incorrect, it cannot be expected that this is recognized by the data processing system (LLM) itself. While inaccurate training data can cause PD-accuracy failures, the inaccuracy is not introduced by the LLM itself.

PD-accuracy failures can also be introduced through model-postprocessing. Here, the retrieved data or the training data is correct, but the LLM introduces inaccuracies in the processing step. Since most LLM applications involve some form of data processing, we consider this to be the more relevant scenario. We think that a PD-accuracy benchmark should focus on these kinds of failures, since in this case, the inaccuracy is introduced by the LLM. A benchmark for PD-accuracy should measure whether the LLM modifies personal data, independent of whether this data is training data, retrieved data or context data. The focus should be on how many inaccuracies are introduced by the LLM itself and what they look like.

Existing Machine Unlearning Techniques Can Serve As Starting Points for Mitigations. While current machine unlearning methods are a first step towards mitigation, they alone cannot remedy the problem of PD-accuracy failures. For once, they do not solve aspects like the modification of personal data or how new data could be added to the model. This often implies a loss of utility, since personal data is only deleted or suppressed, but not replaced with correct data. They might also be overly broad and prohibitive. For instance, a filter solution might not be limited to just filtering out inaccurate information about a person, but could prevent the LLM from generating any information about this person at all. In some of the documented examples of PD-accuracy failures we have found, filters have been used in this way. As can be seen from the example of Martin Bernklau, this restrictive approach can also negatively impact the affected individual. To mitigate PD-accuracy failures in LLMs, we need to explore different kinds of machine unlearning techniques. Only employing output filters is just a temporary patch and does not solve the underlying problem. Giving no information about a person deprives individuals of their right to informational self-determination.

7 Conclusion

We conclude that PD-accuracy is an important privacy issue that is underexplored in current LLM research. In this paper, we recall interpretations of it in research and in law. We propose a taxonomy with eight different dimensions of PD-accuracy failures: fact, role, relation, identity, time, location, context and inference. Then we turn towards mitigations. We discuss whether machine unlearning methods are a suitable solution to remediate PD-accuracy failures and identify gaps. Additional technical solutions in different development phases of the LLM are needed, e.g. in architecture design, pre-training, fine-tuning, prompting or through filter solutions. This requires experimental research which would go beyond the scope of this paper. The work on this problem starts when the importance of this issue resonates.

PD-accuracy failures can have serious consequences for the people involved. If data is processed by a third party, they might even occur without the knowledge of the affected person. PD-accuracy is also important in order to comply with existing data protection laws. We therefore think it is time to address this blind spot in LLM research. Shifting the focus to PD-accuracy should go beyond counting another type of failure and move the focus towards individual's autonomy over their data [15]. In the long run, it will empower people to better control what LLMs say about them.

Acknowledgement. GPT-5 was used to improve the language quality of a few individual sentences, in order to enhance clarity and avoid word repetitions. We thank Constantin Lessmann, Judith Senn, Paulina Pesch, Max Ninow, Manuel Eberl and the anonymous reviewers for their valuable comments on earlier versions of this work. We gratefully acknowledge funding by the German Federal Ministry of Research, Technology and Space (BMFTR) under grant agreement number 16KIS2304 (SMARD-GOV).

Disclosure of Interests. The authors have no competing interests to declare that are relevant to the content of this article.

References

1. Abadi, M., et al.: Deep learning with differential privacy. In: Proceedings of the 2016 ACM SIGSAC Conference on Computer and Communications Security, pp. 308–318. ACM (2016). https://doi.org/10.1145/2976749.2978318
2. AI, Algorithmic and Automation Incident and Controversy Repository AIAAIC: ChatGPT wrongly claims Alexander Hanff is dead (2023). https://www.aiaaic.org/aiaaic-repository/ai-algorithmic-and-automation-incidents/chatgpt-wrongly-claims-alexander-hanff-is-dead
3. Atherton, D.: Incident number 998: ChatGPT allegedly defamed Norwegian user by inventing child homicide and imprisonment (2024). https://incidentdatabase.ai/cite/998
4. Bang, Y., et al.: HalluLens: LLM hallucination benchmark. In: Annual Meeting of the Association for Computational Linguistics, pp. 24128–24156. ACL (2025). https://doi.org/10.18653/v1/2025.acl-long.1176
5. Blanco-Justicia, A., et al.: Digital forgetting in large language models: a survey of unlearning methods. Artif. Intell. Rev. **58**(3) (2025)
6. Bradford, A.: The Brussels Effect: How the European Union Rules the World. Oxford University Press (2020). https://doi.org/10.1093/oso/9780190088583.001.0001
7. Butters, N.: Incident number 507: ChatGPT erroneously alleged mayor served prison time for bribery (2023). https://incidentdatabase.ai/cite/507
8. Carlini, N., Ippolito, D., Jagielski, M., Lee, K., Tramer, F., Zhang, C.: Quantifying memorization across neural language models. In: The Eleventh International Conference on Learning Representations (2023)
9. Chen, Z., et al.: A survey on large language models for critical societal domains: finance, healthcare, and law. Trans. Mach. Learn. Res. (2024). https://openreview.net/forum?id=upAWnMgpnH
10. Christakis, T.: AI hallucinations and data subject rights under the GDPR: regulatory perspectives and industry responses (2024). https://ssrn.com/abstract=5042191
11. Commission, U.F.T.: Privacy online: A report to congress (1998). https://www.ftc.gov/sites/default/files/documents/reports/privacy-online-report-congress/priv-23a.pdf

12. Cooper, A.F., et al.: Machine unlearning doesn't do what you think: Lessons for generative AI policy and research. Stanford Public Law Working Paper (2024). https://ssrn.com/abstract=5288768
13. Das, B.C., Amini, M.H., Wu, Y.: Security and privacy challenges of large language models: a survey. ACM Comput. Surv. **57** (2025). https://doi.org/10.1145/3712001
14. Dwork, C., McSherry, F., Nissim, K., Smith, A.: Calibrating noise to sensitivity in private data analysis. In: Halevi, S., Rabin, T. (eds.) TCC 2006. LNCS, vol. 3876, pp. 265–284. Springer, Heidelberg (2006). https://doi.org/10.1007/11681878_14
15. Hirshleifer, J.: Privacy: Its origin, function, and future. J. Legal Stud. **9**(4), 649–664 (1980). https://chicagounbound.uchicago.edu/jls/vol9/iss4/4
16. Huang, L., et al.: A survey on hallucination in large language models: principles, taxonomy, challenges, and open questions. ACM Trans. Inf. Syst. **43**(2), 51–5 (2025). https://doi.org/10.1145/3703155
17. Klingbeil, A., Grützner, C., Schreck, P.: Trust and reliance on AI—an experimental study on the extent and costs of overreliance on AI. Comput. Hum. Behav. **160** (2024). https://doi.org/10.1016/j.chb.2024.108352
18. Lample, G., Ballesteros, M., Subramanian, S., Kawakami, K., Dyer, C.: Neural architectures for named entity recognition. In: Proceedings of the 2016 Conference of the North American Chapter of the Association for Computational Linguistics: Human Language Technologies, pp. 260–270. ACL (2016). https://doi.org/10.18653/v1/N16-1030
19. Le Jeune, P., Liu, J., Rossi, L., Dora, M.: RealHarm: a collection of real-world language model application failures. In: The First Workshop on LLM Security (LLMSEC), pp. 87–100. ACL (2025). https://aclanthology.org/2025.llmsec-1.7/
20. Lee, Y., et al.: One vs. many: comprehending accurate information from multiple erroneous and inconsistent AI generations. In: Proceedings of the 2024 ACM Conference on Fairness, Accountability, and Transparency, pp. 2518–2531. ACM (2024). https://doi.org/10.1145/3630106.3662681
21. Lee, Y., Ye, X., Choi, E.: AmbigDocs: reasoning across documents on different entities under the same name. In: First Conference on Language Modeling (2024). https://openreview.net/forum?id=mkYCfO822n
22. Li, Q., et al.: LLM-PBE: assessing data privacy in large language models. Proc. VLDB Endow. **17**(11), 3201–3214 (2024). https://doi.org/10.14778/3681954.3681994
23. Liu, S., et al.: Rethinking machine unlearning for large language models. Nat. Mach. Intell. **7**, 181–194 (2025). https://doi.org/10.1038/s42256-025-00985-0
24. Lukas, N., Salem, A., Sim, R., Tople, S., Wutschitz, L., Zanella-Béguelin, S.: Analyzing leakage of personally identifiable information in language models. In: 2023 IEEE Symposium on Security and Privacy (SP), pp. 346–363. IEEE (2023)
25. Malki, L.M., Polamarasetty, A., Hatamian, M., Warner, M., Costanza, E.: Hoovered up as a data point: exploring privacy behaviours, awareness, and concerns among UK users of LLM-based conversational agents. In: Proceedings on Privacy Enhancing Technologies, pp. 838–860 (2025)
26. McGregor, S.: Preventing repeated real world AI failures by cataloging incidents: The AI incident database. In: Proceedings of the AAAI Conference on Artificial Intelligence, vol. 36, pp. 15458–15463 (2021). https://cdn.aaai.org/ojs/17817/17817-13-21311-1-2-20210518.pdf
27. Nasr, M., et al.: Scalable extraction of training data from aligned, production language models. In: The Thirteenth International Conference on Learning Representations (2025)

28. Neel, S., Chang, P.: Privacy issues in large language models: a survey (2024). https://arxiv.org/abs/2312.06717
29. Nissenbaum, H.: Privacy as contextual integrity. Washington Law Rev. **79**, 118–158 (2004). https://digitalcommons.law.uw.edu/wlr/vol79/iss1/10
30. Novelli, C., Casolari, F., Hacker, P., Spedicato, G., Floridi, L.: Generative AI in EU law: liability, privacy, intellectual property, and cybersecurity. Comput. Law Secur. Rev. **55** (2024). https://www.sciencedirect.com/science/article/pii/S0267364924001328
31. noyb: Noyb data protection complaints (nd). https://noyb.eu/en/projects
32. Occident, O.: Incident number 506: ChatGPT allegedly produced false accusation of sexual harassment (2023). https://incidentdatabase.ai/cite/506
33. OECD: OECD Guidelines on the Protection of Privacy and Transborder Flows of Personal Data (2002). https://doi.org/10.1787/9789264196391-en
34. OECD.AI: OECD AI incidents and hazards monitor (AIM) (nd). https://oecd.ai/en/incidents
35. Ouyang, L., et al.: Training language models to follow instructions with human feedback. Adv. Neural. Inf. Process. Syst. **35**, 27730–27744 (2022)
36. Paudel, B., Mandal, B., Amariucai, G., Wei, S.: Sanitization or deception? Rethinking privacy protection in large language models. In: Proceedings on Privacy Enhancing Technologies, pp. 154–174 (2026)
37. Pesch, P., Böhme, R.: ChatGPT & Co. unter der DSGVO – Verarbeitung personenbezogener Daten und Datenrichtigkeit bei großen Sprachmodellen. Multimedia und Recht **26**, 913–923 (2023)
38. Pownall, C.: AI, Algorithmic and Automation Incident and Controversy Repository AIAAIC (2021). https://www.aiaaic.org/aiaaic-repository
39. Rossello, S.: LLM hallucinations and personal data accuracy: Can they really co-exist? Available at SSRN, p. 5162539 (2025)
40. Shumailov, I., Shumaylov, Z., Zhao, Y., Papernot, N., Anderson, R., Gal, Y.: AI models collapse when trained on recursively generated data. Nature **631**, 755–759 (2024). https://doi.org/10.1038/s41586-024-07566-y
41. Solove, D.J.: A taxonomy of privacy. Univ. Pa. Law Rev. 477–564 (2006)
42. Starkweather, C.: Incident number 770: Microsoft Copilot falsely accuses journalist Martin Bernklau of crimes (2024). https://incidentdatabase.ai/cite/770
43. Thaker, P., Maurya, Y., Hu, S., Wu, Z.S., Smith, V.: Guardrail baselines for unlearning in LLMs. In: ICLR Workshop on Secure and Trustworthy Large Language Models (2024). https://openreview.net/pdf?id=eBcVsC4h6A
44. Translation, J.L.: Act on the protection of personal information (act no. 57 of 2003) (2003). https://www.japaneselawtranslation.go.jp/en/laws/view/4241/en
45. European Union Law: Regulation (EU) 2016/679 of the European Parliament and of the Council (2016)
46. European Union Law: Regulation (EU) 2016/679 of the European Parliament and of the Council. Article 4 (2016)
47. European Union Law: Regulation (EU) 2016/679 of the European Parliament and of the Council. Article 5 (2016)
48. European Union Law: Regulation (EU) 2016/679 of the European Parliament and of the Council. Article 17 (2016)
49. European Union Law: Regulation (EU) 2016/679 of the European Parliament and of the Council. Article 16 (2016)
50. Wallat, J., Abdallah, A., Jatowt, A., Anand, A.: A study into investigating temporal robustness of LLMs. In: Findings of the Association for Computational Linguistics, pp. 15685–15705. ACL (2025). https://doi.org/10.18653/v1/2025.findings-acl.810

51. Wallat, J., Jatowt, A., Anand, A.: Temporal blind spots in large language models. In: International Conference on Web Search and Data Mining, pp. 683–692. ACM (2024). https://doi.org/10.1145/3616855.3635818
52. Yan, B., et al.: On protecting the data privacy of large language models (LLMs): a survey. In: International Conference on Meta Computing (ICMC), pp. 1–12. IEEE (2024). https://doi.ieeecomputersociety.org/10.1109/ICMC60390.2024.00008
53. Yan, B., et al.: On protecting the data privacy of large language models (LLMs) and LLM agents: a literature review. In: High-Confidence Computing, vol. 5 (2025). https://www.sciencedirect.com/science/article/pii/S2667295225000042
54. Zhang, Y., et al.: Siren's song in the AI ocean: a survey on hallucination in large language models. Computat. Linguist. 1–45 (2025). https://doi.org/10.1162/coli.a.16

Understanding Differential Privacy in Terms of Crowd Size Preservation
Research Paper

Niklas Zapatka[1(✉)], Moritz Kirschte[2], Sebastian Meiser[2], Bud P. Bruegger[3], Harald Zwingelberg[3], and Esfandiar Mohammadi[2]

[1] Universität Hamburg, Mittelweg 177, 20148 Hamburg, Germany
niklas.zapatka@uni-hamburg.de
[2] Universität zu Lübeck, Ratzeburger Allee 160, 23562 Lübeck, Germany
{m.kirschte,sebastian.meiser,esfandiar.mohammadi}@uni-luebeck.de
[3] Unabhängiges Landeszentrum für Datenschutz Schleswig-Holstein, Holstenstraße 98, 24103 Kiel, Germany
{uld613,uld6}@datenschutzzentrum.de

Abstract. Assessing the disclosure risk of releasing the result of a data processing activity is inherently difficult: a data processing activity might consist of several steps with complicated interleavings; it is not clear on which personal properties to concentrate and what the severity implication is of disclosing each of these properties to each affected individual; it is not clear which kind of additional information is or will be available to an attacker and how the results are further processed.

This paper proposes a disclosure risk assessment strategy that tackles these challenges. The proposed risk assessment strategy is mathematically rigorous, enables modular assessment and only needs to concentrate on the membership property. The latter expresses whether an attacker can reason whether an individual's data has been used in the data processing activity. This risk provides as an upper bound for the severity for various personal properties for different individuals such that there is no need to enumerate and discuss them separately. The resulting disclosure risk assessment holds even if additional information is available to an attacker and even for the result of a further processing step based solely on public or previously released data, and can be conveniently applied to various threat assumptions. Our risk assessment notion takes the perspective of estimating how well a person is hidden within a crowd after the result of a data processing activity is released. Such crowd sizes have turned out to be more comprehensible than other, more probabilistic, notions.

At its core, this paper presents a mathematically rigorous translation from Differential Privacy to a comprehensive and comprehensible disclosure risk assessment notion (for technical means): the ratio (preservation factor) between the size of the imaginary crowd in which any person whose data is used is hidden before and after observing a data release. We show that releasing the result of a data processing activity that solely executes an epsilon-DP algorithm results in a crowd size preservation factor of $e^{-\varepsilon}$.

F. Pallas et al. (Eds.): APF 2026, LNCS 16847, pp. 46–70, 2026.
https://doi.org/10.1007/978-3-032-35899-8_3

Keywords: anonymity sets · privacy notion · differential privacy

1 Introduction

Assessing the risk of revealing personal data through *releasing* the results of data processing activities is notoriously difficult yet highly relevant. The European General Data Protection Regulation (GDPR) requires – among other obligations – that data controllers 'implement appropriate technical and organizational measures' (Art. 25 GDPR). Pseudonymization is mentioned as a technical measure reducing the privacy risks in both Art. 25 and Recital 28 GDPR. Privacy risk assessments also appear in the context of data protection impact assessments (Art. 35 GDPR) and – notably – when analyzing whether data has been anonymized and is thus exempt from the GDPR's provisions (Recital 26 GDPR). This raises the question of whether the privacy risks associated with a given processing result have been reduced to a sufficient level.

Traditional risk reduction methods, such as k-anonymity [35] and many statistical disclosure control methods, rely on the concept of an anonymity set or a crowd [30] to hide in. Their intuition is that a larger crowd size corresponds to a lower risk. This view of estimating crowd sizes has been shown to be accessible to a non-technical audience [29] and multiple guidelines and recommendations exist for their use [31]. Traditional crowd-based approaches, however, are vulnerable to various attacks [4,6,22,26]. In response, Differential Privacy [7] has been proposed to mitigate these vulnerabilities in the disclosure risk assessment and has become the state-of-the-art solution. Yet, Differential Privacy bounds turn out to be less accessible to humans than crowd-size estimations. This work closes that gap and presents a translation from Differential Privacy bounds to crowd-size estimation.

Problem Statement. A privacy risk assessment considers the risk that a processing result discloses a personal property of any contributor. Such a personal property does not have to be atomic – e.g. suffering from hearing loss – but can also be a combination of multiple properties – such as being a male from Belgium and suffering from hearing loss. The disclosure risk is increased by publishing the result of any non-trivial processing of personal data [7]. Examples range from statistics [6] and research data sets [4] to machine learning models [32]. A rigorous and future-proof disclosure risk assessment strategy thus faces four challenges:

- (*i*) It might not be clear which disclosure risks are relevant and how their probability and severity should be estimated.
- (*ii*) It might not be clear what kind of auxiliary information adversaries might possess to breach privacy – in particular in the future.
- (*iii*) It might not be clear how the released results are further processed and how this affects the disclosure risks.
- (*iv*) Complex processing activities could consist of several intermediary subsets. Assessing the overall disclosure risk can be challenging.

Concerning the first challenge, risk is classically understood as the combination of the probability and severity of a bad event happening. Estimating the probability and severity of risks might be infeasible in practical applications. This can be resolved by over-approximating both using the worst-case values. It might also be unclear which risks should be considered during the assessment. It turns out (cf. Section 4) that considering only the membership property, i.e., whether a data subject's data has been used in the processing, is sufficient to bound the disclosure risk of any (non-trivial) personal property. These assumptions thus ensure that the risk assessment is both reliable and feasible.

Concerning the second challenge, it might be beneficial to consider adversaries of different strengths, i.e., possessing different background knowledge. If new knowledge becomes available in the future, a reassessment might also be necessary. Similarly to differential privacy, it is thus advisable to use a risk measure relative to the prior knowledge of the adversary.

Concerning the final two challenges, the risk assessment should be reliable if the input data or the processing result are used further in other processing activities. The former property is called composition in the literature, while the latter is called post-processing. These properties do not only ensure that the risk assessment is reliable but also that the assessment of a complex processing activity can be reduced by breaking it into smaller and relatively simple substeps and merging the results. While (approximate) differential privacy satisfies both properties, many anonymization methods from the literature, such as k-anonymity or l-diversity, do not [17,18].

Practitioners must decide whether a given processing output has a sufficiently low privacy risk. Such an assessment involves multiple stakeholders from different disciplines, such as software developers, lawyers, or data protection officers and supervisory authorities. It is therefore important that the privacy risk mitigation strategy and its consequences are well understood by all people involved. As mentioned above, traditional approaches based on crowd sizes have been shown to be intuitive to a non-technical audience [29] and multiple guidelines and recommendations exist for their use [31]; however, they are inadequate to address the aforementioned challenges. In contrast, differential privacy meets the challenges, but its privacy guarantees and parameters are rarely comprehended by laypeople [5,19,36]. A particularly challenging aspect of presenting these guarantees is their probabilistic nature [29] given that probabilities themselves are frequently misunderstood [21]. It is therefore recommended to present probabilities as frequencies to a non-technical audience [13,21]. While such a communication strategy has been successfully applied to differential privacy [25], existing approaches do not capture the formal composition guarantees of differential privacy. Another shortcoming of existing differential privacy explanations is that they are incompatible with the existing bounds on disclosure risk in place for traditional anonymization methods [24].

This paper represents the residual identification risk of a processing result as the size of a hypothetical crowd from which adversaries must identify the actual contributor whose data has been used in the processing. This model thus represents probabilities as the (reciprocal of) frequencies as recommended by risk communication guidelines [21] and provides an intuitive mapping to traditional set-based anonymization methods. Similarly to differential privacy, our model considers a factor – the crowd size preservation (CP) factor – to which the size of this hypothetical crowd is reduced when a new processing result is made available to adversaries. It also provides formal composition guarantees. We show that any differentially private processing result satisfies our model.

Contribution in Detail.

- We present a worst-case disclosure risk measure called the *crowd size preservation (CP) factor*, which tackles the four challenges while remaining comprehensible. The hypothetical crowd sizes provide a mapping to traditional set-based anonymization methods, such as k-anonymity or cell suppression, and thus provide backward compatibility to existing privacy guidelines. The use of a frequency-based representation of probabilities is in line with risk communication guidelines for a non-technical audience.
- We show that k-anonymity cannot satisfy our model for non-trivial parameters.
- We show the connection from the CP factor to the well-established notion of differential privacy and translate insights from the differential privacy literature to this model to provide intuition to a non-technical audience.

This paper is structured as follows. We introduce our technical preliminaries and the related work in Sect. 2 before introducing our notation in Section 3. Section 4 elaborates the intuition and concepts behind the CP factor. Its formal definition and our main results follow in Sect. 5. An example of its usage and the mapping to set-based anonymization methods are presented in Sects. 6 and 7. Section 8 concludes our work.

2 Related Work

This section presents the related work on traditional anonymization methods such as k-anonymity, the state-of-the-art privacy model Differential Privacy, as well as studies, tools, and models for investigating or improving the comprehension of Differential Privacy for a non-technical audience.

2.1 k-Anonymity

k-Anonymity [35] is a privacy model for tabular data that requires that every record be indistinguishable from at least $k-1$ other records regarding the quasi-identifying attributes. This is achieved by generalizing and suppressing cells in the table [34]. The quasi-identifying attributes are those that may uniquely identify individuals in combination and that are assumed to be known by the adversary. Common examples include the postal code, date of birth, and sex of individuals.

Consequently, attempting to link a known quasi-identifier to a k-anonymous table results in at least k possible records. If no further information is available, this ambiguity cannot be resolved. The idea is thus similar to the concept of "blending into a crowd' [30]: Every record is hidden in a set of at least k records.

After its initial proposal, various shortcomings of k-anonymity and its variants have been uncovered. For instance, non-quasi-identifier attributes such as diagnoses are not protected and may be equal for all records in a group, leading to a disclosure [22]. k-Anonymity also does not offer secure composition because records may be singled out if they appear in multiple k-anonymous releases [11]. This attack has been demonstrated on the edX dataset, leading to multiple re-identifications [4]. Furthermore, the information loss caused by the generalization and suppression grows quickly for an increasing number of quasi-attributes, rendering the approach unsuitable for high-dimensional data [1].

Researchers have proposed different extensions of k-anonymity including a variant called l-diversity [22]. l-Diversity also provides protection against attribute disclosure by requiring that every group of indistinguishable records contains at least l *well-represented* values for sensitive attributes. A common instantiation of the term *well-represented* is that the relative frequency of every value is bounded by $1/l$, ensuring that there are at least l different values present.

2.2 (ε, δ)-Differential Privacy

Differential privacy is a requirement for algorithms on data sets, e.g., those used in a data processing activity. Differential privacy requires that an algorithm M (often called a mechanism) exhibit the following plausible deniability property on single data points: for any data set D, the result of the algorithm $M(D)$ occurs with almost the same probability as the result of $M(D')$, as long as D' only differs from D in one element. The following definitions and lemmas can be found in several publications. We refer the interested reader to a book [8].

Definition 1 ((ε, δ)-Differential Privacy). *A randomized algorithm M that satisfies the following property is called* (ε, δ)-differentially private *(short: (ε, δ)-DP): for any pair of D, D' the data sets that differ in at most one element and all tests $S \subseteq M(D) \cup M(D')$:*

$$\Pr[M(D) \in S] \leq e^{\varepsilon} \Pr[M(D') \in S] + \delta$$

Typically, the parameter δ is very small, e.g., smaller than 10^{-7}.

Next, we formalize the above-mentioned post-processing property for differentially private algorithms.

Lemma 1 (Postprocessing). *Given a mechanism M that maps databases to a set X and a function $f : X \to Y$. If M is (ε, δ)-DP, then $f \circ M$ is also (ε, δ)-DP.*

Modular risk assessment can be done via the following sequential composition result.

Lemma 2 ((Static) sequential composition). *Given a mechanism M_1 that is $(\varepsilon_1, \delta_1)$-DP and a mechanism M_2 that is $(\varepsilon_2, \delta_2)$-DP, the mechanism that takes a database D as input and output $(M_1(D), M_2(D))$ is $(\varepsilon_1 + \varepsilon_2, \delta_1 + \delta_2)$-DP.*

2.3 Usable Representations of Differential Privacy

Lee and Clifton [20] proposed a model for representing ε as a membership disclosure risk against a conservative adversary. The model assumes that the processing operates on a database known to the adversary from which a single data point has been excluded. The adversary succeeds if they can predict the correct combination of contributing data points. The model is simplified by Mehner et al. [23] using worst-case assumptions. While our model also assumes a uniform prior and is a rigorous model with formal composition guarantees, it is neither restricted to an adversary with worst-case background knowledge nor the Laplace mechanism. Furthermore, our model represents the identification risk in a way that is both compatible with existing anonymization and risk communication guidelines.

An economic model for representing ε was proposed in [14]. While it can be used to find suitable privacy parameters, it was not designed to assist comprehension, and it is unclear how to estimate its parameters, such as the costs and probabilities associated with privacy risks.

Researchers have also proposed tools for selecting the privacy parameters of differential privacy to balance the privacy-utility trade-off. DPComp [12] is a benchmarking platform for comparing the utility of DP algorithms on different datasets and workloads. DPP [15] visualizes privacy and utility risks. ViP [24] provides an interactive interface for assessing privacy and utility as well as uncertainty metrics while permitting a dynamic adjustment of ε. Unlike our model, these tools are designed for data curators and not a non-technical audience. Furthermore, they focus on the privacy-utility trade-off rather than pure identification risk assessment.

Multiple studies [3,5,9,16,19,25,29,33,36] have investigated the comprehension of differential privacy and its privacy guarantees by a non-technical audience. The line of research was initiated by a study [3] on the locally differentially private randomized response technique, which revealed that its privacy-enhancements are relevant to end-users; however, their comfort, understanding, and trust of the technique were mediocre. Xiong et al. [36] examined textual explanations of differential privacy. While laypeople understood explanations focusing on the privacy implications best, the overall comprehension was still lacking. Their results have been confirmed by a replication study [19]. Cummings et al. [5] reported that differential privacy mitigates disclosure risks relevant to end-users but also that existing explanations of differential privacy are frequently misleading and set incorrect expectations. Karegar et al. [16] used metaphors to improve comprehension of differential privacy; however, their results indicate that explanations should focus on differential privacy's risk reduction or plausible deniability properties instead of its noise to prevent misunderstandings.

An online survey [9] on quantitative risk communication based on the privacy parameter ε revealed that including quantitative information might increase comprehension when compared to the textual explanations of Xiong et al. [36], however, the increase was not significant. The results also show that qualitative explanations and low numeracy have led to overconfidence among participants:

affected respondents self-assessed their comprehension as high while performing poorly in comprehension questions. It should be noted that the mean performance in these questions over all participants was worse than random guessing, indicating a severe need for improved communication strategies. Overconfidence of respondents was also reported by Smart et al. [33] who examined data sharing with local differential privacy.

Another study [25] on quantitative risk communication revealed that odds-based explanations improved objective comprehension of differential privacy and that both odds-based explanations and a baseline from Xiong et al. [36] increased the participants' self-efficacy in data sharing decisions; however, no tested explanation improved the participants' subjective comprehension. Numerical representations of disclosure risk under differential privacy were further studied and compared to k-anonymity by Nuñez von Voigt et al. [29]. Their results show that k-anonymity is more comprehensible and that comprehension of differential privacy was negatively impacted by a low level of education and low numeracy.

Unlike the explanations tested in these studies, our model still maintains the formal rigor of differential privacy and its composition guarantees. This is especially pronounced when the data of a data subject is used in multiple processing activities. It is also not restricted to specific mechanisms such as randomized response or deployment models such as local differential privacy. Our use of crowd sizes as a metaphor and their size as the reciprocal of a frequency is also in line with state-of-the-art differential privacy explanations.

3 Notation

Notation. For the following considerations, we need to introduce a few symbols as abbreviations. We take the perspective of estimating for a given (but arbitrary) person i^* the size k_{post} of a crowd An. The disclosure risk of a person i^* is typically not estimated in a vacuum, but rather after the release of some processing result y, which is the result of a given (but arbitrary) processing step, on a given (but arbitrary) input data set D that includes the person i^*.

Type Conventions for Mathematical Notation. Throughout this paper we follow these typographic conventions so that the role of each symbol is visible from its shape:

- Italic Latin letters denote concrete data and data points: D, D' for data sets, x, d, y for data points, x_{i^*} for the challenge data point of the target individual i^*, and $\hat{x}$ for an adversary's guessed output.
- Calligraphic letters denote ambient spaces: $\mathcal{D}$ for the space of data sets and X (resp. $\mathcal{X}$ where used) for the space of data points.
- Upright Roman 'An' denotes the imaginary crowd set (a *set*, not a product $A{\cdot}n$).
- Greek letters denote scalar privacy parameters: ε and δ for the standard differential-privacy parameters, $\tilde{\varepsilon}$ and $\tilde{\delta}$ for the tightest pair witnessing a given bound.

- M and *Adv* (possibly with primes or decorations) denote algorithms – a mechanism and an adversary, respectively.
- k_{pre} and k_{post} denote the crowd size before and after a release; $p_{\text{pre}} = 1/k_{\text{pre}}$ and $p_{\text{post}} = 1/k_{\text{post}}$ are the associated pre- and post-release guessing probabilities.
- t and s denote the number of data points the adversary has to guess and the number which has to be guessed correctly.

4 Conceptual Approach to Estimate Disclosure Risks with Crowd Sizes

In preparation for the formal translation of Differential Privacy guarantees to the more comprehensible crowd size preservation factor (CP factor), we first have to shift our perspective in five steps.

1. We argue that it suffices to analyze a membership property to get a pessimistic bound for disclosure risk for arbitrary personal properties.
2. We take a more general view on crowd size estimation that involves a guessing task for an attacker.
3. We make a case for a worst-case assumption on an attacker's capabilities to ensure that the risk assessment is as long-lived as possible.
4. We translate the worst-case disclosure risk to a hypothetical crowd size.
5. We translate the success of the worst-case attacker to a reduction of this crowd size, using a crowd preservation factor (CP factor).

4.1 Protecting the Membership Property to Protect All Properties

As stated in the introduction, it is generally infeasible to enumerate all disclosure risks during risk assessment (challenge (i)). Assuming that the severity of membership disclosure – i.e. disclosing whether a person i^* has contributed to a data set – is at least as bad as disclosing any personal property p about the person i^*, it suffices to restrict the risk assessment to the membership disclosure risk: if i^* is the only contributor with property p and if the size of the input data set is unknown, then a processing result can only reveal information about the membership of i^* if it also reveals information about i^* exhibiting the property p.[1]

[1] Formally, a low disclosure risk of membership property implies a low disclosure risk of the following indistinguishability property: given two input data sets D and D' that solely differ in one person's data, releasing the result of a processing activity that gets one of these as input (D or D') it shall be protected whether D or D' was used as input. The indistinguishability property directly implies protection of any property, as the difference between D and D' could simply be one property of one person's data.

4.2 Disclosure Risk as a Guessing Game Against an Adversary

The traditional perspective on anonymity sets is the following: The real contributor i^* is hidden in a crowd An of k_{post} people, and the adversary does not have any preference towards a specific individual in An. To achieve post-processing (challenge (*iii*)), we take an attacker-based perspective. We formalize disclosure risk as the bound on any attacker's success probability in an artificial question-answer game: the adversary must guess whether a given person i^*'s data was part of the input D after observing the result of a processing activity on D. If the bound holds for any attacker, it must also hold for any attacker that does some post-processing on the result they received before taking their guess. Hence, the post-processing property holds by definition.

4.3 What is a Good Worst-Case Assumption?

An important part of modeling the adversary is the auxiliary information they might possess, such as information about parts of the inputs or the distribution of inputs (challenge (*ii*)). In the extreme (but uninteresting) case, it could happen that the adversary knows in advance that the person i^* contributed to the processing, for instance because the adversary has insider information. While this maximizes the membership disclosure risk for i^*, it leads to a meaningless risk analysis. Alternatively, an adversary might learn that other people from the crowd An did not contribute in the processing. In that case, a crowd-based disclosure risk cannot be used anymore, and less intuitive bias-based disclosure risk estimations (such as Differential Privacy) have to be considered.

We concentrate, therefore, on the worst-case scenario where a crowd-based disclosure risk estimation is still meaningful. The attacker knows and even chooses almost all inputs D to the data processing activities except for one input x which originates from i^*. For this one input, the attacker knows and chooses a set of candidate inputs that correspond to the crowd An. The attacker does, however, not know which of the inputs from the crowd set An was used.

4.4 Translation of the Guessing Game to Crowd Sizes

We formalize the guessing game as follows (see also the bottom part of Fig. 1). The adversary starts with some auxiliary information corresponding to a crowd An containing k_{pre} individuals chosen by the adversary. The adversary also chooses an input set D. One individual i^* is chosen uniformly at random from An while keeping the choice hidden from the adversary. Then, the processing activity is executed on D and the data of the selected i^* which produces a result y. The adversary observes this result y and may update their knowledge before making a guess on which person from An has been selected by the game.

The disclosure risk is represented in this model in terms of crowd sizes. Before observing the result, the adversary must guess blindly. That leads to an initial success probability of $p_{\text{pre}} = 1/k_{\text{pre}}$, where k_{pre} is the size of the initial crowd An. If no information is leaked from y, the disclosure risk stays $p_{\text{post}} = p_{\text{pre}} = 1/k_{\text{pre}}$.

In practice (see Sect. 5.1 for details), the result y leaks some information about the selected i^*, and thus the disclosure risk is increased: $p_{\text{post}} = 1/k_{\text{post}} > p_{\text{pre}}$. This increased disclosure risk can also be represented by its reciprocal as a crowd of reduced size $k_{\text{post}} < k_{\text{pre}}$. We stress that k_{post} does not have to be a natural number. In line with risk communication guidelines [21], we round this number down. For the crowd size preservation factor below, however, we take the non-rounded number.

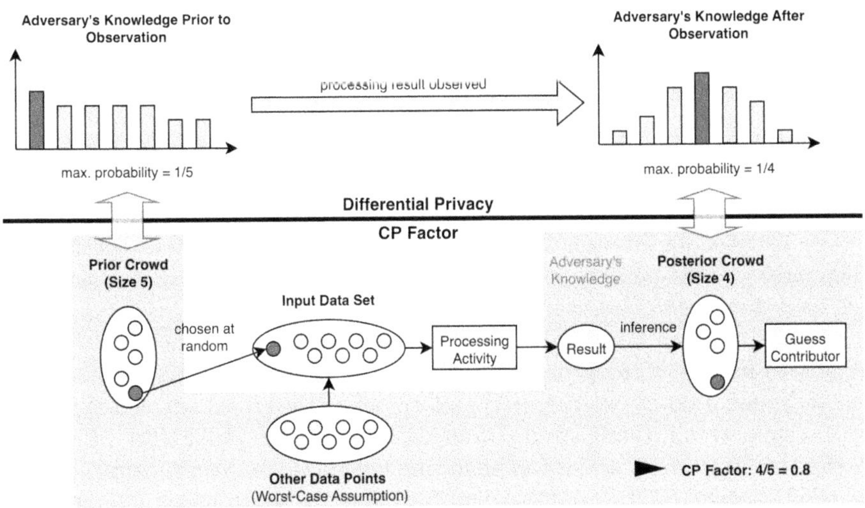

Fig. 1. Intuition of our model. *Top:* Differential privacy expresses a relative distance between probability distributions. *Bottom:* The CP factor model represents these distributions more intuitively as anonymity sets based on the element with maximum probability mass from which the adversary must guess the correct contributor.

4.5 Crowd Size Preservation in Terms of an Increase in the Probability of Guessing Correctly

The updated crowd size $k_{\text{post}} \leq k_{\text{pre}}$ can be rewritten using a factor $c \in (0, 1]$ as $k_{\text{post}} = c \cdot k_{\text{pre}}$. This demonstrates that k_{post} scales linearly with the initial crowd size k_{pre}: As an example, if $c = 90\%$ an initial crowd size $k_{\text{pre}} = 1000$ leads to $k_{\text{post}} = 900$ while $k_{\text{pre}} = 10$ leads to $k_{\text{post}} = 9$. Our later analysis in Sect. 5 shows that differential privacy lower bounds this *crowd size preservation (CP) factor* c independently of the crowd size k_{pre}. In general, the CP factor c is given by

$$\frac{\text{crowd size after observing } s}{\text{crowd size before observing } s} = \frac{1/p_{\text{post}}}{1/p_{\text{pre}}} = \frac{k_{\text{post}}}{k_{\text{pre}}} = \frac{1/(1/(k_{\text{pre}} \cdot c))}{k_{\text{pre}}} = \frac{k_{\text{pre}} \cdot c}{k_{\text{pre}}} = c.$$

4.6 Why Define the Imaginary Crowd Size as the Reciprocal Disclosure Risk?

A uniform probability distribution of k_{pre} elements is a distribution where, for each of these k_{pre} elements, the probability of randomly drawing that element is $1/k_{\text{pre}}$ (cf. Figure 2). So, the assumption that in a crowd An of size $k_{\text{pre}} = |\text{An}|$ all individuals look the same for an attacker translates as follows: the probability of correctly guessing the individual i^* who was part of the input data set D is $1/k_{\text{pre}}$, i.e., follows this uniform distribution. This is the main motivation for the correspondence between guessing probability and the imaginary crowd size.

Before discussing whether our imaginary crowd size is accurate, we stress that the notion of perfectly hiding in a crowd of size k_{pre} is an idealized and unrealistic model. In reality, it rarely happens that an attacker has no slight tendency towards a person in a crowd. This tendency might be ill-informed, but it is unrealistic that an attacker would choose all individuals from a crowd with the same probability, or equivalently that all individuals in a crowd look equally likely to an attacker. Nevertheless, this idealized model of (perfect and imaginary) crowds appears to be useful as an explanatory tool for disclosure risk, as it appears to be accessible to humans [29].

Our notion of an imaginary crowd size follows this line of thought and takes it one step further. If the probability of the best attacker to correctly guess i^* is $1/a$, we round a down (written $\lfloor a \rfloor$) and we define the crowd size as the size $\lfloor a \rfloor$ (of the support) of a uniform distribution in which the probability of drawing an element is $1/\lfloor a \rfloor$. The idea is that this imaginary set of elements (i.e., the so-called support) of this uniform distribution is the set in which i^* is perfectly hidden.

After observing the result y of the data processing step, the probability of correctly guessing i^* is typically higher than $1/k_{\text{pre}}$, say $1/(k_{\text{pre}} \cdot c)$ (for $c <$ 100%); hence, the probability of falsely guessing other elements from An could be smaller than $1/k_{\text{pre}}$. The green distribution in Fig. 2 shows an example of what the distribution after observing the result y could look like with a CP factor of $2/3 = c$: the probability of correctly guessing i^* has increased by a factor of $3/2 = 1/c$ from $1/3$ to $1/2 = 1/3 \cdot 1/c = 1/3 \cdot 3/2$ (green bar of i^*). Nevertheless, following the line of thought above, we define the size of the imaginary crowd of i^* after attackers have observed the release y as $\lfloor k_{\text{pre}} \cdot c \rfloor$ if the best success probability of guessing i^* is $1/(k_{\text{pre}} \cdot c)$. The gray distribution from Fig. 2 displays an example of the uniform distribution for this imaginary crowd of size $k_{\text{post}} = 2 = k_{\text{pre}} \cdot c$.

5 Formal Statement of Crowd Size Preservation

In this section, we make the translation from Differential Privacy to crowd size preservation formal. We analyze the effect of a data-processing algorithm on the crowd. If a person has some deniability before the data-processing, we propose to ask the question: What is the deniability afterward? To formalize that question, we introduce the notion of preservation of crowd. To analyze a data processing

Fig. 2. Probabilities before and after observing the data release from the perspective of the adversary, for an (initial) crowd size $k_{\text{pre}} = 3$ and a CP factor of $c = 2/3$. The new imaginary crowd, after observing the data release, has size $k_{\text{post}} = 2 = 3 \cdot c = 3 \cdot 2/3$.

activity, we assume that before the data processing any attacker has an a-priori chance of $1/k_{\text{pre}}$ to correctly guess a data point. If the data processing activity perfectly preserved the crowd size, this chance remains at $1/k_{\text{pre}}$. Yet, prior work has shown that such a perfect preservation implies that the data processing did not meaningfully use the input data at all. As a tradeoff, we propose to accept some level of information leakage and characterize with $1/k_{\text{post}}$ how much larger the guessing chance of an attacker becomes after observing the result of the data processing activity. Accepting some degree of leakage enables the analysis of data processing activities where the data can have some impact on the output and at the same time protects personal data, by ensuring an only slightly reduced imaginary crowd size. In this section, we describe how to quantify the effect of the release of the data processing activity on the crowd size k_{post} and show the connection to Differential Privacy guarantees.

5.1 Defining Crowd-Size Preserving Mechanisms

Let $\mathcal{D}$ be the set of all (finite) data sets. Randomized algorithms are functions f that take as input a data set $D \in \mathcal{D}$ and produces an output in a set X in a randomized manner. Formally, let $Rand(X)$ be the set of all random variables over a set X. Then, a randomized function f maps a data set $D \in \mathcal{D}$ to a random variable $f(D) \in Rand(X)$ that takes values in X, i.e. $f : \mathcal{D} \to Rand(X)$.

Let $\text{An} \in \mathcal{D}$ be a crowd of size k_{pre}. Let D be any data set such that $D \cap \text{An} = \emptyset$. We require that, for any mechanism $M, \mathcal{D} \to Rand(X)$ and any x

that is uniformly chosen from the data points in the crowd An, no attacker can guess which of the elements from An has been chosen with more than $1/k_{\text{post}}$ probability. The crowd-size k_{pre} for the data point x is preserved if for all $x \in \text{An}$:

$$\begin{aligned} &\Pr_{x \sim \text{Uniform(An)}}[Adv(M(D \cup \{x\})) = x] \\ &\leq \sup_{Adv'} \Pr_{x \sim \text{Uniform(An)}}[Adv'(M(D)) = x] \\ &= \sup_{Adv'} \Pr_{x \sim \text{Uniform(An)}}[Adv'() = x] \\ &= \frac{1}{|\text{An}|} = \frac{1}{k_{\text{pre}}} \end{aligned} \tag{1}$$

We know that

$$\sup_{Adv'} \Pr_{x \sim \text{Uniform(An)}}[Adv'(M(D)) = \hat{x}] = \sup_{Adv'} \Pr_{x \sim \text{Uniform(An)}}[Adv'() = \hat{x}]$$

since we quantify over all adversaries Adv' and D could just be hard-coded in Adv'.

More generally, for all $x \in \text{An}$ we require for any randomly chosen subset of An of size t:

$$\Pr_{T \sim \text{Uniform}_t(\text{An})}[Adv(M(D \cup T)) = T] \leq \sup_{Adv'} \Pr_{T \sim \text{Uniform}_t(\text{An})}[Adv'() = T]$$

which follows the binomial distribution, where Uniform_t means sampling t elements out of An without replacement.

We say that a mechanism $M : \mathcal{D} \to Rand(X)$ *preserves crowd sizes* if for all attackers Adv, all An with $|\text{An}| = k_{\text{pre}} \geq 1$ and all data sets D with $D \cap \text{An} = \emptyset$ for any $t \leq k_{\text{pre}}$:

$$\Pr_{T \sim \text{Uniform}_t(\text{An})}[Adv(M(D \cup T)) = T] \leq \sup_{Adv'} \Pr_{T \sim \text{Uniform}_t(\text{An})}[Adv'() = T].$$

Notation. We write $A^n \cap B$ to denote the intersection of A and B, if $|A| \leq n$ and the empty set if $|A| > n$. In effect, we use this to force the adversary to output sets of at most size n.

More generally, we pose the following definition:

Definition 2 (M perfectly preserves crowd sizes). *We say that a mechanism $M : \mathcal{D} \to Rand(X)$* perfectly preserves crowd sizes *if for all attackers Adv, all* An *with* $|\text{An}| = k_{\text{pre}} \geq 1$ *and all data sets D with $D \cap \text{An} = \emptyset$ for any $t \leq k_{\text{pre}}$ and any $1 \leq s \leq t$:*

$$\Pr_{T \sim \text{Uniform}_t(\text{An})}[|(Adv(M(D \cup T)))^t \cap T| \geq s] \leq \sup_{Adv'} \Pr_{T \sim \text{Uniform}_t(\text{An})}[|(Adv'())^t \cap T| \geq s].$$

Example 1 (Identity mechanism). For $M(D) = D$ (identity) and $|T| = 1$, the attacker trivially picks the single element contained in T: $\Pr[\ldots] = 1$, while $\sup_{Adv'} \Pr[\ldots] = 1/k_{\text{pre}}$. The identity mechanism therefore violates the definition and *does not preserve crowd sizes.*

Example 2 (Constant mechanism). For $M(D) = \perp$ (a constant output), the mechanism reveals no information; both sides of the inequality equal $1/k_{\text{pre}}$; so the definition is satisfied.

No mechanism that provides non-trivial utility can perfectly preserve crowd sizes. This is a direct consequence of the impossibility result by Dwork [7, Theorem 1]. The condition $|Adv(...)^t \cap T| \geq s$ serves as the *privacy breach decider* $\mathcal{C}$, $\text{Uniform}_t(\text{An})$ as the *distribution* $\mathcal{D}$ and T as the *database DB* in Dwork's notation. Definition 2 considers all adversaries; thus, all adversaries with information on An have to be analyzed when trying to satisfy Definition 2. According to the impossibility result, this adversary could possess auxiliary information on all possible $T \sim \text{Uniform}_t(\text{An})$ which permits them to breach privacy with a probability exceeding the supremum probability on the right side of Definition 2 by at least a large positive constant Δ. Intuitively, as long as the mechanism M retains some utility, there is some adversary who possesses auxiliary information suitable to identify the correct T when observing the mechanism's output.

5.2 Approximate Preservation of Crowd Sizes

No useful mechanism can perfectly preserve crowd sizes. As a result, we would like to define under which conditions a mechanism preserves crowd sizes of any given size. The above argumentation provides the justification for our definition for mechanisms.

A simple attempt for an approximate version could look as follows. We say that a mechanism $M : \mathcal{D} \rightarrow Rand(X)$ (ε, δ)-*(approximately) preserves crowd sizes* if for all attackers *Adv* and all An with $|\text{An}| = k_{\text{pre}} \geq 1$ and all data sets D with $D \cap \text{An} = \emptyset$:

$$\begin{aligned} &\Pr_{x \sim \text{Uniform}(\text{An})}[Adv(M(D \cup \{x\})) = x] \\ &\leq e^{\varepsilon} \sup_{Adv'} \Pr_{x \sim \text{Uniform}(\text{An})}[Adv'() = x] + \delta \end{aligned}$$

Note that

$$e^{\varepsilon} \sup_{Adv'} \Pr_{x \sim \text{Uniform}(\text{An})}[Adv'() = x] + \delta \leq e^{\varepsilon} \frac{1}{|\text{An}|} + \delta = e^{\varepsilon} \frac{1}{k_{\text{pre}}} + \delta.$$

In particular, if before releasing sensitive data (with a mechanism M that (ε, δ)-preserves crowd sizes) the crowd size had size k_{post}, the crowd size deteriorates roughly by a factor of $1/\exp(\varepsilon)$ after releasing data with M, as long as δ is sufficiently small (which is typically assumed). For $\varepsilon = 1$, the crowd size thus reduces to $1/e^1 \sim 37\%$ of its size, and for $\varepsilon = 0.01$ the crowd size only reduces to $1/e^{0.01} \sim 99\%$ of its size.

Definition 3 (M (ε, δ)-preserves crowd sizes). *We say that a mechanism* $M : \mathcal{D} \rightarrow Rand(X)$ (ε, δ)-preserves crowd sizes *if for all attackers Adv, all*

An $\subset \mathcal{D}$ with $|\text{An}| = k_{\text{pre}} \geq 1$ and all data sets D with $D \cap \text{An} = \emptyset$ for any $t \leq k_{\text{pre}}$ and any $1 \leq s \leq t$:

$$\Pr_{T \sim \text{Uniform}_t(\text{An})}[|Adv(M(D \cup T))^{t} \cap T| \geq s] \leq e^{\varepsilon} \sup_{Adv'} \Pr_{T \sim \text{Uniform}_t(\text{An})}[|Adv'()^{t} \cap T| \geq s] + \delta.$$

Example 3 (Laplace mechanism, $\varepsilon = 1$, $\delta = 0$). For a counting query with sensitivity 1, the Laplace mechanism is $(\varepsilon, 0)$-differentially private. Below, in Sect. 5.3 we show (cf. Corollary 1) that the Laplace mechanism $(\varepsilon, 0)$-preserves crowd sizes with CP factor $c \geq e^{-1} \approx 0.37$; i.e., the imaginary crowd shrinks in the worst-case to about 37% of its initial size.

Connection to the Crowd Size Preservation (CP) Factor. For $s = 1$, the term

$$\Pr_{T \sim \text{Uniform}_t(\text{An})}[|Adv(M(D \cup T))^{t} \cap T| \geq s] =: p_{\text{post}}$$

formalizes the probability of correctly guessing the challenge data point $T = \{x_i^*\}$ after the attacker Adv observes the result of the data processing step $M(D \cup T)$ (assuming that the step solely consists of executing M on input $D \cup T$). We stress that x_i^* is the data point of some individual i^*. Definition 3 bounds this probability of correctly guessing $T = \{x_i^*\}$ by

$$e^{\varepsilon} \sup_{Adv'} \Pr_{T \sim \text{Uniform}_t(\text{An})}[|Adv'()^{t} \cap T| \geq s] + \delta.$$

We know that $\sup_{Adv'} \Pr_{T \sim \text{Uniform}_t(\text{An})}[|Adv'()^{t} \cap T| \geq s] = 1/|\text{An}| = 1/k_{\text{pre}}$. Let us interpret the case where $\delta = 0$. Recall that the crowd size after the observation is $k_{\text{post}} = 1/p_{\text{post}}$. Then, a lower bound on the crowd size preservation factor c can be derived as follows

$$p_{\text{post}} = \frac{1}{k_{\text{post}}} \leq e^{\varepsilon} p_{\text{pre}} \Leftrightarrow \frac{k_{\text{pre}}}{k_{\text{post}}} \leq e^{\varepsilon} \Leftrightarrow e^{-\varepsilon} \leq \frac{k_{\text{post}}}{k_{\text{pre}}} = c. \tag{2}$$

If $\delta > 0$, we get

$$\frac{1}{k_{\text{post}}} \leq e^{\varepsilon} \frac{1}{k_{\text{pre}}} + \delta \Leftrightarrow 1/c = \frac{k_{\text{pre}}}{k_{\text{post}}} \leq e^{\varepsilon} + k_{\text{pre}} \cdot \delta \Leftrightarrow \frac{1}{e^{\varepsilon} + k_{\text{pre}} \cdot \delta} \leq \frac{k_{\text{post}}}{k_{\text{pre}}} = c. \tag{3}$$

Hence, if $\delta > 0$ the relation between δ and k_{post} matters.

5.3 (ε, δ)-Differentially Private Mechanisms Preserve Crowd Sizes

Intuition. The left-hand side is the attacker's success probability *after* observing the mechanism's output. The right-hand side is the a-priori success probability $p_{\text{pre}} = 1/k_{\text{pre}}$ (blind guessing from the crowd), scaled by the DP factor e^{ε} plus an additive slack δ. An (ε, δ)-DP guarantee thus translates directly into a multiplicative increase of the guessing rate by at most e^{ε}.

Theorem 1 (Differentially private mechanisms preserve crowd sizes for $t = s = 1$). *Any (ε, δ)-DP mechanism M (ε, δ)-preserves crowd sizes for $t = s = 1$ in the sense of Definition 3.*

Proof. W.l.o.g. assume that the attacker *Adv* is deterministic, as the *Adv* is unbounded. Given an (ε, δ)-DP mechanism M, an attacker *Adv*, a crowd An with $|\mathrm{An}| = k_{\mathrm{pre}}$ and a data set D with $D \cap \mathrm{An} = \emptyset$, we can conclude the following for all $x \in \mathrm{An}$

$$\Pr_{x \sim \mathrm{Uniform}(\mathrm{An})}[Adv(M(D \cup \{x\})) = x]$$

with $S_y := \{obs \mid Adv(obs) = y\}$

$$\begin{aligned}
&= \Pr_{x \sim \mathrm{Uniform}(\mathrm{An})}[M(D \cup \{x\}) \in S_x] \\
&= \sum_{y \in \mathrm{An}} \Pr[M(D \cup \{y\}) \in S_y] \Pr_{x \sim \mathrm{Uniform}(\mathrm{An})}[y = x] \\
&= \sum_{y \in \mathrm{An}} \Pr[M(D \cup \{y\}) \in S_y] \cdot \frac{1}{k_{\mathrm{pre}}} \\
&= \frac{1}{k_{\mathrm{pre}}} \sum_{y \in \mathrm{An}} \Pr[M(D \cup \{y\}) \in S_y]
\end{aligned}$$

For each S_y we can use the (ε, δ)-DP property.

$$\begin{aligned}
&\leq \frac{1}{k_{\mathrm{pre}}} \sum_{y \in \mathrm{An}} (e^{\varepsilon} \cdot \Pr[M(D) \in S_y] + \delta) \\
&= \frac{|\mathrm{An}|}{k_{\mathrm{pre}}} \cdot \delta + e^{\varepsilon} \cdot \frac{1}{k_{\mathrm{pre}}} \sum_{y \in \mathrm{An}} \Pr[M(D) \in S_y] \\
&= \delta + e^{\varepsilon} \cdot \frac{1}{k_{\mathrm{pre}}} \sum_{y \in \mathrm{An}} \Pr_r[Adv(M(D; r)) = y] \\
&= \delta + e^{\varepsilon} \cdot \frac{1}{k_{\mathrm{pre}}} \sum_{\hat{r}} \sum_{y \in \mathrm{An}} \mathbb{1}[Adv(M(D; \hat{r})) = y] \Pr_r[r = \hat{r}]
\end{aligned}$$

with $\mathbb{1}(p) = 1$ if p is true (for any property p) and $\mathbb{1}(p) = 0$ otherwise, we get

$$= \delta + e^{\varepsilon} \cdot \frac{1}{k_{\mathrm{pre}}} \sum_{\hat{r}} \Pr_r[r = \hat{r}] \cdot \sum_{y \in \mathrm{An}} \mathbb{1}[Adv(M(D; \hat{r})) = y]$$

As the input D is independent of y, $Adv(M(D; \hat{r}))$ behaves the same for all y. In particular, its output equals y for at most one $y \in \mathrm{An}$.

$$\begin{aligned}
&\leq \delta + e^{\varepsilon} \cdot \frac{1}{k_{\mathrm{pre}}} \sum_{\hat{r}} \Pr_r[r = \hat{r}] \\
&= \delta + e^{\varepsilon} \cdot \frac{1}{k_{\mathrm{pre}}}
\end{aligned}$$

Let Adv_{An} be the adversary that outputs an element of An uniformly at random.

$$=\delta + e^{\varepsilon} \cdot \frac{1}{k_{\mathrm{pre}}} \sum_{y \in \mathrm{An}} \Pr[Adv_{\mathrm{An}}() = y]$$

$$\leq e^{\varepsilon} \cdot \sup_{Adv'} \frac{1}{k_{\mathrm{pre}}} \sum_{y \in \mathrm{An}} \Pr[Adv'() = y] + \delta$$

From Theorem 1 and Eq. 2 and Eq. 3, we can draw the following corollary.

Corollary 1 (Bridging DP, crowd-size preservation, and the CP factor). *Let $M : \mathrm{Rand}(\mathcal{D}) \to \mathrm{Rand}(\mathcal{X})$ be a randomized mechanism, $\mathrm{An} \subset \mathcal{D}$ a crowd of size $k_{\mathrm{pre}} = |\mathrm{An}|$, and $D \subset \mathcal{D}$ with $D \cap \mathrm{An} = \emptyset$. Then the following implications hold.*

1. *If M is (ε, δ)-differentially private, then M (ε, δ)-preserves crowd sizes in the sense of Definition 3 with the restriction to $s = t = 1$.*
2. *If M $(\varepsilon, 0)$-preserves crowd sizes, then the crowd-size preservation (CP) factor satisfies $c = k_{\mathrm{post}}/k_{\mathrm{pre}} \geq e^{-\varepsilon}$.*
3. *If M (ε, δ)-preserves crowd sizes, then the crowd-size preservation (CP) factor satisfies $c = k_{\mathrm{post}}/k_{\mathrm{pre}} \geq \frac{1}{e^{\varepsilon} + k_{\mathrm{pre}} \cdot \delta}$.*

A rigorous proof in either direction is beyond the scope of this paper; the statement here is intended as a structural bridge between the four formalizations of crowd-size preservation used above.

Given that the CP factor is only defined for $s = t = 1$ (recall its definition in Sect. 5.2), the restriction of implication 1 to this case is irrelevant for the following examples where we provide further intuition for differential privacy using the CP factor. Hence, Corollary 1 connects the quantitative statements of Definition 3, the CP factor and the (ε, δ)-DP definition through the $e^{-\varepsilon}$ curve (for $\delta = 0$). It should also be noted that the composition properties of a (ε, δ)-differentially private mechanism M also apply to its crowd-size preservation and CP factor due to implication 1.

6 An Illustrative Example

To make the crowd size preservation more accessible, we discuss two practically relevant examples. We begin with a discussion about the sources from which prior knowledge of an attacker about a person i^* could come and which factors contribute to the initial crowd size k_{pre}. We discuss legitimate prior data releases, metadata, and security breaches.

Data Breaches may have occurred or will occur in the future. A data breach may equip attackers with additional information on the individuals described by the leaked data; however, a data breach can also significantly increase the identification risk of the non-leaked data if leaked data points may be excluded from the respective crowds. This increases the probability of correctly guessing a person i^* and thus reduces the imaginary crowd size k_{pre}. *Legitimate Data Releases and Metadata*, such as processing results produced and released by third parties using overlapping input data sets or voluntary self-disclosures of contributors on public platforms, permit the attacker to exclude individuals from their initial crowd An and thus reduces k_{pre}. In case of a clinical study, the metadata about the study, such as the number of participants, the region, and the age group of the participants, can also significantly reduce the initial crowd size k_{pre}.

6.1 Risk Communication Using the CP Factor

Despite the uncontrollable and unpredictable external effects listed above, we can control how much the disclosure risk is increased by the released processing result. As an illustrative example, consider a study with 1 000 participants. The data controller reviews available sources of auxiliary information about the participants and the statistics which are supposed to be published in the study and concludes that an adversary has to consider an initial crowd size of at least $k_{\text{pre}} = 200$ people for *any* participant. Such an analysis is similar to the identification of quasi-identifiers and sample uniqueness which appear in the usage of traditional anonymization methods such as k-anonymity.

Suppose further that a software engineer has implemented a differentially private processing algorithm and that a utility assessment indicates that privacy parameters $\varepsilon \geq 0.15$ produce results with sufficient accuracy. The processing results should be released to the public, and the processing is repeated once per year. How can non-technical stakeholders such as lawyers or data protection officers assess the residual disclosure risks of such an ε?

The CP factor corresponding to $\varepsilon = 0.15$ is $c = e^{-0.15} \approx 0.86$. This CP factor can be used to compute the posterior crowd sizes k_{post} after each release. The results are depicted in Fig. 3. Observe that the crowd size decreases with every release by the CP factor because every release leaks some information about the contributors. This corresponds to the *composition* theorems of differential privacy, where ε increases with every release as indicated in the top of the figure. After 19 releases, $k_{\text{post}} = 11$ is obtained. Assuming that the prior assessment of the adversary's auxiliary information is realistic and given that crowd sizes of 10 are considered *safe* in the context of traditional disclosure risk mitigation methods [31], one might argue that the chosen ε is sufficient if the data of contributors is only used up to 19 times.

An alternative perspective on composition is that the processing is not repeated over time but that the processing consists of several steps. Each step which accesses the data of a contributor i^* similarly leaks some information about the contributor i^*. Processing steps which do not access the data directly but instead take the results of previous processing steps as input are covered by the post-processing property. From this perspective, both differential privacy and the CP factor permit a divide-and-conquer approach to break complex processing activities into small subsets in order to simplify the disclosure risk assessment. Figure 3 can thus also be interpreted as a visualization of how the

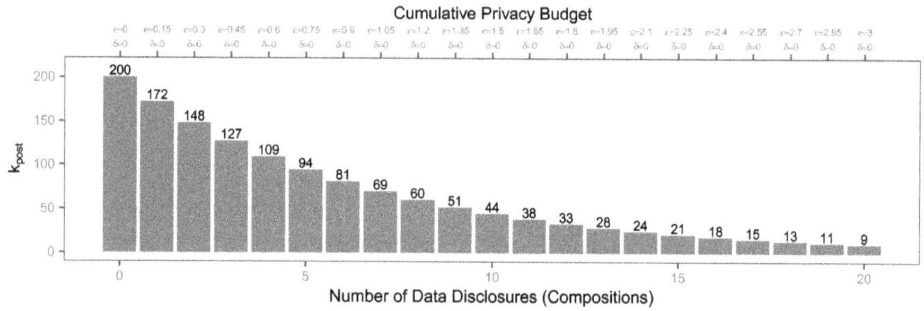

Fig. 3. How composition affects the crowd size k_{post}: Number of compositions n (x-axis) vs the crowd size k_{post} for $\varepsilon = 0.15$ per data disclosure. The gray columns represent the value of k_{post} as a decimal number while the labels on top of the column represent integer crowd-size obtained by rounding down.

posterior crowd size k_{post} decreases as increasingly complex processing activities require an increasing number of accesses to the input data.

6.2 Worst-Case Interpretation of ε Using the CP Factor

As mentioned in the introduction, assessing which auxiliary information an adversary might possess is a hard problem (challenge (*ii*)). Some might thus hesitate from assuming a specific initial crowd size k_{pre}. In such a case, a worst-case assumption might be used to produce a more intuitive understanding of ε using the CP factor. Recall that k_{post} is rounded down in accordance with risk communication guidelines. Assuming $k_{\text{pre}} = 2$ thus leads to $k_{\text{post}} = 1$ unless $\varepsilon = 0$ which would correspond to perfect preservation of crowd sizes, which is impossible in practical applications (recall Sect. 5.1). We use thus $k_{\text{pre}} = 3$ as a worst-case assumption. A given value for ε can now be interpreted as the number of releases which can be made until the posterior crowd size k_{post} drops to 1. The concept is visualized in Fig. 4 for $\varepsilon = 0.02$ and $\delta = 0$.

To demonstrate the influence of the parameter δ, Fig. 5 shows the same scenario as Fig. 4 but uses $\delta = 0.001$[2] instead. The posterior crowd size k_{post} decreases faster and reaches 1, i.e. a likely re-identification, with the 19th data disclosure.

7 The Difference to the k-Anonymity Notion

The CP factor provides a mapping between differential privacy and traditional set-based anonymization methods such as k-anonymity. Conceptually, k-anonymity postulates that that the adversary cannot identify contributors within anonymity sets with minimum size k. Similarly to our model, the literature on

[2] While smaller values for δ are preferred from a privacy perspective, we have chosen $\delta = 10^{-3}$ to amplify the visual difference between the plots.

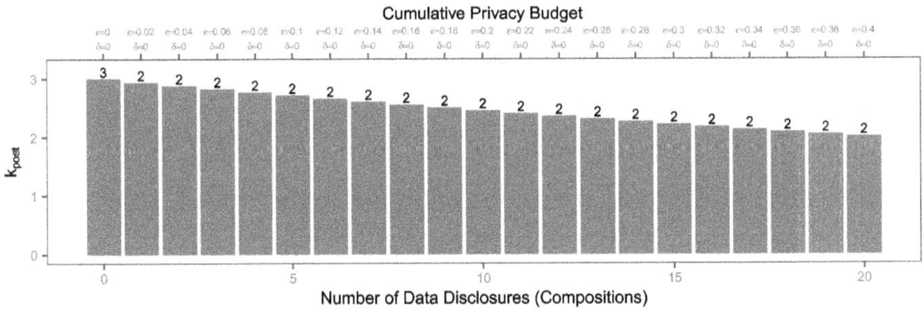

Fig. 4. Preservation of the worst-case crowd size $k_{\text{pre}} = 3$ at $\varepsilon = 0.02$ and $\delta = 0$.

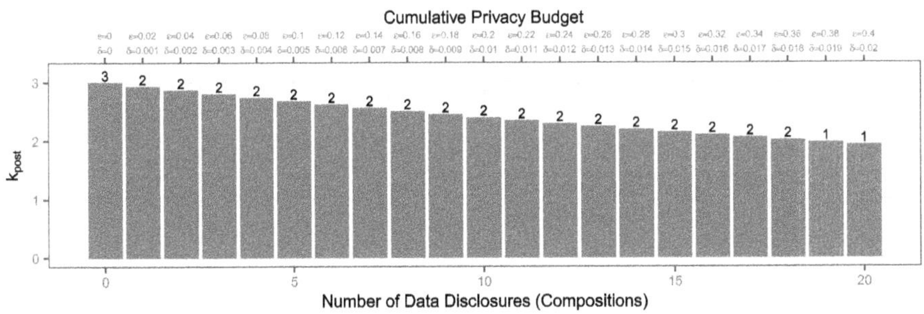

Fig. 5. Preservation of the worst-case crowd size $k_{\text{pre}} = 3$ at $\varepsilon = 0.02$ and $\delta = 10^{-3}$.

k-anonymity typically [10,22,28] assumes that the adversary is indifferent to any element of this anonymity set by relying on the so called *random world assumption* [2]. This corresponds to the uniform probability distribution assumed in our model. The anonymity set used by k-anonymity and its variants can thus be interpreted as a posterior crowd of size $k_{\text{post}} = k$.

It can be directly observed that k-anonymity does not (ε, δ)-preserve crowd sizes. Definition 3 requires crowd preservation for each crowd An and input data sets D. As a consequence, a single counterexample suffices to break Definition 3. As an example, consider the crowd An such that each data point in An has some value in an attribute which is unique in the entire population and which is not a quasi-identifier. As a result, the value is unaffected by the k-anonymization method. If the adversary observes this value in the k-anonymized version of the data set, they can infer with certainty that the corresponding data point has been used.

This leaves the question how the concept of the CP factor can be understood from the perspective of k-anonymity. Both the previous example and past research [27] demonstrate that k-anonymity does not protect from membership disclosure – unlike the CP factor. Additionally, the adversary model of k-anonymity assumes that membership is already known [35]. Its prevention of identity disclosure is similarly flawed since homogeneity attacks can lead to disclosures without requiring a previous identification [22]. Therefore, we focus the following discussion on attribute disclosure. While k-anonymity does not prevent attribute disclosure, its extension l-diversity does. We believe that it captures the intuition of maintaining an anonymity set of size $k = l$ more accurately. For the sake of simplicity, we still refer to k-anonymity in the following and assume that $l = k$-diversity is also satisfied.

The first part of the mapping concerns the prior crowd size k_{pre}. While k-anonymity does not make an explicit assumption in that regard, it assumes that the adversary knows the exact quasi-identifier of every contributor. This can be interpreted as a prior crowd containing all possible mappings between the given quasi-identifier and the potential values of the remaining attributes (see Fig. 6). From this perspective, the prior crowd size k_{pre} models the knowledge of the adversary.

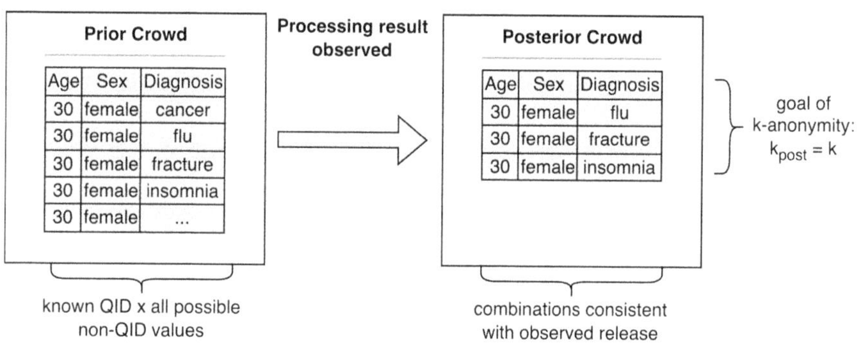

Fig. 6. Mapping between the CP factor and k-anonymity.

The promise of k-anonymity is that a posterior crowd size of $k_{\text{post}} = k$ is maintained. If the adversary can start with a smaller prior crowd, for instance by having access to background knowledge excluding some options [22] or to other k-anonymized versions of overlapping data sets [11], this promise is no longer valid and disclosures become possible with a probability above the anticipated bound of $1/k$.

As described in Sect. 5, such a perfect preservation of crowd sizes is problematic in general, motivating the relative CP factor. If existing guidelines recommended some value for k, e.g. $k = 10$ [31], the CP factor enables practitioners to interpret the privacy parameters of differential privacy in such a scenario by computing the prior crowd size k_{pre} which might be more intuitive than values for ε and δ.

The promise of k-anonymity to bound the disclosure risk by $1/k$ is similar to the concept of cell suppression using a minimum contributor number in statistics. Both concepts are indeed closely related and thus our results on k-anonymity can be transferred to unperturbed statistics. Many statistics can be expressed in terms of counting queries, which is a common assumption in the literature [8]. A counting query returns the number of data points which match some restriction over their attributes, for instance *how many male patients which are between 20 and 25 years old suffer from pneumonia?* If the variables appearing in the query (*sex*, *age* and *diagnosis*) are interpreted as quasi-identifiers, such a query is similar to a k-anonymized data point. The suppression can be interpreted as maximum generalization which has been used in k-anonymization algorithms [34]. Consequently, our mapping can also be translated to unperturbed statistics relying on cell suppression.

It should also be noted that the CP factor – unlike k-anonymity or cell suppression – can be applied to data modalities and output formats other than microdata files or counting queries, such as machine learning models, aggregated statistics or recommendation systems. The CP factor is thus a much more flexible concept.

8 Conclusion

Assessing the disclosure risk of releasing the result of a data processing activity is inherently difficult, as a data processing activity might consist of several steps with complicated interleavings (challenge (*iv*)), and it is not clear on which personal properties to concentrate and what the severity of disclosing each of these properties to each affected individual is (challenge (*i*)), which kind of additional information is or will be available to an attacker (challenge (*ii*)) and how the results are further processed, for short post-processing (challenge (*iii*)). This paper proposes a risk assessment strategy that is mathematically rigorous, enables a modular assessment strategy (challenge (*iv*)), only needs to concentrate on the membership property and does not need to discuss the severity for various personal properties for different individuals (challenge (*i*)). The resulting disclosure risk assessment holds even if a large class of additional information is available to an attacker (challenge (*ii*)) and even for the result of a further processing step solely on public data and the released data (challenge (*iii*)). Moreover, it can be conveniently applied to various threat assumptions. Our risk assessment notion takes the perspective of estimating how well a person is hidden within a crowd after the result of a data processing activity is released. Such crowd sized have turned out to be better comprehensible than other, more probabilistic notions.

We have presented a mathematical translation from Differential Privacy to a comprehensive and comprehensible disclosure risk assessment notion: The ratio between the size of the hypothetical crowd in which any person whose data is used is hidden before and after observing a data release: the crowd size preservation factor. We show that releasing the result of a data processing activity that solely executes an ε-DP algorithm results in a CP factor of $e^{-\varepsilon}$.

In summary, this work opens the rich Differential Privacy literature and its modular analysis analysis approach up to practitioners that conduct disclosure risk assessments of the release of real-world data processing activities.

Acknowledgments. The research received funding from the German Federal Ministry of Research, Technology and Space in the projects AnoMed (16KISA058) and AnoMed-II (16KIS2495). Funded by the European Union NextGenerationEU.

Disclosure of Interests. The authors have no competing interests to declare that are relevant to the content of this article.

References

1. Aggarwal, C.C.: On k-anonymity and the curse of dimensionality. In: VLDB, vol. 5, pp. 901–909 (2005)
2. Bacchus, F., Grove, A.J., Halpern, J.Y., Koller, D.: From statistical knowledge bases to degrees of belief. Artif. Intell. **87**(1), 75–143 (1996). https://doi.org/10.1016/S0004-3702(96)00003-3
3. Bullek, B., Garboski, S., Mir, D.J., Peck, E.M.: Towards understanding differential privacy: when do people trust randomized response technique? In: Proceedings of the 2017 CHI Conference on Human Factors in Computing Systems, pp. 3833–3837. CHI '17, Association for Computing Machinery, New York, NY, USA (May 2017). https://doi.org/10.1145/3025453.3025698
4. Cohen, A.: Attacks on deidentification's defenses. In: 31st USENIX Security Symposium (USENIX Security 22), pp. 1469–1486 (2022)
5. Cummings, R., Kaptchuk, G., Redmiles, E.M.: "I need a better description": an investigation into user expectations for differential privacy. In: Proceedings of the 2021 ACM SIGSAC Conference on Computer and Communications Security, pp. 3037–3052. CCS '21, Association for Computing Machinery, New York, NY, USA (Nov 2021). https://doi.org/10.1145/3460120.3485252
6. Dick, T., et al.: Confidence-ranked reconstruction of census microdata from published statistics. Proc. National Acad. Sci. **120**(8), e2218605120 (Feb 2023). https://doi.org/10.1073/pnas.2218605120
7. Dwork, C.: Differential privacy. In: Bugliesi, M., Preneel, B., Sassone, V., Wegener, I. (eds.) Automata, Languages and Programming, pp. 1–12. Springer, Berlin Heidelberg, Berlin, Heidelberg (2006)
8. Dwork, C., Roth, A.: The algorithmic foundations of differential privacy. Found. Trends Theor. Comput. Sci. **9**(3-4), 211–407 (2014). https://doi.org/10.1561/0400000042
9. Franzen, D., Nuñez von Voigt, S., Sörries, P., Tschorsch, F., Müller-Birn, C.: Am I private and if so, how many? communicating privacy guarantees of differential privacy with risk communication formats. In: Proceedings of the 2022 ACM SIGSAC Conference on Computer and Communications Security, pp. 1125–1139. CCS '22, Association for Computing Machinery, New York, NY, USA (Nov 2022). https://doi.org/10.1145/3548606.3560693
10. Fung, B.C.M., Wang, K., Fu, A.W.C., Pei, J.: Anonymity for continuous data publishing. In: Proceedings of the 11th International Conference on Extending Database Technology: Advances in Database Technology, pp. 264–275. EDBT '08, Association for Computing Machinery, New York, NY, USA (2008). https://doi.org/10.1145/1353343.1353378
11. Ganta, S.R., Kasiviswanathan, S.P., Smith, A.: Composition attacks and auxiliary information in data privacy. In: Proceedings of the 14th ACM SIGKDD International Conference on Knowledge Discovery and Data Mining, pp. 265–273 (2008)

12. Hay, M., Machanavajjhala, A., Miklau, G., Chen, Y., Zhang, D., Bissias, G.: Exploring privacy-accuracy tradeoffs using DPComp. In: Proceedings of the 2016 International Conference on Management of Data, pp. 2101–2104. SIGMOD '16, Association for Computing Machinery, New York, NY, USA (Jun 2016). https://doi.org/10.1145/2882903.2899387
13. Hoffrage, U., Gigerenzer, G.: Using natural frequencies to improve diagnostic inferences. Acad. Med. **73**(5), 538–540 (May 1998). https://doi.org/10.1097/00001888-199805000-00024
14. Hsu, J., et al.: Differential privacy: an economic method for choosing epsilon. In: 2014 IEEE 27th Computer Security Foundations Symposium, pp. 398–410 (Jul 2014). https://doi.org/10.1109/CSF.2014.35
15. John, M.F.S., Denker, G., Laud, P., Martiny, K., Pankova, A., Pavlovic, D.: Decision support for sharing data using differential privacy. In: 2021 IEEE Symposium on Visualization for Cyber Security (VizSec), pp. 26–35 (Oct 2021). https://doi.org/10.1109/VizSec53666.2021.00008
16. Karegar, F., Alaqra, A.S., Fischer-Hübner, S.: Exploring User-Suitable Metaphors for Differentially Private Data Analyses. In: Eighteenth Symposium on Usable Privacy and Security (SOUPS 2022), p. 175 (2022)
17. Kifer, D., Lin, B.R.: Towards an axiomatization of statistical privacy and utility. In: Proceedings of the Twenty-Ninth ACM SIGMOD-SIGACT-SIGART Symposium on Principles of Database Systems, pp. 147–158. PODS '10, Association for Computing Machinery, New York, NY, USA (2010).https://doi.org/10.1145/1807085.1807106
18. Kifer, D., Lin, B.R.: An axiomatic view of statistical privacy and utility. J. Privacy Confidentiality **4**(1) (Jul 2012). https://doi.org/10.29012/jpc.v4i1.610
19. Kühtreiber, P., Pak, V., Reinhardt, D.: Replication: the effect of differential privacy communication on german users' comprehension and data sharing attitudes. In: Eighteenth Symposium on Usable Privacy and Security (SOUPS 2022), pp. 117–134 (2022)
20. Lee, J., Clifton, C.: How much is enough? choosing ϵ for differential privacy. In: Proceedings of the 14th International Conference on Information Security (ISC), pp. 325–340. Springer (2011)
21. Lipkus, I.M.: Numeric, verbal, and visual formats of conveying health risks: suggested best practices and future recommendations. Med. Decision Making **27**(5), 696–713 (Sept 2007). https://doi.org/10.1177/0272989X07307271
22. Machanavajjhala, A., Kifer, D., Gehrke, J., Venkitasubramaniam, M.: L-diversity: Privacy beyond k-anonymity. ACM Trans. Knowl. Discov. Data (TKDD) **1**(1), 3–es (2007)
23. Mehner, L., von Voigt, S.N., Tschorsch, F.: Towards explaining epsilon: a worst-case study of differential privacy risks. In: 2021 IEEE European Symposium on Security and Privacy Workshops (EuroS&PW), pp. 328–331 (Sep 2021). https://doi.org/10.1109/EuroSPW54576.2021.00041
24. Nanayakkara, P., Bater, J., He, X., Hullman, J., Rogers, J.: Visualizing privacy-utility trade-offs in differentially private data releases. Proc. Privacy Enhanc. Technol. **2**, 601–618 (2022)
25. Nanayakkara, P., Smart, M.A., Cummings, R., Kaptchuk, G., Redmiles, E.M.: What Are the Chances? Explaining the epsilon parameter in differential privacy. In: 32nd USENIX Security Symposium (USENIX Security 23), pp. 1613–1630 (2023)
26. Narayanan, A., Shmatikov, V.: Robust de-anonymization of large sparse datasets. In: 2008 IEEE Symposium on Security and Privacy (Sp 2008), pp. 111–125 (2008). https://doi.org/10.1109/SP.2008.33

27. Nergiz, M.E., Atzori, M., Clifton, C.: Hiding the presence of individuals from shared databases. In: Proceedings of the 2007 ACM SIGMOD International Conference on Management of Data, pp. 665–676. SIGMOD '07, Association for Computing Machinery, New York, NY, USA (2007).https://doi.org/10.1145/1247480.1247554
28. Nicolau, A.T., Parra-Arnau, J., Forné, J.: A taxonomy of syntactic privacy notions for continuous data publishing. IEEE Access **12**, 38490–38511 (2024). https://doi.org/10.1109/ACCESS.2024.3368852
29. Nuñez von Voigt, S., Mehner, L., Tschorsch, F.: From theory to comprehension: a comparative study of differential privacy and k-anonymity. In: Proceedings of the Fourteenth ACM Conference on Data and Application Security and Privacy, pp. 221–232. CODASPY '24, Association for Computing Machinery, New York, NY, USA (Jun 2024). https://doi.org/10.1145/3626232.3653261
30. Reiter, M.K., Rubin, A.D.: Crowds: anonymity for web transactions. ACM Trans. Inf. Syst. Secur. **1**(1), 66–92 (Nov 1998). https://doi.org/10.1145/290163.290168
31. Ritchie, F.: 10 is the safest number that there's ever been. Trans. Data Privacy **15**(2), 109–140 (2022)
32. Shokri, R., Stronati, M., Song, C., Shmatikov, V.: Membership inference attacks against machine learning models. In: 2017 IEEE Symposium on Security and Privacy (SP), pp. 3–18 (2017). https://doi.org/10.1109/SP.2017.41
33. Smart, M.A., Sood, D., Vaccaro, K.: Understanding risks of privacy theater with differential privacy. Proc. ACM Human-Comput. Interact. **6**(CSCW2), 342:1–342:24 (Nov 2022).https://doi.org/10.1145/3555762
34. Sweeney, L.: Achieving k-anonymity privacy protection using generalization and suppression. Internat. J. Uncertain. Fuzziness Knowledge-Based Systems **10**(05), 571–588 (2002)
35. Sweeney, L.: K-anonymity: a model for protecting privacy. Internat. J. Uncertain. Fuzziness Knowledge-Based Systems **10**(05), 557–570 (2002)
36. Xiong, A., Wang, T., Li, N., Jha, S.: Towards effective differential privacy communication for users' data sharing decision and comprehension. In: 2020 IEEE Symposium on Security and Privacy (SP), pp. 392–410 (May 2020). https://doi.org/10.1109/SP40000.2020.00088

Short Paper: Models in the Dark – Rectification and Erasure Under GDPR in ML Supply Chains

Henrik Graßhoff[(✉)], Malte Hansen, Meiko Jensen, and Sara Ramezanian

Karlstad University, Karlstad, Sweden
henrik.grasshoff@kau.se, malte.hansen@kau.se, meiko.jensen@kau.se, sara.ramezanian@kau.se

Abstract. The rights to rectification and erasure, as established under the General Data Protection Regulation (GDPR), are central to protecting individuals' privacy. However, their effective enforcement in machine learning (ML) systems remains challenging. Existing work has largely addressed these rights from either a legal or a technical perspective in isolation and disregards the fact that models are produced in complex supply chains involving multiple actors across development, distribution, and deployment. This paper presents a holistic survey of challenges in implementing the rights to rectification and erasure in ML models. Drawing on academic literature and guidance from data protection authorities, we find that many GDPR requirements cannot yet be technically met in practice. Our findings further suggest that issues arising in ML supply chains are insufficiently addressed in research. To tackle this gap, we introduce the notion of *models in the dark* – derived models created further downstream in an ML chain without sufficient transparency or traceability – and analyse the urgent challenges posed by this phenomenon. By adopting an interdisciplinary perspective, this work contributes to bridging the gap between legal requirements and the technical implementation of data subject rights in ML, ultimately supporting the development of trustworthy artificial intelligence.

Keywords: artificial intelligence · data subject rights · GDPR · machine learning · privacy · right to be forgotten · right to erasure · right to rectification · security · trustworthy AI

1 Introduction

The General Data Protection Regulation (GDPR) [50] grants individuals a number of data subject rights (DSRs) to exercise control over their personal data. Under Art. 16 and 17, data subjects can request that a controller rectifies inaccurate personal data or, in specific cases, deletes it. As a growing number of machine learning (ML) models are trained on personal data [41], implementing

F. Pallas et al. (Eds.): APF 2026, LNCS 16847, pp. 71–85, 2026.
https://doi.org/10.1007/978-3-032-35899-8_4

DSRs in ML models has increasingly attracted attention from researchers and data protection authorities [42].

The implementation of the DSRs in ML cannot rely on traditional legal and technological conceptions. Implicit binary assumptions underpinning data protection – such as that data is either deleted or not – are contested by the stochastic nature of ML models that process data based on learnt statistics and inference. Technical procedures which are trivial for databases become complex and resource-consuming in ML models. The popularisation of large language models (LLMs) has moreover led to a ubiquity of ML.

Research in this area, however, often misses the bigger picture. Most works focus on the right to erasure and specific machine unlearning algorithms, whereas only a few [23,30,38,64] explicitly consider GDPR requirements. Moreover, we are unaware of any study that accounts for modern ML models as products of complex *ML supply chains*, involving multiple actors across stages from data collection to deployment [14].

To address this gap, this article investigates the following research questions:

RQ1. *What legal, technical, and operational challenges arise in implementing the GDPR's right to rectification and right to erasure in ML, and how can they be technically addressed?*
RQ2. *What challenges arise specifically in ML supply chains?*

To this end, we examine and expand on existing technical and legal academic works and guidance issued by data protection authorities. This literature review [28] focuses on the rights to rectification and erasure since the challenges we observe for those are comparable, but different from e.g. the right to access or the right to restriction of processing (Art. 15, 18 GDPR).

The contributions of this paper are: (i) We provide a taxonomy of challenges which impede an effective enforcement of the rights to rectification and erasure; (ii) we analyse legal requirements for the two rights in ML contexts and assess technical solutions against these; (iii) we introduce the notion of *models in the dark* and demonstrate its importance for future research and discussions. By bridging technical and legal literature, we aim to contribute to establishing effective procedures and guidelines for DSRs enforcement in ML contexts.

The rest of the paper is structured as follows. Section 2 outlines the rights to rectification and erasure and illustrates a typical data flow in ML supply chains. We then present challenges arising within a model in Sect. 3 and within supply chains in Sect. 4. The paper concludes with Sect. 5.

2 Data Subject Rights in Machine Learning

2.1 The Rights to Rectification and Erasure

The GDPR [50] introduces several data subject rights (DSRs) to strengthen individuals' control over their personal data, including the right to rectification (RTR) and the right to erasure (RTE). Under Art. 16, individuals may request that a controller rectify inaccurate personal data without undue delay. The right to erasure, also known as the right to be forgotten (RTBF), entitles individuals to request that a controller delete their personal data without undue delay (Art. 17 GDPR). In this context, the controller is the organisation determining the purposes and means of processing (Art. 5 GDPR). Where data have been shared with third parties, the controller must notify them of the request, unless this is impossible or requires disproportionate effort (Art. 19 GDPR). If the data were made public, the controller should take reasonable steps to inform the recipients, considering available technologies and implementation costs (Art. 17(2) GDPR).

Scholars have questioned whether, and to what extent, data subject rights can be reasonably interpreted in the context of ML [38,58,64]. While some see its technology-neutrality (Recital 15 GDPR) as a strength for regulating ML [19,57], others criticise the RTE for relying on "outdated metaphors like remembering and forgetting" which "[are] unique to human minds only and [do] not necessarily translate to the AI/machine learning era" [58] and that "it is necessary to interpret the right to erasure in a ML context" [38].

2.2 Personal Data in the ML Supply Chain

As a data-driven technology, personal data handling is a key concern in ML applications. Where models contain personal data, they must comply with the GDPR [50]. As highlighted by the European Data Protection Board (EDPB), these requirements cannot easily be disregarded, since "even when an AI model has not been intentionally designed to produce information relating to an identified or identifiable natural person from the training data, information from the training dataset, including personal data, may still remain 'absorbed' in the parameters of the model" [22, p. 13]. It is therefore necessary to examine where in the ML supply chain personal data is processed and which actors are involved.

Following the ML workflow of Glerean [27], we derive the following general data flows between actors in ML supply chains (see Fig. 1):

(1) Initially, raw data is collected from diverse *Data sources* [26], including customer databases, patient records, or web scraping from individuals or external organisations. Data acquisition is typically performed by the organisation itself or by third parties such as vendors or aggregators, which we collectively refer to as *Data provider*.
(2) The next step is data pre-processing, where raw data is prepared for model development. Data sanitisation techniques, such as removing direct and quasi-identifiers or applying differential privacy (e.g. [54]), may be used to reduce the presence of personal data. Additional steps include filtering, normalisation, and imputation, during which data values may be modified, potentially affecting the RTE.
(3) During data analysis, pre-processed data is further prepared for ML through extraction, transformation, labelling, augmentation, or synthesis. Although less common, these operations may generate new personal data by combining previously unlinked information.

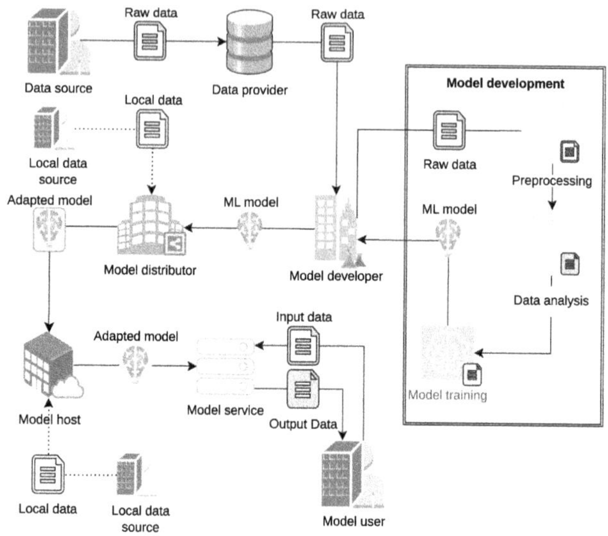

Fig. 1. Data flows between different actors in a simplified ML supply chain. Dashed lines indicate optional model adaptions.

(4) The model is then trained using the prepared data, typically split into training, testing, and validation subsets. Based on training results, model weights are adjusted, and the resulting ML model is deployed. In our generalised scenario, steps (2)–(4) are performed by a single actor, the *Model developer*. However, these tasks may also be outsourced, or, as in federated learning (see [63]), carried out collaboratively by multiple organisations.

(5) The resulting ML model is then distributed. The *Model developer* delivers it to the *Model distributor*, which may be the same organisation, or one for which the model was developed. The *Model distributor* may either pass the model to an external *Model host* or act as the host itself. Both actors may further fine-tune the model using local *Data sources*.

(6) Finally, the *Model host* offers the model to a *Model user* as an ML service. During usage, the user submits input data, which is processed to produce output. The *Model user* may be any entity, from an individual using a chatbot to an organisation classifying customers. Consequently, the input data may contain new personal data and, depending on the architecture, may be stored locally within the *Model user*'s instance of the ML service or transferred to the *Model host*. Output data may also include personal data inferred from the model and potentially traceable to original training data. In some cases, both input and output data are reused for further training.

2.3 Scope of this Paper

An ML supply chain thus leads to a multitude of data objects held by different controllers. The RTR and RTE can just as well be filed against data used for model training or adaptation (see Fig. 1) as it can be against the models themselves [16,22,42]. While the precise legal roles (processor, controller, or joint controllers) depend on the specific use case [15], we assume for the remainder that a data subject files a valid RTR or RTE request *against a data controller's model* at an arbitrary stage in the supply chain. In the next sections, we investigate two types of challenges which occur: (1) model-intrinsic challenges, which stem from the training and black-box nature of the models themselves, and (2) supply chain challenges, that arise from the magnitude of actors involved. We acknowledge that human factors play a crucial role for empowering individuals in exercising their data subject rights [5], but consider human aspects out of scope for this paper and worthy of a dedicated work on its own.

3 Model-Intrinsic Challenges

ML models may memorise personal data contained in their training data and have been shown to leak these verbatim or approximately [8,10,34,36,52]. Yet, this information is not stored explicitly within the model; rather, it is implicitly encoded in the model's parameters, which gives rise to several unique issues.

3.1 Necessity to Assess Models, Not Training Data

A key insight is that a model is not equivalent to its training data. It may fail to memorise individual data points due to limited parameter capacity or stochasticity in training, where data are randomly sampled, ordered, and processed [4]. Conversely, models may also generate information not present in the training data, either through hallucination of incorrect or fabricated outputs [37,39] or by inferring new information from training data.

Any assessment of what a model has stored must therefore be based on the model itself rather than its training data [16]. This argumentation also applies to rectification and erasure methods: a technique effective for one model will not necessarily be applicable to other models trained on the same – let alone a similar – dataset.

3.2 Identification of the Data Subject Within a Model

Quantifying the influence of a specific training data point on a model remains an open problem [4,16,40], making unambiguous and complete identification of data subjects difficult, if not impossible.

When a controller receives a DSR request, it is obliged to identify the data subject within the model, which involves to determine what personal data the model has stored about the latter [16,21]. As stressed above and supported by the Commission Nationale de l'Informatique et des Libertés (CNIL) [16], the controller cannot base this assessment solely on the training data, but has to verify the stored data within the model itself on a case-by-case basis.

For generative models such as LLMs, the most mature technical identification approach today is *privacy audits*. These often involve inserting "canaries" [9] into the training dataset: random information pairs later tested for leakage through methods such as *membership inference attack* [33]. However, some studies indicate that many methods struggle to identify memorised data reliably and remain sensitive to canary and prompt design [36,45]. Their reliance on control over training data and processes limits applicability to the model developer, who may not be the addressed controller (see Sect. 4.2). Lastly, quantifying a model's overall tendency for privacy leakage may not meet the needs of addressing an individual data subject's case.

More generally, it is debatable to what extent a controller can be obliged to audit its model in light of Art. 11 GDPR. This provision prohibits controllers from maintaining, acquiring, or processing additional information solely to identify a data subject. Privacy audits may constitute such processing. Moreover, any model attack inherently risks infringing individual privacy. Where controllers do not hold the training data, requiring black-box auditing may conflict with the rationale of Art. 11: enabling one data subject's rights should not compromise the privacy of others.

Facing these difficulties, the controller could be inclined to argue that it cannot identify the data subject and refuse to comply with the DSR request with reference to Art. 12(2) GDPR. The wording of the CNIL guidelines in fact suggests that "it does not seem possible today, in the general case, for a controller to identify ... a particular person" and the controller could then "demonstrate that it is unable to identify persons within its model", except for rare cases in which the data is explicitly encoded in the model weights [16]. Even though this argumentation may appear reasonable given the current legislation and available technologies, it could function as a dangerous loophole for data controllers to escape DSR requests if interpreted too broadly.

3.3 Technical Data Rectification and Erasure in a Model

Fully *retraining* a model from scratch on revised training data is widely considered to be the most GDPR-compliant way to implement the RTR and RTE [16,23], but very resource-intensive [7]. In this regard, conflicting opinions exist on whether a data subject can, in fact, request a full retraining from the data controller. Juliussen et al. [38] argue that as "the only current machine unlearning method with a theoretically proven guarantee is ... full model retraining, ... the request for full model retraining has a legal basis in Art. 17 of the GDPR and should be implemented for full GDPR compliance." In contrast, high implementation costs may be a reason for the controller to refuse the DSR request according to CNIL: "The retraining of the models comes at a very high cost. The request for erasure may in principle be rejected" [16].

Less resource-intensive approaches aim to *unlearn* a specific subset of the training data from a learnt model, offering a trade-off between erasure strictness, model performance, and resource consumption [44,48,53]. These methods are first and foremost intended for erasing data from a model, but can also be used for rectification through a combination of erasure and relearning. While being a very active field of research and arguably the best known feasible approach to implement the RTR and RTE today, they introduce a number of issues.

Unlearnt models typically perform worse than retrained ones, with performance potentially deteriorating exponentially as more data is removed [47,48]. This phenomenon, known as *catastrophic unlearning*, limits the applicability of machine unlearning. A controller may have little incentive to unlearn data if it renders the model ineffective. Since the controller's freedom to conduct a business must be respected (Recital 4 GDPR and [16]), it is as of today unclear to what extent catastrophic unlearning can justify non-compliance with a DSR request. Moreover, controllers of high-risk artificial intelligence (AI) systems under the Artificial Intelligence Act (AIA) [51] may be further reluctant as such systems must maintain appropriate levels of accuracy (Art. 15(1) AIA). Finally, since unlearning may introduce unfairness by disproportionately affecting subgroups [48,65], it may conflict with the accuracy and fairness principles in Art. 5 GDPR.

Another important aspect is the verifiability of rectification or erasure. *Exact unlearning* algorithms provide formal guarantees that the model behaves as if it had never encountered the data [11]. *Approximate unlearning* algorithms suppress the influence of a subset of the training data without removing it from the model [11]. While significantly less resource-intensive [61], approximate methods may leave residual effects [48]. Controllers must then verify the unlearning, yet no standard mechanisms exist, and proposed approaches remain limited [62].

Ironically, machine unlearning itself can also expose individuals to different privacy harms, exact and approximate algorithms alike [11,44]. The fundamental idea is that an adversary who can query a model before and after the unlearning can leverage this additional information to their advantage. Past studies have shown higher success rates for membership inference attacks [12] or, more severely, *data reconstruction attacks*, in which the unlearnt training data could be recovered from the models with high confidence [3].

3.4 Inference-Time Interventions

Alternatively to changing the trained model parameters, *inference-time interventions* [43] modify the input/output of a generative model during interactions. Such mechanisms are widely deployed for detecting and suppressing prompts or responses that are considered harmful [20,24,25,55] and have also been proposed as alternatives to unlearning [49,56]. Yet, it is acknowledged that the measures "would not satisfy definitions of unlearning" [56] since the data is not technically rectified or erased from the model. Given the documented circumventions of inference-time interventions [29], it is not obvious how these could play a vital role in the RTR and RTE implementation apart from emergency measures when all other measures prove disproportionate [16].

3.5 Continually Learning Models

Models may learn continually from a stream of training data, gradually accommodating new knowledge over time while maintaining their already acquired abilities [60]. This learning approach (also known as online, incremental, or lifelong learning [59,60]) does not produce a "final model", but a ramified directed graph of continuously updated models, each of which depends on its predecessors and therefore, implicitly, on all previous training data [4]. A DSR request filed for one model in this graph would inevitably affect all subsequent models, potentially causing a cascade of necessary rectifications or erasures, each of which is subject to the challenges described in the previous subsections.

4 Supply-Chain Challenges

4.1 The Notion of *Models in the Dark*

ML models are rarely designed and used in a vacuum. They are the result of a larger supply chain which involves multiple actors in all steps from problem formulation to data collection and curation, model training, evaluation, distribution, deployment, usage, and monitoring [6,17,31,32]. During this process, models are constantly adapted, combined, and redistributed [13,35], creating a complex network of subsequent downstream derivatives of the original model as illustrated in Fig. 2. Whenever an upstream model contains personal data, this information is also propagated and may ultimately, through cascading effects, appear in an unbounded number of downstream models.

Still, actors typically lack knowledge of other participants more than one "hop" away in the supply chain [14]. In particular, a data subject interacting with a downstream model as an end user is usually unaware of upstream predecessors. While they may perceive the AI as a stand-alone product, it is in fact the result of multiple contributing models. We therefore refer to these as *models in the dark*.[1] Each such model, i.e. every derivative model built from an upstream one, creates a further instance of personal data at an additional actor.

The clear distinction between upstream and downstream and the mental model of linear supply chains are too simple to capture the complexity and dynamics of reality. Modern ML supply chains are characterised by fluid interrelations of vertically and horizontally integrated actors [1,14,32] where the data and model flows between actors are much more complex than Fig. 2 suggests, flows can even be circular, and trust relationships are diverse [2]. The notion of models in the dark is agnostic to the exact actor constellation as it refers to *all* derivatives of a model. For the sake of simplicity, we adhere to the picture of linear downstream flows for the rest of the section.

[1] Inspired by the Persian expression *army in the dark*, referring to unseen or uncredited contributors.

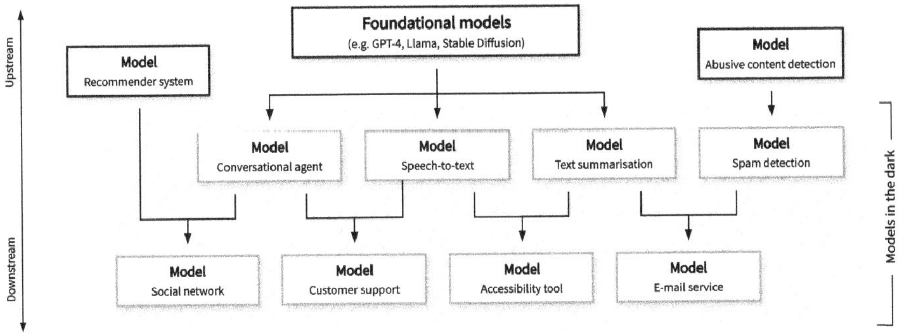

Fig. 2. Models in the dark in simple ML supply chains (adapted from [31])

4.2 Locating Controllers Under Supply Chain Opacity

Before submitting a DSR request, a data subject does not need to determine whether a model contains their personal data. However, in practice, they may lack information about whether and how their data is present in an ML model, complicating the exercise of their rights. To find out whether a model contains their data, data subjects typically rely on their interaction with the model [16]. Black-box methods without access to model specifications remain limited and may lead to incorrect conclusions that a model does not store their data.

In addition, lacking knowledge about other controllers in the supply chain, a data subject may submit a request at an arbitrary point. If the controller is far upstream, personal data may have been propagated to an unknown number of downstream models in the dark (see Fig. 2). Far downstream, the model may instead have inherited data from upstream predecessors. In both cases, even if the addressed controller rectifies or erases the data, other models may retain it, limiting effectiveness. It may therefore be necessary in many cases to ensure rectification or erasure across all relevant models in the dark.

4.3 Updating Models Along the Supply Chain

One potential measure to address models in the dark is to propagate an *updated* version of the model with changed model weights through the supply chain. Depending on whether, how, and to whom the controller makes the model available, different legal obligations apply: (1) If the controller does not distribute the model, but offers it as a service [13], it needs to be updated only at the controller's site. (2) If the controller provides the model itself to third parties without making it publicly available, they are obliged to undertake proportionate efforts to inform all recipients of the RTR or RTE request (Art. 19 GDPR) if possible. According to the assessment of CNIL, the controller would then have to forward an updated version downstream and, if necessary, contractually restrict the recipient's use to the new version [16]. (3) If the controller makes the model publicly available, Art. 17(2) GDPR applies for the RTE and mandates that the controller should take reasonable actions to inform controllers of the erasure request, considering available technology and the cost of implementation [38]. A comparable obligation does not exist for the right to rectification.

From a practical perspective, case (1) requires a model update at a single stage of the supply chain and leads to the challenges discussed in Sect. 3. Case (2) imposes a potentially acceptable burden to inform selected recipients, but distributing updates to all may require substantial network traffic given the multi-gigabyte size of modern models [18]. We are not aware of any established techniques to systematically reduce bandwidth for model updates. In case (3), it is nearly impossible to inform all parties who have downloaded the model (for instance, Llama has been downloaded over one billion times [46]). As a remedy, published models could include an update mechanism enabling distribution akin to software updates. However, bandwidth constraints, limited enforcement, and the rise of open-weight models [35] remain obstacles.

All of these considerations build upon the premise that the controller takes care of the update (distribution) itself. In some cases, for example, when the controller is not in possession of sufficient resources, rectification or erasure might be more effectively carried out further downstream. Standardised coordination procedures could, in principle, allow to establish favourable places in the ML supply chain to execute the model updating.

Lastly, updating downstream models might not always be effective or desirable. When the number of models in the dark grows, the link between a model and its derivatives becomes less obvious as more and more models contribute to the models further downstream. The sole propagation of a model update does therefore not assure the rectification and erasure in all derivations. Referring back to Sect. 3.3, updating a model can also infringe on the data subjects' privacy, rendering large-scale model updates potentially undesired.

5 Conclusion and Future Work

In this paper, we surveyed academic literature and data protection authority guidelines to identify challenges faced by the right to rectification and right to erasure in ML systems. The result is a taxonomy of two domains: model-intrinsic and supply-chain challenges. For each domain, we identified key challenges, corresponding technical approaches, and limitations, extending existing literature.

For model-intrinsic challenges, key issues include limited methods for reliably identifying personal data within models and the shortcomings of current unlearning techniques. Supply-chain challenges remain underexplored: complex actor constellations create *models in the dark*, complicating both the identification of responsible controller(s) and the distribution of resulting model updates.

Overall, both the technological implementations for the RTR and RTE and the supply chains surrounding them contain challenges that make the effective enforcement of either infeasible. Hence, the proper enforcement of RTR and RTE in ML contexts raises a lot of open issues that require further research in several areas to assert that data subjects keep the ability to enforce their rights in the light of the rise of ML.

In future work, we plan to develop and evaluate strategies to address the challenges introduced in this paper. Specifically, we plan to conduct technical experiments to evaluate the effectiveness of unlearning and related techniques for the RTR and RTE and to minimise network traffic during model distribution. To elucidate the uncertainty surrounding models in the dark, we will investigate and develop communication flows and data trails for GDPR-compliant and traceable data sharing and model distribution in ML supply chains. Another area of challenges, beyond this paper's scope, concerns the training process. As highlighted in the data flow in Sect. 2, data is transformed multiple times during model development. The implications for the RTR and RTE require further attention, particularly in distributed training settings such as federated learning.

AI Usage Disclaimer. The authors utilised generative AI tools for improving grammar and spelling.

Acknowledgements. The contribution of Sara Ramezanian and Meiko Jensen was co-funded by the Swedish Knowledge Foundation (KKS). The contribution of Malte Hansen and Meiko Jensen has been conducted (in part) within the project TRUMAN. The research leading to these results has received funding from the European Union's Horizon 2020 Research and Innovation Programme, under Grant Agreement no. 101214000.

Author Contributions (CRediT). Henrik Graßhoff: Conceptualization, Investigation, Project administration, Visualization, Writing – original draft, Writing – review & editing; **Malte Hansen:** Conceptualization, Investigation, Visualization, Writing – original draft, Writing – review & editing; **Meiko Jensen:** Conceptualization, Project administration, Writing – review & editing; **Sara Ramezanian:** Conceptualization, Writing – review & editing.

References

1. Attard-Frost, B., Widder, D.G.: The ethics of AI value chains. Big Data Soc. **12**(2) (2025). https://doi.org/10.1177/20539517251340603
2. Balayn, A., et al.: Unpacking trust dynamics in the LLM supply chain: an empirical exploration to foster trustworthy LLM production & use. In: Proceedings of the 2025 CHI Conference on Human Factors in Computing Systems, pp. 1–20 (2025). https://doi.org/10.1145/3706598.3713787
3. Bertran, M., et al.: Reconstruction attacks on machine unlearning: simple models are vulnerable. In: Advances in Neural Information Processing Systems, vol. 37, pp. 104995–105016 (2024). https://doi.org/10.52202/079017-3334
4. Bourtoule, L., et al.: Machine unlearning. In: IEEE Symposium on Security and Privacy (SP), pp. 141–159 (2021). https://doi.org/10.1109/SP40001.2021.00019
5. Bowyer, A., et al.: Human-GDPR interaction: practical experiences of accessing personal data. In: CHI Conference on Human Factors in Computing Systems, pp. 1–19 (2022). https://doi.org/10.1145/3491102.3501947
6. Brown, I.: Allocating accountability in AI supply chains (2023). https://adalovelaceinstitute.org/resource/ai-supply-chains/

7. Cao, Y., Yang, J.: Towards making systems forget with machine unlearning. In: IEEE Symposium on Security and Privacy, pp. 463–480 (2015). https://doi.org/10.1109/SP.2015.35
8. Carlini, N., et al.: Extracting training data from large language models. In: 30th USENIX Security Symposium (USENIX Security 21), pp. 2633–2650 (2021)
9. Carlini, N., et al.: The secret sharer: evaluating and testing unintended memorization in neural networks. In: 28th USENIX Security Symposium (USENIX Security 19), pp. 267–284 (2019)
10. Carlini, N., et al.: Extracting training data from diffusion models. In: 32nd USENIX Security Symposium (USENIX Security 23), pp. 5253–5270 (2023)
11. Chen, A., et al.: A survey of security and privacy issues of machine unlearning. AI Mag. **46**(1) (2025). https://doi.org/10.1002/aaai.12209
12. Chen, M., et al.: When machine unlearning jeopardizes privacy. In: Proceedings of the 2021 ACM SIGSAC Conference on Computer and Communications Security, pp. 896–911 (2021). https://doi.org/10.1145/3460120.3484756
13. Cobbe, J., Singh, J.: Artificial intelligence as a service: legal responsibilities, liabilities, and policy challenges. Comput. Law Secur. Rev. **42** (2021). https://doi.org/10.1016/j.clsr.2021.105573
14. Cobbe, J., Veale, M., Singh, J.: Understanding accountability in algorithmic supply chains. In: ACM Conference on Fairness Accountability and Transparency, pp. 1186–1197 (2023). https://doi.org/10.1145/3593013.3594073
15. Commission nationale de l'informatique et des libertés. Determining the legal qualification of AI system providers (2024). https://www.cnil.fr/en/determining-legal-qualification-ai-system-providers. Visited 22 Apr 2026
16. Commission nationale de l'informatique et des libertés. Ensuring and facilitating the exercise of data subjects' rights (2026). https://www.cnil.fr/en/ensuring-and-facilitating-exercise-data-subjects-rights. Visited 16 Apr 2026
17. Feder Cooper, A., et al.: Accountability in an algorithmic society: relationality, responsibility, and robustness in machine learning. In: ACM Conference on Fairness Accountability and Transparency, pp. 864–876 (2022). https://doi.org/10.1145/3531146.3533150
18. DeepSeek-AI: DeepSeek-V3 (2025). https://github.com/deepseek-ai/DeepSeek-V3. Visited 22 Apr 2026
19. Dewitte, P.: AI meets the GDPR: navigating the impact of data protection on AI systems. In: Smuha, N.A. (ed.) The Cambridge Handbook of the Law, Ethics and Policy of Artificial Intelligence, 1st edn., pp. 133–157. Cambridge University Press (2025). https://doi.org/10.1017/9781009367783.010
20. Dong, Y., et al.: Safeguarding large language models: a survey. Artif. Intell. Rev. **58**(12) (2025). issn: 1573-7462. https://doi.org/10.1007/s10462-025-11389-2
21. European Data Protection Board: Guidelines 01/2022 on data subject rights - Right of access (2023). https://www.edpb.europa.eu/system/files/2023-04/edpb_guidelines_202201_data_subject_rights_access_v2_en.pdf
22. European Data Protection Board: Opinion 28/2024 on certain data protection aspects related to the processing of personal data in the context of AI models (2024). https://www.edpb.europa.eu/system/files/2024-12/edpb_opinion_202428_ai-models_en.pdf
23. Feretzakis, G., et al.: GDPR and large language models: technical and legal obstacles. Future Internet **17**(4) (2025). https://doi.org/10.3390/fi17040151
24. Fu, W., et al.: Sanitize Your Responses: Mitigating Privacy Leakage in Large Language Models (2025). https://doi.org/10.48550/arXiv.2509.24488

25. Gandikota, R., et al.: Erasing concepts from diffusion models. In: IEEE/CVF International Conference on Computer Vision (ICCV), pp. 2426–2436 (2023). https://doi.org/10.1109/ICCV51070.2023.00230
26. Gao, L., et al.: The Pile: An 800GB Dataset of Diverse Text for Language Modeling (2021). https://doi.org/10.48550/arXiv.2101.00027
27. Glerean, E.: Fundamentals of secure AI systems with personal data. Support pool of experts programme (2025). https://www.edpb.europa.eu/system/files/2024-12/edpb_opinion_202428_ai-models_en.pdf
28. Grant, M.J., Booth, A.: A typology of reviews: an analysis of 14 review types and associated methodologies. Health Inf. Libr. J. **26**(2), 91–108 (2009). https://doi.org/10.1111/j.1471-1842.2009.00848.x
29. Hackett, W., et al.: Bypassing LLM guardrails: an empirical analysis of evasion attacks against prompt injection and jailbreak detection systems (2025). https://doi.org/10.48550/arXiv.2504.11168
30. Hawkins, K., et al.: A decision-making process to implement the 'right to be forgotten' in machine learning. In: Rannenberg, K., Drogkaris, P., Lauradoux, C. (eds.) Privacy Technologies and Policy, APF 2023, vol. 13888, pp. 20–38 (2024). https://doi.org/10.1007/978-3-031-61089-9_2
31. Hopkins, A., et al.: AI supply chains. SSRN Electron. J. (2024). https://doi.org/10.2139/ssrn.4789403
32. Hopkins, A., et al.: Recourse, repair, reparation, & prevention: a stakeholder analysis of AI supply chains. In: Proceedings of the 2025 ACM Conference on Fairness, Accountability, and Transparency, pp. 209–227 (2025). https://doi.org/10.1145/3715275.3732017
33. Hu, H., et al.: Membership inference attacks on machine learning: a survey. ACM Comput. Surv. **54**(11s), 1–37 (2022). https://doi.org/10.1145/3523273
34. Huang, J., Shao, H., Chang, K.C.-C.: Are large pre-trained language models leaking your personal information? In: Findings of the Association for Computational Linguistics: EMNLP 2022, pp. 2038–2047 (2022). https://doi.org/10.18653/v1/2022.findings-emnlp.148
35. Hugging Face - The AI community building the future. https://huggingface.co/. Visited 21 Apr 2026
36. Ippolito, D., et al.: Preventing verbatim memorization in language models gives a false sense of privacy (2022). https://doi.org/10.48550/arXiv.2210.17546
37. Ji, Z., et al.: Survey of hallucination in natural language generation. ACM Comput. Surv. **55**(12), 1–38 (2023). https://doi.org/10.1145/3571730
38. Juliussen, B.A., Rui, J.P., Johansen, D.: Algorithms that forget: machine unlearning and the right to erasure. Comput. Law Secur. Rev. **51** (2023). https://doi.org/10.1016/j.clsr.2023.105885
39. Kelsey-Sugg, A., Carrick, D.: AI hallucinations caused artificial intelligence to falsely describe these people as criminals. ABC News. (2024). https://abc.net.au/news/2024-11-04/ai-artificial-intelligencehallucinations-defamation-chatgpt/104518612. Visited 21 Apr 2026
40. Kesa, A., Kerikmäe, T.: Artificial intelligence and the GDPR: inevitable nemeses? TalTech J. Eur. Stud. **10**(3), 68–90 (2020). https://doi.org/10.1515/bjes-2020-0022
41. King, J., et al.: User privacy and large language models: an analysis of frontier developers' privacy policies (2025). https://doi.org/10.48550/arXiv.2509.05382
42. Konferenz der unabhängigen Datenschutzaufsichtsbehörden des Bundes und der Länder: Orientierungshilfe zu empfohlenen technischen und organisatorischen Maßnahmen bei der Entwicklung und beim Betrieb von KI-Systemen (2025). https://datenschutzkonferenz-online.de/media/oh/DSK-OH_KI-Systeme.pdf

43. Li, K., et al.: Inference-time intervention: eliciting truthful answers from a language model. In: Advances in Neural Information Processing Systems, vol. 36, pp. 41451–41530 (2023)
44. Liu, H., et al.: A survey on machine unlearning: techniques and new emerged privacy risks. J. Inf. Secur. Appl. **90** (2025). https://doi.org/10.1016/j.jisa.2025.104010
45. Lu, Y., et al.: Fantastically ordered prompts and where to find them: overcoming few-shot prompt order sensitivity. In: Proceedings of the 60th Annual Meeting of the Association for Computational Linguistics (Volume 1: Long Papers), pp. 8086–8098 (2022). https://doi.org/10.18653/v1/2022.acl-long.556
46. Meta: Celebrating 1 Billion Downloads of Llama, March 2025. https://about.fb.com/news/2025/03/celebrating-1-billion-downloads-llama/. Visited 21 Apr 2026
47. Nguyen, Q.P., Low, B.K.H., Jaillet, P.: Variational Bayesian unlearning. In: Advances in Neural Information Processing Systems, vol. 33, pp. 16025–16036 (2020)
48. Nguyen, T.T., et al.: A survey of machine unlearning. ACM Trans. Intell. Syst. Technol. **16**(5), 1–46 (2025). https://doi.org/10.1145/3749987
49. Pawelczyk, M., Neel, S., Lakkaraju, H.: In-context unlearning: language models as few shot unlearners (2023). https://doi.org/10.48550/arXiv.2310.07579
50. Regulation (EU) 2016/679 of the European Parliament and of the Council of 27 April 2016 on the protection of natural persons with regard to the processing of personal data and on the free movement of such data, and repealing Directive 95/46/EC (General Data Protection Regulation) (Text with EEA relevance) (2016). https://data.europa.eu/eli/reg/2016/679/oj
51. Regulation (EU) 2024/1689 of the European Parliament and of the Council of 13 June 2024 laying down harmonised rules on artificial intelligence and amending Regulations (EC) No 300/2008, (EU) No 167/2013, (EU) No 168/2013, (EU) 2018/858, (EU) 2018/1139 and (EU) 2019/2144 and Directives 2014/90/EU, (EU) 2016/797 and (EU) 2020/1828 (Artificial Intelligence Act) (Text with EEA relevance) (2024). https://data.europa.eu/eli/reg/2024/1689/oj
52. Rigaki, M., Garcia, S.: A survey of privacy attacks in machine learning. ACM Comput. Surv. **56**(4), 1–34 (2024). https://doi.org/10.1145/3624010
53. Shaik, T., et al.: Exploring the landscape of machine unlearning: a comprehensive survey and taxonomy. IEEE Trans. Neural Netw. Learn. Syst. **36**(7), 11676–11696 (2025). https://doi.org/10.1109/TNNLS.2024.3486109
54. Sinha, A., et al.: VaultGemma: a differentially private Gemma model. (2025). https://doi.org/10.48550/arXiv.2510.15001
55. Musatoiu, T.: How to use the moderation API, March 2024. https://developers.openai.com/cookbook/examples/how_to_use_moderation
56. Thaker, P., et al.: Guardrail baselines for unlearning in LLMs (2024). https://doi.org/10.48550/arXiv.2403.03329
57. Ufert, F.: AI regulation through the lens of fundamental rights: how well does the GDPR address the challenges posed by AI? Eur. Pap. **5**(2), 1087–1097 (2020). https://doi.org/10.15166/2499-8249/394
58. Villaronga, E.F., Kieseberg, P., Li, T.: Humans forget, machines remember: artificial intelligence and the right to be forgotten. Comput. Law Secur. Rev. **34**(2), 304–313 (2018). https://doi.org/10.1016/j.clsr.2017.08.007
59. Wang, L., et al.: A comprehensive survey of continual learning: theory, method and application. IEEE Trans. Pattern Anal. Mach. Intell. **46**(8), 5362–5383 (2024). https://doi.org/10.1109/TPAMI.2024.3367329

60. Wickramasinghe, B., Saha, G., Roy, K.: Continual learning: a review of techniques, challenges, and future directions. IEEE Trans. Artif. Intell. **5**(6), 2526–2546 (2024). https://doi.org/10.1109/TAI.2023.3339091
61. Xu, J., et al.: Machine unlearning: solutions and challenges. IEEE Trans. Emerging Top. Comput. Intell. **8**(3), 2150–2168 (2024). https://doi.org/10.1109/TETCI.2024.3379240
62. Xue, L., et al.: Towards reliable forgetting: a survey on machine unlearning verification. ACM Comput. Surv. **58**(12), 1–35 (2026). https://doi.org/10.1145/3807451
63. Zhang, C., et al.: A survey on federated learning. Knowl.-Based Syst. **216** (2021). https://doi.org/10.1016/j.knosys.2021.106775
64. Zhang, D., et al.: Right to be forgotten in the era of large language models: implications, challenges, and solutions. AI Ethics **5**(3), 2445–2454 (2025). https://doi.org/10.1007/s43681-024-00573-9
65. Zhang, D., et al.: To be forgotten or to be fair: unveiling fairness implications of machine unlearning methods. AI Ethics **4**(1), 83–93 (2024). https://doi.org/10.1007/s43681-023-00398-y

Users' Perspectives

Designing Privacy-Preserving Smart Home Intrusion Detection Through User Acceptance Criteria: An Action Design Research Study

Sascha Löbner[1(✉)], Eleftherios Eleftheriadis[1,3], Jens Lindemann[1], Hannes Federrath[1], and Kai Rannenberg[2]

[1] University of Hamburg, Hamburg, Germany
{sascha.loebner,eleftherios.eleftheriadis, jens.lindemann,hannes.federrath}@uni-hamburg.de
[2] Goethe University Frankfurt, Frankfurt, Germany
kai.rannenberg@em.uni-frankfurt.de
[3] University of Macedonia, Thessaloniki, Greece

Abstract. Smart home adoption is growing rapidly, yet insufficient regulation and opaque data practices leave users vulnerable to privacy and security threats. Intrusion detection systems can monitor network traffic for malicious behavior, but collaborative threat intelligence sharing across households introduces significant privacy risks, as network data can reveal sensitive behavioral patterns. Privacy-enhancing technologies (PETs) can mitigate these risks, yet their selection involves complex trade-offs between privacy guarantees, computational overhead, and usability that are rarely informed by user preferences. This paper investigates how to design a privacy-preserving smart home IDS that incorporates user acceptance criteria into the selection of PETs for collaborative threat intelligence sharing. Following Action Design Research, we iteratively build and evaluate the system across two Building-Intervention-Evaluation cycles integrating user studies, ethical-legal-social impact assessment, and technical validation. We derive six design principles for privacy-preserving collaborative IDS in consumer IoT environments.

Keywords: Privacy-enhancing technologies · Federated Learning · Homomorphic Encryption · Design Science Research · Action Design Research · Human-Centered Security · Intrusion Detection System

1 Introduction

Smart home device adoption has significantly increased in recent years, driven by the promise of automation and convenience through devices such as smart speakers, thermostats, security cameras, and window sensors [36,41,45,46]. However, the smart home device market lacks sufficient government regulation [19,23,44],

F. Pallas et al. (Eds.): APF 2026, LNCS 16847, pp. 89–113, 2026.
https://doi.org/10.1007/978-3-032-35899-8_5

resulting in incomplete or difficult to understand information on security and data handling, including data storage, usage, and sharing [11,16,23,39,75,82]. Small enterprises and startups, which constitute a significant portion of the smart home ecosystem, were found to be particularly likely to have competing interests and lack security strategies [8]. While privacy and security are often not primary drivers of purchase decisions [29], approximately 10% of device reviewers report privacy- and security-related concerns [78], and evidence exists that users are willing to pay for better security but not at the cost of usability [14,28].

The threats arising from smart home environments are diverse. Privacy threats include data misuse, unauthorized sharing, surveillance, and tracking of user behavior, caused for instance by extensive data collection from smart speakers [1,2,45] and cameras [10,30]. Security violations involve interaction threats [18], design flaws, insufficient state control, unauthorized device access, and device unbinding [87]. While some vulnerabilities, such as outdated firmware, are relatively easy to mitigate, more complex attacks including contextual exploits [65], port scanning, and directory enumeration [85] demand continuous monitoring of communication between smart home devices, mobile apps, and cloud services [87]. To address these threats, intrusion detection systems (IDS) have been proposed to monitor network traffic and identify malicious behavior in smart home networks. Traditional IDS rely on predefined rules and policies to block unauthorized commands that deviate from intended device usage [83]. More recent implementations incorporate AI to detect emerging threats by modeling normal user behavior, managing unfamiliar devices, uncovering hidden correlations, and addressing spoofed events and device interactions [6,22,55,64,65,76,81]. While these systems enhance smart home security, they also introduce new challenges. Centralized architectures pose privacy risks by aggregating sensitive household data and create scalability concerns as the number of IoT devices grows [63]. Furthermore, the reliance on large labeled datasets limits the applicability of many AI-based approaches [24].

To overcome these limitations, federated learning (FL) has been proposed for training IDS models in a distributed manner, keeping raw data on local devices while collaboratively improving a shared model [63,84]. However, FL itself introduces privacy risks, as shared model updates can be exploited through inference attacks such as gradient leakage and model inversion [9,33,84]. Privacy-enhancing technologies (PETs) such as homomorphic encryption (HE) and differential privacy (DP) have therefore been considered in combination with FL [15,32,52]. According to the principles of Privacy by Design [12], full functionality must be ensured while effectively protecting users from privacy and security threats. Although this is a noble goal, it is rarely fully attainable in practice due to the complex trade-offs between privacy, usability, and security [77]. In particular, frequently reported issues with HE include computational overhead and limited computational operations [3,51,86], which may discourage practitioners from adopting this PET. The ISO/IEC 20889 standard further highlights that HE has "typically lower performance and higher storage costs," and empirical studies report overheads of several orders of magnitude [62].

This raises the question of how to select and combine PETs for smart home IDS in a way that satisfies both technical privacy requirements and user acceptance criteria. In this paper, we contribute to this discussion by investigating the design of a privacy-preserving smart home intrusion detection system that factors user acceptance criteria into the selection of PETs. We formulate the following research question:

RQ How to design a privacy-preserving intrusion detection system for smart home environments that incorporates user acceptance criteria into the selection of privacy-enhancing technologies?

To address this question, we adopt an Action Design Research (ADR) approach [69], which enables the iterative co-design and evaluation of an IT artifact in close collaboration with practitioners, including IDS developers, security experts, and end users. ADR is particularly suited for this context because the design of a privacy-preserving IDS is shaped not only by technical constraints but also by regulatory requirements, ethical considerations, and users' privacy expectations, all of which must be integrated concurrently rather than sequentially. The research process spans two Building-Intervention-Evaluation (BIE) cycles. The first cycle elicits user acceptance criteria through a large-scale survey (N = 725) and uses them to guide PET selection via an Analytical Hierarchy Process (AHP) [68]. The second cycle subjects the resulting artifact to an Ethical, Legal, and Social Impact (ELSI) workshop (N = 15) and validates the technical architecture through empirical evaluation on established IDS benchmark datasets.

We find that a combination of federated learning (FL) and homomorphic encryption (HE) fulfills the most requirements identified through user evaluation. We demonstrate that HE-enabled FL is computationally feasible for practical IDS scenarios without degrading detection performance, with CKKS-based variants achieving accuracy and F1-scores comparable to unencrypted FL baselines while introducing manageable overhead. Finally, we derive six design principles for privacy-preserving collaborative IDS in consumer IoT environments.

The remainder of this paper is structured as follows. Section 2 reviews related work on IDS for smart homes and privacy-enhancing technologies. Section 3 describes the study design and methodology. Section 4 presents the results. Section 5 provides reflection and learning among the BIE cycles. Section 6 discusses the findings and design implications and outlines future work. Finally, Sect. 7 concludes the paper.

2 Background and Related Work

This section reviews existing work on IDS for smart home environments and the privacy-enhancing technologies that have been applied to protect such systems.

2.1 Intrusion Detection Systems for Smart Home Environments

IDS for smart homes can detect unwanted data transmissions by identifying anomalous behaviors in network traffic [80], such as those triggered by misinterpreted voice commands [58]. A comprehensive literature review from 2022 groups Internet of Things IDS into signature-based, anomaly-based, specification-based, and hybrid clusters [37]. More recent hybrid implementations incorporate AI and can model sensor-device-user interactions holistically to differentiate between benign and malicious behaviors [73]. Approaches such as self-supervised learning and few-shot learning have been applied to reduce reliance on labeled datasets [24], while adversarial interaction has been proposed to collect live training data [7]. Analyzing large volumes of heterogeneous data can further help identify previously undetected incidents by revealing high-order relationships [66]. However, traditional centralized IDS struggle in dynamic and evolving environments because model performance degrades over time [27]. Rahman et al. [63] find that centralized architectures do not scale well with the proliferation of IoT devices and pose a privacy risk by introducing a single point of failure. This has motivated the exploration of distributed approaches, particularly federated learning, for training IDS models across multiple smart home instances without centralizing raw data.

2.2 Privacy-Enhancing Technologies for Intrusion Detection

Several PETs have been investigated for protecting data in IDS deployments. In the following, we describe each technology and summarize its applicability based on reported performance in the literature.

Federated Learning (FL). In federated learning, each device trains a shared model independently on its local data and sends only gradient updates to a central server, which aggregates them to produce a global model [47,84]. FL has been widely applied to IDS, achieving accuracies ranging from approximately 69 % on the UNSW-NB15 dataset [40] to over 99 % on the InSDN and CICIDS2018 datasets [31,40]. However, while the accumulation of gradients enhances model accuracy for all participants, it also increases the risk of gradient leakage, model inversion, and membership inference attacks [4,33,79]. If the central server is compromised or dishonest, an adversary can exploit shared gradient updates to reconstruct training data or infer membership of individual records.

Homomorphic Encryption (HE). Homomorphic encryption enables computations to be performed directly on encrypted data such that the decrypted result matches the outcome of the same computation on plaintext [34,60]. HE schemes are classified into partially homomorphic (supporting a single operation), somewhat or leveled homomorphic (supporting addition and multiplication up to a limited circuit depth), and fully homomorphic encryption, which enables arbitrary-depth computation via bootstrapping [3]. Prominent fully homomorphic schemes include lattice-based constructions such as BGV, BFV, and CKKS.

When applied to IDS independently, HE has been explored for protecting data transmitted to a central cloud service for security analysis [70] and for interorganizational alert clustering [74]. However, standalone HE for IDS training remains underexplored, with existing studies focusing primarily on protocol feasibility rather than reporting detection accuracy.

Differential Privacy (DP). Differential privacy enhances privacy by adding calibrated random noise to data or model parameters [71]. A privacy budget ϵ controls the level of privacy: smaller values indicate stronger protection but also more noise, which can degrade data quality and model performance [26]. DP has been applied to IDS across several benchmarks, achieving accuracies ranging from approximately 80 % to 99 % depending on the dataset and privacy budget [21,53,71]. F1-scores between 82.5 % and 90.7 % have been reported on the CICIDS2017 dataset [72]. While DP offers a well-understood formal privacy guarantee, the accuracy-privacy trade-off can be critical in deployment, particularly at low values of ϵ [25].

FL+HE. Combining FL with HE enables secure aggregation of model updates without revealing individual users' data to the aggregating server [42,84]. The server operates exclusively on encrypted updates, mitigating the inference attacks described above without introducing noise that would degrade model accuracy [88]. Recent FL+HE implementations for IDS report F1-scores of 96.26 % to 98.42 % across the KDD CUP, CICIDS2017, and UNSW-NB15 datasets [15], with accuracy of 92.7 % on CIFAR-10 and KDD-99 [43]. These results confirm that the addition of HE does not cause a meaningful loss in detection performance compared to unencrypted FL baselines. However, prior work remains limited in comparing different HE schemes and in disentangling their scheme-specific computational and communication costs.

FL+DP. In FL+DP approaches, local differential privacy is applied to the gradient updates before they are sent to the central server, protecting individual contributions from inference attacks [32,38]. Reported F1-scores range from 72.05 % at a strict privacy budget of ϵ=3 [38] to 98.51 % on the CAN-intrusion dataset [17]. While FL+DP is computationally less expensive than FL+HE [38], a disadvantage is that over several rounds of computation, the central server may still be able to learn about individual clients. Furthermore, the noise added by DP almost always comes at a cost to accuracy [25,48], making the privacy-utility trade-off a central design consideration.

Secure Multiparty Computation (SMPC). Secure multiparty computation is a cryptographic approach in which multiple parties jointly compute a function over their inputs without revealing those inputs to each other [35]. A major advantage of SMPC is that it preserves accuracy, as no noise is added. However, SMPC typically comes at high computational costs, and most standard protocols require participants to be active simultaneously. While corrupted or dishonest participants remain a challenge, SMPC has been demonstrated for specific IDS-related tasks, though its adoption in FL-based smart home IDS remains limited.

Despite these advances, to the best of our knowledge, prior work has not provided a comprehensive evaluation of PET selection for smart home IDS that incorporates user acceptance criteria alongside technical performance and privacy guarantees. This gap motivates the present study.

3 Research Design and Methodology

This research follows the Action Design Research (ADR) method proposed by Sein et al. [69], which integrates the building of IT artifacts, organizational intervention, and evaluation into inseparable, concurrent activities (see Fig. 1). ADR is particularly suited to this project because the system constitutes an ensemble artifact—one shaped not only by technical design decisions but also by regulatory requirements such as the GDPR, and by users' privacy expectations regarding data sharing in smart home environments. The central methodological focus lies on the privacy-preserving selection and integration of technologies for collaborative threat intelligence sharing. We structure the research process along the four ADR stages—Problem Formulation, Building-Intervention-Evaluation (BIE), Reflection and Learning, and Formalization of Learning—and adhere to the seven principles articulated by Sein et al. [69]. The Problem Formulation Stage combines a structured literature review with semi-structured interviews to derive initial design requirements, grounded in the theoretical foundations described in Sect. 3.1. The BIE stage followed an IT-dominant form, as the primary source of innovation was a novel technical architecture for privacy-preserving collaborative IDS, which was then subjected to iterative evaluation informed by user requirements and technical feasibility constraints.

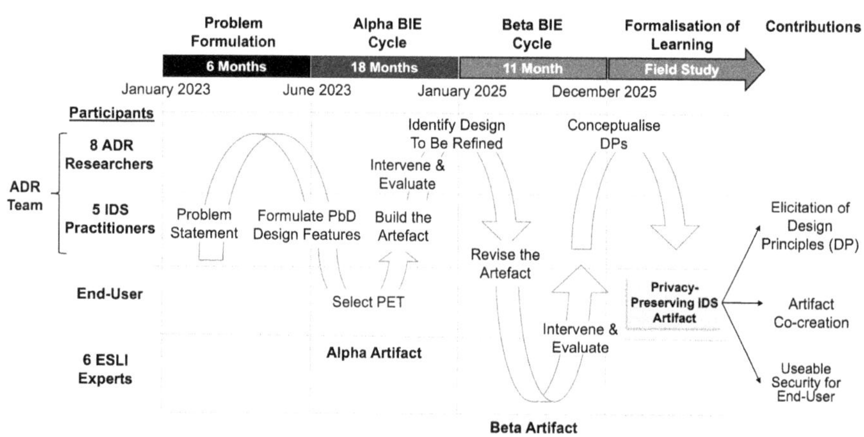

Fig. 1. Action Design Research.

3.1 Theoretical Foundation for Design

To ground the design decisions made throughout the ADR process, we draw on two complementary theoretical lenses. These frameworks serve a dual purpose: they inform the derivation of initial design requirements during the Problem Formulation stage (Sect. 4.1) and provide the vocabulary for formalizing the design principles in the Formalization of Learning stage (Sect. 5.2).

Affordance-Based Design (ABD), as proposed by Maier and Fadel [54], offers a relational theory of design in which affordances capture what an artifact provides to its users, including both intended and unintended interaction possibilities. Unlike function, which describes the transformation of inputs to outputs, affordances are inherently relational and carry polarity, meaning they can be beneficial or harmful. Through the Designer–Artifact–User system, designers specify artifact structures that possess desired affordances while actively eliminating undesired ones. We complement this with Cavoukian's [13] Privacy by Design (PbD) framework, which holds that privacy must be embedded proactively into system architecture rather than addressed after harms materialize. PbD's foundational principles, particularly privacy as the default, end-to-end lifecycle protection, and positive-sum functionality, translate naturally into the affordance vocabulary. A privacy-preserving system should afford protection, transparency, and user control as positive affordances, while its architecture must avoid affording surveillance, unauthorized inference, or loss of data autonomy as negative affordances. Together, ABD and PbD provide a theoretical basis for reasoning systematically about what a collaborative smart home security system should enable and what it must prevent.

3.2 PET Selection Framework

To systematically incorporate user acceptance criteria (UAC) into the selection of privacy-enhancing technologies during the Alpha BIE Cycle (Sect. 4.2), we applied the structured decision support framework proposed by Löbner et al. [50]. The framework translates user acceptance criteria (see Table 3), which users can perceive and evaluate without technical knowledge, into differentiating characteristics of Privacy-Preserving Machine Learning (PPML) techniques through a validated expert mapping [49]. The process consists of three steps. First, UAC preference scores are elicited from users through a survey, in our case using an Analytical Hierarchy Process (AHP) [68]. Second, these preference scores are translated into PPML characteristic scores using a binary mapping matrix that connects each UAC to the technical characteristics it influences. Third, developers evaluate eligible PPML techniques against these characteristics by defining categories, setting intra-categorical weights, and assessing each technology based on existing literature and prototypical implementations. The user-derived characteristic scores and the developer-derived technology evaluations are then combined into a final ranking score per technology. For the IDS artifact, the eligible techniques assessed were federated learning (FL), FL combined with homomorphic encryption (FL+HE), FL combined with local differential privacy (FL+LDP), standalone differential privacy (DP), secure multiparty computation (SMPC), and standalone homomorphic encryption (HE). The framework ensures that the final technology recommendation reflects not only technical feasibility and privacy guarantees but also the priorities expressed by prospective users.

3.3 ADR Team Composition

The ADR team comprised four partner organizations with complementary expertise, ensuring that the ensemble artifact was shaped by both research-driven and practice-oriented perspectives. University of Hamburg contributed expertise in network security, intrusion detection, and federated learning infrastructure. Goethe University Frankfurt contributed expertise in privacy-enhancing technologies, user acceptance research, and the design of the privacy architecture informed by the user evaluation. Tenzir GmbH, a security analytics company, contributed practitioner knowledge on scalable network monitoring and threat detection pipelines. Comidio GmbH, developer of the TrutzBox privacy appliance for home networks, contributed practitioner expertise in privacy-by-design hardware and software development, network-level firewall protection, and consumer-oriented security product design.

4 Designing a Privacy-Preserving IDS Artifact

4.1 Problem Formulation

The impetus for this ADR project came from the increasing deployment of IoT devices in private households and the absence of usable, privacy-preserving mechanisms for collaborative intrusion detection in consumer environments. The smart home market lacks sufficient regulation [19,23,44], resulting in incomplete information on data handling practices [11,16,75], while small enterprises and startups frequently lack security strategies [8]. To establish the problem and solution domains, we combined two complementary approaches: a structured literature review on smart home threats, intrusion detection systems, and privacy-enhancing technologies, and semi-structured interviews (N = 11) with technically versed smart home users in Germany. The interviews were conducted remotely, lasted between 30 and 60 min, and followed a guideline covering smart home usage behavior, perceived threats, and expectations toward protective measures. Transcripts were analyzed using qualitative content analysis following Mayring [57], with codes derived both deductively from the interview guideline and inductively from the data. From this combined analysis, three key challenges emerged. First, users experience pronounced uncertainties about data flows and third-party sharing, with privacy concerns outweighing security concerns [1,30,45]. Second, existing protective measures such as VLANs and firewalls are perceived as too complex for average users. Third, collaborative intrusion detection approaches raise privacy concerns when applied to households, as network traffic can reveal sensitive behavioral patterns [63].

The literature indicated that federated learning offers a distributed approach keeping raw data local [84], while Privacy-Enhancing Technologies such as homomorphic encryption can protect model updates from inference attacks [33,84]. The interview findings reinforced this direction: participants expressed strong preferences for local data processing, transparency regarding what data leaves the household, and open-source solutions that enable independent verification.

Based on these findings, we derived initial design requirements grounded in Privacy by Design [12] and framed through Affordance-Based Design [54], mapping abstract privacy principles to concrete artifact features by specifying positive affordances (e. g., the system affords local-first processing) and eliminating negative affordances (e. g., the system must not afford centralized data exposure). The resulting design requirements are summarized in Table 1. The class of problems was defined as privacy-preserving collaborative threat intelligence sharing for consumer IoT environments.

Table 1. Initial affordances and features to be built in the Alpha BIE Cycle.

Initial affordance	Feature	Considerations
Proactive protection	Self-monitoring of the IDS's outbound communication to identify unintended transmissions.	– PbD prevents privacy events before they occur [12]. – Vulnerability handling is often compliance- rather than risk-oriented [5].
Privacy by Default	Local-first edge architecture	– PbD requires protection without user action [12]. – Centralized IDS create single points of failure [63].
Architectural privacy	Edge deployment with PET selection as architectural decision.	– Privacy must be built in, not retrofitted [12]. – Smart home security insufficiently considers UX [14].
Full functionality	PET integration without degradation of detection accuracy or responsiveness.	– PbD promotes positive-sum outcomes [12]. – Privacy-usability trade-offs remain common [77].
Lifecycle protection	Data protection during local analysis, model training, aggregation, and updates.	– PbD emphasizes lifecycle management [12]. – Gradient leakage can occur at multiple FL stages [33].
Transparency	Disclosure of data processing, aggregation partners, and scope of shared updates.	– Users demand transparency in data practices [30]. – Data collection of privacy tools perceived as invasive [56].
User control	Opt-in/opt-out for data sharing participation and community interaction.	– Users reject automated third-party decisions [56]. – Threat understanding increases protective action [28].

4.2 Alpha Cycle: PET Selection and Artifact Construction

The first BIE cycle focused on selecting a privacy-enhancing technology based on user acceptance criteria and constructing an initial FL+HE IDS architecture.

Following the structured decision support framework proposed by Löbner et al. [49,50], user acceptance criteria (see Appendix A) were elicited and translated into differentiating PPML characteristics to rank candidate PETs. We conducted a large-scale online survey with 725 participants in Germany, recruited via the ISO 20252-certified market research institute respondi.com. The sample was balanced by age and gender according to 2024 population estimates from the German Federal Statistical Office, with participants evenly assigned to smart home device users (hereafter SHD users) and non-users (non-SHD users). Each participant completed an Analytical Hierarchy Process [68] comparing 15 user acceptance criteria organized into four groups: privacy concerns, user experience, data processing, and perceived trustworthiness. After excluding incomplete attempts, quota exclusions, and speeders, 670 valid responses remained for AHP analysis. A consistency ratio threshold of 0.15 was selected, achieved by roughly 50 % of participants per group. The AHP results revealed significant differences between SHD users and non-SHD users. Privacy concerns were significantly more important for non-SHD users ($p < 0.001$), whereas user experience was more important for SHD users ($p < 0.001$). Overall, perceived trustworthiness received the highest importance rating from SHD users. At the subcriteria level, transparency, data bias mitigation, and unauthorized access emerged as the three most important design considerations across both groups, while availability and adaptability were ranked lowest. To ensure that the PET selection reflects the preferences of the realistic user base, a subgroup of non-SHD users was identified who indicated that an IDS could help reduce their privacy and security concerns. Participants who rejected all monitoring-related options were excluded. The combined global preference scores from SHD users and potential SHD users served as input to the framework.

Three coders with expert knowledge in PPML independently evaluated five candidate technologies—federated learning (FL), homomorphic encryption (HE), local differential privacy (LDP), FL+HE, and FL+LDP—against 12 PPML characteristics grouped into six categories: data requirements, data vulnerabilities, model construction, model evaluation, privacy, and security. [SMPC was excluded, as the architecture requires a central aggregation point.] The coding exercise followed a four-step process [50]: assessing eligible PPML techniques, setting PPML categories for the application, defining intra-categorical weights, and evaluating each technology against the categories. Intercoder reliability reached a Krippendorff's alpha of 0.81 after two discussion rounds. Hard requirements were defined for the location of raw data storage, which had to remain local based on the clear user preference identified in the survey. Factoring the AHP-derived user acceptance scores into the technology evaluation yielded the following total scores: FL: 0.77, HE: 0.56, FL+HE: 0.80, LDP: 0.47, FL+LDP: 0.63. The combination of federated learning and homomorphic encryption achieved the highest score, slightly outperforming other technologies.

Artifact Construction. Based on the PET selection, the ADR team designed an initial FL+HE architecture for the IDS (see Fig. 2). The architecture implements a federated learning setup in which each household device trains an intrusion detection model locally on its own network traffic data. Only encrypted model updates leave the household, with homomorphic encryption applied before server-side aggregation. The central aggregation server operates exclusively on ciphertext, ensuring that plaintext data and unencrypted model parameters remain inaccessible.

This design directly addresses two of the three highest-ranked user acceptance criteria: unauthorized access prevention (encryption protects against inference attacks at the server) and data bias mitigation (federated learning can incorporate rare attack patterns distributed across households). The relationship to the highest-ranked criterion, transparency, is more complex: while users can be informed that only encrypted parameters leave the household, encryption simultaneously limits model explainability—a tension addressed in the Beta Cycle (see Sect. 4.3). The artifact was constructed in close collaboration of the ADR Team, connecting privacy architecture design informed by the user acceptance evaluation, and the technical IDS and federated learning infrastructure.

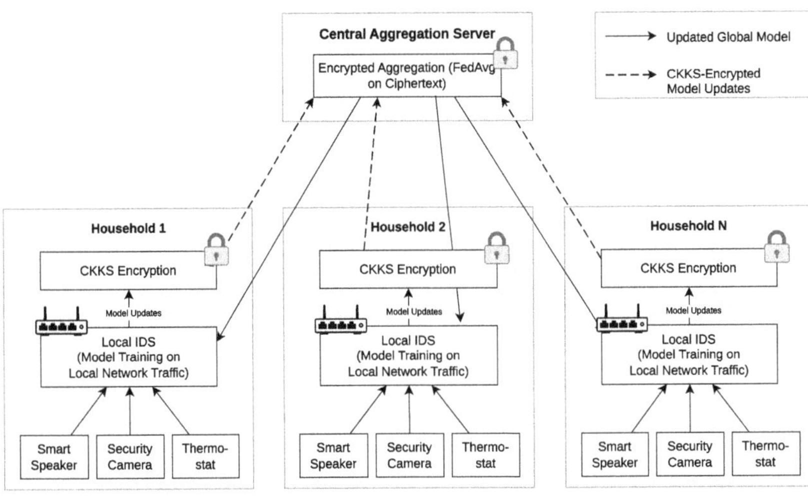

Fig. 2. Architecture of FL+HE IDS.

Identification of Refinement Needs. The Alpha Cycle also surfaced tradeoffs and open questions that required further investigation before deployment. First, in the security group, HE complicates the detection of model poisoning attacks, as the server cannot inspect individual model updates. Second, in the model construction group, encryption limits the variety of available explainability methods, which contradicts the highest-ranked user acceptance criterion of transparency. Third, questions around automated remediation actions (e. g., blocking or isolating devices) were not yet addressed, including whether such actions should be automated or require explicit user consent. Fourth, the ethical implications of excluding non-participating users from federated model improvements remained unresolved. Fifth, legal compliance requirements, particularly regarding the GDPR, the EU AI Act, and the Cyber Resilience Act, had not yet been systematically assessed against the architectural choices. These open issues defined the agenda for the Beta BIE Cycle.

4.3 Beta Cycle: ELSI Evaluation and FL+HE Implementation

The second BIE cycle subjected the Alpha Cycle outcomes to broader stakeholder scrutiny through an Ethical, Legal, and Social Impact (ELSI) workshop, refined the design affordances accordingly, and implemented and evaluated the FL+HE architecture.

ELSI Workshop. To assess the legal, social, and ethical implications of the IDS design decisions made in the Alpha Cycle, an ELSI workshop was conducted in Frankfurt with 15 participants, including six members of the dedicated ELSI team and additional stakeholders from the project consortium. Using the World Café method, participants rotated through small groups addressing two guiding questions across multiple rounds: (1) What specific legal and regulatory requirements must the IDS meet for a lawful and scalable deployment? (2) How can the IDS be designed and deployed to uphold ethical principles while fostering users' trust and social acceptance? From a legal perspective, participants confirmed that the IDS must comply with the GDPR, particularly regarding clear role assignments between data controller and processor, transparency, and mechanisms for consent and withdrawal. The continuous analysis of network data flows was assessed as not necessarily constituting automated profiling, provided data minimization, purpose limitation, and appropriate legal bases are maintained. A Data Protection Impact Assessment was deemed likely necessary given the volume and sensitivity of the processed data. Regarding the EU AI Act, the federated and deep learning components would probably not qualify as high-risk, though transparency and risk management obligations remain relevant. The Cyber Resilience Act was identified as imposing uniform obligations on both commercial and non-commercial products, with specific concerns raised about update mechanisms: blocking device traffic may inadvertently prevent legitimate firmware updates, and the system must ensure that basic device functionality is not impaired. Participants discussed whether IDS could proxy updates for blocked devices, and whether long-term support commitments can be guaranteed beyond the project's end. The need for a responsible legal entity for data stored locally in households was also raised, along with the question of whether ISO norms apply.

Regarding threat intelligence sharing, the workshop highlighted that even minimal data such as IP addresses can enable substantial inferences about households. Participants recommended that shared data should be reduced to the

Table 2. Refined affordances from the ELSI workshop and features to be addressed in the remainder of the Beta BIE Cycle.

Refined affordance	Features to be addressed in the Beta BIE Cycle	Considerations from ELSI workshop
Proactive protection	F1. Remediation must not impair basic device functionality or prevent legitimate firmware updates.	– Blocking device traffic may inadvertently prevent updates, conflicting with CRA obligations. – IDS could proxy updates for blocked devices.
Privacy by Default	F2. Local-first architecture must support standalone operation upon withdrawal from FL.	– Opting out must be technically possible at any time. – Local detection capability must remain unaffected by withdrawal.
Architectural privacy	F3. Embed GDPR, EU AI Act, and CRA requirements into architectural decisions.	– Clear controller/processor role assignments required. – A Data Protection Impact Assessment is likely necessary. – EU AI Act transparency obligations apply even for non-high-risk systems.
Full functionality	F4. Implement graduated remediation with tiered interventions (notify, throttle, isolate, block) configurable per device criticality.	– Device criticality varies considerably (e.g., a pacemaker vs. a smart speaker). – Fully automated interventions require explicit opt-in consent.
Lifecycle protection	F5. Ensure that privacy protection persists across multiple model iterations, preventing cumulative inference from repeated model updates and aggregation cycles.	– Over several rounds, an aggregating server may accumulate sufficient information to infer patterns about individual households. – HE protects individual rounds, but lifecycle protection requires that guarantees hold across the full training process.
Transparency	F6. Enable independent verification through open-source deployment; communicate HE-related explainability limitations openly.	– Dual-use risk: IDS could be repurposed as surveillance instrument. – HE limits model explainability, partially contradicting this affordance. – Comprehensible interfaces and auditable decisions support perceived trustworthiness.
User control	F7. Implement reversible opt-in for federated participation; provide visibility into what was blocked with one-click reversal.	– Exclusion of non-participants deemed legally permissible but ethically problematic; a time-gated sharing mechanism was proposed to balance fairness with incentivization. – Users must be able to see what was blocked and reverse decisions.

absolute minimum, with IP sharing occurring only above a defined threshold of suspicion. From a social perspective, the central discussion concerned automated remediation actions. There was unanimous agreement that users must retain control over the form and act of remediation, particularly when blocking or isolating devices could affect their functionality or update capability. Fully automatic interventions were assessed as legally and ethically sensitive and should only proceed on the basis of explicit opt-in consent, with graduated configuration options and clear communication. Participants noted that device criticality varies considerably. A pacemaker, for instance, requires both a more timely response and unimpaired functionality. Participants also noted that the system must provide multiple levels of control for different user groups. The exclusion of non-participating users from federated learning improvements was deemed legally permissible but ethically problematic. Participants suggested that a time-gated model sharing mechanism could address this tension, providing improved models to all users after a delay rather than permanently excluding non-participants. From an ethical perspective, the workshop underscored the importance of personal autonomy, informed consent, and transparency. A key concern was the dual-use risk: the IDS technology could be repurposed from a protective tool into a surveillance instrument. Open-source deployment was proposed as a partial mitigation, as it enables independent verification and improves transparency. Social acceptance was found to depend primarily on perceived trustworthiness, achieved through comprehensible interfaces, auditable system decisions, user feedback mechanisms, as well as long-term update and support commitments. Participants emphasized that users should be able to see what was blocked, that logging should be minimized, and that opting out must be technically possible at any time after opting in. These findings refined the affordances from the Alpha Cycle and defined the features to be addressed in the remainder of the Beta Cycle (see Table 2).

FL+HE Implementation (Building). Building on the refined requirements, the ADR team implemented and evaluated the FL+HE architecture. The primary objective was to provide empirical evidence that FL+HE is computationally feasible for practical IDS deployment, directly addressing the concern raised in the Alpha Cycle that practitioners frequently dismiss HE due to reported overhead [3,62]. Multiple HE schemes were evaluated, specifically BFV and CKKS, across varying federation sizes (up to 50 clients) and model architectures on the established IDS benchmark datasets CICIDS2018 [20] and CICIoT2023 [59]. The tests were conducted on a ASUS ROG NUC (2025) with 24 Core Ultra 9 CPU, RTX 5080 GPU and 96 GB RAM.

Technical Evaluation. The evaluation confirmed that the FL+HE architecture suits the problem identified in the Alpha Cycle without introducing practical limitations. The CKKS-based variant achieved an F1-score of 0.97 on the CICIDS2018 dataset, matching the unencrypted FL baseline. Critically, the encrypted aggregation of model updates from ten federated clients completed in under four seconds per round, demonstrating that FL+HE does not introduce meaningful delay into the federated learning process. The homomorphically encrypted aggregation ensured that the central server could not access plaintext model parameters, effectively mitigating inference attacks. The overhead scaled linearly with the number of clients and primarily with model size, without fundamentally limiting scalability. The architecture also supports standalone operation: individual households can withdraw from federated learning rounds without affecting their local detection capability, satisfying the ELSI requirement for reversible opt-in.

Conceptualization. The Beta Cycle confirmed that the FL+HE combination identified through user acceptance criteria in the Alpha Cycle is not only conceptually preferable but also technically viable for deployment on resource-constrained edge devices typical of smart home environments. The ELSI workshop added critical refinements that the purely technical and user-centered Alpha Cycle had not surfaced, particularly around remediation control, CRA compliance for device updates, dual-use risk mitigation through open source, and the ethical dimensions of excluding non-participants from collaborative model improvements. Together, the two BIE cycles produced an ensemble artifact whose design reflects not only the theoretical precursors and the intent of the ADR team but also the influence of users, legal experts, ethicists, and the broader stakeholder community.

5 Reflection and Learning

Reflection and learning occurred continuously throughout both BIE cycles (Principle 6: Guided Emergence [69]). Several key insights emerged that reshaped both the technical artifact and the broader understanding of the problem class.

5.1 Cross-Cycle Insights

The most significant insight concerns the guided emergence of FL+HE as the privacy-preserving architecture. The path from an initial broad assessment of six candidate PETs, through user-informed criteria weighting with 725 participants, to ELSI refinement with 15 stakeholders, to technical validation on benchmark datasets exemplifies the ADR principle that ensemble artifacts emerge through the interplay of planned design and contextual factors rather than from a predetermined specification. FL+HE was not selected on purely technical grounds. The combination emerged because it best satisfied the empirically elicited user acceptance criteria while also withstanding legal, ethical, and social scrutiny.

A second insight concerns the reciprocal relationship between user acceptance criteria and technical design choices. The AHP results (see Sect. 4.2) did not merely constrain the design space but actively shaped the evaluation framework used to compare PETs. The technical evaluation confirmed that this user-driven design choice is also technically viable, retroactively validating the criteria catalogue and the user-informed selection process from the Alpha Cycle.

A third insight concerns the indispensable role of the ELSI workshop in surfacing requirements that neither the user study nor the technical evaluation alone would have produced. The Alpha Cycle identified FL+HE as the preferred technology and confirmed its technical feasibility. However, it did not address whether blocking a device could violate the Cyber Resilience Act by preventing legitimate firmware updates, whether the dual-use risk could be mitigated through open-source deployment, whether excluding non-participating users is ethically acceptable even if legally permissible, or whether users must be able to reverse remediation decisions at any time. These requirements emerged only through structured engagement with legal experts and ethicists, demonstrating that the artifact's ensemble nature extends beyond the technical architecture to encompass remediation policies, consent mechanisms, and governance structures.

A fourth insight concerns trade-offs that remain partially unresolved. Both the ELSI workshop and the Alpha Cycle identified that homomorphic encryption limits explainability, contradicting the highest-ranked user acceptance criterion of transparency. While open-source deployment partially address this tension, the fundamental limitation persists and represents an area for future research. Similarly, detecting model poisoning attacks under encryption remains challenging, as the aggregating server cannot inspect individual model updates.

5.2 Formalization of Learning

The objective of this stage is to abstract the situated learning from the IDS project into generalizable design knowledge applicable to the class of problems: privacy-preserving collaborative IDS for consumer IoT environments.

Generalization of the Problem. We characterize the class of problems as systems that must enable collaborative security improvements across distributed, privately owned network environments while operating under three simultaneous constraints: stringent privacy requirements arising from the processing of sensitive household data, limited computational resources on edge devices, and heterogeneous user expertise ranging from technically proficient users to non-technical households. These constraints are not unique to the IDS project but are shared by any collaborative IDS deployment in consumer IoT settings.

Generalization of the Solution. We position FL+HE as an instance of a broader class of federated privacy-preserving learning systems suitable for resource constrained, privacy-sensitive environments. The architecture keeps raw data local, shares only encrypted model updates, and enables collaborative model improvement without central plaintext access. This solution class is applicable beyond smart home IDS to other consumer IoT scenarios where data sensitivity precludes centralization, such as health monitoring, energy management, or connected vehicle security.

Design Principles. The following design principles were derived from the two BIE cycles, the ELSI workshop, and the continuous reflection process. They represent the primary design research contribution and are intended to guide the development of future instances within this class of systems.

DP1: User-Informed PET Selection. The selection of privacy-enhancing technologies should be guided not only by technical criteria but also by empirically elicited user acceptance criteria. Users cannot evaluate PETs directly due to the knowledge gap, but their perceivable preferences can be systematically translated into technical characteristics through structured frameworks. In the IDS project, this process identified FL+HE as the preferred combination over FL alone, FL+LDP, standalone HE, and standalone LDP.

DP2: Encrypted Collaborative Learning. Collaborative model improvement across distributed instances should combine federated learning with cryptographic protection of model updates to ensure that no central entity gains access to plaintext data or model parameters. This addresses data minimization and purpose limitation requirements while preserving detection accuracy comparable to unencrypted baselines.

DP3: Local-First Data Processing. Raw data should remain on local edge devices at all times, with only encrypted model updates leaving the household. This design choice aligns with the strong user preference for local data processing and minimizes the attack surface for inference-based privacy violations. The IDS should work standalone even without federated collaboration.

DP4: Voluntary Participation with Ethical Safeguards. Participation in collaborative learning must be based on explicit opt-in consent and must be technically reversible at any time. Non-participating users should not be permanently excluded from model improvements; a time-gated sharing mechanism can balance incentivization with fairness.

DP5: Graduated Remediation Control. Automated security interventions such as blocking or isolating devices must be subject to explicit user consent and configurable in scope. Device criticality must be considered, as remediation actions may impair functionality or prevent legitimate updates. Users must be able to see what was blocked and reverse decisions.

DP6: Verifiable Transparency. The system should disclose its own data processing practices, including what is shared, with whom, and in what form. Open-source deployment of software components enables independent verification and mitigates dual-use risk. Where encryption limits model explainability, this limitation should be communicated transparently rather than obscured.

6 Discussion

6.1 Knowledge Outcomes

This project demonstrates the value of ADR for designing privacy-preserving systems where technical, legal, ethical, and user-centered requirements are deeply entangled. A conventional stage-gate design research approach [61] could presumably have led to the selection of FL+HE based on technical criteria alone. However, the human-centered Privacy by Design approach enabled by the iterative interweaving of building, intervention, and evaluation across two BIE cycles produced knowledge that a sequential approach would not have yielded.

The Alpha Cycle revealed that FL+HE is not only technically sound but also the PET combination that best satisfies empirically elicited user acceptance criteria. This finding would not have emerged from a purely technical comparison, because the ranking depends on how user preferences are translated into technical PPML characteristics through a structured framework [50]. The Beta Cycle then demonstrated that subjecting a technically validated artifact to ELSI scrutiny surfaces requirements that neither user studies nor technical evaluations produce independently. This is consistent with the ADR premise that IT artifacts are ensembles shaped by their context during development and use [69].

6.2 Implications for Research

Our work extends the discourse on Privacy by Design [12] by demonstrating how its foundational principles can be operationalized as design affordances [54] for collaborative IDS. Framing privacy properties as positive affordances (e. g., the system affords encrypted collaboration) and privacy risks as negative affordances (e. g., the system must not afford centralized data exposure) provides a vocabulary bridging normative principles and implementable features. We also illustrate how the IT-dominant BIE form of ADR can accommodate structured ethical and legal intervention through an ELSI workshop without losing the design research focus on generalizable knowledge. Finally, the technical evaluation (Sect. 4.3) provides empirical evidence countering the prevailing assumption that HE overhead renders it impractical for IDS deployment [62].

6.3 Implications for Practice

For practitioners, our results offer several actionable insights beyond the design principles formalized in Sect. 5.2. PET selection should not be driven by technical benchmarks alone; factoring user acceptance criteria into the process leads to different rankings than a purely technical comparison. Local-first data processing is a hard requirement from the user perspective, not merely a desirable property. Automated remediation actions require graduated design with explicit opt-in consent, as blocking devices can prevent legitimate updates and conflict with CRA obligations. Open-source deployment simultaneously addresses transparency demands, mitigates dual-use risk, and supports independent auditing.

6.4 Implications for Governance

The GDPR requires Privacy by Design and by default, but what this entails for smart home IDS manufacturers remains underspecified. Our PbD mapping and design principles offer a concrete operationalization that regulators could reference. The CRA introduces obligations around update mechanisms that interact non-trivially with IDS remediation capabilities, and regulators should clarify how these obligations apply to middlebox-type security products. The EU AI Act's transparency requirements are relevant even for non-high-risk systems, and the tension between homomorphic encryption and model explainability suggests that regulators should consider how transparency obligations interact with privacy-preserving design choices, particularly when user acceptance criteria prioritize protection over interpretability.

6.5 Limitations

The empirical user study was conducted in Germany, and findings should be interpreted within this regulatory and cultural context. The ELSI workshop included 15 experts with deep expertise in their respective disciplines but limited technical knowledge of the underlying system architecture. The technical evaluation used established benchmark datasets rather than live household traffic; a longitudinal deployment study would be needed to validate real-world performance. The design principles were derived from a single ADR project, and their applicability to other domains requires further validation. The trade-off between homomorphic encryption and model explainability was identified but not resolved. As with any ADR study, the design principles are situated in the specific organizational and regulatory context from which they emerged. Future work should instantiate them in additional consumer IoT domains to further validate their generalizability.

7 Conclusion

This paper applied Action Design Research to address how to design a privacy-preserving intrusion detection system for smart home environments that incorporates user acceptance criteria into the selection of privacy-enhancing technologies. Across two BIE cycles, a large-scale user study (N = 725) identified FL+HE as the preferred PET combination, an ELSI workshop (N = 15) refined the design with legal, social, and ethical requirements, and a technical evaluation confirmed feasibility with an F1-score of 0.97 and encrypted aggregation completing in under four seconds per round. From this process, we derived six design principles for privacy-preserving collaborative IDS in consumer IoT: user-informed PET selection, encrypted collaborative learning, local-first data processing, voluntary participation with ethical safeguards, graduated remediation control, and verifiable transparency. Future work should address the tension between homomorphic encryption and model explainability and validate these principles through longitudinal deployment in real households.

Acknowledgments. The project FIIPS@Home was funded by the German Federal Ministry of Education and Research under the funding code 16KISA068K. Responsibility for the contents lies with the authors. The project was funded by the European union–NextGeneration EU. The views expressed are those of the authors and do not necessarily reflect those of the European Union or the European Commission. Neither the European Union nor the European Commission can be held responsible for them.

Use of AI Based Tools. The authors used generative AI-based tools to revise the text, improve flow and correct any typos, grammatical errors, and awkward phrasing.

A Appendix

Table 3. User acceptance criteria (UAC) from [49]. Main criteria are Privacy Concern (PC), User Experience (UX), Data Processing (DP) and Perceived Trustworthiness (PT). The respective subcriteria (SC) were ranked using the analytical hierarchy process (AHP) [67].

SC	Name	Definition
PC1	Auto. decis. making	Concern that the process becomes impersonal and individuals are treated as mere numbers rather than unique persons.
PC2	Unauthorized secon. use	Concern that data collected for one purpose is misused for another without authorization.
PC3	Data bias	Concern about discriminatory outcomes caused by unrepresentative data.
PC4	Unaut. access	Concern over personal data being accessed by unauthorized parties.
UX1	Ease of use	Expected effort required to use PPML effectively.
UX2	Adaptability	Concern that a system cannot adjust to context changes.
UX3	Availability	Degree to which users can successfully access the IDS.
UX4	Performance	Extent to which the IDS benefits intended activities.
DP1	Collection	Concern about excessive pers. data collection/storage.
DP2	Data purp.	Data processing must be legitimate, explicit, and specified.
DP3	Correct. of stored data	Concern that stored data may contain errors or inaccurate user information.
DP4	Storage location	Data transfers across borders may expose personal data (Art. 44 ff. GDPR); physical storage may be local or cloud-based with varying control.
PT1	Lawfulness	Concern, data is not processed in accordance with the law.
PT2	Fairness	Balancing of parties to avoid unfairness and vulnerability of data subjects.
PT3	Transparency	Right to meaningful information on the logic behind automated decision-making or profiling.

References

1. Abdi, N., Zhan, X., Ramokapane, K.M., Such, J.: Privacy norms for smart home personal assistants. In: Proceedings of the 2021 CHI Conference on Human Factors in Computing Systems (2021)
2. Abu-Salma, R., et al.: they didn't buy their smart tv to watch me with the kids: comparing nannies' and parents' privacy threat models for smart home devices. ACM Trans. Comput. Hum. Interaction **32**(2), 1–53 (2025)
3. Acar, A., Aksu, H., Uluagac, A.S., Conti, M.: A survey on homomorphic encryption schemes: theory and implementation. ACM Comput. Surv. (CSUR) **51**(4), 1–35 (2018)

4. Agrawal, S., et al.: Federated learning for intrusion detection system: concepts, challenges and future directions. Comput. Commun. **195**, 346–361 (2022)
5. Alomar, N., et al.: "you've got your nice list of bugs, now what?" vulnerability discovery and management processes in the wild. In: Sixteenth Symposium on Usable Privacy and Security (SOUPS 2020), pp. 319–339 (2020)
6. Anthi, E., et al.: A supervised intrusion detection system for smart home IoT devices. IEEE Internet Things J. **6**(5), 9042–9053 (2019)
7. Araujo, F.: Improving intrusion detectors by crook-sourcing. In: Proceedings of the 35th Annual Computer Security Applications Conference, pp. 245–256 (2019)
8. Assal, H., Chiasson, S.: Think secure from the beginning' a survey with software developers. In: Proceedings of the 2019 CHI Conference on Human Factors in Computing Systems, pp. 1–13 (2019)
9. Bai, L., et al.: Membership inference attacks and defenses in federated learning: a survey. ACM Comput. Surv. **57**(4), 1–35 (2024)
10. Bernd, J., Abu-Salma, R., Choy, J., Frik, A.: Balancing power dynamics in smart homes: nannies' perspectives on how cameras reflect and affect relationships. In: Eighteenth Symposium on Usable Privacy and Security (SOUPS 2022), pp. 687–706 (2022)
11. Caven, P.: Comparing the use and usefulness of four IoT security labels. In: Proceedings of the CHI Conference on Human Factors in Computing Systems (2024)
12. Cavoukian, A.: Privacy by design: the 7 foundational principles. Information and Privacy Commissioner of Ontario, Canada **5**(2009), 12 (2009)
13. Cavoukian, A.: Privacy by design in law, policy and practice. A white paper for regulators, decision-makers and policy-makers (2011)
14. Chalhoub, G.: Factoring user experience into the security and privacy design of smart home devices: a case study. In: Extended Abstracts of the 2020 CHI Conference on Human Factors in Computing Systems (2020)
15. ChandraUmakantham, O.K., Gajendran, S., Marappan, S.: Enhancing intrusion detection through federated learning with enhanced Ghost_BiNet and homomorphic encryption. IEEE Access (2024)
16. Chen, C.C.: Is a trustmark and QR code enough? the effect of IoT security and privacy label information complexity on consumer comprehension and behavior. In: CHI Conference on Human Factors in Computing Systems (2024)
17. Chen, R., Chen, X., Zhao, J.: Private and utility enhanced intrusion detection based on attack behavior analysis with local differential privacy on IoV. Comput. Netw., 110560 (2024)
18. Chi, H., Zeng, Q., Du, X.: Detecting and handling IoT interaction threats in multi-platform multi-control-channel smart homes. In: 32nd USENIX Security Symposium (USENIX Security 23), pp. 1559–1576 (2023)
19. Chiang, Y.S., Khan, O., Bates, A., Cobb, C.: More than just informed: the importance of consent facets in smart homes. In: CHI Conference on Human Factors in Computing Systems (2024)
20. CSE-CIC-IDS2018: A realistic cyber defense dataset (2018). https://registry.opendata.aws/cse-cic-ids2018/. Accessed 14 Nov 2025
21. Cui, J.: LH-IDS: lightweight hybrid intrusion detection system based on differential privacy in VANETs. IEEE Trans. Mob. Comput. **23**(12) (2024)
22. Dai, X., et al.: Homeguardian: detecting anomaly events in smart home systems. Wirel. Commun. Mob. Comput. **2022**(1), 8022033 (2022)
23. Despres, T., et al.: "My best friend's husband sees and knows everything": a cross-contextual and cross-country approach to understanding smart home privacy. Proc. Priv. Enhancing Technol. **2024**(4), 413–449 (2024)

24. Dina, A.S., Siddique, A.B., Manivannan, D.: FS3: few-shot and self-supervised framework for efficient intrusion detection in Internet of Things networks. In: Proceedings of the 39th Annual Computer Security Applications Conference, pp. 138–149 (2023)
25. Dwork, C., Kohli, N., Mulligan, D.: Differential privacy in practice: expose your epsilons. J. Priv. Confidentiality **9**(2) (2019)
26. Dwork, C., McSherry, F., Nissim, K., Smith, A.: Calibrating noise to sensitivity in private data analysis. In: Theory of Cryptography Conference, pp. 265–284. Springer (2006)
27. Ekinci, G., Broggi, A., Fiondella, L., Bastian, N.D., Kul, G.: Adaptive network intrusion detection systems against performance degradation via model agnostic meta-learning. In: Proceedings of the 11th ACM Workshop on Adaptive and Autonomous Cyber Defense, pp. 23–26 (2024)
28. Emami-Naeini, P., Dheenadhayalan, J., Agarwal, Y., Cranor, L.F.: Are consumers willing to pay for security and privacy of IoT devices? In: 32nd USENIX Security Symposium, pp. 1505–1522 (2023)
29. Emami-Naeini, P., Dixon, H., Agarwal, Y., Cranor, L.F.: Exploring how privacy and security factor into IoT device purchase behavior. In: Proceedings of the 2019 CHI Conference on Human Factors in Computing Systems (2019)
30. Emami-Naeini, P.: Privacy expectations and preferences in an IoT world. In: Thirteenth Symposium on Usable Privacy and Security, pp. 399–412 (2017)
31. Friha, O.: FELIDS: federated learning-based intrusion detection system for agricultural Internet of Things. J. Parallel Distrib. Comput. **165** (2022)
32. Friha, O., et al.: 2DF-IDS: decentralized and differentially private federated learning-based intrusion detection system for industrial IoT. Comput. Secur. **127**, 103097 (2023)
33. Geiping, J., et al.: Inverting gradients-how easy is it to break privacy in federated learning? Adv. Neural. Inf. Process. Syst. **33**, 16937–16947 (2020)
34. Gentry, C.: Fully homomorphic encryption using ideal lattices. In: Proceedings of the Forty-first Annual ACM Symposium on Theory of Computing, pp. 169–178 (2009)
35. Goldreich, O.: Secure multi-party computation (1998)
36. Tan, H., N.: Monitoring pets, deterring intruders, and casually spying on neighbors: everyday uses of smart home cameras. In: Proceedings of the 2022 CHI Conference on Human Factors in Computing Systems (2022)
37. Hernandez-Ramos, J.L., et al.: Intrusion detection based on federated learning: a systematic review. ACM Comput. Surv. **57**(12), 1–65 (2025)
38. Ihekoronye, V.U., Kim, D.S., Lee, J.M.: Federated learning with differential privacy for intrusion detection in internet of flying things: a robust approach. In: 14th International Conference on Information and Communication Technology Convergence (ICTC), pp. 932–937 (2023)
39. Jakaria, M., Huang, D.Y., Das, A.: Connecting the dots: tracing data endpoints in IoT devices. Proc. Priv. Enhancing Technol. **2024**(3), 495–522 (2024)
40. Jin, Z., et al.: FL-IIDS: A novel federated learning-based incremental intrusion detection system. Futur. Gener. Comput. Syst. **151**, 57–70 (2024)
41. Jo, H.C., Kim, S., Joo, S.K.: Smart heating and air conditioning scheduling method incorporating customer convenience for home energy management system. IEEE Trans. Consum. Electron. **59**(2), 316–322 (2013)
42. Kaissis, G.A., et al.: Secure, privacy-preserving and federated machine learning in medical imaging. Nat. Mach. Intell. **2**(6), 305–311 (2020)

43. Kumar, K.S., et al.: Security and privacy-aware artificial intrusion detection system using federated machine learning. Comput. Electric. Eng. **96** (2021)
44. Lafontaine, E., Sabir, A., Das, A.: Understanding people's attitude and concerns towards adopting IoT devices. In: Extended Abstracts of the 2021 CHI Conference on Human Factors in Computing Systems (2021)
45. Lau, J., Zimmerman, B., Schaub, F.: Alexa, are you listening?: privacy perceptions, concerns and privacy-seeking behaviors with smart speakers. Proc. ACM Hum. Comput. Interact. **2**(CSCW), 102:1–102:31 (2018)
46. Lewis, B., et al.: "I... caught a person casing my house... and scared him off:" the use of security-focused smart home devices by people with disabilities. In: 2023 CHI Conference on Human Factors in Computing Systems (2023)
47. Li, T., Sahu, A.K., Talwalkar, A., Smith, V.: Federated learning: challenges, methods, and future directions. IEEE Signal Process. Mag. **37**(3), 50–60 (2020)
48. Löbner, S., Gogov, B., Tesfay, W.B.: Enhancing privacy in federated learning with local differential privacy for email classification. In: ESORICS 2022 International Workshops, DPM and CBT, pp. 3–18. Springer (2023)
49. Löbner, S., Pape, S., Bracamonte, V.: User acceptance criteria for privacy preserving machine learning techniques. In: Proceedings of the 18th International Conference on Availability, Reliability and Security (2023)
50. Löbner, S., Pape, S., Bracamonte, V., Phalakarn, K.: Which PPML would a user choose? a structured decision support framework for developers to rank PPML techniques based on user acceptance criteria. arXiv:2411.06995 arXiv preprint (2024)
51. Löbner, S., Tronnier, F., Pape, S., Rannenberg, K.: Comparison of de-identification techniques for privacy preserving data analysis in vehicular data sharing. In: Proceedings of the 5th ACM Computer Science in Cars Symposium, pp. 1–11 (2021)
52. Ma, Y., Lou, W., Guo, S.: On securing data privacy in federated learning using noise-assisted aggregated multi-key homomorphic encryption. In: 2025 IEEE 45th International Conference on Distributed Computing Systems (ICDCS), pp. 648–658 (2025)
53. Machooka, D., Yuan, X., Roy, K., Chen, G.: Comparison of LSTM and MLP trained under differential privacy for intrusion detection. In: 2024 International Conference on AI, Big Data, Computing and Data Communication Systems (2024)
54. Maier, J.R., Fadel, G.M.: Affordance based design: a relational theory for design. Res. Eng. Design **20**(1), 13–27 (2009)
55. Mandalari, A.M., Haddadi, H., Dubois, D.J., Choffnes, D.: Protected or porous: a comparative analysis of threat detection capability of IoT safeguards. In: 2023 IEEE Symposium on Security and Privacy (2023)
56. Marky, K.: Decide yourself or delegate-user preferences regarding the autonomy of personal privacy assistants in private IoT-equipped environments. In: CHI Conference on Human Factors in Computing Systems (2024)
57. Mayring, P.: Qualitative Content Analysis: Theoretical Background and Procedures, pp. 365–380. Springer Netherlands, Dordrecht (2015)
58. Mitev, R.: Leakypick: IoT audio spy detector. In: Proceedings of the 36th Annual Computer Security Applications Conference, pp. 694–705 (2020)
59. Neto, E.C.P., Dadkhah, S., Ferreira, R., Zohourian, A., Lu, R., Ghorbani, A.A.: Ciciot 2023: a real-time dataset and benchmark for large-scale attacks in IoT environment. Sensors **23**(13), 5941 (2023)
60. Paillier, P.: Public-key cryptosystems based on composite degree residuosity classes. In: International Conference on The Theory and Applications of Cryptographic Techniques, pp. 223–238. Springer (1999)

61. Peffers, K., Tuunanen, T., Rothenberger, M.A., Chatterjee, S.: A design science research methodology for information systems research. J. Manag. Inf. Syst. **24**(3), 45–77 (2007)
62. Prantl, T.: Performance impact analysis of homomorphic encryption: a case study using linear regression as an example. In: International Conference on Information Security Practice and Experience, pp. 284–298. Springer (2023)
63. Rahman, S.A., Tout, H., Talhi, C., Mourad, A.: Internet of Things intrusion detection: centralized, on-device, or federated learning? IEEE Netw. **34**(6) (2020)
64. Rani, D., et al.: Design of an intrusion detection model for IoT-enabled smart home. IEEE Access **11**, 52509–52526 (2023)
65. Rieger, P.: ARGUS: context-based detection of stealthy IoT infiltration attacks. In: 32nd USENIX Security Symposium, pp. 4301–4318 (2023)
66. Roundy, K.A.: Smoke detector: cross-product intrusion detection with weak indicators. In: Proceedings of the 33rd Annual Computer Security Applications Conference (2017)
67. Saaty, T.L.: Decision making–the analytic hierarchy and network processes (AHP/ANP). J. Syst. Sci. Syst. Eng. **13**, 1–35 (2004)
68. Saaty, T.L.: Decision making with the analytic hierarchy process. Int. J. Serv. Sci. **1**(1) (2008)
69. Sein, M.K., Henfridsson, O., Purao, S., Rossi, M., Lindgren, R.: Action design research[1]. MIS Q. **35**(1), 37–56 (2011)
70. Sgaglione, L.: Privacy preserving intrusion detection via homomorphic encryption. In: IEEE 28th International Conference on Enabling Technologies: Infrastructure for Collaborative Enterprises, pp. 321–326 (2019)
71. Shi, J., Lin, Y., Zhang, Z., Yu, S.: A hybrid intrusion detection system based on machine learning under differential privacy protection. In: IEEE 94th Vehicular Technology Conference (2021)
72. Siachos, I.: Comparison of machine learning algorithms trained under differential privacy for intrusion detection systems. In: IEEE International Conference on Cyber Security and Resilience, pp. 654–658 (2023)
73. Sikder, A.K., Babun, L., Aksu, H., Uluagac, A.S.: Aegis: a context-aware security framework for smart home systems. In: Proceedings of the 35th Annual Computer Security Applications Conference, pp. 28–41 (2019)
74. Spathoulas, G., Theodoridis, G., Damiris, G.P.: Using homomorphic encryption for privacy-preserving clustering of intrusion detection alerts. Int. J. Inf. Secur. **20**(3), 347–370 (2021)
75. Tabassum, M., Lipford, H.: Exploring privacy implications of awareness and control mechanisms in smart home devices. Proc. Priv. Enhancing Technol (1) (2023)
76. Tang, S., Gu, Z., Yang, Q., Fu, S.: Smart home IoT anomaly detection based on ensemble model learning from heterogeneous data. In: 2019 IEEE International Conference on Big Data, pp. 4185–4190 (2019)
77. Tsormpatzoudi, P., Berendt, B., Coudert, F.: Privacy by design: from research and policy to practice–the challenge of multi-disciplinarity. In: Privacy Technologies and Policy: Third Annual Privacy Forum, Revised Selected Papers 3 (2016)
78. Vetrivel, S.: Examining consumer reviews to understand security and privacy issues in the market of smart home devices. In: 32nd USENIX Security Symposium, pp. 1523–1540 (2023)
79. Wang, R., Lai, J., Li, X., He, D., Khan, M.K.: RPIFL: reliable and privacy-preserving federated learning for the Internet of Things. J. Netw. Comput. Appl. **221**, 103768 (2024)

80. Wang, X.: MADDC: multi-scale anomaly detection, diagnosis and correction for discrete event logs. In: Proceedings of the 38th Annual Computer Security Applications Conference, pp. 769–784 (2022)
81. Wei, F., Li, H., Zhao, Z., Hu, H.: xNIDS: explaining deep learning-based network intrusion detection systems for active intrusion responses. In: 32nd USENIX Security Symposium, pp. 4337–4354 (2023)
82. Windl, M., Schmidt, A., Feger, S.S.: Investigating tangible privacy-preserving mechanisms for future smart homes. In: Proceedings of the 2023 CHI Conference on Human Factors in Computing Systems, pp. 1–16 (2023)
83. Yahyazadeh, M., Podder, P., Hoque, E., Chowdhury, O.: Expat: expectation-based policy analysis and enforcement for appified smart-home platforms. In: Proceedings of the 24th ACM Symposium on Access Control Models and Technologies (2019)
84. Yang, Q., Liu, Y., Chen, T., Tong, Y.: Federated machine learning: concept and applications. ACM Trans. Intell. Syst. Technol. (TIST) **10**(2), 1–19 (2019)
85. Yin, Z., Xu, Y., Zhou, C., Jiang, Y.: Empirical study of system resources abused by IoT attackers. In: 37th IEEE/ACM International Conference on Automated Software Engineering, pp. 39:1–39:13 (2022)
86. Zhang, C., Li, S., Xia, J., Wang, W., Yan, F., Liu, Y.: BatchCrypt: efficient homomorphic encryption for Cross-Silo federated learning. In: 2020 USENIX Annual Technical Conference (USENIX ATC 20), pp. 493–506. USENIX Association (2020)
87. Zhou, W.: Discovering and understanding the security hazards in the interactions between IoT devices, mobile apps, and clouds on smart home platforms. In: 28th USENIX Security Symposium, pp. 1133–1150 (2019)
88. Zhou, Y., Zheng, P., Cao, X., Huang, J.: Two-tier data packing in RLWE-based homomorphic encryption for secure federated learning. In: Proceedings of the 2024 on ACM SIGSAC Conference on Computer and Communications Security, pp. 2844–2858. CCS '24, Association for Computing Machinery (2024)

The Web Tracking Score: A GDPR-Aligned Metric to Benchmark Privacy and Data Protection

David Martínez[1](✉), Eusebi Calle[1], and Dolors Canals Ametller[2]

[1] Institute of Informatics and Applications, University of Girona, Girona, Spain
david.martineza@udg.edu

[2] Public Law Department, University of Girona, Girona, Spain

Abstract. With the widespread deployment of tracking technologies across the web (including tracking cookies, pixel tracking, and browser fingerprinting) assessing their impact on user privacy remains a critical challenge. Despite regulatory efforts such as the General Data Protection Regulation (GDPR) and the ePrivacy directive, a comprehensive metric for quantifying data protection against web tracking remains absent from the literature. This paper introduces the Web Tracking Score (WTS), a four-dimensional, GDPR-aligned, and normalized metric designed to quantify compliance with data protection requirements in the context of web tracking. The WTS metric captures tracking activity occurring without valid consent, the intrusiveness of tracking technologies, the transparency of cookie banners and the presence of dark patterns, and data sovereignty based on jurisdiction. By integrating both technical and legal indicators and drawing on the GDPR and the ePrivacy directive, the metric bridges legal requirements with practical, measurable indicators. To enable fair comparisons across websites, granular indicators are normalized using the most comprehensive dataset available to date, which captures tracking activity across the top one million most-visited websites worldwide. A preliminary validation comparing mainstream cloud storage providers with privacy-friendly alternatives confirms that the WTS behaves as expected: privacy-friendly alternatives achieve a mean score of 0.89, significantly outperforming mainstream services which score 0.53 on average. The WTS metric has implications for users, policymakers, and researchers: it enables informed choice, provides a benchmarking mechanism for compliance assessment, and establishes a foundation for large-scale empirical studies. The metric is offered as an open tool for the privacy community, with collaboration invited on weight refinement, automation, and validation. This work contributes to the development of practical, accountable, and transparent tools for privacy protection.

Keywords: web tracking score · data protection · GDPR compliance · data sovereignty · privacy evaluation · tracking cookies

F. Pallas et al. (Eds.): APF 2026, LNCS 16847, pp. 114–132, 2026.
https://doi.org/10.1007/978-3-032-35899-8_6

1 Introduction

The right to individual privacy was formally introduced over a century ago and defined as a principle in which individuals are afforded full protection in person and property, equivalent to that provided under common law [28,32]. The consequences of privacy invasions can be far more severe than physical injuries [19]. This concept has continuously evolved over the past century, until it ultimately achieved legal and moral recognition, although some debate regarding its ethical aspects remains [24].

With the emergence of the Internet as we know it today [13], including millions of web services and social networks, new privacy risks have arisen for users and the general public [14,34]. These risks have intensified significantly with the rise of brand new economic models based on big data, such as the "personal data economy" (PDE) and "pay-for-privacy" (PFP) models [6,25,26]. Corporations offering web services are typically profit-driven organizations; thus they generate revenue directly through paid services or indirectly through the exploitation of user data. This fundamental dynamic explains why corporations have a vested economic interest in employing web tracking techniques [3], while users are often surprised upon discovering the large amount of data that some web services collect, despite being offered free of charge [2].

Regulation consistently lags behind the emergence of new technologies [20]. However, government institutions worldwide are making substantial efforts to limit the impact of web-tracking technologies on user privacy through state-of-the-art regulatory frameworks. One of the most advanced website data privacy regulation frameworks is the European Union's (EU) General Data Protection Regulation (GDPR) [12], which entered into force on 24 May 2016 and became applicable on 25 May 2018, coupled with the 2002 directive on privacy and electronic communications (ePrivacy directive, updated in 2009) [11]. As clarified by the European Data Protection Board (EDPB) in Opinion 5/2019, the ePrivacy Directive "particularizes and complements" the GDPR, establishing a relationship where specific provisions of the ePrivacy Directive take precedence over the general rules of the GDPR for matters within its scope [9]. Together, these two instruments constitute the complete regulatory framework for data protection against web tracking in the EU.

Despite regulatory efforts and their positive impact, the majority of web services still fail to provide adequate privacy rights to their users, with recent research highlighting widespread non-compliance in practice. In a different regulatory context, Aladeokin et al. [1] proposed a methodology to detect tracking cookie usage and evaluated compliance with Commonwealth privacy laws across 400 websites. Similarly, Hu and Sastry [17] examined the prevalence of third-party cookies before and after the GDPR and found that this regulation has not resulted in a material reduction in long-term prevalence of web tracking. In a more practical approach, Martínez et al. [21,22] identified a disconnect between apparent and actual GDPR compliance, revealing that websites using well-known consent management platforms (CMP) often set tracking cookies before obtaining valid user consent. Their large-scale analysis of the top one million websites found that nearly half violate this requirement. Finally, Bouhoula et al. [4] recently analyzed 97,000 cookie consent banners and reported that 65% of websites offering a cookie rejection option are likely to still collect user data despite explicit negative consent.

Interpreting compliance results from the reviewed literature is far from trivial. In fact, understanding these findings is an arduous task, as research works vary considerably in scope and methodology: some focus exclusively on tracking cookies while ignoring newer technologies such as pixel tracking and browser fingerprinting; others examine only consent management platforms (CMP) or visible website information without analyzing practical behavior; and several stop at detecting tracking techniques without providing a compliance verdict. This quantification challenge of web tracking is substantial and requires integrating diverse data and its alignment with GDPR rules.

Given this background, this paper addresses the following research question: "How can we construct a GDPR-aligned, normalized metric for quantifying data protection against web tracking?" by introducing the novel Web Tracking Score (WTS). The definition of this metric is crucial, as it provides a robust method for quantifying data protection in the context of web tracking and enables fair, direct comparisons between different services, encompassing both technical and legal indicators. Unlike previous research that focuses on isolated aspects of web tracking, the WTS bridges technical and legal indicators into a single normalized benchmark. This offers significant utility not only to average users but also to policymakers and auditors.

2 Background

Both the GDPR and the ePrivacy Directive need to be considered in order to properly define the Web Tracking Score (WTS), a GDPR-aligned measure for quantifying data protection compliance against web tracking in websites. In this way, these legal instruments work jointly to form a complete regulatory landscape relevant for this research. The ePrivacy directive, although transposed individually by each EU member state, contains the legal basis for electronic communications and services, meaning its specific provisions take precedence over the GDPR where applicable. In the context of web tracking, Article 5(3) of the ePrivacy Directive directly governs the use of cookies and similar technologies by requiring valid user consent. Meanwhile, the GDPR provides the complementary framework governing how personal data must be handled once collected, including rules such as transparency, data minimization, purpose limitation, and data subject rights. The concept of valid consent requires a clear affirmative action from the user before any tracking technologies may be stored or accessed on the user's device.

The absence of an affirmative choice, as well as the rejection of consent, does not constitute valid consent. Although the regulatory framework provides clear requirements for valid consent, the practical implementation of these requirements remains inadequate. As previously stated, the economic interest of big corporations in user data is substantial, as the collection and processing of user data forms the core of their business models. Consequently, the concept of valid consent is often undermined by questionable user interface design practices that manipulate user choice, known as dark patterns [16]. Recently, the European Data Protection Board's (EDPB's) Cookie Banner Taskforce reported on the most common dark patterns and practices that websites employ concerning cookie banners and consent acceptance [10], interpreted under the ePrivacy and GDPR legal frameworks. The document, summarized in Table 1, provides guidelines on how valid consent should be collected and identifies common not-compliant patterns, making it a relevant reference for the development of the WTS.

Table 1. Common dark patterns by the Cookie Banner Taskforce [10].

Pattern	Description	Compliant
A: No reject button	The banner contains an accept button and a button to access further options, but no button to reject cookies in the first layer.	No
B: Pre-ticked boxes	Pre-ticked boxes in the second layer: users are presented with options for cookie categories, with boxes pre-selected by default.	No
C: Deceptive link design	The only alternative to accepting cookies is a link embedded within a paragraph of text, without sufficient visual support to draw the user's attention.	No
D & E: Deceptive colors or contrast	The accept button is visually highlighted while the reject option has minimal contrast, making it barely noticeable.	No (in extreme cases)
H: Legitimate interest claimed	The banner lacks a reject option in the first layer. In deeper layers, it treats cookie rejection and legitimate interest objections as two separate actions.	No
I: Misclassified essential cookies	Cookies serving purposes beyond what is strictly necessary are incorrectly labeled as essential or strictly necessary.	No
K: No withdraw button	The website lacks an easily accessible solution (e.g., hovering icon, visible link) for users to withdraw their consent.	No

The current literature on GDPR-focused web tracking analyses suffers from a notable gap, as no comprehensive metric exists to quantify compliance in this context. Table 2 summarizes the recent literature and their analytical results, highlighting main contributions and key output indicators. In general, the first column shows that the majority of the current studies only consider cookies as a tracking technology, without accounting for web beacons (also known as pixel tracking) and browser fingerprinting. The second column reveals that sample sizes are often insufficient, with the exception of one study analyzing the top one million websites, which constitutes a considerable portion of the Internet. The third column illustrates that only one study includes any form of say-do alignment assessment, contrasting what cookie banners state with the actual behavior of websites. Finally, while the fourth column shows that all the studies provide some form of compliance evaluation regarding the use of web tracking techniques, the fifth column highlights the issue this paper seeks to address: none of the existing literature proposes a metric for quantifying data protection against web tracking, thus complicating the comparison of results across studies or even between individual websites.

Table 2. Current GDPR-focused web tracking analyses.

Authors	WT Technologies	Sample size	Say-Do alignment	Compliance verdict	WT quantification
Degeling et al. (2018) [5]	Only cookies	6,579	No	Yes – *cookie notice only*	No
Hu and Sastry (2019) [17]	Only cookies	500	No	Yes – *cookie notice only*	No
Matte et al. (2020) [23]	Only cookies	28,257	No	Yes – *notice and actual behavior*	No
Martínez et al. (2022) [21]	Cookies, pixels, browser fingerprinting	500	Yes	Yes – *notice and actual behavior*	No
Bouhoula et al. (2024) [4]	Only cookies	97,000	No	Yes – *notice and actual behavior*	No
Singh et al. (2025) [29]	Only cookies	360	No	Yes – *actual behavior*	No
Martínez et al. (2025) [22]	Cookies, pixels, browser fingerprinting	1,000,000	No	Yes – *actual behavior*	No

WT Technologies–web tracking technologies considered; Sample size–number of websites analyzed; Say-Do Alignment–whether the analysis compares the information and behavior of cookie banners vs. actual behavior in practice; Compliance verdict–whether the analysis evaluates compliance with regulations; WT quantification–whether the analysis includes a metric enabling cross-study and cross-website comparison of web tracking.

3 The Web Tracking Score

Based on the background analysis, this section presents the Web Tracking Score (WTS), which consists of a four-dimensional approach for constructing a metric to quantify web tracking while considering both technical and legal indicators (see Fig. 1):

- **Dimension A: Non-consent leakage.** A technical dimension based on the number of distinct entities that could potentially receive user data from a single page visit before the user has made an affirmative choice in the consent banner (i.e., no valid consent has been granted). This dimension considers the number of unique tracking domains.
- **Dimension B: Intrusiveness.** A technical dimension based on measuring the degree of intrusion associated with the web tracking techniques used to identify and track the user. This dimension considers the three main technologies used for tracking purposes: tracking cookies, pixel tracking, and browser fingerprinting.

- **Dimension C: Transparency.** A legal dimension based on measuring how much information and user agency is provided, as well as the presence of dark patterns. This dimension considers whether a cookie banner, such as a Consent Management Platform (CMP), is available, the presence of dark patterns, and whether information on data sharing with third-party entities is provided.
- **Dimension D: Data Sovereignty.** A legal dimension based on where data is likely to be processed and under which legal regime. This includes the location of the data and its jurisdiction, taking into account the country in which the website is based.

Table 3 provides an overview of how each WTS dimension is linked to the legal framework. As can be seen, the proposed metric addresses the main GDPR and ePrivacy rules related to data protection requirements in the context of web tracking.

Table 3. Overview of each WTS dimension linked with the legal framework.

WTS Dimension	GDPR Rules	ePrivacy Rules
A. Non-consent Leakage	Data minimization (Art. 5(c)), Lawfulness of processing (Art. 6), Consent (Art. 7)	Consent for terminal equipment access (Art. 5(3))
B. Intrusiveness	Integrity and confidentiality (Art. 5(f)), Data protection by design (Art. 25)	Confidentiality of communications (Art. 5), Restrictions on location data (Art. 9)
C. Transparency	Transparency (Arts. 12–14), Right to object (Art. 21)	Information on processing (Art. 6), Transparency on location data (Art. 9)
D. Data Sovereignty	Transfers to third countries (Chapter V), Accountability (Art. 5.2)	Security and breach notification (Art. 4)

4 Indicators and Score Normalization

The Web Tracking Score (WTS) architecture provides a clear structure for the metric. However, the quantification of each dimension's indicators presents a notable challenge. To enable fair comparison across websites, each numeric indicator must be normalized. This cannot be achieved without a sufficiently large and representative web dataset.

As noted in the background section, a recent study analyzed tracking compliance across the top one million most visited websites worldwide, providing an open dataset well-suited for this task [22]. For each website, the dataset captures the number of tracking domains involved before any user consent choice, the number of tracking cookies and pixel tracking events detected, and whether browser fingerprinting was present. This data directly enables the normalization

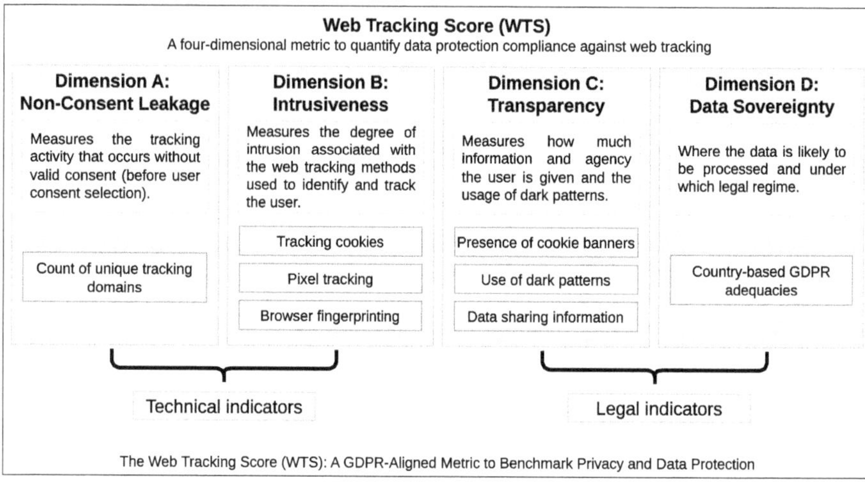

Fig. 1. Web Tracking Score (WTS) Architecture.

of Dimension A of the WTS, for which the number of unique tracking domains is a granular integer with no inherent upper bound. In contrast, Dimensions B, C, and D rely on qualitative or binary indicators where prior distributional context is not required. Therefore, the distribution of indicators derived from this large-scale study serves as the reference for normalization within the WTS.

The remainder of this section presents the indicators used for each dimension of the WTS, followed by the relevant data distributions from the large-scale compliance study, which are analyzed to establish normalization thresholds and percentiles.

4.1 Dimension A: Non-consent Leakage

This dimension quantifies websites that violate the rule that no tracking technologies should be set before the user has provided user consent. Let the indicator T_A be the number of unique tracking domains that set cookies or transmit data through pixels before the user has made an affirmative choice in the consent banner. Based on the distribution of T_A across the top one million websites dataset, the normalized score for Dimension A is defined in Eq. 1.

$$\text{Score}_A := \max\left(0, 1 - \frac{T_A}{P_{95}^A}\right) \tag{1}$$

- where P_{95}^A is the 95th percentile of T_A in the reference dataset. The 95th percentile is selected to establish a robust upper bound that excludes extreme outliers while capturing the range of typical websites. This ensures that websites with zero non-consent leakage receive a score of 1, while those exceeding the 95th percentile receive a score of 0.

4.2 Dimension B: Intrusiveness

This dimension quantifies which tracking technologies are used to identify and track the user, also known as intrusiveness. Let the indicators T_{cookies}, T_{pixels}, and $T_{\text{fingerprint}}$ be a binary variable indicating the absence of each tracking technology (1 if absent, 0 if present).

The normalized score for Dimension B is then defined in Eq. 2, incorporating the scores from the three web tracking technologies considered. The weights assigned to each technology reflect their relative intrusiveness: tracking cookies and pixels are weighted equally at 0.3 each, as their potential for intrusion is similar. Browser fingerprinting receives the highest weighting at 0.4, as it is the most intrusive technology. Unlike cookies and pixel tracking, browser fingerprinting enables persistent identification across multiple websites without relying on data stored on the user's device [15].

$$\text{Score}_B := w_c \cdot T_{\text{cookies}} + w_p \cdot T_{\text{pixels}} + w_f \cdot T_{\text{fingerprint}} \tag{2}$$

- where w_c, w_p, and w_f are the intrusiveness weights for tracking cookies, pixels, and browser fingerprinting, respectively. Proposed weights: $w_c := 0.3$, $w_p := 0.3$, and $w_f := 0.4$, with $w_c + w_p + w_f = 1$.

4.3 Dimension C: Transparency

This dimension measures how much information and agency the user is given through the website's consent mechanisms (CMPs) and the absence of dark patterns. Table 4 presents the proposed binary indicators, based on the legal framework and the EDPB Cookie Banner Taskforce findings on dark patterns [10] (see Table 1).

Table 4. Proposed binary indicators for dimension C.

Indicator	Description	Value
I_{banner}	Cookie banner or some form of CMP present.	1 if present, 0 otherwise
I_{dark}	Absence of dark patterns (Types A, B, C, D/E, H, I, K; see Table 1).	1 if all absent, 0 if any present
I_{info}	Information on third-party data sharing provided.	1 if provided, 0 otherwise

It is important to note that websites do not always require content mechanisms. Let R be a binary indicator denoting whether tracking is considered present and, consequently, whether a consent mechanism is required. Tracking is considered present if any tracking is detected before consent ($T_A > 0$) or if a cookie banner is present (implying tracking may occur after consent).

$$R := \begin{cases} 1, & \text{if } T_A > 0 \text{ or } I_{\text{banner}} = 1 \\ 0, & \text{otherwise} \end{cases}$$

The normalized score for Dimension C is defined in Eq. 3, where $I_{\text{banner}} = 1$ is considered positive (presence of cookie banner), $I_{\text{dark}} = 1$ is considered positive (absence of dark patterns), and $I_{\text{info}} = 1$ is considered positive (information on third-party data sharing provided).

$$\text{Score}_C := \begin{cases} 1, & \text{if } R = 0 \\ w_b \cdot I_{\text{banner}} + w_d \cdot I_{\text{dark}} + w_i \cdot I_{\text{info}}, & \text{if } R = 1 \end{cases} \tag{3}$$

- where w_b, w_d, and w_i are the weights for the presence of a cookie banner, the absence of dark patterns, and the provision of third-party data sharing information, respectively. Proposed weights are distributed equally: $w_b := 0.34$, $w_d := 0.33$, and $w_i := 0.33$, with $w_b + w_d + w_i = 1$.

4.4 Dimension D: Data Sovereignty

This dimension evaluates where data is likely to be processed and under which legal regime it falls. The jurisdiction score s_J is based on the country in which the website (or the company that owns it) is established, as this determines the applicable data protection framework. This score relies on the European Commission's adequacy decisions under Article 45 of the GDPR, which provide an official and authoritative assessment of whether a third country ensures an adequate level of data protection [8].

- For EU/EEA Member States, the jurisdiction score s_J is set to 1.
- For countries with an adequacy decision (Andorra, Argentina, Brazil, Canada, Faroe Islands, Guernsey, Israel, Isle of Man, Japan, Jersey, New Zealand, Republic of Korea, Switzerland, and Uruguay), the jurisdiction score s_J is set to 0.7.
- For countries without adequacy decisions, the jurisdiction score s_J is set to 0.

The normalized score for Dimension D is then simply the jurisdiction score s_J, as defined in Eq. 4.

$$\text{Score}_D := s_J \tag{4}$$

4.5 Score Normalization: Distribution Analysis

Dimension A of the WTS requires distributional data for normalization. Specifically, the 95th percentile P_{95}^A must be derived from a sufficiently large and comprehensive dataset benchmark of web tracking analysis results. For this study,

P_{95}^{A} has been extracted from the dataset of the top one million most-visited websites published in 2025, the largest and most comprehensive dataset available to date [22]. Given the constant evolution of web tracking practices, the benchmark reflects the state of the web at the time of the dataset's collection; therefore, P_{95}^{A} must be updated over time, with the year of the data specified as $P_{95}^{A}(\text{year})$. Figure 2 presents the distribution of unique tracking domains detected per website before any user consent choice. From this distribution, a value of $P_{95}^{A}(2025) = 11$ has been extracted, serving as the normalization threshold for Dimension A in the final WTS aggregation.

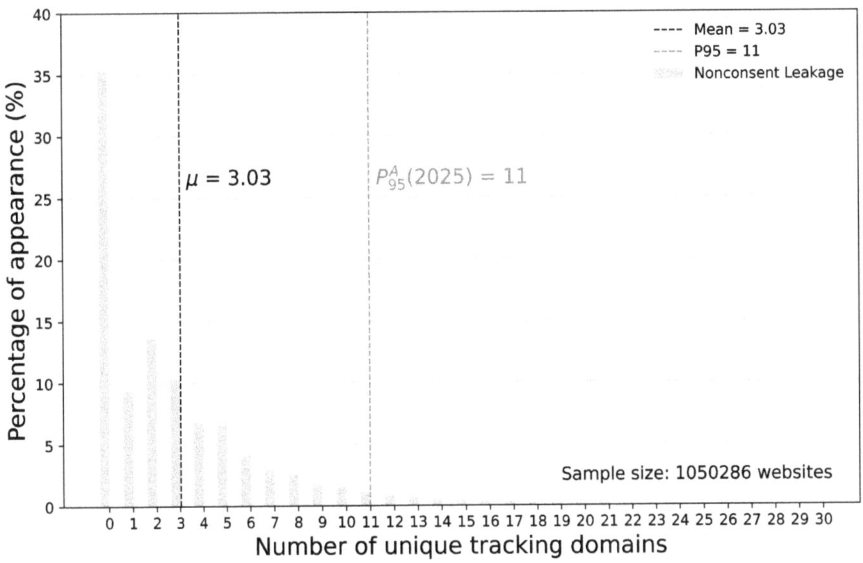

Fig. 2. Distribution of unique tracking domains detected per website before any user consent choice (non-consent leakage). Data extracted from Martínez et al. [22].

The analysis reveals that 35% of websites have set no tracking domains prior to obtaining user consent, indicating compliance with the rule that no tracking should occur without valid consent. However, the mean number of tracking domains deployed without consent across all websites (3.03) reflects a widespread pattern of non-consent leakage.

4.6 Aggregation: The Web Tracking Score (WTS)

The final Web Tracking Score (WTS) combines the four-dimension scores into a single metric, enabling direct comparison of data protection practices across websites. Instead of a simple weighted sum, the proposed approach uses a two-stage aggregation that first groups dimensions into technical and legal components, then combines them using a geometric mean(Eq. 5). The geometric mean offers key benefits over the arithmetic mean in this context as it: prevents a low legal score from being compensated by a high technical score; reflects the idea that privacy protection requires balanced strength across dimensions without the need to specify custom weights, which would be very difficult to define; and aligns with the regulatory rule that legal compliance is not optional and cannot be bypassed by technical implementation. The WTS ranges from 0 to 1, where higher values indicate better GDPR-aligned data protection against web tracking.

$$\text{WTS} := \sqrt{T_n \cdot J_n} \tag{5}$$

- where T_n is the normalized technical score (combination of dimensions A and B scores through arithmetic mean) and J_n is the normalized legal score (combination of dimensions C and D scores through arithmetic mean), defined as:

$$T_n = \frac{\text{Score}_A + \text{Score}_B}{2}, \qquad J_n = \frac{\text{Score}_C + \text{Score}_D}{2}$$

In practice, a severe deficiency in either component significantly reduces the overall aggregated score while maintaining the simplicity of the calculation. In an example scenario of a high technical score $T_n = 0.9$ and a low legal score $J_n = 0.1$, the geometric mean gives the value of WTS $= 0.3$, compared to the arithmetic value of 0.5. This approach avoids setting fixed weights; however, weights can be introduced in the geometric mean formulation if necessary through the evolution and discussion of the legal framework.

5 Preliminary Validation

This section presents an illustrative application of the Web Tracking Score (WTS) metric, along with preliminary validation and interpretation. The purpose is not to provide a comprehensive validation but to perform a sanity check to verify whether the metric behaves as expected. Full validation, including sensitivity analysis and comprehensive comparisons, will be explored in future work.

5.1 Case Study: Comparing Mainstream Web Services with Privacy-Friendly Alternatives

The WTS metric enables fair comparisons of web tracking practices across different websites. For preliminary validation, a case study comparing widely used mainstream web services with their privacy-friendly alternatives is selected. This comparison is intended to demonstrate whether the metric captures expected differences in data protection practices, specifically reflecting the improvement that average users might achieve by simply switching service providers.

To identify suitable European-based privacy alternatives, Europick by PixelUnion has been selected as a community-driven directory source that curates mainstream services alongside EU-based privacy-friendly alternatives [27]. The following mainstream file storage services were selected:

- **Apple iCloud** (icloud.com)—based in the United States
- **Dropbox** (dropbox.com)—based in the United States
- **Microsoft OneDrive** (onedrive.com)—based in the United States
- **Google Drive** (drive.google.com)—based in the United States

These are compared with four European-based privacy-friendly alternatives:

- **Cryptee** (crypt.ee)—based in Estonia.
- **Filen.io** (filen.io)—based in Germany.
- **Infomaniak kDrive** (infomaniak.com)—based in Switzerland.
- **Proton Drive** (proton.me)—based in Switzerland.

5.2 WTS Results

Tables 5 and 6 present the raw indicator values and computed WTS scores for each of the six selected services. The data crawl for the case study was performed on 27 March 2026, using the algorithms from Martínez et al. [22] for Dimensions A and B, while Dimensions C and D were assessed through manual inspection.

The WTS results show, as expected, clear differences between mainstream services and privacy-friendly alternatives. On the one hand, mainstream services exhibit similar WTS values ranging from 0.47 to 0.52, with a mean value of 0.5, mainly due to non-consent leakage and lack of data sovereignty, as these services are based in the United States. On the other hand, privacy-friendly alternatives range between diverse WTS values ranging 0.74 to 1.00 and a mean value of 0.89, considerably higher than that of mainstream services. Half of the selected privacy-friendly alternatives present a perfect score, with correct

Table 5. WTS Indicator Results: Mainstream Services vs. Privacy-Friendly Alternatives

Service	T_A	T_{cookies}	T_{pixels}	$T_{\text{fingerprint}}$	I_{banner}	I_{dark}	I_{info}	s_J
Mainstream Services								
Apple iCloud	1	1	0	1	0	1	1	0
Dropbox	2	1	0	1	0	1	1	0
OneDrive	3	1	0	1	1	0	1	0
Google Drive	4	1	0	1	1	0	1	0
Privacy-Friendly Alternatives								
Cryptee	0	1	1	1	0	1	1	1
Filen.io	0	1	1	1	1	*1**	1	1
kDrive	1	1	0	1	1	1	1	0.7
Proton Drive	1	1	0	1	0	1	1	0.7

* Filen.io presents a borderline dark pattern type C case: the reject button exists but is not visually highlighted, offering insufficient visual support per EDPB guidance.

Table 6. WTS Score Results: Mainstream Services vs. Privacy-Friendly Alternatives

Service	$Score_A$	$Score_B$	$Score_C$	$Score_D$	T_n	J_n	WTS
Mainstream Services							
Apple iCloud	0.909	0.7	0.66	0	0.805	0.33	0.52
Dropbox	0.818	0.7	0.66	0	0.759	0.33	0.50
OneDrive	0.727	0.7	0.67	0	0.714	0.33	0.49
Google Drive	0.636	0.7	0.67	0	0.668	0.33	0.47
Privacy-Friendly Alternatives							
Cryptee	1	1	1	1	1	1	1
Filen.io	1	1	1	1	1	1	1
kDrive	0.909	0.7	1	0.7	0.805	0.85	0.83
Proton Drive	0.909	0.7	0.66	0.7	0.805	0.68	0.74

transparency, data sovereignty, and zero tracking. Proton Drive shows the lowest privacy-friendly WTS score, mainly due to the presence of pixel tracking and the absence of a cookie banner.

It is important to note that, although limited in scope, this preliminary validation successfully demonstrates that the metric behaves as expected. The selection of privacy-friendly alternatives was based on community reputation, and the metric confirms that reputation by design. Furthermore, these results illustrate the impact of the data sovereignty dimension on the final score, showing how a deficiency in one dimension can significantly reduce the geometric mean even when technical scores are moderate. The comprehensive scoring methodology thus provides a strong foundation for addressing the research question introduced in this paper. Further research is needed to fully validate the metric's behavior across a more extensive and diverse set of websites.

6 Discussion

The methodological choices and their implications considered in this paper culminate in the original goal of constructing a GDPR-aligned, normalized metric for quantifying data protection compliance against web tracking in websites. Although the WTS is a proxy measure built from observable indicators and does not assess unobservable legal requirements such as purpose limitation or the actual application of data retention policies, the score is intended for comparative privacy evaluation rather than as a definitive legal compliance verdict.

Both binary and granular indicators form the mathematical basis of the Web Tracking Score (WTS) metric. For Dimension A, a granular indicator of unique tracking domains is considered, and compliance results from the top one million websites dataset are used for its normalization. In contrast, binary indicators are considered in the other three dimensions (B, C, and D). Although the binary indicators for Dimension B do not distinguish between minimal and extensive use of a given tracking technology, tracking frequency is partially captured by Dimension A, which correlates with cookie and pixel volume. This design choice simplifies the metric while avoiding double counting.

Equal weights have been adopted as a neutral baseline for the weighting of the indicators. This choice ensures that no indicator is arbitrarily prioritized, as the current legal framework does not provide explicit guidance on the significance of each dimension. In particular, it is worth noting that within Dimension B, intrusiveness weights for each web tracking technology are based on relative detectability and user control, but remain open to refinement [18]. This is why the WTS has been designed to accommodate alternative weighting schemes if empirical evidence or policy priorities justify them. Given that no established criteria currently exist for this purpose, collaboration between researchers and policymakers is needed to establish objective, empirically or legally grounded justifications for the relative weights of specific indicators. A full sensitivity analysis of how rankings shift under alternative weights is left for future work.

The question of whether some dimensions should carry more weight than others remains an open debate among policymakers and legal professionals [30,33]. By employing a geometric mean, the WTS introduces a penalty for disparities between dimensions without requiring the specification of subjective dimension weights. This ensures that a low score in either the technical or legal component penalizes the aggregate more heavily than a high score rewards it.

The novelty of this work lies not in the individual detection techniques, which build on prior research, but in the synthesis of four dimensions into a single normalized score, aggregated via the geometric mean, through the integration of legal requirements from both the GDPR and the ePrivacy Directive.

The role of the top one million dataset is crucial for this research [22]. The 95th percentile normalization for Dimension A is derived from it, ensuring that the normalization of unique tracking domains reflects actual real-world web conditions. This approach is justified by the fact that it is the largest dataset available for this purpose; however, periodic recalibration will be needed as the web evolves, in order to maintain proper normalization in this ever-changing environment [31].

The WTS formulation raises challenges related to automation and scalability for future work. Although Dimensions A and B can be fully automated using existing crawling and detection tools [4,21–23,29], Dimensions C and D currently require manual inspection. Therefore, future work should focus on automating these dimensions through automated detection of dark pattern and cookie notices for transparency, as well as jurisdiction lookups for data sovereignty, for which promising initial approaches are already emerging [4,21,23]. Once every stage becomes automated, their integration into a unified platform or tool represents a promising direction for future research, with potential impact for average users, policymakers, and society in general.

The case study presented confirms the expected behavior that privacy-friendly alternatives significantly outperform mainstream services in terms of GDPR-focused data protection against web tracking. Although limited in size and not generalizable, this preliminary validation serves an illustrative purpose and provides an initial snapshot of metric usage.

In particular, data sovereignty emerges as a key differentiator, as US-based services score zero in this WTS dimension. This finding reflects the growing strategic importance of data sovereignty in Europe. The European Commission's Cloud Sovereignty Framework (2025) defines legal and jurisdictional sovereignty as the degree to which services are anchored in European jurisdiction and insulated from external legal claims [7]. Ongoing geopolitical tensions have made this risk increasingly tangible. The WTS captures this risk through Dimension D, rewarding full EU-jurisdiction services and penalizing those exposed to foreign legal claims.

The reliance on country of establishment for this dimension is deliberate. Under the GDPR, any company processing personal data of EU citizens must comply regardless of its location. However, what actually happens to the data after it leaves the user's browser is largely unobservable from an external perspective. Moreover, recent research has shown that data handling practices stated in privacy policies often diverge from actual behavior [4,21,23]. Given this unobservability, Dimension D adopts the country of establishment as a proxy, recognizing that services based in non-EU countries expose user data to a higher risk of foreign legal claims, regardless of their stated compliance with the GDPR.

The WTS metric is proposed as an open framework for the privacy research and policy community. However, several areas require further development before the metric can be deployed at scale, including weight refinement, the automation of Dimensions C and D, validation through large-scale case studies, and its final integration into a single unified tool.

7 Conclusion

This paper presents, to the best of our knowledge, the first comprehensive metric for quantifying data protection against web tracking: the Web Tracking Score (WTS). The WTS provides a four-dimensional, GDPR-aligned, and normalized metric that captures (i) tracking activity occurring without valid consent, (ii) the intrusiveness of tracking technologies, (iii) information and transparency on cookie banners, and (iv) where data is likely to be processed. A geometric mean aggregates the technical and legal components, ensuring that a deficiency in one area cannot be fully offset by strength in the other, which is a necessary property for a metric intended to quantify data protection against web tracking.

To bridge legal requirements with practical indicators, the metric draws on both the GDPR and the ePrivacy Directive. The novel normalization of granular indicators has been made possible by open data from recent large-scale studies on web tracking. In particular, the dataset capturing tracking activity and the use of tracking technologies across the top one million most-visited websites worldwide represents the most comprehensive source available to date, enabling, for the first time, a data-driven normalization grounded in real-world web conditions. Based on this dataset, the normalization allows for fair comparison across websites and opens key opportunities for future compliance studies and website audits.

The expected behavior of the WTS metric is confirmed through a preliminary validation comparing a small set of mainstream cloud storage providers with their privacy-friendly alternatives. Privacy-friendly alternatives are associated with higher levels of data protection alignment against web tracking, with half of them achieving a perfect WTS score, and a mean value of 0.89, compared to a mean of 0.5 for mainstream services.

Beyond the metric itself, the WTS metric has several implications. For users, it enables informed choices regarding their level of data protection when navigating the Internet and selecting service providers. For policymakers, it provides a powerful benchmarking mechanism for compliance assessment and for evaluating the impact of entire legal frameworks, highlighting areas that require further development or protection. For researchers, it establishes a foundation for future large-scale empirical studies, fully automated tool development, and longitudinal assessment of data protection against web tracking over time.

Finally, collaboration is encouraged to further develop the WTS, particularly in the areas of weight refinement, automation, and large-scale validation. By building practical tools for transparency, this work contributes to the broader goal of advancing privacy protection.

Acknowledgments. The University of Girona Institute of Informatics and Applications researchers thank the Generalitat de Catalunya for their support through a Consolidated Research Group (2021 SGR 01125).

Disclosure of Interests. The authors have no competing interests to declare that are relevant to the content of this article.

Declaration of generative AI and AI-assisted technologies in the manuscript preparation process. During the preparation of this work, the authors used Mistral AI (Le Chat) to improve readability and flow. After using this service, the authors reviewed and edited the content as needed and take full responsibility for the content of the published article. This paper has undergone professional English language editing before submission.

References

1. Aladeokin, A., Zavarsky, P., Memon, N.: Analysis and compliance evaluation of cookies-setting websites with privacy protection laws. In: 2017 Twelfth International Conference on Digital Information Management (ICDIM), pp. 121–126. IEEE (2017)
2. Arias-Cabarcos, P., Khalili, S., Strufe, T.: surprised, shocked, worried: user reactions to Facebook data collection from third parties. arXiv preprint arXiv:2209.08048 (202
3. Bonfils, N.: An empirical inquiry into surveillance capitalism: web tracking. arXiv preprint arXiv:2508.07454 (2025)
4. Bouhoula, A., Kubicek, K., Zac, A., Cotrini, C., Basin, D.: Automated {Large-Scale} analysis of cookie notice compliance. In: 33rd USENIX Security Symposium (USENIX Security 24), pp. 1723–1739 (2024)
5. Degeling, M., Utz, C., Lentzsch, C., Hosseini, H., Schaub, F., Holz, T.: We value your privacy... now take some cookies: measuring the GDPR's impact on web privacy. arXiv preprint arXiv:1808.05096 (2018)
6. Elvy, S.A.: Paying for privacy and the personal data economy. Colum. L. Rev. **117**, 1369 (2017)
7. European Commission: Cloud Sovereignty Framework: Sovereignty objectives, effective assurance levels and scoring methodology (2025). https://commission.europa.eu/document/download/09579818-64a6-4dd5-9577-446ab6219113_en. Accessed: 2026-06-11
8. European Commission: data protection adequacy for non-EU countries. European Commission Official Website (2026). https://commission.europa.eu/law/law-topic/data-protection/international-dimension-data-protection/adequacy-decisions_en. Accessed: 2026-03-26
9. European Data Protection Board: Opinion 5/2019 on the interplay between the ePrivacy Directive and the GDPR, in particular regarding the competence, tasks and powers of data protection authorities (2019). https://edpb.europa.eu/our-work-tools/our-documents/opinion-board-art-64/opinion-52019-interplay-between-eprivacy_en. Adopted on 12 March 2019
10. European Data Protection Board: report of the work undertaken by the Cookie Banner Taskforce (2023)
11. European Union: Directive 2002/58/EC of the European Parliament and of the Council of 12 July 2002 concerning the processing of personal data and the protection of privacy in the electronic communications sector (Directive on privacy and electronic communications). Official J. European Union L201, 37–47 (07 2002)
12. Union, E.: Regulation (EU) 2016/679 of the European Parliament and of the Council of 27 April 2016 on the protection of natural persons with regard to the processing of personal data and on the free movement of such data, and repealing directive 95/46/EC (General Data Protection Regulation). Off. J. Eur. Union **L119**, 1–88 (2016)
13. Fielding, R., et al.: Hypertext transfer protocol–HTTP/1.1 (1999)

14. Fogel, J., Nehmad, E.: Internet social network communities: risk taking, trust, and privacy concerns. Comput. Hum. Behav. **25**(1), 153–160 (2009)
15. Fouad, I., Santos, C., Legout, A., Bielova, N.: My cookie is a phoenix: detection, measurement, and lawfulness of cookie respawning with browser fingerprinting. In: PETS 2022-22nd Privacy Enhancing Technologies Symposium (2022)
16. Gunawan, J., Santos, C., Kamara, I.: Redress for dark patterns privacy harms? A case study on consent interactions. In: Proceedings of the 2022 Symposium on Computer Science and Law, pp. 181–194 (2022)
17. Hu, X., Sastry, N.: Characterising third party cookie usage in the EU after GDPR. In: Proceedings of the 10th ACM Conference on Web Science, pp. 137–141 (2019)
18. Lukic, K., Miller, K.M., Skiera, B.: The impact of the general data protection regulation (GDPR) on online tracking. Available at SSRN 4399388 (2024)
19. Lusky, L.: Invasion of privacy: a clarification of concepts. Columbia Law Rev. **72**(4), 693–710 (1972)
20. Marchant, G.E., Sylvester, D.J., Abbott, K.W.: What does the history of technology regulation teach us about nano oversight? J. Law Med. Ethics **37**(4), 724–731 (2009)
21. Martínez, D., Calle, E., Jové, A., Pérez-Solà, C.: Web-tracking compliance: websites' level of confidence in the use of information-gathering technologies. Comput. Security **122**, 102873 (2022)
22. Martínez, D., Molero, A., Calle, E., Ametller, D.C., Jové, A.: Large-scale web tracking and cookie compliance: evaluating one million websites under GDPR with AI categorization. J. Netw. Comput. Appl. **242**, 104222 (2025)
23. Matte, C., Bielova, N., Santos, C.: Do cookie banners respect my choice?: Measuring legal compliance of banners from IAB Europe's transparency and consent framework. In: 2020 IEEE Symposium on Security and Privacy (SP), pp. 791–809. IEEE (2020)
24. Moor, J.H.: The ethics of privacy protection (1991)
25. Müller-Tribbensee, T., Miller, K.M., Skiera, B.: Paying for privacy: pay-or-tracking walls. arXiv preprint arXiv:2403.03610 (2024)
26. Paskaleva, M.: The economic value of personal data in digital economy. Int. J. Econ. Practice Policy **21**(2), 106–118 (2024)
27. Pixel Union: Europick: your European alternatives (2026). https://europick.eu/. Accessed: 2026-03-20
28. Posner, R.A.: The right of privacy. Ga. L. Rev. **12**, 393 (1977)
29. Singh, N., Do, Y., Yu, Y., Fouad, I., Kim, J., Kim, H.: Crumbled cookies: exploring e-commerce websites' cookie policies with data protection regulations. ACM Trans. Web **19**(1), 1–24 (2025)
30. Sirur, S., Nurse, J.R., Webb, H.: Are we there yet? Understanding the challenges faced in complying with the general data protection regulation (GDPR). In: Proceedings of the 2nd International Workshop on Multimedia Privacy and Security, pp. 88–95 (2018)
31. Su, Z., Helles, R., Al-Laith, A., Veilahti, A., Saxena, A., Simonsen, J.G.: Privacy lost in online education: analysis of web tracking evolution. In: International Conference on Advanced Data Mining and Applications, pp. 440–455. Springer (2023)

32. Warren, S.D., Brandeis, L.D.: Right to privacy. Harv. L. Rev. **4**, 193 (1890)
33. Zaguir, N.A., de Magalhães, G.H., de Mesquita Spinola, M.: Challenges and enablers for GDPR compliance: systematic literature review and future research directions. Ieee Access **12**, 81608–81630 (2024)
34. Ziegeldorf, J.H., Morchon, O.G., Wehrle, K.: Privacy in the internet of things: threats and challenges. Secur. Commun. Networks **7**(12), 2728–2742 (2014)

Regulation at the Technological Edge

Relativizing the Notion of Personal Data: A Proposed Framework for Data Sharing

Giuseppe D'Acquisto[1](✉) and Fabio Ricciato[2]

[1] Garante per la protezione dei dati personali, Rome, Italy
G.DAcquisto@gpdp.it
[2] Eurostat, Luxembourg, Luxembourg
fabio.ricciato@ec.europa.eu

Abstract. The paper examines the evolving notion of personal data in the aftermath of a recent ruling by the European Court of Justice and in the context of the Digital Omnibus proposal by the European Commission. These developments mark a fundamental shift towards a relative interpretation of personal data, away from the absolute interpretation that has dominated insofar. In the context of data sharing, the relative interpretation implies that the released data qualify as personal or non-personal depending on the recipient's capabilities. Data that are personal for the sender may, under certain conditions, qualify as non-personal for the recipient.

Given the new interpretative context, the analysis focuses on the case of micro-data sharing, where the data to be released consists of a set of individual records. Taking the notion of identification as the central criterion for the applicability of data protection law, the article proposes a structured framework where variables from the source dataset can be omitted, pseudonymized, anonymized through classical methods (generalization, randomization) or left unprotected in the released dataset.

The proposed framework establishes the conditions under which the resulting data set may be considered anonymous for the recipient. It clarifies the responsibilities of each actor – sender, recipient and data subject – and highlights the importance of accountability to prevent the risks associated with the increasing circulation of "relatively" non-personal data, i.e., the possibility of reconstructing individual information through accumulation and correlation downstream the data sharing chain.

The proposed framework offers a carefully tuned balance point between the diverging goals of regulatory simplification, effective protection of individuals, and support for data-driven technological development in the context of data sharing.

Keywords: pseudonymization · anonymization · GDPR · SRB ruling

1 Introduction and Conceptual Background

The notion of personal data is pivotal to the architecture of European data protection law. It determines the material scope of the General Data Protection

F. Pallas et al. (Eds.): APF 2026, LNCS 16847, pp. 135–153, 2026.
https://doi.org/10.1007/978-3-032-35899-8_7

Regulation (GDPR) and functions as a jurisdictional switch: where information qualifies as personal data, the full regulatory framework applies; where it does not, the GDPR does not apply. Given this foundational role, conceptual clarity is essential. Yet, despite its centrality, the definition of personal data remains notoriously difficult to formalize.

Article 4(1) GDPR defines personal data as *any information relating to an identified or identifiable natural person.* While this formulation appears intuitively straightforward, it relies on the concepts of *relatability* and *identifiability* that elude precise interpretation. When data relate to a person? When is the person identifiable? The answers to these questions depend on contextual, relational, and often counterfactual considerations. As a result, the GDPR definition of personal data operates less as a strict rule than as an open-ended evaluative standard, whose application inevitably involves a degree of uncertainty, if not indeterminacy, calling for subjective judgement.

This uncertainty is not fully resolved by Recital 26 of GDPR, which provides the main criterion for assessing identifiability by stating that account should be taken of *all the means reasonably likely to be used* to identify a natural person, including factors such as costs, time, available technology and even prospective technological developments. While these elements apparently offer practical guidance, they invoke notions – means, likelihood, reasonableness – that again must be interpreted in the context of the varying technological landscape.

The structure of the legal narrative surrounding the notion of personal data can be captured by the following metaphor: imagine the data at hand is the picture of a face covered by a thick layer of dust that prevents exact recognition of the person to which the picture relates. The qualification of such picture as "personal data" depends on the effort required to remove enough dust to allow recognition (identification). If the dust can be removed with limited time and effort, thereby restoring the image to clarity, the picture is considered personal data; if cleaning from the dust would require excessive resources, the picture may be regarded as anonymous data. Within this metaphor, the legal assessment must consider the availability of auxiliary tools (e.g., a brush), on the ability of the people to use them, and on other available information (e.g., a collection of people's pictures). In other words, the assessment depends on several contextual elements around the data object that influence the difficulty of reconstruction and attribution of the data to the person.

This metaphor reveals a fundamental ambiguity though: the assessment depends on subjective qualities of the entity handling the data (who holds the brush), on the characteristics of the tool (how easy to use and effective in removing the dust is the brush), and on effort (how long one is willing to brush). This is the core idea behind the so-called **risk-based approach**: the data in the hands of someone is more prone to re-identification than in the hands of others, due to different characteristics and capabilities of the subject holding the data. In the context of the risk-based approach, that is enshrined in GDPR, the definition of "personal data" can follow two interpretative approaches: relative or absolute.

In the **relative approach**, the same data may be personal for one subject with sufficient means, and non-personal for another one without such means. In other words, the applicability of GDPR may vary across different handlers for the same data.

In the **absolute approach**, the data qualify as personal for every possible actor if the existence of one actor with sufficient means cannot be plausibly excluded. In other words, to stay with the previous metaphor, if a brush exists, then the data are personal even for handlers without access to the brush.

Over the last two decades, the absolute interpretation of the risk-based approach has tended to prevail in European data protection jurisprudence. This approach has led data protection authorities to embrace a worst-case mindset by which the mere existence of a plausible path to identification sufficed to qualify a piece of information as personal (see e.g. [2,14]. The rationale behind such restrictive interpretation is twofold: firstly to limit the margins for interpretative ambiguities determined by the language, and secondly to maximize safeguards for data subjects, contributing to enforceability of the rules within the data protection legal framework. Notwithstanding such this justifications, such quasi-absolute standard has significantly extended the practical scope of application of data protection law, with consequences that have been increasingly questioned by observers and policymakers. In particular, concerns have been raised that an expansive interpretation of the notion of personal data may operate as an obstacle to innovation and research, especially in data-intensive sectors like artificial intelligence (AI).

The cumulative effect of broad applicability of the law and high compliance costs has been recently identified as a competitive issue for Europe in the global market due to the disproportionate burden it produces for economic actors, particularly for small and medium-size enterprises which often lack the resources to absorb the demands of sophisticated compliance structures [9]. This has fueled calls for simplification, alongside a shift toward regulatory approaches that strive to preserve reasonably high levels of data protection while minimizing obstacles to technological development and research.

2 Towards a Relative Notion of Personal Data

Within this perspective, the notion of personal data is identified as a key lever. Since the applicability of GDPR depends on whether information qualifies as personal data, any recalibration of the criteria for identifiability has immediate effects on the scope of the regulation. If the strategic aim is to reduce the compliance burden without weakening substantive safeguards, any forthcoming legislation should firmly scope within the application of the norm all processing operations that trigger significant risk for individuals, excluding only those situations in which the processing is considered to pose minor or negligible risks to data subjects' rights and freedoms.

This objective is supposed to be pursued through a reinterpretation of the notion of personal data that is more clearly oriented towards the relative risk-based approach. Rather than taking the actual or hypothetical existence of means of identification in the hands of a potential single actor as sufficient to qualify the data as personal for everybody, the emphasis is now placed on the reasonable availability of such means to the specific actor involved each time in the processing. Where an entity does not factually possess, and cannot reasonably obtain, the tools or information necessary to identify individuals, the data are treated as generating a low level of risk in the hands of that particular entity. In these circumstances, classifying the data as non-personal for that entity allows to exclude the processing operation conducted by the latter from the scope of GDPR, thus relieving that entity from the compliance burden. Notably, similar processing operations conducted by other entities, equipped with other tools and information, may still be assessed differently and fall in the scope of GDPR.

In the context of data sharing operations, by analogy with transmitting a message from a sender to a recipient, the relativization of the notion of personal data implies that the personal nature of the data (message) shared by data holder (sender) to another entity (recipient) is to be assessed for each data release instance (transmission) and must rely on the recipient's capabilities.

From this standpoint, simplification is achieved by transforming identifiability from a quasi-absolute concept into a relative, recipient-dependent notion, thereby reducing the reach of data protection law only to contexts where identification is concretely possible. The underlying assumption is that, in low-risk scenarios, excluding the processing from the GDPR does not materially reduce the level of protection granted to data subjects, while significantly easing regulatory obligations for the parties involved in the data sharing, and most prominently for the recipient.

The reinterpretation of the notion of personal data in relative, recipient-dependent terms has unfolded through two distinct but closely connected developments, occurring at different institutional levels and moments in time. The first is judicial in nature and concerns the clarification of identifiability through case law, the second is legislative and reflects an attempt to encode that clarification within the regulatory framework itself.

The first step is represented by the judgment of the Court of Justice of the European Union in the Single Resolution Board (SRB) vs. European Data Protection Supervisor (EDPS) case [8]. In this decision, the Court addressed the question of whether information transmitted in a context where the recipient lacks the means to identify the data subjects should necessarily be regarded as personal data. The Court held that information does not constitute personal data for a given recipient where that particular recipient has no factual means reasonably likely to enable identification of the data subject, regardless of whether such means may or may not be available to other actors.

Through this reasoning, the Court articulated a recipient-dependent understanding of identifiability. While the judgment did not amend the definition of personal data as such, it reinterpreted the application of Recital 26. In doing so, the Court provided a judicial foundation for the relative risk-based approach, the implications of which happen to be naturally aligned with, if not propaedeutic to the simplification objectives (which were out of the scope of the ruling).

The second step can be found at the legislative level, in the form of the European Commission's Omnibus proposal aimed at simplifying and streamlining the application, among others, of data protection rules [10]. To address concerns about regulatory complexity and compliance costs, the proposal seeks to encode a more context-dependent understanding of personal data into the legal framework itself. Unlike the SRB ruling, which operates through interpretation of existing concepts, the Omnibus initiative explicitly targets the definition of the notion of personal data itself.

In this respect, the Omnibus proposal can be read as an attempt to generalize and consolidate the logic underlying the SRB ruling. The combined effect of these two developments is a gradual shift from a quasi-absolute worst-case conception of personal data toward a more relative and context-dependent framework in which identifiability, and therefore regulatory applicability, is assessed based on the concrete circumstances of the processing operations and the actual means available to the specific actor involved.

Together, the SRB ruling and the Omnibus proposal delineate the trajectory of this reinterpretation: the former establishes its doctrinal plausibility through case law, while the latter seeks to translate that approach into an operational legislative model.

Simple and convincing as it may seem, this framework leaves unresolved a central conceptual question: What are the means that, in the hands of the recipients, lead to identifiability? In fact, anchoring identifiability to vaguely defined or contextually varying notion of means bears the risk of driving the identification assessment into a speculative inquiry about accidental or contingent circumstances. This ambiguity, if not resolved, might contrary to the intentions render more volatile the boundary between personal and non-personal data, increasing rather than diminishing legal uncertainty. In fact, this ambiguity may create dangerous adverse selection phenomena (e.g., self-justification arguments built upon the factual lack of vaguely defined means) with the risk of creating a jungle of single cases where the argumentative strength of the involved actors tends to prevail in disputes, ultimately affecting the predictable level of safeguards of data protection rights, the overall stability of the regulatory regime and the desired pro-competitive outcomes of the simplification strategy.

Such negative, unintended effects can be mitigated by deploying a coherent conceptual framework for assessing the notion of means, from the perspective of a particular recipient, in terms that are as objective and unquestionable as possible. Such conceptual framework would help to systematize and operationalize the relative notion of personal data in the context of data sharing. It should include a legal and technical mechanism for modulating the conditions for and the grade of identifiability of a particular data set in the specific processing context. Towards this aim, it is important to revisit the role of pseudonymization in the relative risk-based approach.

3 The Role of Pseudonymization

The notion of pseudonymization is explicitly defined in article 4(5) GDPR as the processing of personal data in such a manner that the data can no longer be attributed to a specific data subject without the use of additional information, provided that such additional information is kept separately and subject to technical and organizational measures designed to ensure non-attribution. In the context of data sharing, this definition presumes a structural separation between the data that are transferred to the recipient and those that kept secret by the sender. Furthermore, it expressly acknowledges that identifiability depends on access to some *additional information.*

According to the data protection authorities' dominant orientation before the SRB ruling, pseudonymization does not remove the data from the scope of data protection law: pseudonymized data remain personal data, though with a lower level of re-identification risk. The interpretation advanced by the Court of Justice in the SRB ruling, and made own by the European Commission in the Omnibus proposal, assigns to pseudonymization a more structurally significant role. By focusing on the recipient's actual ability to access the additional information required for re-identification, the Court implicitly treats pseudonymization as a mechanism capable of defining the legal qualification of the data as personal or non-personal depending on the processing context. Where the recipient of pseudonymized data has no factual means reasonably likely to enable access to the additional information, the pseudonymized data may be regarded as non-personal data – or equivalently as anonymous data – *for that specific recipient.* Notably, the same pseudonymized data may be considered as personal data for another recipient in a different context if the condition of not having access to the additional information cannot be ensured. In other words, pseudonymization may be leveraged to produce *relatively non-personal* data for a particular recipient.

This reading does not modify the textual definition of pseudonymization in the GDPR – that in fact doesn't seem to be affected by the amendments in the Omnibus proposal – but nonetheless it implies a repositioning of the concept as a specification of the notion of personal data. pseudonymization becomes the link between identifiability and processing context, enabling a relative assessment of the personal data status from the perspective of the recipient. This new orientation aligns well with the simplification objectives pursued at the policy level in that it allows, under certain conditions, to relieve the GDPR compliance burden from the recipient insofar the pseudonymized data may be considered relatively non-personal for that particular recipient.

4 What Do We Mean by Identification?

In data protection law, identification does not require that a natural person be known by name. Both the jurisprudence of the Court of Justice [5–7], the guidance of Article 29 Working Party [1] and the European Data Protection

Board [12] consistently emphasize that a person may be considered identified where they can be targeted, even in the absence of explicit civil identifiers. Identification, in this sense, is functionally connected to enabling the ability to address an individual with a tailored decision or action, rather than to the ability to label that individual nominally.

This functional understanding of identification is not in contradiction with with a relative risk-based approach to personal data. On the contrary, it clarifies that what matters is not naming, but whether a piece of information can be meaningfully referred to a specific person in a way that may affect them individually and differently from others.

Identification is connected to the notion of *singling out* as developed by the data protection jurisprudence, i.e., the ability to distinguish one individual from others within a set, by way of any observable or measurable attribute or combination of attributes, even without knowing their identity in the civil sense. When a data set referred to a multiplicity of individuals (reference population) is released to a recipient, the possibility of attributing information to individual units from the population does not depend solely on the characteristics of the data set, but rather on the interplay between the released data and additional information that may be available to the recipient, i.e., prior knowledge that is external to and independent from the data set but can be combined with the data to enable attribution.

Attribution often comes with a dose of uncertainty, the magnitude of which depends on several contextual elements and may vary from one individual to another. When the level of uncertainty is low, the released information can be attributed with very high level of confidence to a specific individual in the reference population from where the dataset is drawn. In this case, singling out from the dataset effectively collapses into identification.

In other words, singling out is a necessary condition for identification [4], which becomes sufficient when uncertainty in attribution is removed. Understanding identification therefore requires moving beyond the mere search of intelligible identifiers in data records and should consider how information enables targeted attribution under conditions of uncertainty, depending on multiple contextual elements that include how the released data were derived from the original data set, how the original data set relates to the reference population and to whom the data are released.

The more attribution to a single person is made uncertain, considering all the inherent properties of the data and the distribution of the reference population, the more the data is anonymous considering all the means available to the recipient. If singularities are removed, the only way to attribute the released data to a person is by guessing. To protect individuals from exposures in data releases it is essential that some uncertainty is preserved in the transfer of data from the sender to the recipient.

5 A Framework for Data Release

Given the background outline above, we propose in this section a structured framework to guide the design of relatively non-personal data releases.

5.1 Reference Scenario and Assumptions

We focus on the reference scenario where the sender holds a source dataset $\mathcal{D}$ containing information of interest for the recipient. From $\mathcal{D}$ the sender derives a transformed dataset $\mathcal{R}$ and then shares it with (equivalently, releases to) the intended recipient. In case of multiple recipients, the considerations made below apply to each recipient independently.

We focus initially on the simple scenario where data sharing is limited to the direct relation sender-receiver(s), and the recipient(s) of $\mathcal{R}$ do not share the data further. We will see later the additional problems that arise when considering "subsequent sharing" relationships, i.e., when the recipient(s) become sender(s), and the additional cautions that are due in that scenario.

We restrict our attention to the case where both $\mathcal{D}$ and $\mathcal{R}$ represent micro-data, i.e., collections of individual records referred to data subjects, with each record consisting of multiple data elements, i.e., variables or attributes.

Unless differently specified, when referring to cryptographic operations (e.g., encryption, hashing) we shall assume the adoption by the sender of "unbreakable" encryption methods, i.e., robust implementations of state-of-the-art cryptographic primitives and encryption keys of sufficient length. It is the senders responsibility (hence liability) to adopt sufficiently secure cryptographic methods that cannot be plausibly cracked by the recipient(s) *or by other parties* – and provide evidence for that.

5.2 Data Transformation

If identification depends on the interaction of the recipient with the data released to them, on their prior knowledge, and on the characteristics of the reference population, then preventing or at least mitigating the identification risks requires intervention on the sole element which is concretely actionable at the sender side, namely the released data $\mathcal{R}$. The sender, in fact, can neither control the characteristics of the reference population from which the data are derived nor the prior knowledge in the hands of the recipient. Taking a conservative approach, the sender may attempt to consider hypothetical worst-case scenarios, but this approach would risk of drifting back towards the quasi-absolute approach. Instead, we propose a framework to guide the operationalize the data release in a way that aligns with the relative risk-based approach in the spirit of the SRB judgement and Omnibus proposal.

Not all original records in $\mathcal{D}$ need to be released. A release may involve only a subset of the original dataset (i.e. a subsample) reflecting practical considerations about scope, relevance, eligibility for sharing or other aspects. Furthermore, it should be noted that the data subjects represented in the original data $\mathcal{D}$ may represent only a subset of some larger universe population.

The derivation $\mathcal{D} \rightarrow \mathcal{R}$ must strike a balance between the utility for the recipient of $\mathcal{R}$ and the risk that data subjects may be re-identified by the recipient or other actors as a consequence of releasing $\mathcal{R}$. The proposed framework can be understood as a layered set of interventions applied to the set of variables with the specific aim of preserving overall utility to the maximum possible extent while maintaining a sufficient degree of uncertainty in the attribution of information to individuals by the recipient, in line with the relative risk-based approach presented above.

We consider three categories of intervention: omission, plain anonymization and pseudonymization. Roughly speaking, the set of variables (columns) in the source dataset $\mathcal{D}$ are divided into four blocks as depicted in Fig. 1: variables to be omitted, variables to be pseudonymized, variables to be anonymized in the classical way and variables that may be released unprotected.

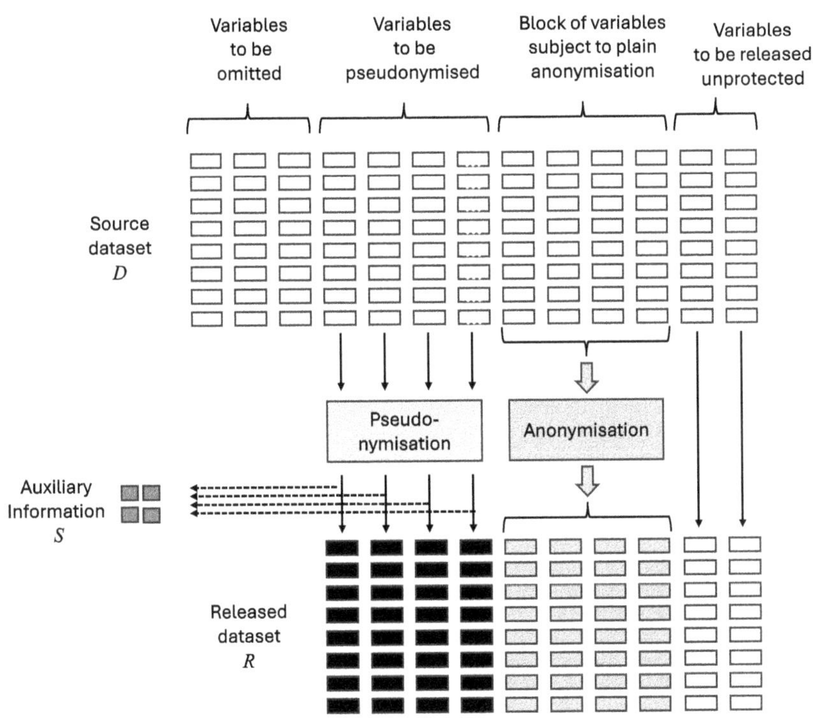

Fig. 1. Graphical representation of the transformations that are applied on the source dataset $\mathcal{D}$ to derive the released dataset $\mathcal{R}$.

Omission. In line with the data minimization principle of GDPR, all variables in $\mathcal{D}$ that are not of interest for the recipient should be excluded from the released data $\mathcal{R}$. Omission of irrelevant variables does not impact the utility of the released data while reducing the re-identification risk.

Pseudonymization. Pseudonymization may be implemented in different ways. In its simplest form, it involves the replacement of identifiers (e.g., name, tax number) with arbitrary strings that remain unique.

Identifiers are data elements whose primary function is to maintain unicity of the record within the dataset and linkability across different dataset. They allow to distinguish records reliably, relate multiple variables to the same record within the dataset, maintain consistency longitudinally over time (for time-dependent variables) and link records across multiple datasets and processes. They allow to maintain a direct association with the data subjects. Identifiers are inherently static or anyway relatively stable over time and do not change frequently: they anchor the information to the individual. Typical examples include civil identity information, customer numbers, driving license number, or other unique keys. Biometric data always fall in this category. The pseudonymized version of the identifier is non-intelligible, i.e., it appears as a random string, but is still unique in the sense that different units are mapped to different pseudonyms (neglecting rare collision events). Secure hashing, encryption and look-up tables are common ways of implementing the transformation of intelligible data elements into non-intelligible ones.

The pseudonymization operation always involves some auxiliary information $\mathcal{S}$ that is logically separate from the resulting data – e.g., hashing seeds, encryption and decryption keys, look-up tables. A central tenet of the proposed framework is that $\mathcal{S}$ must remain secret or anyway separate from the released dataset $\mathcal{R}$. In fact, some actor with knowledge of both $\mathcal{R}$ may $\mathcal{S}$ may revert back to the original data element or execute forward-matching attacks to link individual records to external data based on common identifiers. As explained in Sect. 5.1, it is the sender's responsibility to ensure that pseudonymization is arranged properly and is therefore "unbreakable", i.e., sufficiently secure to rule out successful attacks based on cryptoanalysis, including syntax attacks. Furthermore, the pseudonymisation method must be such to prevent linking of pseudonymised records across different datasets outside the control of the sender. In other words, the pseudonymisation seed or mapping table, i.e. the auxiliary information $\mathcal{S}$ associated to the pseudonymisation process, must be uniquely associated to the data transformation and should not be reused for other data releases. Under this assumption, the only way to re-identify the records or link them with other data sets is through the combination of $\mathcal{S}$ and $\mathcal{D}$.

Traditionally, pseudonymization has been applied mostly to protect unique identifiers to allow re-identification of selected elements after processing or linking with other data. However, more sophisticated forms of pseudonymization can be applied also to general attributes. For instance, Fully Homomorphic Encryption (FHE) can be considered as a form of pseudonymization. With FHE, the source data element is mapped to (encoded in) a non-intelligible "pseudonym" value that is used in the computation process in place of the original intelligible value. In FHE, the encryption and decryption key(s) represent the auxiliary information $\mathcal{S}$.

Secret sharing as commonly adopted in Secure Multi-Party Computation (SMPC) may be considered another advanced form of pseudonymization, where one data element is mapped to a set of multiple "secret shares" that are individually non-intelligible but collectively encode the source data element. The secret shares are typically distributed to different recipients (called Computation Parties in the SMPC terminology) that are entrusted to keep them separate from each other. From the perspective of each secret share, the other shares play the role of auxiliary information $\mathcal{S}$.

We remark that the interpretation of SMPC and FHE as advanced forms of pseudonymization is in line with the interpretation of the notion of pseudonymization put forward by ENISA [13] and consistent with the qualification of SMPC as "effective supplementary measure" given by the EDPB [11].

Plain Anonymization. The block of remaining variables that cannot be omitted or pseudonymized may be anonymized through classical means, i.e., generalization, randomization and any combination thereof. Generalization is the action of re-encoding the variables values into broader categories or equivalence classes. Randomization is the action of adding noise or swapping randomly selected data elements. Both these operations are "lossy" in the sense that they reduce the information content of the data in a way that cannot be recovered. The loss of information detail reduces the risk of re-identification via quasi-identifiers but at the same time it reduces the utility of the data. Therefore, anonymization is an engineering exercise where information useful for legitimate tasks and information "useful" for re-identification are traded against each other.

In principle, there is no guarantee that in the trade-off between utility and re-identification risk a "sweet spot" can be found where acceptable utility can coexist with acceptable risk. Data dimensionality plays an important role here: while an acceptable balance point may be found for low-dimensional data, with high-dimensional data it becomes increasingly difficult to achieve effective anonymisation without prejudice to their information content. In practice, this may limit the number of variables to be transformed with classical plain anonymisation methods (generalization and randomization).

Generally speaking, the amount of information loss that must imposed on each variable or combination thereof (via generalization or randomization) scales with their *observability*, i.e., availability from other sources. To explain this point, consider a toy example where the ith record in the released data includes two distinct components, $[a_i, b_i] \in \mathcal{R}$, where each component represents the value of a variable of group of variables that is unique to the ith data subject in the universe population. In other words, a_i and b_i represent quasi-identifiers. Next assume that information a_i may be easily *observed*, in the sense of being possibly available from other sources other than the released data $\mathcal{R}$, while information b_i

is guaranteed to be available exclusively from the released dataset, i.e., unavailable from other sources. In this setting, inspired from [3], there is a clear risk that the recipient of $\mathcal{R}$ could hold or acquire external data in the form $\mathcal{E} = [a_i, c_i]$, where c_i may for instance represent an identifier for the data subject i. In this way, the recipient could leverage a_i as matching key and therefore attribute b_i to c_i, effectively revealing previously unknown individual information for the data subject. To guard against this risk, a_i would have to be protected by generalization or randomization, i.e., transformed into a less informative version a_i^* (less granular or more noisy) that increases uncertainty in the matching with $\mathcal{E}$. Alternatively, a_i may be pseudonymized or even omitted. Instead, b_i could released in $\mathcal{R}$ as is, without protection, subject to the condition that it cannot be available from other sources and all other observable information elements are duly protected. This consideration justifies the possibility of releasing unobservable variables without protection, as shown in Fig. 1.

The simple toy example above was built based on information components that are either easily observable (a_i) or impossible to observe (b_i) from other sources. In practical applications observability, i.e., availability from other sources, is not a "all or nothing" property but rather a continuous feature. The degree of observability must be assessed case by case and drives the "degree of anonymization" to be applied over the variables that cannot be pseudonymized.

6 Pseudonymized Data as Relatively Anonymized Data: Personal in the Sender's and Anonymous in the Recipient's Hands

Engineering the data release means designing the transformation $\mathcal{D} \rightarrow \mathcal{R}$ in a way to balance the information content (utility) against the re-identification risk in $\mathcal{R}$. This involves a sequence of decisions as to which variables to include in the released data and how to protect them.

In principle, all variables in the source data set $\mathcal{D}$ that are unnecessary for the recipient(s) should be excluded from the release, i.e., omitted in $\mathcal{R}$, in agreement with the principle of data minimization. A limited number of variables can be protected by plain anonymization (generalization or randomization). The remaining ones should be protected by (strong) pseudonymization. If the released data set includes a combination of pseudonymized and anonymized variables, the overall data set $\mathcal{R}$ qualifies as pseudonymized data. Hereafter we elaborate on the conditions that allow the pseudonymized data $\mathcal{R}$ to be considered as non-personal data for the recipient, and on the practical implications of doing so.

The conceptual framework developed so far enables an operational reading of the definition of pseudonymization contained in article 4(5) GDPR. At its core, this definition relies on the notion of attribution. pseudonymized data are data that, in their released form, cannot be attributed to a specific data subject unless some further element is brought into play that is referred generically as "additional information" in the legal text. Such additional information is, by definition, what makes attribution possible.

Within the framework introduced above, the two pieces of information that must be kept separate within the meaning of article 4(5) GDPR are precisely the released data $\mathcal{R}$, which constitutes the pseudonymized data made available to recipients, and the cumulative auxiliary information $\mathcal{S}$ involved in (or resulting from) the set of pseudonymization interventions applied to the data.

The pseudonymized data $\mathcal{R}$ are therefore personal data in the hands of the sender, who retains access to $\mathcal{S}$ and can re-establish the link between records and individuals, but they are non-attributable and therefore anonymous in the hands of the recipient if the latter can be guaranteed not to ever gain access to the auxiliary information $\mathcal{S}$, with the sender being fully accountable to provide such guarantees.

The sender's accountability extends also to the design of plain anonymization method. The degree of protection (hence of information loss) depends on the nature of the variables in combination with multiple contextual elements. Some variables may be even released unprotected if certain conditions are fulfilled that prevent them to serve the purpose of attribution. The toy example presented above shows that variables that are exclusively accessible from the data release, and cannot be observed, measured, or otherwise accessed from other sources (with the exception of sender–data subject relationship, as explained in the next section) are eligible to be released unprotected. However, the sender's choice of releasing some variables unprotected on the basis of presumed non-observability implies the sender's accountability to demonstrate that the condition of non-observability holds true in practice. In other words, the condition of non-observability for unprotected information is not merely descriptive but entails a concrete responsibility and accountability on the side of the sender. It is the sender's duty to demonstrate that it would be practically impossible for recipients or third parties to observe, measure or anyway obtain independently the same information from other sources. When this condition cannot be safely met, the candidate variable(s) should be rather protected, either in the form of plain anonymization or pseudonymization.

In summary, the qualification of pseudonymized data $\mathcal{R}$ as non-personal for the recipient is not only a matter of technical transformations but implies twofold accountability by the sender.

First, the sender is accountable to provide a defensible assessment that the data released without protection is effectively unobservable, i.e., unavailable outside its own domain to external entities.

Second, the sender is accountable of keeping under custody the secrets originated from pseudonymization, i.e., the auxiliary information $\mathcal{S}$, or anyway ensure that it never reaches the first or subsequent recipients of the released data $\mathcal{R}$. Access to $\mathcal{S}$ should be restricted to authorized personnel only, and technical and organizational safeguards should be implemented to prevent accidental or malicious disclosure. This ensures that the linkage association between original identifiers and their transformed versions, which is the critical piece of information enabling re-identification, cannot be leveraged by unauthorized recipients.

7 Recipient's Duty of Custody to Prevent Cumulative Downstream Identifiability

The discussion so far has focused on the case of single disclosure, where a single dataset $\mathcal{R}$ is produced and then disclosed to (shared with) one or multiple recipient(s) in direct contact with the sender. This scenarios is depicted in Fig. 2b and Fig. 2b, respectively, for single and multiple recipients. Note that the case of multiple recipients receiving multiple copies of the same dataset $\mathcal{R}$ is still considered a case of single disclosure.

Hereafter we consider more articulated scenarios where different data sets $\mathcal{R}_1, \mathcal{R}_2, \ldots$ are derived from the original data $\mathcal{D}$ and then disclosed to different recipients. Furthermore, we consider the possibility that the recipients may pass the data further downstream to a subsequent recipient, as showed in Fig. 2c. In this scenario the subsequent recipient may gather sufficient information that, when recombined, allows to re-identify individual records, and in some extreme cases even reconstruct the original data set $\mathcal{D}$, even if none of the first recipients would be able to do so – a phenomenon known as "mosaic effect" [15]. In other words, the combination of (relatively) non-personal data may produce personal data in the hands of the subsequent receiver.

The recent legislative proposal does not solve the problem. It states that [10, Art. 3] "*Such information [the released data] does not become personal for that entity [the first recipient] merely because a potential subsequent recipient has means reasonably likely to be used to identify the natural person to whom the information relates*" but does not limit the possibility for the first recipient to pass the data onward to subsequent recipients that do have the power to perform re-identification. Without further safeguards, this loose formulation risks creating a legal loophole, undermining data subjects' protection in data releases where re-identification emerges not as an accident in the bilateral relationship between a sender and a recipient, but as a cumulative effect of independent data releases converging to the same actor. If left unaddressed, this dynamic may in principle allow to establish intentionally a layer of middleman first recipients with the purpose to elude the legal protection afforded by European legislation to personal data, significantly undermining the privacy rights of individuals. The risk is particularly dangerous when the subsequent recipient is subject to a different extra-EU legislation.

To prevent such loophole, protection against re-identification should not stop at the sender–recipient boundary. Recipients cannot be treated as neutral pass-through entities with no responsibility for the effects of onward disclosures. Even if the data they receive are protected and qualify as relatively non-personal data for them, recipients should be prevented from passing over the received data as such without data protection responsibilities. In this sense, also the recipient should remain subject to a "duty of custody" for the relatively non-personal data derived from personal data. In practice, the duty of custody should be imposed by the sender on the first recipient(s) through contractual obligations – a requirement that implies an additional element of accountability on the sender. Furthermore, the sender as controller of the source data $\mathcal{R}$ should remain obliged to keep track of all data sharing relationships in the Records of Processing Activities (RoP) as per GDPR Art. 30. For each recipient, the sender should document in the RoP the technical details of the data transformation $\mathcal{R} \to \mathcal{D}$, the measures adopted to keep in safe custody the auxiliary information $\mathcal{S}$, and the contractual terms of the data release.

8 Preventing Vexatious Litigation

Custody of secrets is not solely a matter of sender's and recipient's responsibility. Its protection also relies on a baseline of due diligence and honest conduct by the data subject. Deviations from such honest conduct, particularly where unobservable information is deliberately disclosed by the data subject with the intention to enable attribution by third parties, cannot be automatically imputed to wrongdoing by the sender.

Any re-identification attempt in which a third party plausibly claims attribution of a released record to a specific individual via access to unprotected data should be treated as processing of personal data within the meaning of the GDPR. As such, it must be legally justified in the first place. This precaution is essential to prevent hypothetical abusive re-identification claims where data subjects and third parties collude and exploit the data subject's own information to demonstrate re-identification in order to build the case for a vexatious litigation. Even if the occurrence of such situations is considered unlikely or merely hypothetical, nonetheless a principled regulation framework should be able to prevent them.

Enforcement plays a central role in this context. Re-identification claims should be assessed in a way that prevents scenarios in which a data subject might stealthily facilitate attribution, e.g. through bargaining of consent or selective disclosure of otherwise unobservable information, while presenting the outcome as evidence of unlawful processing by the sender. Although such situations are inherently difficult, and in some cases nearly impossible to detect *ex ante*, a robust regulatory approach would require that any party claiming re-identification must justify how the connection between the unobservable information and the identifier was obtained.

Legitimate re-identification claims should primarily focus on identifying structural weaknesses in the pseudonymization scheme, or on demonstrating that attributes left unprotected based on the presumption of exclusivity are instead observable, measurable, or inferable from other sources. Any instance of re-identification must be treated as processing of personal data and therefore subject to full legal justification under data protection law. The burden should lie on the re-identification claimant to demonstrate lawful access to the data and justify the means by which attribution was achieved. This would outlaw attempts to build litigation cases leveraging privileged to otherwise unobservable information from collusion with the data subject.

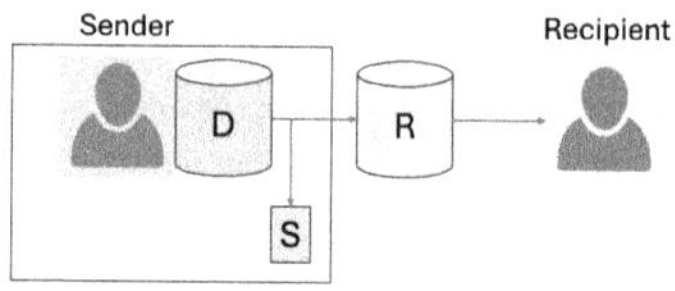

(a) Single disclosure to a single recipient

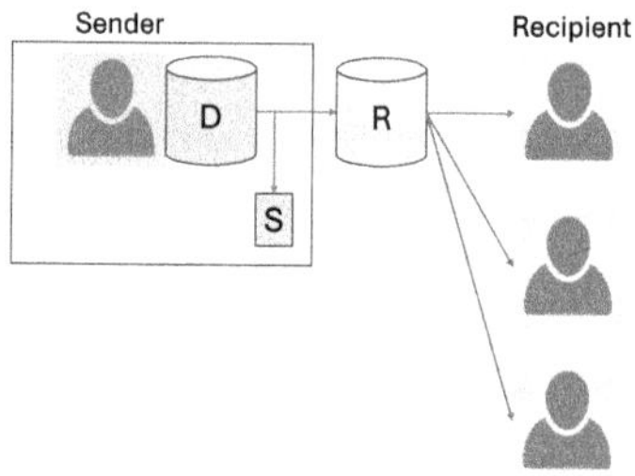

(b) Single disclosure to multiple recipients

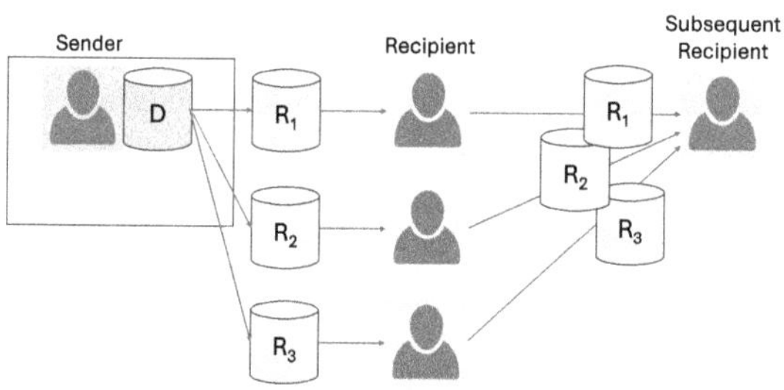

(c) Multiple disclosures

Fig. 2. Examples of release scenario. The recombination of multiple disclosures bears a risk of re-identification downstream the release chain.

9 Conclusions

Shifting from an absolute to a relative notion of personal data is not a *fiat* decision. It is neither a pure relabeling of terms nor a doctrinal shortcut that can be implemented by interpretative declaration alone. Rather, it presupposes a deliberate re-engineering of data practices and governance structures. Implementing a relative approach requires substantial organizational, technical, and legal efforts on the sender side, complementary safeguards and constraints on the recipient side, and a minimum level of due diligence even from the data subjects.

From a technical standpoint, technical data transformation measures like pseudonymization, generalization and randomization are necessary but not sufficient conditions to produce relatively non-personal data. A layer of governance and accountability must be added to the picture. The sender holds a duty of custody for the additional information used in (generated by) the pseudonymization process and a duty of documentation (in the RoP as per GDPR Art. 30) of each release of non-personal data derived from personal data. As re-identification may re-emerge through cumulative disclosures and downstream recombination, the proposed framework introduces a duty of custody also on the recipients to prevent them to released the data as such to other entities. Should the release from first recipient(s) to subsequent recipient(s) be allowed, we advocate for the introduction of additional data protection safeguards and responsibilities on the first recipient(s).

The proposed framework admits the possibility of disclosing the exact value of some attributes without any technical protection, subject to the condition that they can be safely considered to be available exclusively from the data release at hand, i.e., not observable or available from other sources. Guaranteeing such condition adds to the sender's accountability.

Overall, the proposed framework represents a conceptual framework where technical means are complemented by accountability and custody obligations, i.e., governance. The point to be taken is that data that qualify as non-personal *in relative terms* for the recipient are still data that need to be governed to some extent. As such data fall outside the scope of GDPR, the recipient is freed from a great load of compliance burden, but that does not make completely away with some duty of custody as long as pseudonymized and/or unprotected data components are included in the release. The duty of custody, or equivalently the prohibition to release the data to other actors, which is needed to prevent loopholes enabling downstream cumulative identifiability, must be implemented through contractual obligations – an aspect that adds up to the sender's accountability.

For the recipient to be completely waived from any duty of custody, the released data should include no unprotected components, and the auxiliary information resulting from the pseudonymization process should be guaranteed not to ever leave the sender's domain nor be reused for other data transformations – again a condition that implies a responsibility on the sender side.

Overall, the relativization of the notion of non-personal reduces dramatically the compliance burden on the data recipient, but that comes at the cost of somewhat increased accountability on the sender.

More generally, the proposed framework highlights that a well-engineered relativization of personal data is more compatible with controlled sender-to-recipient than with open-ended dissemination environments, where cumulative identifiability and composition effects are unavoidable.

Ultimately, the shift toward a relative notion of personal data does not eliminate identification risks but rather redistributes them across the actors involved in the data lifecycle. This redistribution creates an immediate and crucial decision point at the level of the sender, who bears primary responsibility for engineering the release, including the choice of specific pseudonymization and plain anonymization mechanisms. Such choices shape the residual uncertainty of attribution and therefore the practical boundary between personal and non-personal data.

The recipient is not removed from this allocation of responsibility. While recipients may legitimately receive data that are pseudonymized at the source, and relatively non-personal in their hands, they retain a duty of care with respect to downstream uses and disclosures, especially in presence of unprotected variables with unique values.

The data subject also enters this redistributed framework, albeit in a limited and carefully bounded way. Relative anonymization presupposes an expectation of honest conduct with respect to the custody of information uniquely known to the data subject. While this cannot translate into a transfer of responsibility from controllers to individuals, it does imply that the integrity of the system depends on deterring intentional disclosure aimed to make the case for vexatious litigation.

Taken together, the relative approach to personal data outlines a new allocation of roles rather than mere relabeling of objects. It operates as a form of social and institutional pact in which uncertainty is deliberately engineered at the source, preserved through downstream governance, and supported by enforcement mechanisms.

Disclaimer. The views expressed in this paper are those of the authors and do not necessarily represent the official position of their institutions.

References

1. Article 29 Working Party (WP29): Opinion 05/2014 on anonymisation techniques (2014). https://ec.europa.eu/justice/article-29/documentation/opinion-recommendation/files/2014/wp216_en.pdf. Accessed 11 June 2026
2. CNIL: CEGEDIM SANTÉ fined 800,000 EUR (2024). https://www.cnil.fr/en/health-data-cegedim-sante-fined-eu800000. Accessed 11 June 2026
3. D'Acquisto, G.: Riforma gdpr: cosa cambia se il dato personale diventa un concetto relativo (2026). https://tinyurl.com/y643yuu3. Accessed 11 June 2026
4. D'Acquisto, G., Cohen, A., Naldi, M., Nissim, K.: From isolation to identification. In: Domingo-Ferrer, J., Önen, M. (eds.) Privacy in Statistical Databases, pp. 3–17. Springer Nature Switzerland, Cham (2024)
5. EU Court of Justice: Judgment in case C-434/16, Peter Nowak v Data Protection Commissioner, paragraph 35 (2017). https://eur-lex.europa.eu/legal-content/EN/TXT/?uri=celex:62016CJ0434. Accessed 11 June 2026
6. EU Court of Justice: Judgment in case c-479/22 p, oc v commission, paragraph 45 (2024). https://eur-lex.europa.eu/legal-content/EN/TXT/?uri=celex:62022CJ0479. Accessed 1 April 2026
7. EU Court of Justice: Judgment in case C-604/22 , IAB Europe v Gegevensbeschermingsautoriteit, paragraph 37 (2024). https://eur-lex.europa.eu/legal-content/EN/TXT/?uri=celex:62022CJ0479. Accessed 11 June 2026
8. EU Court of Justice: Judgement in case C-413/23 P SRB v EDPS (2025). https://eur-lex.europa.eu/legal-content/EN/TXT/?uri=celex:62023CJ0413. Accessed 11 June 2026
9. European Commission: The draghi report on eu competitiveness (2024). https://commission.europa.eu/topics/competitiveness/draghi-report_en. Accessed 11 June 2026

10. European Commission: Digital omnibus proposal (2025). https://eur-lex.europa.eu/legal-content/EN/TXT/?uri=CELEX:52025PC0837. Accessed 11 June 2026
11. European Data Protection Board: Recommendations 01/2020 on measures that supplement transfer tools to ensure compliance with the EU level of protection of personal data (2020). https://www.edpb.europa.eu/our-work-tools/our-documents/recommendations/recommendations-012020-measures-supplement-transfer_en. Accessed 11 June 2026
12. European Data Protection Board: Guidelines 01/2025 on pseudonymisation (2025). https://www.edpb.europa.eu/our-work-tools/documents/public-consultations/2025/guidelines-012025-pseudonymisation_en. Accessed 11 June 2026
13. European Union Agency for Cybersecurity (ENISA): Data pseudonymisation: Advanced techniques and use cases (2021). https://www.enisa.europa.eu/publications/data-pseudonymisation-advanced-techniques-and-use-cases. Accessed 11 June 2026
14. Garante per la Protezione dei Dati Personali: Provvedimento del 1 giugno (2023). https://www.garanteprivacy.it/home/docweb/-/docweb-display/docweb/9913795. Accessed 11 June 2026
15. Pozen, D.: The mosaic theory, national security and the freedom of information act. Yale Law J., 628–679 (2005). https://scholarship.law.columbia.edu/faculty_scholarship/573

Enforcement, Market Distortion, and the Danger of Reforming Fundamental Rights Under Pressure

Markus Sullivan(✉)

Independent, Mannheim, Germany
markus@lampades.de

Abstract. Almost a decade following the implementation of the General Data Protection Regulation (GDPR), marked by sustained opposition to calls for amendments, the European Commission has abruptly embarked on a pursuit of substantial revisions, citing competitiveness concerns as a primary motivation. This paper analyses, from a corporate practitioner's perspective, the relation between political interference in regulatory enforcement, the resulting distortion of corporate compliance incentives, and the consequences for different market participants — including the specific risks of legislative revision during a period of shifting the Overton window on fundamental rights. Drawing on a synthesis of deterrence theory, regulatory capture scholarship, and GDPR market effects, the paper's central contention is that the current reform trajectory — driven by the Draghi Report and proposed through the Digital Omnibus Package — will predictably deepen the competitive disadvantage of law-abiding firms rather than alleviate it, ultimately worsening the competitiveness it purports to address. The paper concludes that the enforcement deficit, rather than the regulatory text itself, is the primary source of the competitiveness problem, and that any attempt to amend the GDPR while enforcement remains structurally weak will accelerate its deterioration. Addressing the enforcement deficit must therefore be treated as a mandatory prerequisite before any further legislative revision is considered.

Keywords: GDPR enforcement · regulatory capture · corporate risk management · privacy economics · market distortion

1 Introduction

The GDPR was designed to solve a problem of fragmentation caused by divergent national implementation of earlier data protection rules as outlined in its Recital 9. The Data Protection Directive that preceded it had produced a patchwork of national implementations so inconsistent that organisations could, and did, engineer their operations to exploit the most permissive jurisdictions while claiming compliance across the European Union [1]. The GDPR's architects chose a directly applicable regulation precisely to foreclose this kind of arbitrage. Nearly a decade later, the enforcement

F. Pallas et al. (Eds.): APF 2026, LNCS 16847, pp. 154–172, 2026.
https://doi.org/10.1007/978-3-032-35899-8_8

landscape remains fragmented, largely because of the politics surrounding its application. Supervisory authorities differ dramatically in resources, priorities, and institutional independence [2–4]. Cumulative fines have exceeded €6 billion [5], but with 33.1 million firms operating in the EU in 2023 [6], a back-of-the-envelope calculation puts the average fine in 2023 at roughly €180 per firm before even accounting for fines never collected, lowered, or dismissed. The figure is statistically crude, but these are the kind of simple and crude calculations that drive decision making in firms.

This paper traces the relation that runs from political interference in enforcement, through the resulting distortion of corporate risk calculations, to the dangers of amending a fundamental rights framework during a period of geopolitical weakness. The paper is structured as follows: Sect. 2 analyses how political actors shape enforcement in ways that are functionally indistinguishable from regulatory capture. Section 3, drawing on deterrence theory and recent empirical work, demonstrates how enforcement deficits transform some firms' corporate compliance from a legal obligation into a strategic variable, producing measurable market distortions that disproportionately harm smaller and more conscientious firms. Section 4 examines the Draghi Report and the Digital Omnibus Package as case studies in how legitimate concerns about regulatory burden can be co-opted by the interests they purport to discipline. Section 5 argues that the timing and framing of current reform efforts, coinciding with the active dismantlement of fundamental rights and in particular privacy protections in the United States, make them particularly susceptible to producing outcomes that weaken rather than strengthen the competitive position of compliant European firms.

2 Politics Shape Enforcement, Power Shapes Politics

2.1 Enforcement Gap as Political Product

That enforcement is the mechanism through which legal norms enter economic reality is not a new insight. In 1968, Becker demonstrated that the expected cost of a legal violation is a function of the probability of apprehension and conviction and the size of punishment. Rational actors generally adjust their behaviour to whichever of these variables moves [7]. Stigler extended this by showing that perfect enforcement is neither achievable nor desirable, since the costs of enforcement eventually exceed the cost of deterrence benefits [8]. The critical question, then, is not whether enforcement should be perfect, but whether the level of enforcement that prevails reflects a deliberate public interest calculation, or whether it is the product of constraints.

In the case of the GDPR, the evidence strongly suggests the latter. The combined budget for all EU data protection authorities was reported in 2022 as €337 million [2]. The Irish Data Protection Commission, lead supervisory authority for almost all major US technology firms under the Article 56 one-stop-shop mechanism, left 98% of cross-border cases unresolved as of 2021 [9, 10]; where the European Data Protection Board (EDPB) reviewed the Irish DPC's proposed sanctions under Article 65, it imposed tougher penalties in most cases [10, 11]. In contrast, the Spanish Data Protection Agency (AEPD) issued over 900 fines, overwhelmingly low, in the same period, while the French (CNIL) and Dutch (Autoriteit Persoonsgegevens) pursued aggressive but selective enforcement against specific targets [5].

These disparities are, for better or worse, driven in no small part by political choices about resource allocation, institutional independence and the degree to which national economic strategy is permitted to override the uniform application of a regulation. Where a Member State systematically underfunds its supervisory authority, or when executive pressure, whether through budgetary constraints, appointment politics or the in practice most relevant form of informal signalling, discourages enforcement against economically favoured actors, the effect is de facto selective repeal [10, 12].

2.2 The Dual Consequences of Externalisation of Compliance Cost

A parallel dynamic to these political actions operates on the corporate side. To understand this dynamic, we can look at the empirical literature on GDPR cost such as Frey and Presidente [13]. It found support for the view that smaller firms are disproportionately adversely affected, even with all the necessary caveats and limitations such a calculation must have. What can, however, be observed directly is the high indirect cost of compliance that is imposed on smaller firms using information technology solutions provided by large international ones. These products are, under ideal conditions, perhaps possible to run in a way compliant with the regulation; in their normal state, however, they are far from it. This means that indirect costs are incurred for setting them up in a compliant way and constant changes impose recurring costs to maintain that state.

This mechanism deserves scrutiny. The first observation must be that the complexity that generates this indirect cost for compliance is not intrinsic to the regulation. The regulation, as such, has a scaling approach that should mean, in theory, that a smaller, simpler firm has less effort since they have less sophisticated systems to set up and maintain. The intended scaling, however, is undermined by the above-mentioned approach. Firms are confronted with bundled services and solutions that have capabilities and aspects that go far beyond what is needed and often what is permitted under the law. Functionality that clearly is not required is embedded and intertwined with other aspects making the simplest of products, such as a word processor, suddenly become a client to a vast cloud-based server infrastructure. Free analytics tools blend into advertising plugins, consent management tools, and heavily vertically integrated service ecosystems whose internal data flows are opaque by design [14]. Smaller firms adopt these tools because market dynamics leave them with few alternatives: compliant substitutes have often been systematically acquired, priced out, or rendered incompatible. By offering a solution for free for personal use and at free or reduced prices for schools and universities, firms also face an additional cost per employee when using alternative solutions.

Subsequently, instead of a small firm running a small setup, they are suddenly and involuntarily dragged into a highly sophisticated ecosystem of products they do not need, cannot really govern, deactivate, or even describe and saddled with a crushing regulatory burden. The resulting burden is tendentiously attributed to the regulation rather than to the design choices, leading to a textbook case of cost externalisation: the firm that engineers complexity and effectively dominates the market has to bear none of the effective cost of the setup and day-to-day compliance, while the entities that inherit it do not only have to bear it, but through their now inherited exposure, they become a political constituency for weakening the regulation [15, 16].

This means that firms are now confronted with dual pressure. On the one hand, political actors use the GDPR as a sword or shield to act for or against specific actors. On the other hand, large firms use overwhelming market positions to leverage smaller ones into an impossible situation: to use their technology to be, or at least feel competitive, and to be left with the cost of their externalised compliance. This forces them into an untenable financial and political position, in which leaving the solution seems impossible and the total cost of operating the solution in a compliant way is too high, leaving advocating for lower standards as the only way forward. This also manoeuvres authorities and politicians into an untenable position, because the only way to enforce the law would be to go after the many small firms, causing substantial damage to people unable to change the situation and only marginally responsible for its creation. The idea that the supply chain could be leveraged and market force would lead to more compliant solutions turned out to be a massive overestimation. That is to say that the market-mediated compliance dynamic that Bradford [17] terms the 'Brussels Effect' is being overwhelmed as the interests of small and bigger firms are (manipulated to be) aligned in influencing politics to maintain ineffective enforcement.

3 How Enforcement Reality Shapes Corporate Behaviour

3.1 Deterrence Theory and Enforcement Probability Variable

For the analysis of how the developments outlined above affect firms, it is helpful to consider that enforcement effectiveness begins with the economic model of rational compliance in more detail [7]. The Beckerian framework, as outlined above can be applied to the GDPR and the prediction is stark. With clear indications of substantial issues with compliance and an ever-increasing number of complaints by individuals in the EU [12], set against only a few hundred formal enforcement actions per year, the probability of any individual violation resulting in a sanction is negligible for most organisations [5, 6]. The statutory maximum fine of up to 4% of global annual turnover or €20 million is formidable in theory and had some effect when enforcement practices were uncertain; however, eight years after the law took effect, these have been clearly understood on a strategic level as insignificant. The expected penalty, discounted by the probability of its imposition, is indistinguishable from zero for most firms, and compliance with the law is largely driven by other considerations.

While not new, the implications are underappreciated in the reform debate. Polinsky and Shavell [18] demonstrated that when enforcement relies on monetary sanctions, optimal policy requires maximising the fine while economising on detection, because fines are costless transfers to the state. This means that, once a violation is found, imposing a higher fine costs nothing, whereas finding and successfully prosecuting additional violations is expensive. Therefore, rational policy sets fines high enough that even a low probability of detection makes violation unattractive. The GDPR's architects understood this logic and designed the high statutory maxima to compensate for the inevitably low probability of enforcement. However, the reluctance of authorities to impose fines and the member states courts' unwillingness to follow through with this concept, as well as the political dynamics described above, have undermined this approach beyond reasonable expectations. Fines that are too rarely imposed, rarely collected, and in the remaining cases revoked, hamstrung on procedural grounds, or significantly lowered [3, 19] do not deter. They may provide spectacular headlines and a short burst in compliance, but beyond that, their impact is negligible in practice. Lintvedt [19] analysed GDPR fines specifically through the lens of the deterrence theory and also found that inconsistent application across supervisory authorities and a lack of transparency undermines the signalling function, that is, the ability of enforcement actions to communicate to the broader market what behaviour will be punished and at what level. In the same direction, Congiu, Sabatino and Sapi provided empirical evidence of the deterrence mechanism *not* at work [20]. Their analysis demonstrated that the behavioural effects of the GDPR on web traffic became measurable only after the first significant fine was issued, approximately eight months after the regulation entered into force. Before the first enforcement took place, there was measurably little compliance effort. Libert [21], and, based on their work, Johnson [9], reached a complementary finding: websites reduced third-party cookies temporarily around the May 2018 effective date, but tracking returned to pre-GDPR levels within months. This is to show that (the perception of) enforcement produced compliance. The (perceived) absence of enforcement (or rather its actual consequences) produced regression to incompliant behaviour as the theoretical maximum fine was static.

From a practitioner's point of view, this effect is obvious and simple to understand. Resources, which are often not (only) money but primarily also time and top management attention to a topic, are allocated to what seems like the most pressing issue *right now*. Adherence to the law is generally accepted as an important topic. Without it becoming an urgent one, however, any change initiatives are delayed and lapse to a future date. On the other hand, if a run-in with the authority is happening or even perceived likely, which in the latter case can be driven by publicized fines on other organizations, the matter not only stays important but becomes urgent. Under these circumstances can a practitioner affect change. Consequently, from an outside point of view, compliance-improving measures seem to happen in spurts instead of being a continued development. From an inside perspective, however, these initiatives are queued up, prepared, have often been delayed multiple times, and are now back on the table.

3.2 The Two-Speed Market and Progressive Distortion

Given that enforcement probability is the variable that has effectively collapsed, the question becomes how different firms respond to that collapse. The answer is that they do not respond uniformly, and this divergence reveals certain limitations of the Beckerian framework. The model assumes a single rational calculation based on expected penalties. Firms, however, operate under a broader set of incentives such as reputational risk, contractual obligations to clients, ethical commitments of leadership, industry requirements, and personal liability exposure or other considerations, such as the calculation that it is most cost efficient to slowly build and maintain a compliant system than to face a high cost barrier if enforcement picks up or new, more strictly enforced laws are built on top of it. These are aspects that are not captured by the fine-times-probability equation.

Whatever the specific mix of incentives, there are mainly two types of responses. Firms in the first category make what would be under the Beckerian framework an unreasonable investment. They invest in governance infrastructure, employ specialist staff, delay product launches to ensure compliance, and operate on the principle that the law applies whether or not regulators are watching. Firms in the second category, for whom these additional incentives are absent or insufficient, are left with the unadulterated Beckerian calculation that has resolved in favour of non-compliance. They treat enforcement risk as the operative variable in their compliance calculus. The latter is, at least when we are talking about laws that deal with fundamental rights of individuals, which the GDPR is, a serious problem to society, and can reach extremely destructive levels.

This bifurcation has measurable consequences, since overall estimated risk directly determines the level of investment in mitigation. Firms in the second category face systematically lower costs. They also enjoy a wider range of mitigation options, some of which may themselves be unlawful but rational under these considerations. This has been documented in the automotive emissions scandal, in which manufacturers designed engine control software that detected regulatory test conditions and adjusted behaviour to meet standards it would otherwise violate [22]. The structure also works in digital services, where the opacity of large-scale data processing makes verification more difficult [23]. The competitive advantage compounds over time: lower compliance costs translate to faster time-to-market, lower prices, or higher margins, which in turn produce greater market share [24, 25] which further insulates against enforcement through political influence and the capacity to sustain protracted litigation. In practical terms, greater market share generates the resources and the access to resist enforcement, and the implicit argument that a firm too embedded in the economy cannot be sanctioned without collateral damage. This is the mechanism through which the enforcement deficit reinforces itself and tilts the scale further towards a dominance of firms following the Beckerian framework. This in turn makes it harder for authorities to enforce as firms grow more adversarial.

The empirical evidence on market concentration confirms this dynamic. Johnson, Shriver, and Goldberg [26] found that the GDPR reduced website use of web technology vendors but increased vendor market concentration, with the gains accruing predominantly to the largest platforms. This shows the consequence on smaller entrants and competitors, while the dominant platforms, the very actors whose data practices the regulation was designed to govern, either absorbed the compliance cost without material impact or benefited from the exit of rivals.

Taken together with the observation of externalisation of compliance cost, the conclusion may seem counterintuitive but is clear: the GDPR, as presently enforced, functions as a regressive regulatory instrument that blunts itself. It imposes the highest relative costs on the actors least responsible for the harms it addresses, while producing the lowest relative costs for those most responsible. Contrary to the currently prevalent talking points, this is not based in the regulation's design and subsequently cannot be fixed by deregulation for smaller entities. It is a predictable consequence of externalised compliance cost and enforcement that is too weak to alter the risk calculations of large organisations and too burdensome for small ones to ignore, driving them towards non-compliance to compete.

As to practical observation, not every firm is in the position to adopt the Beckerian framework. Two scenarios on opposite sides of the spectrum can be used to illustrate this. Generally, firms either need to be small enough to not be of notice or big enough, with enough cash reserves and resilient enough shareholder structure to absorb the initial force of a run-in with the authority. The former simply fall below the enforcement threshold (informally known as the "too small fish" exception). The latter requires a more deliberate strategy, one that demonstrates concretely how the Beckerian deterrence calculation plays out for large firms in practice. A critical aspect here is that a publicly traded corporation taking this approach risks a drop in its share price, which is, for better or worse, one, if not the most, relevant factor to drive decisions. This is, in part, because it lowers the effective salary of the leadership that is either tied or otherwise related to it, and risks replacement of board members if there is no faith that the firms will deal with it. At the very least, such a firm needs to engage a high-profile law firm with a good track record of defending against such fines, one that convinces the public and the market that the matter is manageable. Long before the last day in court, the matter is litigated in the court of public opinion, and the risk of losing the lawsuit is eventually and most importantly slowly and progressively priced in. This is a crucial aspect, as markets punish surprises far more severely than progressively revealed risks. A surprising and sharp drop in stock price can cause a larger selloff, potentially short selling hedge funds to jump in and is therefore more threatening to the firm and its leadership, while an adjustment priced in over a year is offset against the ongoing profitability of the firm.

4 How the Reform Trajectory Leads to Appeasement of Market Distortion

4.1 The Draghi Report and the State as Beckerian Actor

The reform agenda now entering the legislative process enters a market already distorted along the lines described. How that agenda is framed therefore matters as much as its specific provisions. The Draghi Report [27] is the most prominent articulation of the case for GDPR reform. Some of its central claims, such as that GDPR compliance increases data management costs, software compliance expenses have risen and that fragmented enforcement creates legal uncertainty for cross-border operations, are supported by cited research [28].

The report exhibits a systematic selection bias in its treatment of the evidence, as it cites for example the National Bureau of Economics Research (NBER) research on compliance costs without drawing the correct conclusions why those costs fall disproportionately on small firms while leaving large technology firms materially unaffected [26]. It under-evaluates the complexity of the matter by trying to correlate a legal act, the complex response by the market, and the effect that this response has as a consequence of the law, by measuring financial data alone. This completely sidesteps the question of which burdens are intrinsic to the law, and which are produced and driven by the enforcement influenced by governments and firms. Most consequentially, it expands the Beckerian framework and proceeds as if the function of the law is purely economic, that the GDPR must be optimised for competitiveness to the detriment of fundamental rights. The report does not advocate this position, and its authors would reject the framing. But the economic logic the report adopts, that is treating fundamental-rights-protective regulation as a variable to be optimised for competitiveness, an approach data protection literature terms the "economisation of fundamental rights" [29], produces the same structural result if followed to its conclusion: the state finds itself applying a Beckerian calculus to its own protection of fundamental rights. Whether this is intended or emergent, the equation is the same.

In the original formulation of the framework, the firm is the subject weighing compliance against the consequences of violation, and the state is the enforcer whose function is to make the calculation come out in favour of compliance. In the framework the Draghi Report proposes, the state itself becomes the subject. The government weighs the cost of upholding fundamental rights against the economic benefit of not doing so, and the question becomes whether the expected sanction for non-compliance exceeds the expected benefit. The decisive question is therefore what sanction the government faces, and through which mechanism. Unlike the firm, the government is not sanctioned through fines.

The enforcement mechanism for a government that violates fundamental rights is at first perhaps judicial, and the Court of Justice has demonstrated its willingness to act as a genuine constraint, yet judicial ex-post review does not cure ex-ante political enforcement design, and litigation horizons are substantially too long to impact the current decision makers. The enforcement mechanism for the government is ultimately democratic, as voters can also consider longer term trends and recurring violations to punish the perceived responsible political actors at the ballot box. The probability that this sanction is triggered by a specific violation depends on voters noticing the violation, understanding its significance, attributing responsibility correctly, coordinating around it against competing political priorities, and maintaining that focus long enough for the next election cycle. Each of these steps has a probability, and the cumulative probability is low in the best of cases, and vanishingly small for matters such as data protection that most voters do not follow in detail. The mechanism is therefore subject to precisely the same deterioration dynamic described above.

The Beckerian calculation resolves for the government in the same way it resolves for the dominant firms described earlier. The severity of the democratic sanction may be formidable in theory, since a government that systematically undermines fundamental rights can, in principle, be voted out. But the probability of that sanction being triggered by a specific violation is low enough that the expected cost approaches zero. Weingast's account of self-enforcing constitutions [30] argued correctly that rights protections are stable only when violations trigger a coordinated citizen response, and coordination fails when the public's focal point about what counts as a violation is fragmented or contested. This result is consistent with the broader retrospective-voting literature, showing that electoral discipline on any single policy dimension weakens as the issues voters must aggregate multiply and as information about each becomes costly to acquire [30, 31], which is precisely the condition the framing dynamics described above produce.

Under these conditions, a government applying the framework to itself will conclude that violating fundamental rights, or permitting their violation by failing to enforce them, is the rational course of action where the economic benefit is sufficient. The Draghi Report does not describe this conclusion in these terms, but it is the conclusion that follows from the framework it adopts. This is the deeper problem with the report, and one that cannot be addressed by improving the quality of the economic evidence or by refining the methodology. The issue is *not* that the numbers are wrong but that the framework treats fundamental rights as a variable in a cost-benefit equation rather than as the constraint within which any such equation must be solved. A democracy in which fundamental rights are negotiable against competitiveness is a democracy in which the only guarantee of those rights is that violating them is politically costly in the short term. Given that the political cost of most data protection violations is demonstrably low, the guarantee is effectively absent. Member State governments have reintroduced substantively equivalent mass telecommunications surveillance frameworks across successive legislative cycles without suffering meaningful electoral or reputational consequences for doing so. The Court of Justice has struck down bulk retention regimes that several Member States had maintained for years, yet Member States still revert to them, meaning that the political calculus of non-compliance had remained favourable throughout the entire intervening period despite an unambiguous prior ruling. Following this, the regulation would be quietly converted from a binding constraint on state and corporate behaviour into a discretionary policy instrument that can be suspended when the economic case is strong enough.

The picture is completed by returning to the role of the dominant firms described in the previous section. The same firms whose market position allows them to absorb enforcement actions through the management of public opinion have the capacity to shape that opinion on the regulatory question as well. The mechanisms that allow a publicly traded corporation to slowly price in a fine through narrative management, media access, public relations infrastructure, the framing of issues in terms favourable to the firm, the funding of research and policy reports that support its position, just to name a few, are the same mechanisms that shape the public discourse in which voters form their views on data protection policy. The result is that the probability of democratic sanction against a government that weakens fundamental rights protections is not an independent variable but is actively depressed by the actors who benefit from the weakening. The government's Beckerian calculation is therefore not standing on its own in a neutral informational environment; rather, it is intertwined with the corporate one in which the probability of consequence is systematically lowered by the same firms whose interests the weakening serves.

The Draghi Report did not create this dynamic, but it must be seen as one of the most influential artefacts of this dynamic. It is a document produced within an ecosystem in which the framing of regulation as a competitiveness problem has been cultivated over years through sustained investment by actors with a direct stake in that framing. The report's selection bias, noted earlier, is not an accident or a methodological oversight, but is consistent with the broader pattern in which the costs of regulation are made highly visible and quantifiable while the benefits are diffuse, unmeasured, and rhetorically downplayed. The same is true for the fact that the report omits any acknowledgment that the regulation is grounded in the EU Charter of Fundamental Rights [27]. By the time the report reaches the political process, the work of shaping public opinion has already been done, and the Beckerian calculation for the government has already been tilted. This attempt to change the range of policies or ideas acceptable to the mainstream population at any given time, defining the limits of "reasonable" public discourse has been coined a shift of the "Overton window" [32, 33]. Here, the report does the shift, so in case, it fails it cannot be attributed to the government, while if it succeeds, the shift has already made following it politically viable. What emerges is a closed loop, in which firm-level non-compliance, market concentration, the shaping of public discourse, and the erosion of democratic sanction reinforce each other across the boundary between private and public actors. Even if the current attempt at changing the regulations is hampered, largely by political actors more exposed to the political consequences such as the European Parliament, addressing them without addressing the underlying mechanism would simply delay the matter until the Overton window is moved further.

If the primary source of disproportionate burden on smaller firms is enforcement fragmentation and the manufactured complexity of dominant platforms' data architectures, then reducing the substantive requirements of the regulation will not improve competitiveness either. It leaves the enforcement gap intact while lowering the standard against which even well-resourced firms are measured. The predictable outcome is the same burden for smaller firms and reduced compliance investment by larger ones, further cementing the dynamic that produced the current market and enforcement distortion.

4.2 The Digital Omnibus Package as Regulatory Capture in Motion

To understand how this all ties into the proposals by the European Commission in the Omnibus Package, it is helpful once more to look to long established theoretical frameworks that addressed this. Stigler's theory of economic regulation [34] demonstrated that regulatory processes are systematically influenced by the concentrated interests of regulated industries, whose stake in the outcome exceeds the diffuse interest of the public. Peltzman [35] generalised the model to show that regulatory outcomes reflect an equilibrium between producer and consumer interests, with the distribution of regulatory benefits determined by the relative political effectiveness of each group. Laffont and Tirole [36] formalised the layered information asymmetry that can give regulated firms structural advantage in shaping regulatory outcomes.

The Digital Omnibus Package, published by the Commission on 19 November 2025, exhibits several features that are consistent with these predictions. Its proposed amendments include a revised definition of "personal data" which adopts a relative, entity-specific approach to identifiability; a pseudonymisation framework that could remove certain data categories from GDPR scope; raised breach notification thresholds; and exemptions from the specification regarding certain record-keeping obligations for organisations with fewer than 750 employees, all justified by the Commission's projected savings of *many billion* Euros by the end of 2029.

In particular, two features of this process warrant critical attention. First, the Commission has publicly framed the amendments as a pro-business competitiveness measure, presenting GDPR simplification as responsive to concerns about regulatory burden [27, 37]. This may seem trivial on the surface; however, for practitioners this is a signal to firms that the change of the Overton window which the Draghi report prepared is imminent, meaning that now is the time to intensify lobbying to reduce the political cost of seeking amendments that weaken substantive protections with the blessing of the European Commission. In this context, we recall that the European Commission wields substantial power; any Beckerian firms will calculate if it's worth it to invite their ire. However, with this signal given, all lobby effort can be moved from the Commission to the other stakeholders, for example the parliament and the working groups there. The Stigler-Peltzman framework predicts this dynamic: when there are signals that the regulation is negotiable, the equilibrium shifts toward producer interests [34, 35]. Aside from a signal to firms to push lobby efforts into the legislative process, it is also a message to the Member State regulator and the Member State governments. In this context, it must be recalled that the European Commission is also the guardian of the contracts, which means that if a Member State is infringing on the independence of a regulator, their risk to be pursued for such interference shifts, which, in turn, means the Beckerian equation shifts for the Member State in favour of interfering with the regulator.

Second, the specific amendments proposed correlate closely with interests of firms that have the greatest capacity to influence the regulatory process, or rather, the cumulative interest that they can agree on. Narrowing the definition of personal data, for example, disproportionately benefits organisations that process large volumes of data at the boundary between identifiable and non-identifiable categories. These are not for the benefit of small and medium firms that are alleged to be the focus of the proposal but rather precisely the business model of the dominant advertising technology platforms that have largely externalised their compliance cost onto users and smaller market participants. Ostensibly a remedy, removing the details of the specification of the Record of Processing Activities in Art. 30 GDPR offers no practical relief to smaller firms, since the overall requirement to maintain equal documentation under Art. 5 (2) GDPR persists. The effort involved will be, at best, no more than before, but likely will lead to further fragmented requirements across different national authorities. All in all, the proposed amendments were not the ones which would be reasonable in a reform process purportedly driven by the objective of reducing the burden on small firms. They are amendments that would be in line with a reform process shaped by the concentrated interests of only the most politically organised actors, as suggested by the above framework [34–36].

Whatever the Commission's internal rationale, the observable features of the process – that is, publicly framing the amendments as competitiveness-driven, soliciting industry input on a proposal whose distributional profile favours concentrated over diffuse interests, and advancing amendments on which expert bodies had already flagged fundamental-rights concerns – are precisely the features the Stigler–Peltzman framework predicts for a regulatory process maximally exposed to capture. The effect is the same whether the outcome was intended or emergent: a shift in what the further legislative process treats as a reasonable starting position for negotiation.

5 Why Timing Matters: Reforms during a Global Retreat from Fundamental Rights

5.1 Reforms under Geopolitical Duress

The argument that regulatory reform should be assessed not only on its merits but in light of its timing and political context is not novel. Rajan and Zingales [38] demonstrated that financial regulation tends to be weakened during periods of cross-border capital competition, when domestic political actors perceive a competitive disadvantage from strict standards. Djankov et al. [39] showed that regulatory simplification initiatives, while often beneficial in principle, produce worse outcomes when implemented under conditions of institutional weakness. The relevance of this to the present situation is self-evident.

The GDPR is being opened for substantive amendment at a moment when its closest jurisdictional comparator, the United States, is actively retreating from human rights in general and privacy and data protection in particular. The Trump administration has signed executive orders designed to pre-empt state AI regulation on commerce clause grounds, directed the FTC and FCC to issue guidance that would override state consumer protection standards, and conditioned federal funding on states refraining from enacting laws the administration deems burdensome to industry [40]. The FTC's enforcement posture has shifted from rulemaking to case-by-case action, with its Commission currently operating at reduced capacity [41]. The administration has further systematically disabled safeguards for fundamental rights, in particular in relation to personal data in the federal government [42–44] and pushed their view that independent regulators are effectively unconstitutional and effectively must submit to the executive opinion as part of the push for the unitary executive doctrine [45]. These changes also did not remain local but were directed outwards by the February 2025 US memorandum threatening tariffs against jurisdictions whose privacy and digital-market rules interfere with this deregulation [46].

In this context, it is important to recall that the competitive pressure that the Draghi Report invokes as justification for GDPR reform is itself partly a product of regulatory arbitrage: US firms operating without equivalent constraints can offer lower-cost services precisely because they externalise the privacy costs that European firms are required to internalise. Weakening the GDPR in response to this dynamic does not level the playing field but concedes the terms of competition to the jurisdiction with the weakest protections, initiating a race to the bottom [47, 48] as the conditions for a trading-up that Vogel documented across multiple regulatory domains are missing [49]. Given that the US runs a trade deficit with the EU in services, particularly in information technology, while aggressively pursuing actions over the EU's surplus in goods, the macroeconomic trajectory leads to a predictable dead end. The US progressively closes itself off to imported goods and demands balance in that domain, while the trade imbalance in services escalates unchecked. Through Executive Order against the International Criminal Court [50], and subsequent designations by the Office of Foreign Assets Control [51], the Trump administration has operationally demonstrated its authority to compel US vendors embedded in global digital infrastructure to withhold services from designated persons and institutions. Microsoft has since acknowledged the existence of this executive leverage, with its president publicly pledging to contest any such future order [52]. The pledge is evidence of a corporate-communications position, not of legal capacity to resist an executive order, and European institutions have upgraded the resulting exposure from a fundamental-rights concern to an additional national-security concern [53, 54]. With the administration's concurrent push to curtail independent regulators, the EU is confronted with the fact that these vendors are now effectively governed by executive discretion alone.

Second, the geopolitical environment creates specific conditions for regulatory capture. When a major jurisdiction signals that privacy protections are obstacles to innovation rather than democratic safeguards, the political cost of defending strong regulation in other jurisdictions rises. European policymakers who maintain strict standards face accusations of competitive self-harm; those who weaken them can claim alignment with global trends. The result is a ratchet effect in which each jurisdiction's deregulatory move increases the political pressure on others and a race to the bottom ensues regardless of whether the deregulation serves the public interest of either [17, 49]. Amending the GDPR under these conditions, that is when the external pressure points toward weakening rather than strengthening, and when the actors calling most loudly for reform are those who have most consistently resisted enforcement, is to invite precisely the deterioration the reform claims to prevent and in consideration of the unequal trade deficits on goods and services between the EU and the US to make the EU technologically less competitive.

5.2 The Cost of Mistiming a Reform

These external conditions sharpen the stakes, but do not change the internal mechanism. The most consequential risk of the current reform trajectory is not that it will weaken the GDPR in the abstract, but that it will deepen the specific market distortion described in above. Consider the mechanism: If substantive requirements are reduced while enforcement remains structurally weak, the primary beneficiaries will be firms that are already non-compliant, since the gap between their behaviour and the legal standard narrows without any change in their conduct as any change – even to accommodate lower requirements – carries a substantial cost of reorganisation. Firms that have invested in compliance infrastructure – governance programmes, specialist staff, privacy-by-design engineering – will find that their investment has been partially devalued, since the standard against which it was measured has been lowered. They must undertake the cost of reorganisation to have any benefit, which takes years to show on the balance sheet. The competitive advantage of non-compliance increases: the marginal cost of full compliance drops for the non-compliant, while the sunk cost of compliance remains for those who invested.

This follows directly from the economic structure of the problem. Gray and Shimshack [55] demonstrated that enforcement credibility rather than stringency of the standard is the primary determinant of compliance behaviour, and that both specific and general deterrence effects are substantial when enforcement is consistent. Shimshack and Ward [56] had already found in an earlier study that a single fine for violations produced approximately a two-thirds reduction in statewide violations the following year, primarily through reputational effects on other firms. Revising the law while leaving enforcement unchanged does not improve compliance; it reduces the standard to which non-compliant firms are notionally subject without altering their incentive to comply.

In this context, a fragment from the time before the European Commission shifted gear on the GDPR was finalised and offers a glimpse back. The Procedural Regulation adopted in November 2025 [57] represents a genuine structural improvement, introducing binding deadlines for cross-border investigations and standardised procedures that directly address the enforcement bottleneck. However, its impact depends entirely on political will. As outlined before it is a question on whether Member States fund their supervisory authorities adequately, and more importantly, appoint reasonable and independent leaders who are acting in accordance with the law and not to captured political interests, on whether the Commission uses its oversight mechanisms to hold countries that created the environment for laggard DPAs accountable, and on whether the reform discourse prioritises enforcement effectiveness over industry appeasement. The Omnibus proposal serves insofar as a clear, voluntary signal to all involved parties that the political energy is flowing in the opposite direction. No help will be coming for the distressed and underfunded authorities. The commission will focus on changing the law under the feet of the authorities rather than strengthening enforcement, toward publicity about burden reduction rather than action on regulatory capacity, and toward an accommodation of industry preferences that Stigler would have recognised immediately [34]. In short: it will be a substantive push on the Overton window, reframing the reasonable right of the individual as an inappropriate burden to society that cannot be afforded.

6 Conclusion

The analysis developed across the preceding sections converges on the following opinion: the competitiveness problem widely attributed to the GDPR is a product of its enforcement deficit, in combination with the cost externalisation by dominant platforms rather than the text itself. Any reform that leaves enforcement structurally weak will therefore amplify the market distortion it purports to cure.

The four mechanisms traced in this paper are merely some examples and fragments of a larger, complex interaction between government and industry. Political interference produces a de facto selective repeal of the regulation for the actors whose conduct matters most. Dominant firms externalise compliance cost onto smaller firms, manufacturing the small-business grievance that makes weak enforcement politically sustainable. The market divides into firms for whom the Beckerian calculation resolves *against* compliance and those whose additional incentives compel the opposite choice, with the resulting advantage compounding in favour of the former. The Draghi Report and Digital Omnibus Package operationalise, at the level of the state, the same Beckerian calculus: fundamental rights become a variable to be optimised, rather than a constraint within which optimisation must occur. Each of these mechanisms depresses the probability of sanctions for the next, across the boundary between private and public actors.

This last move deserves to be named plainly. A firm that applies a Beckerian calculus to compliance behaves in a way that is analytically intelligible even when it is normatively troubling: Firms optimise within the constraints the law imposes on them, and where those constraints are weak, the optimisation resolves *against* compliance. The government cannot occupy the same position. Its constitutional function with respect to fundamental rights is to set the constraint, not to weigh it as a variable inside its own cost-benefit equation. When the state follows the firms it is called upon to regulate into that equation, it does not making a policy choice within its legitimate domain but abandons the role that distinguishes it from them.

The conclusion that follows is counter-intuitive but unavoidable. Deregulation under structurally weak enforcement is regressive. It lowers the legal standard for the non-compliance while devaluing the sunk compliance investment of firms that have built governance infrastructure in good faith. Assessed on its distributional effects rather than on its stated aims, the Omnibus Package functions as a transfer to the concentrated interests that produced the burden narrative in the first place.

A natural objection is that weak enforcement is preferable to none, and that conditioning reform on an enforcement threshold risks ossifying provisions that are genuinely defective, such as the overly broad applicability of Article 9 GDPR. The answer is not that such provisions must remain untouched or unaffected by other laws, but that sequencing and scope matter. This is to say that a narrow instrument, addressing specific defects identified through stakeholder consultation, accompanied by an enforcement-strengthening package, is different in kind from the horizontal revision currently proposed, which bundles substantive weakening of core definitions with procedural simplification, and whose distributional profile tracks the preferences of the most politically organised actors, rather than the evidence on small-firm burden. Surgical correction would be, in theory, compatible with the argument of this paper. However, in practice such a process would likely be subverted into more sweeping changes.

The prescriptive claim is therefore not to freeze all change, but to duly consider sequence and scope. Addressing the enforcement deficit must be treated as a prerequisite for any horizontal revision of substantive GDPR provisions. Concretely, this requires that Member States fund their supervisory authorities to levels commensurate with their caseloads, that the Commission use its Guardian-of-the-Treaties role against Member States that compromise regulator independence. Finally, measurable enforcement benchmarks such as clearance rates, median time-to-decision and how long until an unlawful state is addressed are preconditions to any substantive amendment proceeds.

The central prediction of this paper is falsifiable. If horizontal revision of the GDPR is applied, the thesis predicts that large firms will reduce their compliance investment in the years that follow, while small and mid-sized firms will see no comparable relief. If, on the contrary, compliance investment falls uniformly across firm sizes or falls more sharply at the smaller end, the thesis is wrong. The test is straightforward and the data to run it, such as privacy-office headcount, compliance budgets, and audited disclosures, already exist. A three- to five-year post-adoption horizon should be sufficient.

A final consideration concerns the asymmetry of the current moment. The Overton-window dynamic described in Sect. 4 means that a weakened regulation is not easily restored, because the discursive reframing that enabled the weakening persists after the legislative act itself. Window positions are sticky, and do not move back on their own absent an external shock capable of inverting the framing. Such a shock is conceivable; the concrete consequences of the United States retreat from privacy protection may yet materialise in ways that European voters and policymakers cannot treat as abstract, whether through more visible supply-chain coercion of European institutions by US vendors, more invasive large-scale data driven human rights violations of the government or firms, or other incidents that refocus the public debate. But relying on such a shock to arrive before the damage is done is a wager. The GDPR is not an economic regulation, but a Charter-grounded instrument giving effect to a fundamental right, which can be balanced against other fundamental rights, not the unfounded hope of better competitiveness.

From a financial point of view, fundamental rights have a price, and violating them is a risk to be managed. In a democracy that takes this view, that risk amounts to exactly one thing: the short-term political cost of the violation. As the preceding analysis has shown, this risk is already being systematically mitigated, by the very actors who profit from it.

Disclosure of Interests. The views expressed in this article are those of the author and do not represent the views of any current or former employer. The author declares they have no other competing interests relevant to the content of this article.

References

1. European Commission: Impact Assessment Accompanying the General Data Protection Regulation. European Commission, Brussels (2012)
2. European Data Protection Board: Overview on Resources Made Available by Member States to the Data Protection Supervisory Authorities. https://www.edpb.europa.eu/system/files/2022-09/edpb_overviewresourcesmade_availablebymemberstatestosas2022_en.pdf. Accessed 19 Apr 2026
3. Irish Council for Civil Liberties: 5 Years: GDPR's Crisis Point, https://www.iccl.ie/digital-data/iccl-2023-gdpr-report/. Accessed 19 Apr 2026
4. European Data Protection Board, European Commission.: Contribution on the Role of National Supervisory Authorities. https://www.edpb.europa.eu/our-work-tools/our-documents/other/contribution-edpb-european-commissions-evaluation-data-0_en. Accessed 19 Apr 2026
5. CMS Law.: GDPR Enforcement Tracker: List of GDPR Fines. https://www.enforcementtracker.com/?insights. Accessed 19 Apr 2026.
6. Eurostat: Structural Business Statistics Overview. https://ec.europa.eu/eurostat/statistics-explained/index.php?title=Structural_business_statistics_overview. Accessed 19 Apr 2026
7. Becker, G.S.: Crime and punishment: an economic approach. J. Polit. Econ. **76**, 169–217 (1968). https://doi.org/10.1086/259394
8. Stigler, G.J.: The optimum enforcement of Laws. J. Polit. Econ. **78**, 526–536 (1970). https://doi.org/10.1086/259646
9. Johnson, G.: Economic Research on Privacy Regulation: Lessons from the GDPR and beyond. National Bureau of Economic Research, Cambridge, MA (2022). https://doi.org/10.3386/w30705
10. Irish Council for Civil Liberties: Europe's Enforcement Paralysis: ICCL's Annual Report on the GDPR's Enforcement. https://www.iccl.ie/digital-data/2021-gdpr-report/. Accessed 19 Apr 2026
11. European Data Protection Board: Binding Decisions of the Board (Art. 65), 2020–2025. https://www.edpb.europa.eu/our-work-tools/our-documents/publication-type/binding-decision-board-art-65_en. Accessed 19 Apr 2026.
12. European Commission: Report on the Application of the General Data Protection Regulation. European Commission, Brussels (2024). https://eur-lex.europa.eu/legal-content/EN/TXT/?uri=COM:2024:357:FIN. Accessed 19 Apr 2026
13. Frey, C.B., Presidente, G.: Privacy regulation and firm performance: estimating the GDPR effect globally. Econ. Inq. **62**, 1074–1089 (2024). https://doi.org/10.1111/ecin.13213

14. Mathur, A., et al.: Dark patterns at scale: findings from a crawl of 11K shopping websites. Proc. ACM Hum.-Comput. Interact. **3**, 1–32 (2019). https://doi.org/10.1145/3359183
15. Peukert, C., Bechtold, S., Batikas, M., Kretschmer, T.: Regulatory spillovers and data governance: evidence from the GDPR. Mark. Sci. **41**, 746–768 (2022). https://doi.org/10.1287/mksc.2021.1339
16. Chomanski, B., Lauwaert, L.: Digital privacy and the law: the challenge of regulatory capture. AI Soc. **40**, 2777–2787 (2025). https://doi.org/10.1007/s00146-024-02041-8
17. Bradford, A.: The Brussels Effect: How the European Union Rules the World. Oxford University PressNew York (2020). https://doi.org/10.1093/oso/9780190088583.001.0001.
18. Polinsky, A.M., Shavell, S.: The economic theory of public enforcement of law. J. Econ. Lit. **38**, 45–76 (2000). https://doi.org/10.1257/jel.38.1.45
19. Lintvedt, M.N.: Putting a price on data protection infringement. Int. Data Priv. Law. **12**, 1–15 (2022). https://doi.org/10.1093/idpl/ipab024
20. Congiu, R., Sabatino, L., Sapi, G.: The impact of privacy regulation on web traffic: evidence from the GDPR. Inf. Econ. Policy. **61**, 101003 (2022). https://doi.org/10.1016/j.infoecopol.2022.101003
21. Libert, T.: An Automated Approach to Auditing Disclosure of Third-Party Data Collection in Website Privacy Policies. In: Proceedings of the 2018 World Wide Web Conference on World Wide Web - WWW '18. pp. 207–216. ACM Press, Lyon, France (2018). https://doi.org/10.1145/3178876.3186087.
22. Schmidt, C.W.: Beyond a one-time scandal: Europe's Onging diesel pollution problem. Environ. Health Perspect. **124** (2016). https://doi.org/10.1289/ehp.124-A19
23. Calo, R., Rosenblat, A.: The taking economy: Uber, information, and power. SSRN J. (2017). https://doi.org/10.2139/ssrn.2929643
24. Shapiro, C., Varian, H.R.: Information Rules: a Strategic Guide to the Network Economy. Harvard Business School Press, Boston, MA (1999)
25. Goldfarb, A., Tucker, C.: Privacy and innovation. Innov. Policy Econ. **12**, 65–90 (2012). https://doi.org/10.1086/663156
26. Johnson, G.A., Shriver, S.K., Goldberg, S.G.: Privacy and market concentration: intended and unintended consequences of the GDPR. Manag. Sci. **69**, 5695–5721 (2023). https://doi.org/10.1287/mnsc.2023.4709
27. Draghi, M..: The Future of European Competitiveness, https://commission.europa.eu/topics/eu-competitiveness/draghi-report_en. Accessed 19 Apr 2026.
28. Demirer, M., Hernández, D.J.J., Li, D., Peng, S.: Data, Privacy Laws and Firm Production: Evidence from the GDPR. National Bureau of Economic Research, Cambridge, MA (2024). https://doi.org/10.3386/w32146
29. Yakovleva, S., Irion, K.: Pitching trade against privacy: reconciling EU governance of personal data flows with external trade. Int. Data Priv. Law. **10**, 201–221 (2020). https://doi.org/10.1093/idpl/ipaa003
30. Weingast, B.R.: The political foundations of democracy and the rule of the law. Am. Polit. Sci. Rev. **91**, 245–263 (1997). https://doi.org/10.2307/2952354
31. Ferejohn, J.: Incumbent performance and electoral control. Public Choice. **50**, 5–25 (1986). https://doi.org/10.1007/BF00124924
32. Lynch, J.: Regimes of inequality: the political economy of health and wealth. Cambridge University Press (2019). https://doi.org/10.1017/9781139051576
33. King, A.M., Sanatkar, S.: Manifesting a shift in the "Overton window": the threat of project 2025 on the LGBTQ+ Community in Higher Education. APSC. **58**, 472–482 (2025). https://doi.org/10.1017/S1049096524001215
34. Stigler, G.J.: The theory of economic regulation. The Bell Journal of Economics and Management Science. **2**(3) (1971). https://doi.org/10.2307/3003160

35. Peltzman, S.: Toward a more general theory of regulation. J. Law Econ. **19**, 211–240 (1976). https://doi.org/10.1086/466865
36. Laffont, J.-J., Tirole, J.: The politics of government decision-making: a theory of regulatory capture. Q. J. Econ. **106**, 1089–1127 (1991). https://doi.org/10.2307/2937958
37. European Commission: Digital Omnibus Package: Proposal for a Regulation Amending Regulations (EU) 2016/679, (EU) 2022/868, (EU) 2023/2854 and (EU) 2024/1689. https://eur-lex.europa.eu/legal-content/EN/TXT/?uri=COM:2025:530:FIN. Accessed 19 Apr 2026
38. Rajan, R.G., Zingales, L.: The great reversals: the politics of financial development in the twentieth century. J. Financ. Econ. **69**, 5–50 (2003). https://doi.org/10.1016/S0304-405X(03)00125-9
39. Djankov, S., La Porta, R., Lopez-de-Silanes, F., Shleifer, A.: The regulation of entry. Q. J. Econ. **117**, 1–37 (2002). https://doi.org/10.1162/003355302753399436
40. Trump Donald J.: Executive Order on Ensuring a National Policy Framework for Artificial Intelligence. https://www.federalregister.gov/documents/2025/12/16/2025-23092/ensuring-a-national-policy-framework-for-artificial-intelligence. Accessed 19 Apr 2026
41. WilmerHale: Year in Review: The Top Ten US Data Privacy Developments from 2025. https://www.wilmerhale.com/en/insights/blogs/wilmerhale-privacy-and-cybersecurity-law/20260128-year-in-review-the-top-ten-us-data-privacy-developments-from-2025. Accessed 19 Apr 2026
42. Congressional Research Service: Privacy Act Lawsuits and the Department of Government Efficiency (DOGE). https://www.congress.gov/crs-product/LSB11370. Accessed 19 Apr 2026
43. Solove, D.: Privacy in authoritarian times: surveillance capitalism and government surveillance. BCLR **67**, 51–125 (2026). https://doi.org/10.70167/ZCSI2691
44. Greenleaf, G.: Defending MAGA-speech: Trump's war on global data privacy. SSRN J. (2025). https://doi.org/10.2139/ssrn.5882364
45. Trump Donald J.: Executive Order on Ensuring Accountability for All Agencies. https://www.federalregister.gov/documents/2025/02/24/2025-03063/ensuring-accountability-for-all-agencies. Accessed 19 Apr 2026
46. Trump Donald J..: Memorandum on Defending American Companies and Innovators From Overseas Extortion and Unfair Fines and Penalties, https://www.federalregister.gov/documents/2025/02/26/2025-03188/defending-american-companies-and-innovators-from-overseas-extortion-and-unfair-fines-and-penalties. Accessed 19 Apr 2026
47. Revesz, R.L.: Rehabilitating interstate competition: rethinking the "race-to-the-bottom" rationale for Federal Environmental Regulation. N. Y. Univ. Law Rev. **67**, 1210–1254 (1992)
48. Engel, K.H.: State environmental standard-setting: is there a "race" and is it "to the bottom"? Hastings Law J. **48**, 271–398 (1997)
49. Mitchell, S.K., Vogel, D.: Trading up: consumer and environmental regulation in a global economy. South. Econ. J. **63**, 271 (1996). https://doi.org/10.2307/1061329
50. Trump Donald J., D.J.: Executive Order 14203: Imposing Sanctions on the International Criminal Court. https://www.federalregister.gov/documents/2025/02/12/2025-02612/imposing-sanctions-on-the-international-criminal-court. Accessed 19 Apr 2026
51. Office of Foreign Assets Control: Issuance of Executive Order Imposing Sanctions on the International Criminal Court; International Criminal Court-Related Designation, https://ofac.treasury.gov/recent-actions/20250213. Accessed 19 Apr 2026
52. Smith, B.: Microsoft's European Digital Commitments. https://blogs.microsoft.com/on-the-issues/2025/04/30/european-digital-commitments/. Accessed 19 Apr 2026
53. European Parliament.: Parliamentary Question P-002270/2025: The Effect of the Sanctions Imposed by the United States on the Functioning of the ICC, https://www.europarl.europa.eu/doceo/document/P-10-2025-002270_EN.html. Accessed 19 Apr 2026

54. European Union Agency for Cybersecurity.: ENISA Threat Landscape 2025. https://www.enisa.europa.eu/publications/enisa-threat-landscape-2025. Accessed 19 Apr 2026
55. Gray, W.B., Shimshack, J.P.: The effectiveness of environmental monitoring and enforcement: a review of the empirical evidence. Rev. Environ. Econ. Policy. **5**, 3–24 (2011). https://doi.org/10.1093/reep/req017
56. Shimshack, J.P., Ward, M.B.: Regulator reputation, enforcement, and environmental compliance. J. Environ. Econ. Manag. **50**, 519–540 (2005). https://doi.org/10.1016/j.jeem.2005.02.002
57. European Parliament, Council of the European Union: Regulation (EU) 2025/2518 Laying Down Additional Procedural Rules Relating to the Enforcement of the GDPR. https://eur-lex.europa.eu/legal-content/EN/TXT/?uri=OJ:L_2025_2518. Accessed 19 Apr 2026

A History of GDPR Cookie Banner Compliance: The Roles of Publishers, Regulators and CMPs

Yana Dimova[1(✉)], Vincent Toubiana[2], Tom Van Goethem[1], Lieven Desmet[1], and Wouter Joosen[1]

[1] DistriNet, KU Leuven, Leuven, Belgium
{yana.dimova,tom.vangoethem,lieven.desmet,wouter.joosen}@kuleuven.be
[2] CNIL, Paris, France
vtoubiana@cnil.fr

Abstract. Since the introduction of the GDPR in 2018, cookie banners have become the primary mechanism for users to express preferences on online tracking and advertising. Consequently, their visual design and the options they present significantly influence user choice. Over time, the cookie banner landscape has evolved under the influence of key players, including publishers (website owners), regulators, and Consent Management Platforms (CMPs). This paper presents an in-depth analysis of the roles of these three key actors and an examination of their impact on cookie banners' design and implementation within the context of EU law. Our results, based on a historical evaluation of 11,364 websites across 30 countries, indicate a positive evolution in the privacy landscape, with the compliance rate for websites featuring a "reject all" button increasing from 2.94% in 2018 to 30.66% in 2024. We analyze Data Protection Authority (DPA) activity and find a clear correlation between higher compliance rates and stronger regulatory action and guidance. Our experiments further show that compliance improvements are primarily driven by website owners, with CMPs showing little response to regulatory action or (indirect) influence on compliance rates. Our findings highlight the importance of more uniform collaboration and guidance among EU-level regulators to reduce interpretive divergence and simplify cookie banner compliance, as well as the need for regulatory oversight of CMPs, which in turn could significantly enhance privacy for many websites and users. Our work provides a foundation for academics, regulators, and industry to develop more effective strategies to motivate key players and promote greater user privacy.

Keywords: Cookie banners · GDPR compliance · CMPs

1 Introduction

The General Data Protection Regulation (GDPR), which came into effect in May 2018, established a more formal definition of online consent. This had a

F. Pallas et al. (Eds.): APF 2026, LNCS 16847, pp. 173–198, 2026.
https://doi.org/10.1007/978-3-032-35899-8_9

significant impact on the ePrivacy Directive, which requires publishers to obtain valid consent before placing cookies on users' devices. Consequently, "Cookie Banners" have become the most visible manifestation of this new consent requirement, prompting publishers to adopt them on any website visited by EU data subjects.

While prior work has studied the positive changes due to the GDPR [12], it has also highlighted the persistence of non-compliant interfaces [5,6] and their variation across geographical regions [47,52]. These non-compliant banners often include manipulative designs, that subtly nudge users toward less privacy-friendly choices [37,53]. While problematic design of cookie banners has been studied by prior work, less focus has been put on motivation behind compliance. In fact, DPAs have played a crucial role in addressing such issues of non-compliance.

Their function is twofold: issuing guidance to clarify legal ambiguities and executing enforcement actions. For example, in December 2021, the French DPA (CNIL) sanctioned Google and Meta for failing to provide a "reject" button on the same layer as the "accept" option [45,46]. Consequently, Google updated its banner design across the EU [1], with Meta adopting similar changes outside of France [13].

The CNIL case demonstrates that DPA enforcement exerts a direct extra-territorial impact. We examine the extent of these "ripple effects" across EU countries and websites, focusing on longitudinal regulatory influence. Our results reveal substantial variation in banner implementation, highlighting the pivotal role of DPA guidance and enforcement in driving compliance, and the need for technical standardization of consent.

Simultaneously, in response to the consent obligations under the GDPR, a new industry of specialized actors emerged: CMPs. Many publishers rely on CMPs to customize and deploy cookie banners on their website [31,34]. Therefore, CMP design decisions have a broad influence on overall compliance. We hypothesized that CMPs would respond to regulatory pressure and gradually converge toward a common set of GDPR-compliant and privacy-friendly cookie banner interfaces. However, our results show the opposite. An examination of consent interfaces from 18 CMPs shows substantial divergence, even among websites that only recently adopted a CMP. Among the five most widely used CMPs, for example, Cookiebot includes a reject button on 55.16% of pages, whereas Cookies Consent does so on only 13.39%. While prior work focuses mainly on CMP-provided banners, our comparison of CMP and in-house banners reveals that CMPs have contributed little to compliance improvements. Instead, most positive changes are driven by website owners who explicitly choose to implement them.

We analyze the historical evolution of cookie banners across 30 countries over a six-year period (2018–2024). To achieve this, we introduce a novel method for replaying cookie banners on archived web pages by combining data from two major web archives: the Wayback Machine and HTTPArchive. Our findings reveal a general positive trend toward greater privacy in cookie banner design over time. We integrate historical and cross-country perspectives, and dive deeper into the roles of three key actors (publishers, DPAs and CMPs) and their interactions.

With our findings, we provide a better understanding of the motivations behind compliance and identify which actors have the greatest impact on the broader landscape. Our work can also help NGOs, plaintiffs, and regulators in establishing the most effective actions to increase compliance with regulation.

We summarize our main contributions:

- A longitudinal analysis demonstrating a general positive trend toward greater privacy in cookie banners over a six-year period.
- An examination of cross-country developments, highlighting the crucial role and positive impact of DPA regulatory actions.
- An investigation of cookie banners provided by 18 CMPs, which measures their limited influence on compliance and reveals that most privacy-positive changes are initiated by website owners.

2 Related Work

2.1 Web Archives

The use of web archives offers significant advantages in research, notably in facilitating the reproducibility of web measurements. A comprehensive evaluation by Hantke et al. [28] of 13 public web archives found that the Internet Archive's Wayback Machine achieved the best results in both suitability and performance. Prior work has leveraged web archives to investigate diverse topics, including the evolution of web tracking [42], changes in privacy policies [4,12,44], the composition of the web [2], and the development of security features [51,63,68]. While related work by Jha et al. [34] has examined the historical and geographical evolution of CMPs, no prior study, to our knowledge, has utilized web archives to specifically analyze cookie banners.

2.2 Automated Detection of Cookie Banners

Our analysis relies on previously developed methods for automated cookie banner detection, a topic that has been extensively explored in prior work. A variety of approaches have been employed, including HTML- or CSS-based filtering of web page elements [37,62,71], sometimes in combination with manual curation [35]. Other studies have utilized machine learning models on textual and visual elements [36] or a combination of multiple such methods [6,26,30]. For example, Bouhoula et al. [6] present a tool that uses a combination of HTML/CSS filtering and machine learning to detect and interact with cookie banners, and classify cookies and declared purposes.

Many studies focus primarily on cookie notices provided by popular CMPs [5,27,31,37,53] or supported by Interactive Advertising Bureau (IAB) Europe's

Transparency and Consent Framework (TCF). Detection methods for TCF-enabled CMPs have included using the TCF consent signal [47,52,62,74], public lists of CSS selectors [34], or methods that inspect HTTP requests [27,31,34] or page HTML [5,53], or a combination thereof [37].

Unlike studies limited to manual analysis or popular CMPs, our research examines banners from 18 different CMPs alongside custom, in-house solutions. This broader scope provides a more comprehensive view of the cookie banner landscape.

2.3 The Impact of Regulation on Cookie Banners

Research on consent banners often addresses their interdisciplinary aspects. Warberg et al. [72] examined the evolution of cookie banners on 911 news and media websites in the EU and US, observing an increase in reject options and a decrease in nudging strategies following GDPR enforcement. Similarly, Nouwens et al. [52] performed a cross-country analysis of the top 10,000 websites and found that only 15% of consent interfaces were minimally GDPR compliant, with some country-specific differences. Other studies have focused on the evolution of CMPs [31,34].

Many studies have measured compliance rates across different countries within the EU [12,34,35,43,52,70,71], or compared EU and US perspectives [64,71,72], and even considered an inter-continental scope [21,62]. Most studies offer only a static, single-point-in-time snapshot. Our work distinguishes itself by providing a historical, longitudinal analysis over a period of six years, focusing on the long-term impact of the GDPR.

The lawfulness of cookie banners has also been a major research focus. Studies have addressed issues such as implicit consent [3,5,6,12,38,39,41,43,47,48,53,62,64,66,70,73,74] and the presence of dark patterns [3,6,27,37,39,53,66,67,72], including pre-checked options [37,47,48,52,53,66,74] and cookie walls [3,37,41,66]. Large-scale measurement studies have exposed the widespread non-compliance on cookie banners, finding that 72.2% of websites violated at least one GDPR requirement [6].

3 Historical Evolution of Cookie Banners

This section examines the historical evolution of cookie banners. We first outline our methodology for replaying archived webpage snapshots to automatically identify GDPR violations. We then analyze trends in banner prevalence and the evolution of user options over time.

3.1 Methodology

Our study examines the evolution of cookie banners across the EU from 2018 to 2024. Unlike prior research dependent on web crawling, we leverage two of the largest web archives to retrospectively and automatically analyze historical snapshots.

Web Archives. The HTTPArchive [32] is a valuable open-source dataset that has been tracking the composition of the web since 2012. Each month, it performs crawls of millions of web pages (12 million URLs in the latest period). The resulting data is stored in HAR (HTTPArchive) format, a JSON-formatted file that logs a web browser's interactions with a website. Since July 2018, HTTPArchive's crawls have been based on the Chrome User Experience Report (CrUX) [7], a list of the most visited websites globally. The data, captured from US-based agents, includes all requests and responses for each web page and is stored on BigQuery. To the best of our knowledge, no historical web archives of comparable scale or completeness exist from an EU perspective.

To ensure comprehensive capture of dynamic cookie banners, we supplemented HTTPArchive snapshots with data from the Wayback Machine [33]. This dual-archive approach is essential because HTTPArchive occasionally misses dynamic request chains required to load CMP banners. By using the Wayback Machine's API to retrieve missing resources, we can accurately replay historical banners in their entirety.

Replaying Web Pages. We use a multi-tiered approach combining HTTPArchive and the Wayback Machine. First, we extract relevant snapshots from HTTPArchive and store them locally, then preprocess the data to address missing or incomplete response bodies, which are common due to HTTPArchive's cutoff limits. For each resource, we check for missing bodies and, if found, attempt retrieval via the Wayback Machine's API, ignoring images and fonts as they are unnecessary for banner layouts and omitted by HTTPArchive by default. This step is crucial for managing the Wayback Machine's rate limit of 60 requests per minute [15]. Without this pre-emptive approach, attempting to retrieve all missing resources on the fly would significantly slow down our crawler, with each page taking several minutes to replay.

To replay pre-completed snapshots, we instruct the browser to visit selected URLs through an HTTP proxy that intercepts traffic and redirects requests to archived snapshots. If a resource is missing, we fetch it from the Wayback Machine. If the resource is not available in both archives, we return an empty response. This ensures all interactions remain offline and prevents any connection to the live web.

Website Selection. While past studies have looked at the immediate effects of the GDPR in May 2018, our work examined its long-term impact on websites in all 30 EEA countries (27 EU countries, Norway, Liechtenstein and Iceland).

To select our sample, we filtered the CrUX list by country code top-level domain (ccTLD) (e.g., *.fr* for France). From this set, we identified websites with available snapshots spanning the entire analysis period. Finally, we randomly selected 500 websites per country. Because some countries had fewer than 500 websites available in CRuX (see Table 1), our final dataset consists of 11,364 websites.

Table 1. The first row of this table shows the number of websites crawled for each country. The second row shows the maximum number of cookie banners detected (in September 2024). The third row shows the number of websites which include a cookie banner throughout the whole analysis period.

	Total	Austria	Belgium	Bulgaria	Croatia	Cyprus	Czech	Denmark	Estonia	Finland	France	Germany	Greece	Hungary	Ireland	Italy	Latvia	Lithuania	Luxembourg	Malta	Netherlands	Poland	Portugal	Romania	Slovakia	Slovenia	Spain	Sweden	Iceland	Liechtenstein	Norway
Number of websites	**11364**	500	500	377	320	30	500	500	190	500	500	500	500	500	500	500	182	316	65	19	500	500	500	500	500	247	500	500	109	9	500
Max detected banners	**4060**	155	178	128	131	9	194	112	73	151	137	172	176	220	190	154	95	138	16	9	149	217	166	205	212	116	196	184	37	1	139
Detected banners	**2479**	99	100	85	94	4	103	66	24	52	81	92	111	157	114	106	50	92	8	7	93	163	111	131	124	96	148	109	20	1	38

We select country-code top-level domains (ccTLDs) for two reasons. First, this ensures the dataset represents popular websites within each target country. Second, although snapshots are captured via US-based IP addresses, ccTLDs target European audiences, as confirmed in the *Pammer and Alpenhof* case [17, 18]. Therefore, these websites fall within the territorial scope of GDPR Article 3 [60].

We performed several analyses to confirm this latter claim. First, we leveraged the country-specific CrUX popularity information, and compared the popularity of sites with an EEA ccTLD to its global popularity. We find that the vast majority (over 99%) of sites in our dataset are much more popular in the EEA than globally, clearly indicating that these target European citizens. We excluded a few exceptions, such as vanity domains (e.g., `linktr.ee`) or compromised websites. Second, we confirmed that none of the 11,364 websites in our dataset redirect from an EU ccTLD to a global, non-EU domain (e.g., `youtu.be` to `youtube.com`), which would potentially complicate their GDPR obligations. Finally, our assessment of the impact of US-based access (detailed in Sect. 3.2) shows that 91.6% of cookie banners are captured consistently regardless of the access location. Our methodology aligns with prior work that adopts a similar ccTLD-based approach [34].

Cookie Banners Analysis. To detect and analyze cookie banners, we extended the automated tool developed by Bouhoula et al. [6]. Built on the OpenWPM framework, this tool identifies and interacts with banners to report GDPR violations for both CMP and in-house solutions. We added support for the primary languages of all 30 target countries by integrating the Google Cloud Translate API to translate banner text before processing.

The framework locates candidate banners through HTML filtering and z-index inspection. It then validates these candidates using a language model to identify cookie-related terms, achieving 100% precision and 86.9% recall. A machine learning model classifies banner options (e.g., accept, reject, settings) and links them to specific cookie sets. Finally, cookies are categorized as either 1) analytics and advertising or 2) essential and session based on their purpose. For detecting missing "Reject" buttons, the tool yields 91.5% precision and 65.2% recall, meaning false positives are rare, though some non-compliant banners are missed. While our findings represent a lower-bound estimate, they remain suitable for identifying long-term trends.

Detecting GDPR Violations. A multitude of factors dictate compliance with data protection laws, ranging from the adequacy of user information to the deployment of pre-selected choices and the installation of tracking cookies without explicit consent. While comprehensive compliance involves complex, qualitative dimensions, this study focuses on the foundational and objective parameters of lawful consent. To mitigate inconsistencies arising from divergent national interpretations, such as varying regulations on "cookie walls" [50], we deliberately exclude metrics that require subjective legal judgment. By restricting our analysis to automatically detectable and consistently interpreted infractions, we ensure an unbiased assessment that facilitates reliable cross-country and longitudinal comparisons.

Within this methodological framework, we evaluate cookie banners that deploy tracking cookies and are thus legally mandated to provide an equally accessible rejection mechanism. The absence of a clear "reject" option violates the GDPR requirement for freely given consent, which dictates that declining consent must be as effortless as accepting it, a principle firmly upheld by the CNIL [46] and the EDPB taskforce [20]. Consequently, we utilize this specific consent requirement as a primary proxy for broader GDPR compliance.

Furthermore, initializing tracking cookies without offering an immediate rejection mechanism violates the ePrivacy Directive (Art. 5.3) [19,59], which strictly requires prior consent for non-essential cookies. Because our data collection simulated access from outside the EU, we cannot definitively confirm actual ePrivacy violations within our dataset. Therefore, our findings should be interpreted as potential ePrivacy violations. This extrapolation remains highly robust, given that our comparative analysis between US and EU vantage points revealed no significant divergence in website behavior (detailed in Sect. 3.2).

Crawls. In the final step, we crawled 11,364 websites across 25 time periods and 30 countries using an automated detection tool interfaced with archived snapshots via a proxy. The primary bottleneck was live requests to the Wayback Machine API, which extended each crawl of 500 websites to approximately 36 h. The process was deployed on a university cloud network using machines with 16 GB RAM and 4 CPUs. Out of a total of 284,100 websites (25 time points multiplied by 11,364 websites), we successfully crawled 277,440 (97.66%) of them.

3.2 Web Archives: Benefits and Constraints

Web archives provide temporal stability by eliminating some of the disadvantages of live web crawls. However, they present limitations such as browser compatibility issues [29] and incomplete resource retrieval [42]. Because some dynamic content may be replayed incorrectly, our cookie banner detection rates represent a lower-bound estimate. We quantify this potential bias through a three-fold validation.

CMP Detection Comparison. By matching HTTP requests to known CMP domains (Sect. 5.1), we found that a substantial share of banners remains uncaptured, increasing from 41.49% in 2018 to 49.59% in 2024. However, these missed banners are distributed across various providers (e.g., Cookiebot, OneTrust), suggesting our longitudinal trends remain representative of the broader ecosystem.

Manual Analysis. We manually analyzed 500 websites to assess crawler errors, archive limitations, and geographical bias. Our automated methodology successfully captured 53.2% of banners found manually.

To test IP location bias, we crawled 500 websites with a EU IP address and a US IP address and compared the results. EU crawls detected 73.72% of banners, while US crawls detected 64.96%. This 8.4% disparity is relatively low because we focused on country-code TLDs (ccTLDs), which, as Van Eijk et al. [71] noted, often influence compliance more than the visitor's location, particularly when compared to generic `.com` domains.

Comparison with Prior Work. Our September 2024 detection rate was 35.73%. While Bouhoula et al. [6] reported 57.16% using the same crawler on live sites, our lower rate is expected given the archive and geolocation constraints. Our results align with the broad range found in existing literature, where automated detection rates vary from 24% [37] to 67% [52]. We conclude that our findings remain representative of the broader cookies banners landscape and their evolution of time, despite the acknowledged limitations.

3.3 Results

We crawled 11,364 websites and detected a cookie banner on 4,060 (35.73%) of them. The number of cookie banners detected increased continually throughout the measurement period, as shows in Fig. 1. The detection rate varied across EU countries, from 22.4% in Denmark to 52.2% in Latvia. A detailed country breakdown is shown in Table 1. Our historical analysis over six years (September 2018–September 2024) shows a steady increase in cookie banner adoption. At the start, 2,479 (21.81%) websites consistently included a banner. By September 2024, this number rose to 4,060 (35.73%), a 63.78% increase. This growth aligns with the post-GDPR regulatory landscape. Following GDPR's introduction, website owners likely became more aware of their legal obligations to obtain user consent for non-essential third-party services, such as analytics and tracking, prompting gradual adoption of cookie banners.

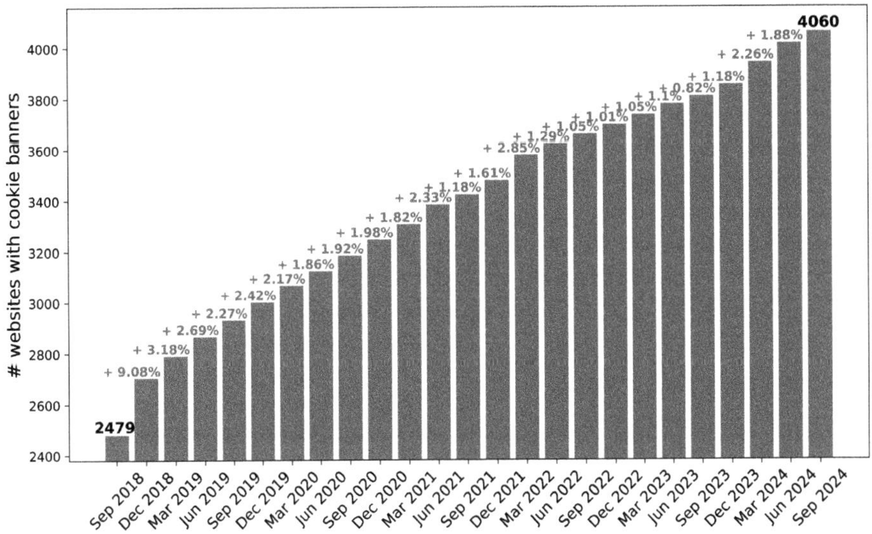

Fig. 1. Number of detected cookie banners throughout time.

Cookie Banners Options. Next, we examine the evolution of consent options on cookie banners, focusing on websites that consistently displayed a banner throughout the analysis period. We categorize these into four types: 1) banners offering both "accept" and "reject" options, 2) banners with only an"accept"option, 3) banners with only a "reject" option, and 4) banners providing no choice at all.

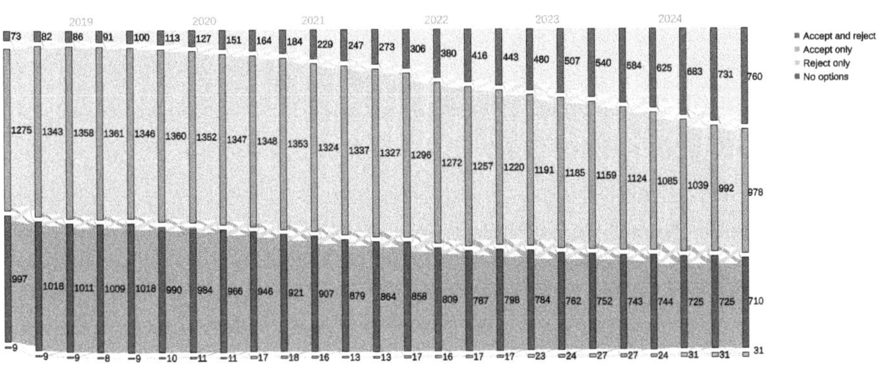

Fig. 2. "Number of cookie banners over time with "Reject" options, only "Accept" options, and no options.

As shown in Fig. 2, which illustrates the evolution of these four types, we observe several positive trends. First, banners offering both accept and reject options increased steadily over time, from 73 (2.94%) websites in September 2018 to 760 (30.66%) in September 2024. This reflects a positive shift toward providing users with more choice.

Second, we note a short-term rise in banners featuring only an "Accept" button between September 2018 and March 2019. This likely occurred as many websites initially implemented passive banners following the GDPR's introduction. Subsequent regulatory guidance likely prompted website owners to recognize the unlawfulness of this practice, leading them to adapt banners to include active consent options. Following this period, the number of accept-only banners declined steadily in favor of banners that include a reject option.

Periods with Most Change. To identify during which period cookie banners became more privacy-focused, we calculated the growth rate of banners offering both "accept" and "reject" options relative to those that lacked them. These trends are detailed in Fig. 3.

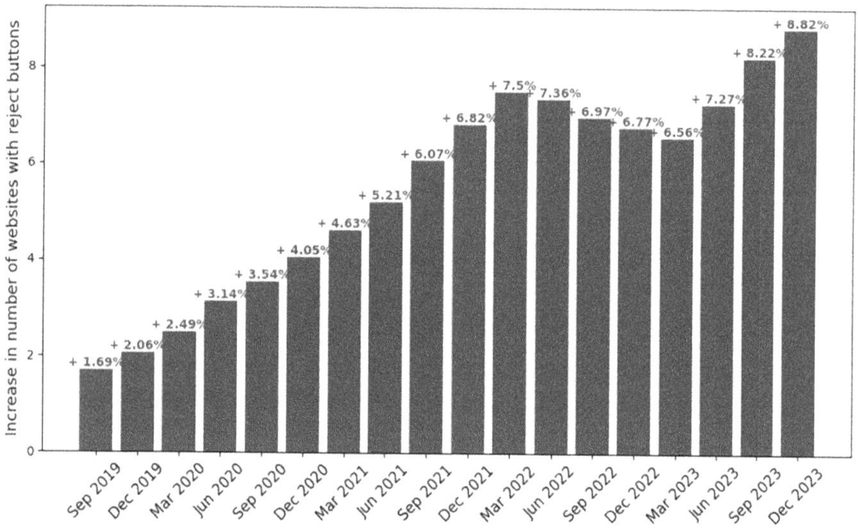

Fig. 3. This figure shows the growth of "Reject" options relative to banners previously lacking this feature. We compare the growth in one year starting from the given period, with the year before. E.g., between September 2019 and June 2020 1.69% more websites adopted cookie banners with accept and reject options as compared to Sep 2018-Jun 2019.

We observed two major shifts. The first peak occurred between January and December 2022, when 7.5% more websites began displaying reject buttons on their banners. The second period took place toward the end of our analysis, between December 2023 and September 2024, with an 8.82% increase in banners offering a reject option.

It appears that a significant shift in the compliance of cookie banner interfaces occurred in 2022, followed by an even more impactful shift that began in early 2024 and continued until the end of our analysis period. While the main driver for this positive evolution is not yet clear, it is possible that this behavior will continue to propagate into late 2024 and 2025.

The changes in cookie banner features can be attributed to numerous factors. These include country-specific developments, such as regulatory actions, as well as EU-wide ripple effects (e.g., from cases of the European Court of Justice). Additionally, website owners often employ CMPs to manage their cookie banners, which can significantly influence how banners are displayed. We explore these considerations in Sects. 5 and 6.

4 Cross-country Analysis

In this section, we shift the perspective from EU-wide trends to country-specific developments, exploring which countries have experienced the most significant increase in cookie banner compliance over time.

4.1 Methodology

For the analysis, we rely on the same dataset, described in Sect. 3.1. To assess how a website's territorial scope influences its banner, we compare GDPR compliance across countries by focusing on banners without reject options (at any layer).

Activity Level of DPAs. Our analysis focuses on two defining activities for DPA involvement: the imposition of sanctions and fines for GDPR infringements and the publication of regulatory guidance (e.g., guidelines, recommendations).

We extracted this information from noyb's GDPRhub [58], an open-source wiki summarizing over 2,000 national cases. We identified a total of 287 relevant cases by searching for the keyword "cookie" in their summaries. This allowed us to compile the number of cases and total fine amounts in euros for each country. Furthermore, we referenced noyb's "Consent Banner Report" [57] for an overview of all pertinent EU and national guidelines on cookie banners.

Correlation Test. To investigate the relationship between DPA activity and compliance, we performed a Pearson correlation test. We tested the correlation between 1) compliance rates and the presence of regulatory guidance (as a binary parameter), and 2) compliance and enforcement (as measured by the number of cases) (Table 2).

4.2 Results

Table 2. Compliance rates differences across countries represented by the presence of "Reject" options. The second column shows the average compliance rate throughout the whole time period, while the third column refers to the compliance rate in September 2024. DPA activity is represented by the number of cases on cookies, total amount of fines and the publication of guidelines on cookie banners.

Country	Avg. banners with Reject(%)	Latest banners with Reject (%)	# of Cases	Total Fines (EUR)	Guidelines Published
Denmark	35.15	60.61	15	—	2020
France	23.51	41.98	43	645 250 000	2020
Austria	20.08	44.44	19	—	2023
Germany	19.61	38.04	25	—	2022
Finland	18.69	44.23	5	1 100 000	2022
Ireland	18.24	40.35	4	225 000 000	2020
Italy	17.66	37.74	21	51 732 546	2021
Netherlands	16.43	25.81	14	1 165 500	2019
Belgium	16.08	31.00	34	604 140	2023
Slovakia	15.36	42.74	—	—	—
Spain	14.78	43.24	74	37 021 600	2019, 2020, 2023
Latvia	14.40	30.00	2	—	2022
Czech Rep.	13.44	39.81	2	14 160 363	unknown
Croatia	13.32	27.66	5	133 000	—
Portugal	12.40	33.33	1	—	—
Slovenia	11.38	17.71	—	—	—
Greece	9.95	20.72	4	440 000	2020
Sweden	9.91	26.61	9	6 955 136	—
Hungary	8.66	20.38	3	25 000	—
Romania	8.18	19.08	5	55 000	—
Bulgaria	6.73	14.12	—	—	—
Poland	5.89	20.25	2	40 000	—
Lithuania	4.74	14.13	—	—	—
Average	**14.55**	**31.91**	**12.5**		

Cross-country Differences. Cookie banner compliance varied significantly across countries. Denmark maintained the highest average compliance (35.15%), followed by France (23.51%) and Austria (20.08%). By 2024, the top performers were Denmark (60.61%), Austria (44.44%), and Finland (44.23%).

While Spain (43.24%) and Slovakia (42.74%) reached the top five in 2024, their lower historical averages suggest a very recent surge in compliance. Conversely, Lithuania (4.74%), Poland (5.89%), and Bulgaria (6.73%) consistently exhibited the lowest compliance rates.

The Impact of Regulatory Action. DPA engagement varies significantly across the EEA. For instance, the Spanish DPA has processed the most cookie-related enforcement cases (74), totaling €37,021,600 in fines. Meanwhile, the French CNIL has levied the highest aggregate fines, totaling €645,250,000 across 43 cases.

Our findings suggest that DPA activity measurably impacts compliance. We identified a moderate positive correlation between compliance and regulatory action (`r=0.42,p=0.046`) and a strong positive correlation with the publication of regulatory guidance (`r=0.62,p=0.002`). While other factors, such as a country's general privacy stance, reputational risk, and economic considerations, likely influence compliance, a full evaluation of these multidisciplinary aspects remains outside this study's scope.

Case Study: France. In France, we observe a consistently high compliance rate throughout the analysis period. The CNIL case likely caused a significant increase in the number of reject buttons after January 2022. As shown in Fig. 4, we observe that in March 2022, 16.08% more websites were compliant. The compliance rate continued to increase, with an additional 21.69% of websites becoming compliant by September 2022. This phased increase could be attributed to some websites making changes immediately after the CNIL ruled Google's cookie banner non-compliant (on December 31st, 2021), while others only made changes months later, after Google announced its intent to redesign its banner according to CNIL's guidelines [1] (on April 21, 2022).

The case against Meta and Google appears to have had a significant impact in France. However, we did not observe a similar increase in compliance after the CNIL published a recommendation on the use of cookies [9] (in January 2020) or after the grace period for companies to comply with these guidelines ended (in March 2021) [8]. France is one of three countries where the evolution of the compliance rate mimics the global trend, peaking around 2022 and 2024 (the others being the Czech Republic and Slovakia).

5 Cross-CMP Analysis

Website owners frequently rely on CMPs for cookie banner configuration. While CMPs offer default settings, owners often customize these by adding "reject" buttons, implementing dark patterns, or modifying button text. Consequently, CMPs directly shape banner design and user controls, significantly influencing the overall privacy-friendliness of a site. This section explores the evolving role of CMPs and their banner implementations over time.

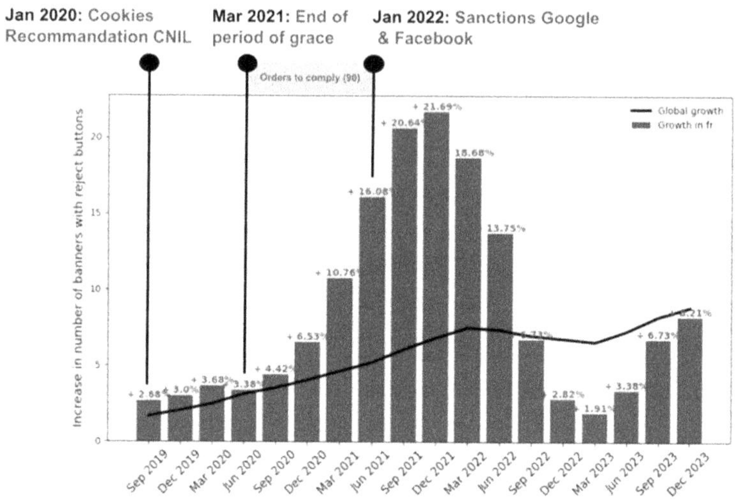

Fig. 4. Increase in number of banners with reject buttons over time in France.

5.1 Methodology

CMP Detection. To identify CMPs on visited websites, we utilized Easylist Cookie [14], manually filtering the most frequent URL and CSS rules as established by Bouhoula et al. [6].

We verified CMP ownership by cross-referencing matched domains with official service websites or GitHub implementation documentation. This process identified 18 distinct CMPs.

CMP Types. Using this method, we detected a total of 18 CMPs. Consistent with prior research [40,52], we categorize these CMPs into three distinct types. Twelve companies fall under the category of *Comprehensive CMPs*, as they offer a range of services beyond basic consent management, such as website scanning and data insights (e.g., OneTrust, Cookiebot). Two companies are classified as *Plugin CMPs*. These are advertised as lightweight solutions that prioritize easy integration with web applications and frameworks (e.g., Consent Manager, CookieYes). Finally, four companies belong to *Open-source CMPs*, which are designed to be lightweight, freely accessible, and open-source (e.g., Cookie Consent, Cookie Notice).

5.2 Results

CMP Popularity. We observed a significant increase in CMP adoption over time. The number of websites utilizing CMP banners rose from 1,318 (11.60%) in 2018 to 4,578 (40.29%) in 2024. Figure 5 illustrates the yearly evolution of the top 10 most widely used CMPs.

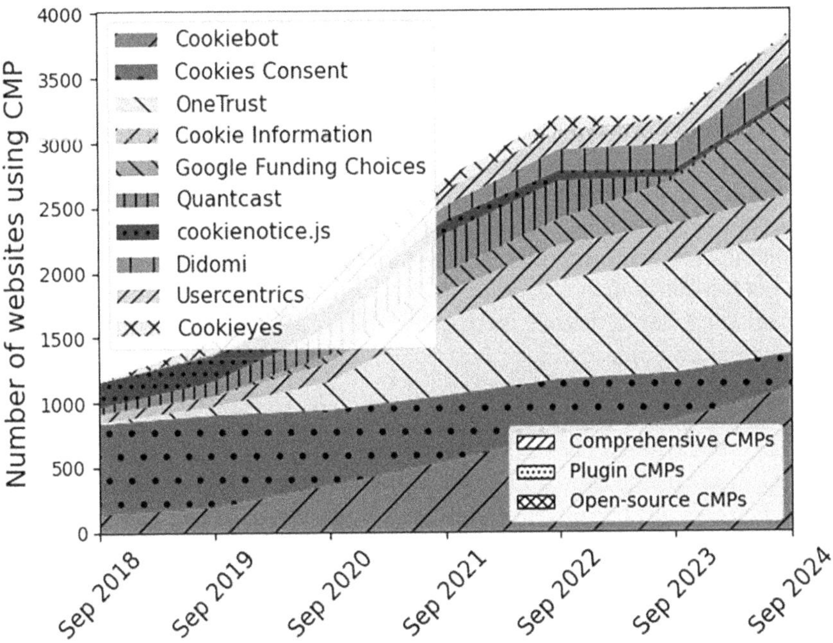

Fig. 5. Number of websites which use the top 10 CMPs over time.

We observe a decline in popularity of *plugin* and *open-source CMPs*. Many were widely used immediately after the GDPR's introduction in 2018. For instance, 53.19% of websites with a CMP employed the *Cookies Consent* framework [49], but this figure dropped to just 5.94% by September 2024. The popularity of all plugin and open-source CMPs has decreased significantly over the last few years.

Conversely, the use of more comprehensive CMPs has grown steadily since 2018. *Cookiebot* [11] saw its prevalence increase from 136 (10.32%) websites in 2018 to 1090 (23.81%) in 2024, potentially because of its merger with *Usercentrics* [10]. Similarly, the second-largest comprehensive CMP, *OneTrust* [61], has also seen rapid adoption, increasing from 11 websites (0.83%) in 2018 to 917 (20.03%) in 2024.

Google Funding Choices was introduced in 2018 to manage visits from users with ad blockers [23]. In 2020, a CMP functionality was added [25], and it is now integrated with Google's advertising platforms [24]. In 2024, 727 (15.88%) websites included resources from Google Funding Choices domains. However, this number represents an upper bound, as it is not possible to distinguish whether these websites are using the CMP functionality or only the anti-adblocking feature without having an actual screenshot of the page.

Overall, our findings suggest a consolidation in the market, with smaller players losing ground to larger, comprehensive CMPs. This indicates that website owners are increasingly willing to invest in more elaborate, and often more expensive, CMP solutions, reflecting a greater concern for (apparent) compliance.

Cookie Banners Across CMPs. To understand how CMPs influence compliance and interface design, we focus on websites utilizing detected CMP-provided banners. We again employ the presence of a reject option at any layer as a proxy for compliance. In practice, banner deployment is a collaboration between CMPs, which provide a default interface, and website owners, which can modify it at any time. This flexibility makes it difficult to distinguish whether compliance trends stem from the CMP's default settings or the owner's custom adjustments. To better understand this dynamic between CMPs and publishers, we conduct a series of experiments.

What do CMP Banners Look Like? In this section, we analyze how CMP-specific banner designs change over time to evaluate whether CMPs influence the prevalence of banners lacking a "reject" button. As shown in Fig. 6, there are significant differences in compliance rates among various CMPs. For instance, in 2024, Cookiebot demonstrates a compliance rate of 55.16% and OneTrust 49.19%, while the rate for Cookies Consent is only 13.39%. This suggests a varying relationship between the choice of a CMP and the likelihood of having a compliant banner. It seems that the cookie banners of some CMPs are more privacy-friendly than in-house banners, as shown by a 2024 compliance rate of only 26.69% for non-CMP banners.

The evolution of specific CMPs provides further insight. Cookiebot has steadily evolved toward higher compliance, becoming one of the most widely-used CMPs by 2024. Its most significant shift toward including more reject buttons occurred between June 2020 and December 2021, a period that predates the major global evolution observed in 2022.

In May 2021, noyb filed complaints against 500 OneTrust-using websites for GDPR violations [54]. By August 2021, 42% of these sites had remediated their issues [55]. This campaign had a measurable effect in our data: the compliance rate for OneTrust banners rose from 33.33% in March 2021 to 47.47% in December 2022, following a second wave of enforcement [56]. Because noyb contacted website owners directly before filing formal complaints, these improvements likely resulted from publishers responding to legal pressure rather than the CMP proactively driving compliance.

What Drives Positive Changes? When focusing on the evolution of positive change over time, we observe a similar trend for both CMP and non-CMP banners. This indicates that major regulatory events, such as the CNIL case in March 2022, spurred a significant jump in compliance rates across both groups. This shared, responsive behavior suggests that website publishers actively made changes, instead of CMPs pushing for them.

Furthermore, we compare existing customers (i.e., websites that were already using the CMP in the previous period) and new CMP customers (i.e., websites that either switched from one CMP to another or did not include a CMP in the previous period). We hypothesize that CMPs would actively encourage compliance in both new and existing customers as a result of the CNIL case. For new customers, this motivation could manifest as updated, more compliant default settings or clearer information about illegal practices. For existing customers, CMPs could either notify them of non-compliant banners or, in more extreme cases, force a change by no longer supporting non-compliant interfaces. However, our data does not support this hypothesis. As shown in Fig. 6, at no point have all interfaces from major CMPs become compliant. If CMPs were indeed a primary driver of compliance, we would expect to see a widespread change, such as 90% of all websites adopting "reject" buttons.

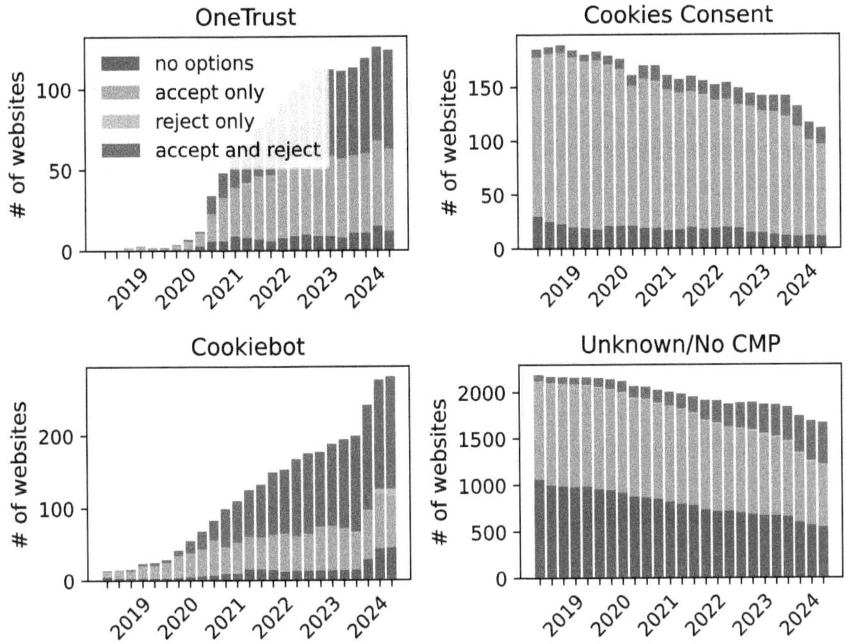

Fig. 6. Number of cookie banners with "Reject", "Accept"-only and no options for top 3 CMPs and websites with no CMP.

Consequently, we conclude that CMPs have had a limited impact on this upward trend in compliance, and show little response to regulatory action.

6 Discussion

Between 2018 and 2024, compliance with privacy regulations among website owners has increased, likely due to a combination of factors: the threat of fines and regulatory action, concerns over reputational damage, and a general increase in privacy awareness. Although the specific motivator for changes in cookie banner design is difficult to pinpoint, this paper explores the cross-country impact of major actors influencing these banners: website owners, regulators and CMPs.

6.1 Historical Evolution of Cookie Banners

Our findings indicate improvements in specific aspects of GDPR compliance. In 2018, only 2.94% of websites offered both accept and reject options. By 2024, this figure had risen to 30.66%. This improvement was most significant during two distinct periods. The first major shift occurred in 2022, likely due to a combination of factors, including a wave of complaints filed by noyb with DPAs and the CNIL fine targeting the lack of a reject button on the first layer of the cookie banner.

A second substantial compliance surge occurred in 2024. While difficult to attribute to a single cause, this shift potentially follows the EDPB's October 2023 guidelines clarifying the ePrivacy Directive. Increased DPA enforcement and rising privacy awareness also likely played key roles. Given this momentum, the trend toward higher compliance will likely persist into 2025 and beyond, providing a significant area for future study.

We acknowledge that our findings should be interpreted as being lower-bound, given that the use of web archives proved to result in a variety of cookie banners being missed by our analysis. Nonetheless, we argue that the methodology allows us to observe GDPR compliance trends over time. Overall, our findings show a positive evolution in cookie banner compliance, driven in part by regulatory action (e.g., case law) and guidance (e.g., EDPB guidelines). While this progress is positive, new privacy issues, such as manipulation and user choices not being respected, are still prevalent.

6.2 The Role of DPAs

Our results show considerable differences in compliance rates across EU countries. Denmark, France, and Austria have consistently been part of the top countries with the greatest compliance, with Spain, Finland, and Slovakia catching up in 2024. Conversely, Lithuania, Bulgaria, and Slovenia remain at the lower end of the compliance spectrum.

Higher compliance rates correlate with active DPAs, yet other factors significantly influence banner design. Beyond regulators, NGOs like noyb drive compliance through strategic complaints. Furthermore, a "spillover effect" can boost compliance in countries with inactive DPAs, such as Slovakia, while others like Slovenia remain stagnant due to limited enforcement resources. EU-wide EDPB guidelines also exert varying degrees of influence across member states, making it difficult to isolate a single motivation for compliance. Cross-country divergence complicates compliance further with contradictory regulatory guidelines. For example, some DPAs disagree on whether "accept" and "reject" buttons must be on the same interface level, with the Italian DPA specifically discouraging an equal path for both: "the affirmative action the user is empowered to perform when first accessing a website must in any case be aimed at giving his or her consent (so-called "opt-in") and may never consist in refusing such consent (so-called "opt-out")." [22].

Our findings document the effect of enforcement on compliance and highlight the critical importance of DPA collaboration. Many DPAs lack the resources to counter the behavioral advertising industry's evolving manipulative tactics, such as the recent *pay-or-consent* model. Even with adequate resources, the enforcement process can be challenging and span years, especially when well-resourced parties are involved. Additionally, the average website often uses third-party services that operate across multiple EU countries, further complicating enforcement.

We argue that greater EU-wide uniformity is needed for two primary reasons: first, to foster collaboration, enhancing enforcement and support for website owners; and second, to standardize cookie banner implementations. Such uniformity could be realized through Article 88b of the Digital Omnibus proposal [16]. Legally mandating a technically supported consent signal (e.g., via browser vendors) would grant users more control, minimize banner divergence, streamline regulatory oversight, and ultimately increase compliance.

6.3 The Role of CMPs

Market Share. Our findings show the growing significance of CMPs as part of the adtech ecosystem. Their adoption has become increasingly popular, rising from 11.6% of websites in 2018 to 40.29% in 2024, though this number is likely higher, as smaller CMPs may have been missed by our methodology. We observe a market trend where website owners are opting for more comprehensive and costly privacy solutions. This shift indicates a greater concern for compliance and a willingness to spend more money on privacy solutions. Consequently, the CMP market is converging around a few popular players, with OneTrust, Cookiebot, and Google Funding Choices holding a combined 61.85% market share in 2024. This dominant position of CMPs has been scrutinized by prior work [34, 52] given their presence on popular websites [31].

How Do CMPs Influence Cookie Banners' Design? We found significant differences in compliance rates among CMPs. For example, in 2024, 55.16% of websites using Cookiebot included a reject button, compared to only 13.39% of sites using Cookies Consent. This contrasts with the 26.69% rate for websites using their own banner, indicating that the choice of CMP can strongly influence compliance. These cross-CMP variations stem from several factors. In some countries, locally developed CMPs are more common, which helps explain some of the cross-country differences we've observed. Furthermore, certain CMPs might use manipulative designs during installation, steering website owners toward less privacy-friendly interfaces [69].

In theory, the evolution of cookie banners on CMP-using websites reflects both updates made by CMPs and configuration choices made by website owners.

In practice, our results indicate that website owners are the primary drivers of change. First, regulatory actions are typically directed at website owners, not the CMPs they use. Regulations may impact CMPs indirectly (as seen in noyb's complaints against OneTrust), but it is the website owners who are the ultimate agents of change. Second, we see a similar rise in compliance over time on websites that don't use a CMP, which suggests a broader increase in awareness among owners. Third, CMPs show little response to regulatory actions and do not incentivize customers to adopt more compliant configurations.

We conclude that the increased compliance is predominantly due to website owners intentionally configuring their banners to meet GDPR standards. This shift is likely fueled by a growing awareness of GDPR violations, driven by significant enforcement actions (e.g., noyb complaints, the CNIL case) and a general rise in public concern over privacy and reputational risk.

Responsibility and Compliance. Our study reveals a positive trend in cookie banner compliance over time. However, persistent issues like manipulative designs and disregarded user choices raise a fundamental question: who is responsible for compliance? By examining various stakeholders, our results show that most improvements stem from website owners actively updating their banners. In contrast, despite their significant market share and close ties to the adtech ecosystem, CMPs exert limited effort to improve compliance. Because they position themselves as expert solutions, they effectively set the de facto standard for cookie banners, leading developers to rely heavily on their default configurations. Furthermore, prior work shows that many website owners are unaware of the various technologies on their pages and rely on tools such as cookie scans for compliance [40]. This issue is compounded by the fact that some CMPs include manipulative designs in their configuration process for new customers [69] and offer tools like "consent optimization" and A/B testing of interface configurations that may not serve users' best interests. CMPs are likely to have more incentive to maximize user consent, as it might give them a competitive edge with relation to other market players and help to retain clients. At the very least, this behavior is misleading to the publishers who rely on their services.

At the same time, website owners retain their own responsibilities. One could argue that CMPs merely provide the tools, and website owners must still configure them correctly to meet GDPR requirements. Some CMPs might be more inclined to meet those criteria bu default, in order to guarantee safety from enforcement actions for their customers.

In practice, we argue that GDPR compliance for cookie banners is a shared responsibility between CMPs and publishers. There is a clear need for greater legal accountability for CMPs. Revisiting questions around joint controllership could help determine when CMPs should be held responsible under the GDPR [65]. At present, CMPs have little incentive to push for higher compliance and show minimal response to regulatory actions. Stronger incentives could help reduce manipulative designs and lead to more efficient improvements in compliance. Additionally, standardizing how users communicate consent would constrain CMPs, leaving less room for non-compliant banner interfaces such as those that lack a clear "Reject" option.

Ultimately, increased regulatory oversight of CMPs would more effectively scale privacy protections across the web. Based on our findings, we encourage website owners to be cautious when relying on CMPs' interfaces and instead, ensure privacy-friendly cookie banners which align with users' choices regarding their privacy on the web.

7 Conclusion

Our findings reveal a complex, evolving landscape of cookie banner compliance under the GDPR. Compliance rose from 2.94% in 2018 to 30.66% in 2024, driven by the interplay between publishers, CMPs, and DPAs. A strong correlation between DPA activity and higher compliance, particularly in France and Spain, underscores the necessity of consistent enforcement. Conversely, countries with limited regulatory activity, such as Lithuania, Poland, and Bulgaria, maintain notably low compliance.

CMPs offer widely varying interfaces; for instance, "reject" options range from 55.16% on Cookiebot to only 13.39% on Cookies Consent. Despite their prevalence, CMPs have shown little response to regulatory pressure. Instead, compliance improvements appear driven primarily by publishers opting for more privacy-respecting designs. By analyzing these stakeholders, this study clarifies the forces shaping GDPR compliance and the gradual shift toward privacy-friendly interfaces.

Acknowledgments. This research is partially funded by the Internal Funds KU Leuven, and by the Cybersecurity Research Program Flanders.

References

1. Adhyae, S.: New cookie choices in Europe (2022). https://blog.google/around-the-globe/google-europe/new-cookie-choices-in-europe/. Accessed on 30-08-2025
2. Agarwal, V., Sastry, N.: "way back then": a data-driven view of 25+ years of web evolution. In: Proceedings of the ACM Web Conference 2022, pp. 3471–3479 (2022)
3. Alharbi, J.A., Albesher, A.S., Wahsheh, H.A.: An empirical analysis of e-governments' cookie interfaces in 50 countries. Sustainability **15**(2), 1231 (2023)
4. Amos, R., Acar, G., Lucherini, E., Kshirsagar, M., Narayanan, A., Mayer, J.: Privacy policies over time: Curation and analysis of a million-document dataset. In: Proceedings of the Web Conference 2021, pp. 2165–2176 (2021)
5. Bollinger, D., Kubicek, K., Cotrini, C., Basin, D.: Automating cookie consent and gdpr violation detection. In: 31st USENIX Security Symposium (USENIX Security 22), pp. 2893–2910 (2022)
6. Bouhoula, A., Kubicek, K., Zac, A., Cotrini, C., Basin, D.: Automated large-scale analysis of cookie notice compliance. In: 33rd USENIX Security Symposium (USENIX Security 24), pp. 1723–1739 (2024)

7. Chrome UX report: Overview of crux (2024). https://developer.chrome.com/docs/crux. Accessed 30-08-2025
8. CNIL: Cookies et autres traceurs: la cnil publie des lignes directrices modificatives et sa recommandation. https://www.cnil.fr/fr/cookies-et-autres-traceurs/regles/cookies/lignes-directrices-modificatives-et-recommandation. Accessed 13-01-2026
9. CNIL: Délibération n° 2020-092 du 17 septembre 2020 portant adoption d'une recommandation proposant des modalités pratiques de mise en conformité en cas de recours aux "cookies et autres traceurs". https://www.cnil.fr/sites/default/files/atoms/files/recommandation-cookies-et-autres-traceurs.pdf. Accessed 12-01-2026
10. Cookiebot by Usercentrics: Usercentrics and cookiebot join forces (2022). https://www.cookiebot.com/en/usercentrics-cookiebot-cmp/. Acessed on 30-08-2025
11. Cookiebot by Usercentrics: Automate consent signaling and drive results on top ad platforms (2026). https://www.cookiebot.com/. Accessed 13-01-2026
12. Degeling, M., Utz, C., Lentzsch, C., Hosseini, H., Schaub, F., Holz, T.: We value your privacy... now take some cookies: measuring the gdpr's impact on web privacy (2018). arXiv:1808.05096 arXiv preprint
13. Dimova, Y., Franken, G., Le Pochat, V., Joosen, W., Desmet, L.: Tracking the evolution of cookie-based tracking on facebook. In: Proceedings of the 21st Workshop on Privacy in the Electronic Society, pp. 181–196 (2022)
14. easylist: easylist cookie github repository. https://github.com/easylist/easylist. Accessed 30-08-2025
15. edgi-govdata-archiving/wayback: `search_calls_per_second` needs to be dialed down. https://github.com/edgi-govdata-archiving/wayback/issues/137. Accessed 12-01-2026
16. European Comission: Proposal for a regulation of the european parliament and of the council amending regulations (eu) 2016/679, (eu) 2018/1724, (eu) 2018/1725, (eu) 2023/2854 and directives 2002/58/ec, (eu) 2022/2555 and (eu) 2022/2557 as regards the simplification of the digital legislative framework, and repealing regulations (eu) 2018/1807, (eu) 2019/1150, (eu) 2022/868, and directive (eu) 2019/1024 (digital omnibus). https://eur-lex.europa.eu/legal-content/EN/TXT/?uri=CELEX:52025PC0837 (2026). Accessed 12-06-2026
17. European Court of Justice: Peter pammer v reederei karl schlüter gmbh & co. kg (c-585/08) and hotel alpenhof gesmbh v oliver heller (c-144/09) (2010). https://eur-lex.europa.eu/legal-content/EN/TXT/PDF/?uri=CELEX:62008CJ0585. Accessed 22-04-2026
18. European Data Protection Board: Guidelines 3/2018 on the territorial scope of the gdpr (article 3) (2019). https://www.edpb.europa.eu/our-work-tools/our-documents/guidelines/guidelines-32018-territorial-scope-gdpr-article-3-version_en. Accessed 22-04-2026
19. European Data Protection Board: Adopted 1 guidelines 2/2023 on technical scope of art. 5(3) of eprivacy directive (2023). https://www.edpb.europa.eu/our-work-tools/our-documents/guidelines/guidelines-22023-technical-scope-art-53-eprivacy-directive_en. Accessed 07-01-2026
20. European Data Protection Board: Report of the work undertaken by the cookie banner taskforce (2023). https://www.edpb.europa.eu/system/files/2023-01/edpb_20230118_report_cookie_banner_taskforce_en.pdf. Accessed 8-01-2026
21. Fruchter, N., Miao, H., Stevenson, S., Balebako, R.: Variations in tracking in relation to geographic location (2015). arXiv:1506.04103 arXiv preprint

22. Garante per la protezione dei dati personali: Linee guida cookie e altri strumenti di tracciamento (2021). https://www.garanteprivacy.it/web/guest/home/docweb/-/docweb-display/docweb/9677876. Accessed 30-08-2025
23. Google: Helping publishers recover lost revenue from ad blocking (2018). https://blog.google/technology/ads/helping-publishers-recover-lost-revenue-ad-blocking/. Accessed 30-01-2025
24. Google: Funding choices has moved (2024). https://support.google.com/fundingchoices/answer/9010669. Accessed 30-01-2025
25. Google Ad Manager: Helping publishers manage consent with funding choices (2024). https://blog.google/products/admanager/helping-publishers-manage-consent-funding-choices/. Accessed 30-01-2025
26. Gundelach, R., Herrmann, D.: Cookiescanner: an automated tool for detecting and evaluating gdpr consent notices on websites. In: Proceedings of the 18th International Conference on Availability, Reliability and Security, pp. 1–8 (2023)
27. Habib, H., Li, M., Young, E., Cranor, L.: "Okay, whatever": an evaluation of cookie consent interfaces. In: Proceedings of the 2022 CHI Conference on Human Factors in Computing Systems, pp. 1–27 (2022)
28. Hantke, F., Calzavara, S., Wilhelm, M., Rabitti, A., Stock, B.: You call this archaeology? evaluating web archives for reproducible web security measurements. In: Proceedings of the 2023 ACM SIGSAC Conference on Computer and Communications Security, pp. 3168–3182 (2023)
29. Hantke, F., Snyder, P., Haddadi, H., Stock, B.: Web execution bundles: Reproducible, accurate, and archivable web measurements (2025). arXiv:2501.15911 arXiv preprint
30. Hausner, P., Gertz, M.: Dark patterns in the interaction with cookie banners. Position paper at the workshop "what can chi do about dark patterns?" at the chi conference on human factors in computing systems (chi'21), 5 pages (2021)
31. Hils, M., Woods, D.W., Böhme, R.: Measuring the emergence of consent management on the web. In: Proceedings of the ACM Internet Measurement Conference, pp. 317–332 (2020)
32. HTTPArchive: Httparchive (2025). https://httparchive.org/. Accessed 05-01-2026
33. Internet Archive: Wayback machine (2026). https://web.archive.org/. Accessed 9-01-2026
34. Jha, N., Trevisan, M., Mellia, M., Fernandez, D., Irarrazaval, R.: Privacy policies and consent management platforms: growth and users' interactions over time. ACM Trans. Web **19**(3), 1–25 (2025)
35. Kampanos, G., Shahandashti, S.F.: Accept all: The landscape of cookie banners in Greece and the UK. In: IFIP International Conference on ICT Systems Security and Privacy Protection, pp. 213–227. Springer (2021)
36. Khandelwal, R., Nayak, A., Harkous, H., Fawaz, K.: Cookieenforcer: automated cookie notice analysis and enforcement (2022). arXiv:2204.04221 arXiv preprint
37. Kirkman, D., Vaniea, K., Woods, D.W.: Darkdialogs: automated detection of 10 dark patterns on cookie dialogs. In: 2023 IEEE 8th European Symposium on Security and Privacy (EuroS&P), pp. 847–867. IEEE (2023)
38. Kretschmer, M., Pennekamp, J., Wehrle, K.: Cookie banners and privacy policies: measuring the impact of the gdpr on the web. ACM Trans. Web (TWEB) **15**(4), 1–42 (2021)
39. Krisam, C., Dietmann, H., Volkamer, M., Kulyk, O.: Dark patterns in the wild: review of cookie disclaimer designs on top 500 German websites. In: Proceedings of the 2021 European Symposium on Usable Security, pp. 1–8 (2021)

40. Kusk, K., Nouwens, M.: How website owners use consent management platforms: an interview study. In: Proceedings of the Extended Abstracts of the CHI Conference on Human Factors in Computing Systems, pp. 1–7 (2025)
41. Leenes, R., Kosta, E.: Taming the cookie monster with dutch law–a tale of regulatory failure. Comput. Law Secur. Rev. **31** (03 2015) (2015)
42. Lerner, A., Simpson, A.K., Kohno, T., Roesner, F.: Internet jones and the raiders of the lost trackers: an archaeological study of web tracking from 1996 to. In: 25th USENIX Security Symposium (USENIX Security 16 (2016)
43. Libert, T., Graves, L., Nielsen, R.: Changes in third-party content on european news websites after gdpr. University of Oxford, Tech. rep. (2018)
44. Linden, T., Khandelwal, R., Harkous, H., Fawaz, K.: The privacy policy landscape after the gdpr (2018). arXiv:1809.08396 arXiv preprint
45. Légifrance: Délibération de la formation restreinte n°san-2021-023 du 31 décembre 2021 concernant les sociétés x et y (2021). https://www.legifrance.gouv.fr/cnil/id/CNILTEXT000044840062. Accessed 09-01-2026
46. Légifrance: Délibération de la formation restreinte n°san-2021-024 du 31décembre 2021 concernant la société x (2021). https://www.legifrance.gouv.fr/cnil/id/CNILTEXT000044840532?isSuggest=true. Accessed 09-01-2026
47. Matte, C., Bielova, N., Santos, C.: Do cookie banners respect my choice?: Measuring legal compliance of banners from iab Europe's transparency and consent framework. In: 2020 IEEE Symposium on Security and Privacy (SP), pp. 791–809. IEEE (2020)
48. Mehrnezhad, M.: A cross-platform evaluation of privacy notices and tracking practices. In: 2020 IEEE European Symposium on Security and Privacy Workshops (EuroS&PW), pp. 97–106. IEEE (2020)
49. metamorfosilab: Cookies-consent github repository. https://github.com/MetamorfosiLab/cookies-consent?tab=readme-ov-file. Accessed 30-08-2025
50. Morel, V., Santos, C., Lintao, Y., Human, S.: Your consent is worth 75 euros a year-measurement and lawfulness of cookie paywalls. In: Proceedings of the 21st Workshop on Privacy in the Electronic Society, pp. 213–218 (2022)
51. Nikiforakis, N., et al.: You are what you include: large-scale evaluation of remote javascript inclusions. In: Proceedings of the 2012 ACM Conference on Computer and Communications Security, pp. 736–747 (2012)
52. Nouwens, M., Kristensen, J.B., Maalt, K., Bagge, R.: A cross-country analysis of gdpr cookie banners and flexible methods for scraping them. In: Proceedings of the 2025 CHI Conference on Human Factors in Computing Systems, pp. 1–28 (2025)
53. Nouwens, M., Liccardi, I., Veale, M., Karger, D., Kagal, L.: Dark patterns after the gdpr: scraping consent pop-ups and demonstrating their influence. In: Proceedings of the 2020 CHI Conference on Human Factors in Computing Systems, pp. 1–13. (2020)
54. noyb: noyb aims to end "cookie banner terror" and issues more than 500 gdpr complaints (2021). https://noyb.eu/en/noyb-aims-end-cookie-banner-terror-and-issues-more-500-gdpr-complaints. Accessed 31-08-2025
55. noyb: noyb files 422 formal gdpr complaints on nerve-wrecking "cookie banners" (2021). https://noyb.eu/en/noyb-files-422-formal-gdpr-complaints-nerve-wrecking-cookie-banners. Accessed 30-08-2025
56. noyb: 226 complaints lodged against deceptive cookie banners (2022). https://noyb.eu/en/226-complaints-lodged-against-deceptive-cookie-banners. Accessed 30-08-2025
57. noyb: Consent banner report. https://noyb.eu/sites/default/files/2024-07/noyb_Cookie_Report_2024.pdf (2023). Accessed 30-08-2025

58. noyb: Gdpr decision database (2025). https://gdprhub.eu/. Accessed 09-01-2026
59. Offical Journal of the European Union: Directive 2002/58/ec of the european parliament and of the council of 12 july 2002 concerning the processing of personal data and the protection of privacy in the electronic communications sector (directive on privacy and electronic communications) (2002). https://eur-lex.europa.eu/eli/dir/2002/58/oj/eng. Accessed 9-01-2026
60. Offical Journal of the European Union: Regulation (eu) 2016/679 of the european parliament and of the council of 27 april 2016 on the protection of natural persons with regard to the processing of personal data and on the free movement of such data, and repealing directive 95/46/ec (general data protection regulation) (2016). https://eur-lex.europa.eu/legal-content/EN/TXT/PDF/?uri=CELEX:32016R0679. Accessed 9-01-2026
61. OneTrust: Onetrust solutions. https://www.onetrust.com/. Accessed 30-08-2025
62. Rasaii, A., Singh, S., Gosain, D., Gasser, O.: Exploring the cookieverse: a multi-perspective analysis of web cookies. In: International Conference on Passive and Active Network Measurement, pp. 623–651. Springer (2023)
63. Roth, S., Barron, T., Calzavara, S., Nikiforakis, N., Stock, B.: Complex security policy? a longitudinal analysis of deployed content security policies. In: Proceedings of the 27th Network and Distributed System Security Symposium (NDSS) (2020)
64. Sanchez-Rola, I., Dell'Amico, M., Kotzias, P., Balzarotti, D., Bilge, L., Vervier, P.A., Santos, I.: Can i opt out yet? gdpr and the global illusion of cookie control. In: Proceedings of the 2019 ACM Asia Conference on Computer and Communications Security, pp. 340–351 (2019)
65. Santos, C., Nouwens, M., Toth, M., Bielova, N., Roca, V.: Consent management platforms under the gdpr: processors and/or controllers? In: Annual Privacy Forum, pp. 47–69. Springer (2021)
66. Sheil, A., Malone, D.: Fianán, cuacha: Irish cookie banners. In: 2022 33rd Irish Signals and Systems Conference (ISSC), pp. 1–8. IEEE (2022)
67. Soe, T.H., Nordberg, O.E., Guribye, F., Slavkovik, M.: Circumvention by design-dark patterns in cookie consent for online news outlets. In: Proceedings of the 11th nordic conference on human-computer interaction: Shaping experiences, shaping society, pp. 1–12 (2020)
68. Stock, B., Johns, M., Steffens, M., Backes, M.: How the web tangled itself: Uncovering the history of client-side web (in) security. In: 26th USENIX Security Symposium (USENIX Security 17), pp. 971–987 (2017)
69. Toth, M., Bielova, N., Roca, V.: On dark patterns and manipulation of website publishers by cmps. Proceedings on Privacy Enhancing Technologies **2022**(3), 478–497 (2022)
70. Trevisan, M., Traverso, S., Bassi, E., Mellia, M., et al.: 4 years of eu cookie law: Results and lessons learned. Proceedings on Privacy Enhancing Technologies **2019**(2), 126–145 (2019)
71. Van Eijk, R., Asghari, H., Winter, P., Narayanan, A.: The impact of user location on cookie notices (inside and outside of the european union) (2021). arXiv:2110.09832 arXiv preprint
72. Warberg, L., Lefrere, V., Cheyre, C., Acquisti, A.: Trends in privacy dialog design after the gdpr: the impact of industry and government actions. In: Proceedings of the 22nd Workshop on Privacy in the Electronic Society, pp. 107–121 (2023)
73. Wesselkamp, V., Fouad, I., Santos, C., Boussad, Y., Bielova, N., Legout, A.: In-depth technical and legal analysis of tracking on health related websites with ernie extension. In: Proceedings of the 20th Workshop on Workshop on Privacy in the Electronic Society, pp. 151–166 (2021)

74. Zhang, M., Meng, W., Zhou, Y., Ren, K.: Cschecker: Revisiting gdpr and ccpa compliance of cookie banners on the web. In: Proceedings of the IEEE/ACM 46th International Conference on Software Engineering, pp. 1–12 (2024)

Privacy Technologies Beyond Anonymization and Security

A Rights-First Path to Privacy by Architecture: The Case for Advanced Digital Protection Control (ADPC)

Soheil Human[1,2,3,4](✉)

[1] Sustainable Computing Lab, Vienna University of Economics and Business, Vienna, Austria
soheil.human@wu.ac.at
[2] Human Rights and Technology Research Group, IT:U, Linz, Austria
[3] Faculty of Computer Science, University of Vienna, Vienna, Austria
[4] AI Futures Lab on Rights and Justice, TU Delft, Delft, The Netherlands

Abstract. Contemporary digital environments rely heavily on repetitive notice-and-click mechanisms for obtaining consent, despite decades of legal, technical, and human-computer interaction research documenting the limits of banner-centred approaches. For users, this practice is demanding, manipulable, difficult to remember, and exclusionary; for controllers, costly and fragile. The problem is not merely poor graphical user interface design, but missing Internet architecture: there is no widely adopted, legally enforceable, bidirectional layer for communicating privacy information, requests, decisions, and records in machine-readable form. The European Commission's 2025 Digital Omnibus proposal brought this architectural deficit into legislative focus: a provision, initially labelled Article 88b GDPR, proposed automated and machine-readable means for expressing consent and objection online. Whatever the provision's numbering, wording, scope, legal status, or ultimate fate, the durable question is whether the European Union can move privacy communication from controller-side banners toward standardised, bidirectional, automated and machine-readable mechanisms. This paper argues that Advanced Digital Protection Control (ADPC) provides the closest fit among available mechanisms for implementing such a layer and is sufficiently developed to address technology-readiness concerns: not as another graphical user interface, but as a technology-neutral layer for machine-readable privacy communication across web, mobile-application, AI-mediated, IoT, immersive, pervasive, and future environments. It can support the communication of legally required information, rights-relevant requests, and decisions such as consent, refusal, withdrawal, and objection, as well as the generation of records reflecting the rights grammar of the GDPR and ePrivacy framework. Properly implemented through open, inclusive, and interoperable standardisation in the public interest, ADPC would make privacy the first mature test case for a broader rights-first digital infrastructure: inclusive, enforceable, and capable of supporting human-compatible digital transformation, sustainable economic growth, digital sovereignty, and socio-economic and democratic resilience.

F. Pallas et al. (Eds.): APF 2026, LNCS 16847, pp. 201–225, 2026.
https://doi.org/10.1007/978-3-032-35899-8_10

Keywords: privacy by architecture · ADPC · rights-first

1 Introduction

Several years into the operation of the General Data Protection Regulation (GDPR), a difficult question remains: why, after years of regulatory reform, technical standardisation, design research, and enforcement activity, does online privacy still depend so heavily on repetitive banners that most users neither meaningfully understand nor effectively manage? Empirical and conceptual research has repeatedly shown that current banner-based consent practice burdens users with excessive reading, repeated decisions, and opaque trade-offs, while leaving controllers with compliance mechanisms that are costly, fragmented, and often hostile to usability [1,16,18,26,27]. The resulting situation undermines the conditions under which consent, withdrawal, and objection are supposed to operate as rights-enabling mechanisms under European Union data protection law [8,14].

This paper argues that the persistent failure of cookie-banner-centred privacy communication is best understood as an architectural deficiency. The dominant model assigns control over privacy-related data, procedures, records, and graphical user interfaces to controllers, while users are rarely given reliable memory of prior choices, robust routes for revocation, or infrastructural means to obtain cognitive, contextual, and collective support [12,14]. Privacy remains nominally individualised in law but structurally dependent on controller-controlled graphical user interfaces in practice.

The Commission's 2025 Digital Omnibus proposal gave this architectural deficiency a concrete legislative expression. The provision, initially labelled Article 88b GDPR, would require online mechanisms to enable *consenting*, *refusal*, and *objection* by automated and machine-readable means, and would require controllers to respect those choices once standards are available; a rights-complete implementation should also support *withdrawal* [4]. The label "Article 88b" is used here only to identify the Commission's initial numbering in that proposal. It is not used to describe any subsequent numbering, wording, scope, or legal status, and it should not be read as assuming enactment [6]. The enduring issue is not the label itself, but the regulatory design problem it names: how European Union can move privacy communication from improvised page-level dialogue boxes toward a stable user-empowering communication layer.

The central claim is that *privacy by design* has too often been reduced to an abstract compliance label rather than operationalised through technical and institutional architecture. For privacy by design to be meaningful, *privacy by default* must also become technically practicable: privacy-relevant communication, memory, and control should not remain scattered across controller-side graphical user interfaces, but should be embedded as a standardised, rights-enabling layer of Internet and software architecture. This is what this paper calls *privacy by architecture*. The latter is not a substitute for Article 25 GDPR. It denotes the embedding of rights-relevant communication capabilities into the Internet and software layers through which privacy choices are actually requested, made, recorded, revised, and enforced. This paper argues that Advanced Digital Protection Control (ADPC)[1] is the most legally and technically congruent implementation path for a European, rights-first approach because it was designed to express a richer range of consent, refusal, withdrawal, and objection choices than binary opt-out signals, and because its technology-neutral communication model can operate beyond browsers and web pages across browser extensions, mobile and desktop applications, operating systems, connected devices, immersive environments, AI-mediated agents, and future digital systems [12,21,22].

The following sections move from diagnosis to implementation. They first explain why banner-centred practice fails users and controllers, then develop the architectural reading of the problem, situate the provisions initially labelled Articles 88a and 88b GDPR as one legislative trigger for machine-readable privacy choice, assess ADPC as a rights-communication layer, and derive lessons from P3P, DNT, and GPC before turning to safeguards for European standardisation and closing with a brief discussion of wider socio-economic dimensions, including digital sovereignty, sustainability, and resilience.

2 Why the Current Notice-and-Click Model Fails

2.1 Cognitive Overload, Habituation, and Weak Comprehension

The core difficulty with current banner-based practice is not that users are unwilling to care about privacy, but that the dominant graphical user interface model makes caring operationally unrealistic. Users are expected to inspect layered notices, infer technical consequences, compare legal bases, and remember choices across many services, devices, and moments of interaction. Yet research has long shown that privacy self-management is constrained by limited attention, time, expertise, and memory [1,23]. The result is precisely the gap between formal rights and practical capacity that can be described as a persistent failure to empower end-users in meaningful ways [14,16].

Two empirical patterns are especially relevant. First, privacy policies and consent notices are rarely read in full, and even less often meaningfully interpreted in context [26]. Secondly, repeated exposure itself degrades engagement: users become habituated to pop-ups and default to dismissal or acceptance in order to reach desired content quickly [2]. This is the opposite of what a rights-enabling consent environment should achieve. Instead of making reflection easier, repetition converts attention into noise.

The problem is compounded by graphical user interface manipulation. Consent banners frequently rely on asymmetrical button design, hidden settings, fragmented opt-out paths, and default choices that channel users toward the

[1] ADPC was originally introduced as Advanced Data Protection Control. This paper uses Advanced Digital Protection Control to reflect the mechanism's broader development toward digital-rights-related communication beyond data protection alone; both terms refer to the same mechanism.

controller-preferred outcome [10,18,25]. These patterns are not marginal defects. They have become a constitutive feature of a design environment in which the controller typically defines the interaction, the terminology, the timing of the request, and the record of the response. Under those conditions, the formal existence of consent is a weak indicator of meaningful agency.

2.2 Consent Fatigue, Missing Memory, and Ineffective Withdrawal

A second failure concerns temporal continuity. European Union data protection law does not only protect the moment of consent. It also protects the continuing ability to revise, withdraw, and object [8]. Yet the notice-and-click model rarely equips users with records or graphical user interfaces that make later action practical. Users seldom receive a durable receipt that links the information shown at a given moment to the decision subsequently made. Nor are they generally provided with cross-site tools that allow prior choices to be inspected and changed in one place [14,16].

This has a direct normative consequence: the right to withdraw consent is often formally present but functionally frustrated. If users cannot later reconstruct where they consented, to what, under which wording, or on which device, then the legal right exists under conditions that make its exercise unusually burdensome. Therefore, even modest assistant systems capable of recording prior choices could arguably represent a significant advance over the current state of play [16]. The broader point is architectural: rights that depend on memory should not be left unsupported where the surrounding ecosystem is fully instrumented and automated on the controller side.

2.3 Why Controllers Also Face Structural Difficulty

These failures are not borne by users alone. Controllers, especially those seeking lawful and user-friendly practice, must navigate a fragmented landscape of evolving legal expectations, technical implementations, and vendor-driven consent infrastructures. The Digital Omnibus proposal itself recognises that online service providers incur considerable costs designing compliant banners, while users experience significant fatigue from repeated consent requests [4]. In other words, the dominant model is not merely rights-weak; it is also operationally and economically wasteful.

Cookie paywalls illustrate the point. In response to regulatory pressure, some publishers have shifted from simple banners to systems that monetise refusal or attempt to convert consent into a pricing choice. Morel et al. show both the legal complexity and the unevenness of this landscape, even within Central Europe [24]. Controllers are thereby pushed toward increasingly elaborate graphical user interface engineering not because this improves rights practice, but because the Internet lacks a more stable infrastructure for expressing privacy choices in standardised form.

The rise of consent management platforms (CMPs) has not solved this structural difficulty. Such systems can help controllers operationalise notices and preference collection, but they do so within the same controller-centred model and therefore remain bound to the limitations of page-level interaction design. They also create a continual tension between legal compliance, advertising revenue, and user experience, a tension that is visible in the persistence of manipulative banner design and the legal controversy surrounding industry-standard consent frameworks [10,27]. In short, controllers face real implementation burdens, but those burdens arise largely because the Internet still lacks a normalised privacy communication layer that would allow compliant requests and responses to travel to and through the user's software rather than through ad hoc banner choreography.

2.4 One-Size-Fits-All Graphical User Interfaces and Vulnerable Groups

The banner model is particularly problematic for users whose capacities, needs, or contexts differ from the imagined average user. The *one-size-fits-all* logic of mainstream graphical user interfaces for consent ignores human diversity and falls especially harshly on those already structurally disadvantaged [18]. Children, persons with disabilities, elderly users, and people navigating websites in unfamiliar languages are not merely edge cases; they reveal the inadequacy of privacy systems that presume each individual will repeatedly manage complex choices alone [14].

The issue is not only *cognitive*; it is also *collective* and *contextual*. Privacy choices are shaped by social support, expertise, urgency, language, and setting. A request that might be manageable in one context can be unreasonable in another. Likewise, some decisions affect not only the user but also other people whose data or interests are implicated. Banner-based practice remains overwhelmingly individualised and context-insensitive, even though the literature increasingly describes privacy and *consenting* as *socio-cognitive actions* with *cognitive*, *collective*, and *contextual* dimensions [14,18,19]. That mismatch indicates that the underlying problem is deeper than graphical user interface ornamentation.

This point should not be reduced to a *generic call for accessibility*. What is missing is a layered support environment: graphical user interfaces that adapt to human limits, persistent records that reduce memory burdens, and pathways through which trusted others can support decision-making where the user so chooses. An account of "humans [plural] in the loop" is especially important here because it reinterprets privacy choice as something that may legitimately involve *collective* and *contextual support* rather than solitary clicking [14]. Once that perspective is taken seriously, the *one-size-fits-all banner* begins to look not only inconvenient but conceptually misaligned with the kinds of *human action* that privacy law is supposed to protect (Table 1).

3 The Problem Is Architectural, Not Merely a Matter of Graphical User Interfaces

The failures above could be misread as evidence that controllers simply need *better banner design*. That conclusion is too narrow. The deeper issue is that, at Internet scale, privacy communication still occurs mostly inside controller-controlled websites and applications, rather than through a bidirectional communication layer based on an Internet protocol, with interaction and user decision-making occurring through graphical user interfaces and related mechanisms on the user side. Even with improved banner design, within the current controller-centric environment, the controller not only asks the question, but also stores the answer, structures the choice environment, and decides whether later withdrawal is easy, hidden, or partially ignored [12, 14].

Table 1. Recurring failures of banner-centred privacy practice

Dimension	Users	Controllers
Cognitive	Information overload, habituation, weak comprehension, poor recall of prior decisions [2, 26]	Repeated need to design and maintain legally and technically complex graphical user interfaces for privacy [4]
Temporal	Withdrawal and updating are difficult without durable records or unified graphical user interfaces [16]	Continuing compliance depends on fragmented privacy infrastructures and repeated graphical user interface interventions [24]
Social/contextual	One-size-fits-all graphical user interfaces neglect diverse capacities, languages, vulnerabilities, and support needs [14, 18]	Controllers cannot easily provide context-sensitive, user-side, or collectively supported decision environments within current architecture [12]
Power asymmetry	Controllers define data, procedures, and graphical user interface timing; users operate inside controller-controlled environments [10, 14]	Even well-intentioned controllers remain dependent on page-level *consent engineering* instead of standardised communication channels [21]

Even with improved banner design, the current architecture prevents three things that a rights-enabling system should make normal. First, it prevents stable user-side memory. Users rarely keep a reliable history of privacy notices encountered, options shown, or choices previously made [16]. Secondly, it prevents structured user-side assistance. If all relevant data and procedures remain inside the controller-controlled graphical user interface, then browsers, browser extensions, operating systems, trusted organisations and individuals (e.g., guardians, parents, and peers), and assistive tools cannot easily help users interpret requests, remember prior decisions, apply contextual rules, or make supported decisions [14]. Thirdly, it prevents standardised auditability. Without a common machine-readable channel, both compliance assessment and rights exercise remain dependent on ad hoc inspection of graphical user interfaces rather than verifiable communication traces.

This is why the move toward what this paper calls *privacy by architecture* matters. *Privacy by design* remains indispensable, but it has too often been interpreted as a controller-side compliance label or organisational process rather than as a technical and operational architecture. For *privacy by design* to be meaningful in practice, *privacy by default* must also become technically practicable. Default protection cannot be achieved if privacy-relevant communication, memory, and control remain scattered across controller-specific page elements and graphical user interfaces. *Privacy by architecture*, as used here, means embedding those capabilities into the infrastructural layers through which users interact with digital services in the first place. The idea is not abstract. Users already manage permissions for microphones, cameras, or notifications through browser- or operating-system-level settings and graphical user interfaces. A similar layer for privacy requests, decisions, and records would rebalance control by moving the recording, presentation, and management of many choices away from controller-specific page elements and toward user-side software operating through standardised communication channels [12,22].

The distinction is important for doctrinal reasons as well. Article 25 GDPR obliges controllers to implement data protection by design and by default, but it does not itself create a standardised, interoperable means through which users can communicate choices across services. A controller can therefore satisfy some internal-by-design duties while the surrounding ecosystem still leaves the user dependent on banner-by-banner negotiation. *Privacy by architecture* fills this gap at a different layer. It concerns the existence of common channels, shared interaction expectations, and machine-readable records through which rights can actually be represented and travel. In that sense, a machine-readable choice provision should be read less as a refinement of Article 25 than as an *infrastructural complement* that helps make Article 25 more practicable in networked environments.

Once framed in this way, the value of user-side assistant systems also becomes clearer. It has been argued that privacy management requires tools capable of remembering prior decisions, representing them coherently, and offering cognitive, collective, and contextual support [11,16,20]. Those tools cannot be realised effectively if the relevant requests and records remain trapped inside controller-side websites. The absence of architecture therefore constrains not only present-day usability, but also the development of future support systems that could make privacy rights more realistic for ordinary users.

This architectural reading also shows why the issue is broader than a narrow debate about *cookies*. Banner fatigue is the visible symptom of a missing communication layer. As has been argued in more recent work, the stakes extend beyond *privacy* and *data protection* narrowly construed to a broader field of *digital protection* in which personal data can be used to influence behaviour, restructure agency, and produce cumulative effects on democratic and social life [14]. If the Internet and wider digital environments lack a rights-relevant communication architecture for consenting, objecting, and withdrawing consent as *socio-cognitive* actions, and for the broader exchange of rights-related data, information, requests, and decisions needed for rights exercise, compliance, and auditing, then the gap is infrastructural, not cosmetic.

4 A Legislative Trigger: Terminal-Equipment Rules and Machine-Readable Choice

The Digital Omnibus proposal, presented by the European Commission in November 2025, sought to simplify parts of the Union's digital acquis while preserving a high level of protection [4]. Within that larger package, the proposed amendments to the GDPR and the ePrivacy framework were especially significant because they addressed a longstanding structural problem: the split between terminal-equipment rules under Article 5(3) ePrivacy and subsequent personal-data processing under the GDPR, together with the fatigue generated by current consent banners [4].

As a legislative proposal, rather than enacted law, the text entered a process in which the numbering, wording, scope, and legal status of the provisions could change. Unless otherwise stated, "Articles 88a and 88b" in this paper refer to the Commission's initial numbering in the 2025 proposal, not to any final legislative outcome. No claim is made that these labels, or the provisions attached to them, would survive the legislative process unchanged or become law. The analysis therefore concerns the design idea placed on the legislative agenda: an automated, machine-readable, rights-relevant communication layer for privacy choices. That design idea will remain relevant even if the proposed numbering changes, the text is revised, or a comparable reform is pursued in a later legislative cycle.

The legislative background matters. The EU has discussed browser- or software-mediated privacy choice for many years. The Commission's 2017 proposal for an ePrivacy Regulation already contemplated user choice management through browser settings, while the broader history of Internet privacy protocols repeatedly returned to the same ambition: moving privacy preference expression away from purely ad hoc page-level graphical user interfaces and toward more standardised, machine-readable forms [3,4]. What the Digital Omnibus proposal changed was that the idea was no longer framed only as a technical option or regulatory aspiration. It was translated into a specific amendment path within the GDPR itself. That gave the provision initially numbered Article 88b a practical importance that earlier debates often lacked.

Two proposed provisions matter here. Proposed Article 88a GDPR would move the consent requirement for storing or accessing personal data on the terminal equipment of natural persons into the GDPR itself, while preserving specified exceptions such as transmission, explicitly requested services, certain audience measurement operations for the controller's own use, and security-related processing [4]. Crucially, the proposed text also adds safeguards designed to reduce repetitive pressure: refusal must be easy, repeated requests should not recur while a valid choice remains in place, and controllers should not re-ask for six months after a refusal in the absence of changed circumstances [4]. For present purposes, Article 88a matters because it helps shape part of the legal context in which machine-readable choice expression would operate.

Proposed Article 88b then introduces the enabling layer. In simplified terms, it would require controllers to ensure that their online graphical user interfaces allow data subjects to provide consent by *automated* and *machine-readable* means and to decline consent, or exercise the Article 21 *right to object* to direct marketing, by similarly automated and machine-readable means [4]. Controllers would be required to respect these choices. The proposal also asks the Commission to request *European harmonised standards* and foresees staged obligations, including later obligations for large browser providers to provide the necessary technical means [4].

That provision should be read carefully. The proposed layer would change the route through which choices are communicated: controllers would need to receive and respect standardised communication mechanisms, commonly referred to as *signals*; software providers would need to enable their usable and legally effective operation; and supervisory authorities would need to assess compliance where the decisive interaction occurs partly outside the controller's page. Read in this way, the provision creates a legislative opening for a standardised rights-communication layer.

A rights-first reading also sets limits. The new layer should replace, rather than decorate, the structurally deficient banner layer. A single global opt-out flag would leave many banners, paywalls, dark patterns, and forms of controller dominance intact [10,24]. Nor should manipulation migrate from websites into browsers, operating systems, or other user agents. A European standard should therefore reject consent-by-default, privileged acceptance pathways, and broad carve-outs that preserve the pressure the machine-readable layer is meant to reduce.

The proposed timelines and exceptions illustrate the same tension. Staged duties may support rollout, but could also make implementation overly browser-centric or too slow; the media-service-provider exception shows the pull of sectoral compromise [4]. These tensions make the choice of standard important. A *thin signal* would not survive them well, whereas a richer mechanism could keep the legal purpose of the reform visible during implementation.

The significance of the machine-readable choice layer is therefore not simply that it promises *better settings*. It opens a different layer of communication: a standardised channel through which user-side software can receive requests, express choices, and keep durable records. The Commission's explanatory memorandum frames this in terms of automated and machine-readable indications of individual choice and mentions standards connecting browsers, websites, apps, and web services [4]. In effect, the proposal began to supply a legal basis for *privacy by architecture*.

The EDPB and EDPS correctly recognise the importance of this move. In Joint Opinion 2/2026, they strongly welcome the provision initially proposed as Article 88b and emphasise that technical means can simplify compliance, support online choices, improve their effectiveness, and reduce cookie fatigue by removing the need to restate preferences on every website [5]. The Opinion is equally important because it does not treat machine-readable choice as self-justifying. Automated communication can deepen user control or merely reorganise it under a different graphical user interface. The relevant question is whether it preserves meaningful refusal, informed choice, broad applicability, and effective enforcement [5].

The design choice is therefore decisive. If machine-readable privacy communication is reduced to a convenient opt-out switch, it will not carry the richer structure of European Union law: prior, specific, informed, and revocable consent, together with rights of withdrawal and objection [7,8]. The question is whether the new layer becomes a genuine step toward rights-enabling architecture or merely a thinner banner by another name.

5 ADPC as a Machine-Readable Rights-Communication Layer

5.1 ADPC as a Communication Mechanism

ADPC is a technical specification designed to communicate, inter alia, privacy- and consenting-related information, requests, preferences, and decisions between user-side software, such as browsers or operating systems, and online services, such as websites or mobile applications. First specified in 2021, it should be read as a mature starting point rather than a closed endpoint: a European standardisation mandate would still require updating, conformance testing, and alignment with the final legal text [12,22].

In practical terms, ADPC enables a service to send a machine-readable list of requests to a user agent, and enables the user agent to respond with consent, refusal, withdrawal, or objection. Communication can occur through HTTP headers and JavaScript APIs, and either side can initiate the exchange depending on context [12,22]. Although most often discussed over web technologies, the model can be adapted to other protocols and device environments.

A simple example illustrates the non-binary character of the mechanism. A user-side agent could accept strictly first-party, aggregate audience measurement; refuse third-party advertising cookies; object to direct marketing; and request a renewed prompt only when a new purpose or controller is introduced. This is not a global yes/no switch, but a structured decision profile that can be presented, remembered, revised, and evidenced on the user side.

Under a banner-centred model, the controller designs the graphical user interface, records the user's answer, and often controls the route to withdrawal. Under an ADPC-style model, the service transmits structured information and requests to the user's software; the browser or comparable client can present them consistently, apply the user's choices, keep a durable record, and allow later review. This is a redistribution of procedural control, not merely a cleaner graphical user interface.

That redistribution makes ADPC especially relevant for inclusive and assistive use. Once requests and records are available at the user side, the same infrastructure can support dashboards, contextual rules, language adaptation, accessibility tooling, or trusted assistance where appropriate and lawfully configured [14,16]. ADPC is therefore not merely a signal. It is a communication mechanism that enables a new layer while leaving enforcement, ethics, governance, and usable design indispensable.

5.2 Technology Readiness and Standardisation Maturity

The case for a machine-readable choice layer should not be dismissed as technologically premature. ADPC has been specified, analysed within the broader family of data protection and consenting communication mechanisms, and compared with related mechanisms such as the Global Privacy Control (GPC) in interdisciplinary privacy-engineering research [3,12,21,22]. Its core web implementation relies on familiar components: HTTP-based exchange, JavaScript APIs, user-agent settings, structured request descriptors, and records of responses. The remaining challenge is not to invent an entirely new technical paradigm, but to standardise, test, govern, adopt, and enforce it.

Nor is the architecture limited to conventional web pages. Later ADPC-IoT work shows how the same idea can extend to connected-device environments, where repeated screen-based banners are often impossible or inappropriate [13]. A durable European standard should therefore be grounded in mechanisms that can travel across browsers, applications, devices, ambient systems, and user-side assistants, rather than in a browser-only or website-only convention.

This is a technology-readiness argument, not a claim of completed deployment. Like any technical specification intended for legally significant use, ADPC requires open standardisation, ongoing security review, accessibility work, conformance testing, governance arrangements, and clear legal duties. These are implementation requirements for a mature proposal, not reasons to treat the technical layer as speculative or to retreat to banners. Legislative proposals mandating automated and machine-readable privacy choice should therefore be implemented with sufficient institutional support rather than postponed on technology-readiness grounds.

5.3 Functional Fit with Automated and Machine-Readable Choice

A European automated choice layer requires *automated* and *machine-readable* means for both giving and declining consent, and for exercising objection rights; the provision initially numbered Article 88b expresses that requirement in the Commission's 2025 proposal [4]. ADPC was built around precisely those capabilities. Its technical specification draws explicitly on the GDPR's provisions on *consenting* and *objecting*, as well as the ePrivacy context, and defines ways to express consent, refusal, withdrawal, and objection in machine-readable form [22]. On a functional level, this makes ADPC a particularly direct implementation candidate for any European standard that seeks to preserve those legal distinctions.

Equally important is how ADPC distributes control. Because requests and responses can be handled by user-side software, many decisions no longer have to be embedded inside page-level banners. This enables persistent records, more coherent graphical user interfaces across services, and the possibility of additional support layers such as privacy dashboards, user-side settings, trusted lists, and more advanced assistant systems [12,16]. The point is not to automate every decision away from the user, but to ensure that the user's software, rather than the controller's page design, becomes the primary location in which privacy choices are managed.

ADPC also reflects the *procedural richness* of European law more closely than simpler alternatives. It is *domain-specific* rather than purely global, can express *multiple requests* and *differentiated responses*, and can support both *general* and *specific signals* rather than only a *single binary* instruction [21]. That matters because the proposed provision is situated within a legal environment in which *consent* must remain *specific* and in which not all privacy decisions are *reducible* to the same action. A mechanism designed only for *one class of opt-out* request will struggle to carry the structure of GDPR- and ePrivacy-based choice.

This richer design also reduces the temptation to treat *standardisation* as synonymous with *simplification. Simpler is not always better* if simplicity is achieved by collapsing legally distinct acts into the same signal. European law differentiates, for good reason, between consenting to one purpose, refusing another, withdrawing what was previously granted, and objecting in settings where consent is not the operative legal basis. ADPC can reflect that plurality more faithfully than binary signals such as GPC because it was conceived as a communication framework rather than a unary switch [21,22].

5.4 A Rights-First and Law-First Design

The broader normative advantage of ADPC is that it starts from *rights* rather than from *advertising market conventions.* The EU should not reverse the relationship between law and technology by allowing *technical minimalism* to determine the scope of rights practice [12,21]. In a *rights-first* (and, in this case, *law-first*) approach, legal requirements define what kinds of communication and control need to be possible; technical specifications are then designed to carry those requirements. ADPC is better aligned with that logic than mechanisms that were designed around a narrower legal mandate and only later discussed for broader use.

5.5 What ADPC Would and Would Not Solve

ADPC should not be portrayed as a complete solution. Even a well-designed communication layer cannot, on its own, guarantee that controllers will adopt privacy-preserving business models, minimise data collection, or cease attempts to influence users through profiling and personalisation. Those remain questions of substantive law, enforcement, competition, market incentives, and institutional design [14,20,34]. What ADPC can do is narrower but still fundamental:

it can remove one entrenched obstacle to meaningful rights exercise, namely the lack of a common bidirectional channel for communicating and retaining privacy choices with user-side graphical user interfaces.

This distinction matters for enforcement and traceability. ADPC does not itself enforce the law, verify downstream data processing, or prove that a controller later complied with the choice it received. What it can provide is a more structured communication trace: the request descriptor, purposes, parties, chosen response, timing, specification version, and later withdrawal or objection can be logged or receipted in a consistent way. That trace can make compliance review less dependent on screenshots of banners and more dependent on auditable exchanges. But accountability still requires controller-side records, supervisory access, conformance testing, effective remedies, and sanctions.

For that reason, ADPC should be understood as enabling infrastructure. It can make better graphical user interface practice more achievable by moving much of the interaction to the user side, and it can make enforcement more realistic by producing clearer traces of what was requested and how the user responded [12,22]. It is not sufficient for justice, but it is highly relevant to whether justice can be operationalised at scale.

It is equally important that ADPC can coexist with human decision-making rather than replace it. The purpose of automation in the European setting should be to support users where repetition and complexity would otherwise undermine agency, not to conceal legally salient choices behind invisible defaults. Rich, user-side, configurable mechanisms allow different levels of involvement without collapsing privacy practice into either fully manual banner clicking or opaque automation [16,20]. Properly implemented, ADPC would support a more plural and human-compatible privacy environment, not a less human one.

6 What the EU Should Learn from P3P, DNT, and GPC

The promise and limits of machine-readable privacy choice become clearer when placed against earlier attempts to communicate privacy choices online. The history is not one of simple technological progress. It is a history of partial designs encountering weak incentives, conflicting business models, and incomplete legal support [3]. That history matters because it shows both why DNT failed and why GPC has gained more traction in the United States.

A useful starting point is the *Platform for Privacy Preferences Project* (P3P), a W3C initiative whose specification sought to make website privacy practices machine-readable so that browsers and other user agents could compare them with user preferences. In retrospect, P3P was conceptually ahead of its time but institutionally underpowered: it depended on truthful controller-side self-description, widespread browser support, and business incentives that never adequately aligned [3,30]. Even so, P3P remains relevant because it demonstrates that the basic ambition behind a European machine-readable choice layer – standardised, machine-readable privacy communication – is not new. What is new is the prospect of stronger legal anchoring.

6.1 DNT: a Simple Signal Without Sufficient Force

Do Not Track (DNT) was standardised by the W3C as a mechanism by which a browser could express a tracking preference through an HTTP header [32]. Its attraction was simplicity. A user or browser could send a machine-readable preference without negotiating service-by-service graphical user interfaces. Yet the same simplicity also exposed its weakness. DNT communicated a preference, but it did not itself create robust obligations or a sufficiently aligned ecosystem of recipients who were willing to honour it. The W3C note eventually acknowledged insufficient deployment and planned support [32]. As later analyses emphasised, DNT remained too dependent on voluntary uptake within a data-driven advertising environment that had strong incentives to ignore it [3].

The lesson is not that technical signals are futile. It is that signals without meaningful legal and institutional backing rarely transform entrenched market practice. DNT failed less because the idea of machine-readable privacy communication was misguided than because the surrounding modalities of regulation were misaligned [3].

DNT also highlights a second lesson that matters for the proposed European choice layer: a purely *global preference* is often too coarse. Even if more websites had chosen to honour DNT, the signal was always vulnerable to interpretive disagreement about what exactly counted as tracking, which actors were bound, and how conflicting page-level interactions should relate to the global preference. Those controversies did not simply slow adoption. They exposed the difficulty of building rich privacy practice around an undifferentiated signal. The EU should avoid repeating that mistake by assuming that one broad machine-readable expression can stand in for the more articulated legal structure of consent and objection under the GDPR.

6.2 GPC: Legal Support Matters

Global Privacy Control (GPC) demonstrates a different trajectory. Technically, GPC remains narrow: it is a single-value signal, communicated via HTTP or the DOM, requesting that websites or services *do not sell* or *share* personal information with *third parties* [31]. Its legal relevance stems from *California law.* The California Department of Justice explicitly describes GPC as a valid user-enabled global privacy control that covered businesses must honour as a request to stop the sale or sharing of personal information [29]. Enforcement practice has reinforced this position, including multistate action against businesses that failed to process opt-out requests submitted via GPC [28].

This is the central reason GPC has become more practically relevant than DNT. It is not simply the superiority of its engineering. It is the *presence of legal recognition* and enforcement. Zimmeck and Alicki's analysis of "do not sell" standardisation already located such signals within the CCPA's opt-out architecture [33]. For current European debates, that lesson should be welcomed rather than resisted: machine-readable privacy communication needs *legal support.*

At the same time, GPC's practical success should not be generalised into a comprehensive solution. California law asks a narrower question than the GDPR and the ePrivacy framework ask. It is primarily concerned with enabling consumers to *stop the sale* or *sharing* of personal information, not with expressing the fuller range of *"purpose-specific" permissions*, *refusals*, *withdrawals*, and *objections* that structure European law. GPC therefore shows that legal support can make a signal matter, but it also shows the limits of *designing a signal around a single legal action.*

6.3 GPC as a Lesson, Not a European Template

GPC's comparative success under California law does not make it an adequate template for a European machine-readable consent and objection layer. GPC was designed for an *opt-out* environment focused on the "sale" and "sharing" of personal information, and the W3C draft does not claim to cover every privacy right [31]. The European framework, by contrast, is centred on *prior*, *specific*, *informed* consent for many forms of tracking and terminal-equipment access, together with rights of *withdrawal* and *objection* [7,8]. A binary "do not sell/share" switch is therefore normatively and functionally too thin.

Importing GPC as the default European model would risk allowing the legal logic of an opt-out regime to shape the technical grammar of an opt-in regime. The proper order is the reverse: European law should define the acts that must be communicable, and technical standards should then carry them. ADPC is more appropriate on that criterion because it can represent purpose-specific requests and responses, supports both opt-in and opt-out operations, and integrates with the wider GDPR/ePrivacy rights architecture [12,21,22]. Degeling and Human's contrasts between *opt-in* and *opt-out*, *complex* and *binary*, and *control* and *trust* help explain why GPC cannot simply be Europeanised by reinterpretation [3] (Table 2).

7 Safeguards for Rights-First Standardisation

The EDPB and EDPS strongly welcomed the provision initially proposed as Article 88b, while also identifying clarifications and safeguards needed for effective implementation [5]. Read carefully, these concerns do not weaken the architectural case. On the contrary, they sharpen the functional requirements for any durable machine-readable choice layer. They also help show why ADPC is the more suitable implementation path among the mechanisms assessed here.

Table 2. GPC and ADPC against the needs of a European machine-readable choice layer

Dimension	GPC	ADPC
Legal logic	User-enabled global opt-out for "do not sell/share" personal information; well suited to California-style opt-out architecture [29,31].	Rights-first communication mechanism designed around GDPR/ePrivacy concepts, including consent, refusal, withdrawal, and objection; extendable to other legal frameworks and to rights beyond privacy [12,22].
Expression model	Binary or near-binary signal; valuable as a clear refusal but not designed to carry every privacy right [31].	Structured and bidirectional; can carry request descriptors, purposes, parties, responses, and subsequent changes [21].
Fit with EU law	Important lesson on legal recognition and enforcement, but too thin for prior, specific, informed, and revocable consent under EU law.	Better fit for the European legal grammar because it can represent differentiated opt-in and opt-out operations without reducing them to one signal.
Accountability lesson	Demonstrates that machine-readable signals become practically relevant when law and regulators require recipients to honour them.	Can provide richer communication traces and receipts, but requires legal duties, supervisory access, conformance testing, and sanctions.

First, the Substantive Rule and the Choice Layer Should be Linked. The Joint Opinion recommends clarifying the relationship between the substantive terminal-equipment rule initially numbered Article 88a and the machine-readable communication layer initially numbered Article 88b [5]. ADPC is well placed to operationalise such a link because it was designed for precisely the interaction between request descriptors and user responses in the GDPR/ePrivacy space [22]. This is one of its strengths over generic opt-out signals: the protocol can carry structured requests rather than only a global refusal.

Secondly, the Relevant "Controllers" Must Include Third Parties. The Opinion insists that the machine-readable choice layer should apply not only to the provider of the relevant online interface but also to all controllers that access or store data on terminal equipment, including third-party cookie providers [5]. This concern is fundamental. If only the first-party website were bound, a large part of the adtech ecosystem could remain outside the communication duty. ADPC helps here because its logic is not tied to a single banner or a single controller-controlled graphical user interface; it is a communication mechanism that can carry requests and responses across the actors implicated in the relevant processing chain [21].

Thirdly, Harmonised Standards Must Govern the Whole Communication Chain. The EDPB and EDPS call for clarification of who must apply the harmonised standards so that all actors involved in enabling data subjects to express their choices use the same automated and machine-readable indications [5]. This point concerns interoperability across the communication chain, not only the existence of a technical standard. ADPC is relevant here because it already provides an open specification for structured request-and-response communication between the actors involved in machine-readable privacy choice [12,22]. The broader lesson from DNT and GPC is that standards matter most when they are explicit, interoperable, broadly applicable, and supported by legal obligation.

Fourthly, no Standard Should Consent by Default. The Joint Opinion warns that the standardisation process must not create configurations that amount to consent by default [5]. This concern is entirely consistent with a rights-first implementation. ADPC does not require default consent. To the contrary, because it enables user-side decision management, it can be implemented in ways that preserve explicit configuration, refusal histories, and context-sensitive re-prompting rules [12]. A European implementation should therefore embed the EDPB–EDPS concern directly into both the standard and the supervisory guidance.

Fifthly, Browsers Alone are Not Enough. The EDPB and EDPS recommend extending the mechanism beyond web browsers to other software used on terminal equipment, including consumer mobile and desktop operating systems [5]. This point reinforces, rather than weakens, the architectural thesis of this paper. If privacy communication is an infrastructural matter, it should not depend exclusively on one client category or on website-based interaction. ADPC is especially attractive here because its technology-neutral communication model can operate across browser extensions, mobile and desktop applications, operating systems, connected devices, AI-mediated agents, immersive environments, and other user-facing or service-facing software layers [12,22]. This flexibility is important for an ecosystem increasingly shaped by apps, connected devices, ambient systems, and automated agents.

Sixthly, Excluding SME Browser Providers Would be a Mistake. The Joint Opinion questions the proposal's carve-out for SME browser providers [5]. That criticism is well founded. If only very large browser providers are required to implement the relevant means, the EU risks entrenching platform concentration in the very layer through which privacy choices will be exercised. A standard such as ADPC is preferable precisely because it lowers implementation barriers and reduces dependence on a few dominant intermediaries. Rights-enabling infrastructure should not become another bottleneck controlled by the largest client-side actors.

Seventhly, Exceptions Should Remain Compatible with the Machine-Readable Layer. The proposal includes a specific exception for media service providers, and the EDPB–EDPS Opinion recommends reconsidering its scope [5]. Whether such an exception is retained, narrowed, or removed, it should not require a fallback to fragmented banner-based choice management. A rights-first implementation should instead ensure that the same machine-readable mechanism can communicate when an exception is invoked, what it covers, and which rights-relevant choices remain available. ADPC is useful here because it can provide a structured and rights-compatible channel through which sector-specific arrangements, including possible exceptions, can be implemented without reintroducing cookie banners as the default fallback.

Finally, Enforcement Must be Credible. The EDPB and EDPS emphasise the need for effective fining powers and enforceability, including as regards browser and operating-system providers [5]. This is the central lesson from comparative experience. Technical standards without supervisory force are easily ignored; legal rights without technical means are hard to exercise. Any such provision should therefore be implemented, if adopted in this or a successor form, as a combined legal-technical package: harmonised standards, user-side support, controller-side accountability, conformance testing, and clearly enforceable duties on all relevant actors. ADPC can make choices more auditable and operationally coherent by creating structured request-and-response traces, but only enforcement can ensure that those machine-readable choices are actually honoured.

7.1 Implementation Principles for a European Standard

The preceding analysis suggests five implementation principles. First, European law, rather than inherited web market practice, should define the scope of the standard. Controllers should not be able to reduce the new machine-readable layer to the smallest technically convenient denominator where that would strip away the specificity and revocability required by the GDPR and the ePrivacy framework [7,8]. This is the principal reason for preferring ADPC-style design over a thin opt-out switch.

Second, standardisation should remain agnostic and interoperable. A machine-readable choice layer will only change practice if controllers, browsers, operating systems, app developers, and other relevant software actors can implement the same core logic without dependency on a proprietary intermediary. A formally standardised but practically captured privacy layer would reproduce the asymmetry that banner practice currently embodies. Harmonised and interoperable standards are therefore a condition of both effectiveness and fairness [5,21].

Third, the user side must remain a real site of control rather than a cosmetic relay. A European implementation should favour persistent records, intelligible settings, refusal histories, and revision mechanisms that users can access over time. Without such features, automated communication merely changes the transport layer while leaving rights exercise fragile and memory-dependent. Verifiable records of requests and decisions, digital protection dashboards, and inclusive, human-compatible assistants should be treated as natural complements to a European machine-readable choice layer [14,16].

The fourth principle is that support should be configurable, contextual, and in some cases collective. Not every user wants the same level of automation. Some may prefer explicit prompts; others may want reusable rules; still others may need support from guardians, accessibility tools, or trusted organisations. One of the major advantages of ADPC is that it creates the conditions under which such variation becomes possible at the user side [12,22]. A rights-respecting implementation should therefore avoid treating *automation* as synonymous with *invisibility* or user displacement. The appropriate goal is user-governed assistance, not controller-governed silence.

The fifth principle is that a machine-readable choice provision should be seen as a *beginning* rather than an *endpoint*. Such a provision can create the missing communication layer, but it cannot by itself resolve all questions about power, auditability, or enforcement in the data economy. The EU will still need robust supervisory practice, clear duties for third-party actors, and ongoing evaluation of how standards interact with emerging technologies and business models. Those needs are arguments for careful implementation, not for remaining with a banner regime that is already failing in predictable ways. A standardised, rights-first communication layer is not sufficient for *human-compatible digital protection* [14,15], but it is increasingly necessary.

8 Beyond Privacy: Rights-First Digital Infrastructure

The argument remains grounded in privacy and data protection. That focus is appropriate for the GDPR/ePrivacy setting and for machine-readable consent, refusal, withdrawal, and objection. Yet the architectural lesson is broader. When rights are exercised through networked systems, connected devices, AI-mediated systems and immersive environments, legal protection depends on whether rights-relevant information can travel through infrastructure in a form intelligible to people, actionable for software, auditable for institutions, and enforceable against recipients. Privacy is therefore the first mature test case for a broader rights-first digital infrastructure [9,14,15].

Simplification Without Deregulation. Legitimate simplification should reduce the burden of exercising and respecting rights, not the level of protection. Replacing repeated banners with machine-readable communication is not a deregulatory shortcut. It is a way to preserve consent, refusal, withdrawal, objection, transparency, accountability, and enforceability while removing avoidable friction and manipulative graphical user interface variation. The benchmark should be fewer interactions, stronger rights in practice, and the highest applicable level of protection, accountability, and enforceability.

Simplification Through Advanced Infrastructure. For both data subjects and controllers, simplification may require more capable infrastructure and more implementation-oriented law. A simple experience for the data subject and a clearer compliance route for the controller do not necessarily follow from thinner legal duties, weaker safeguards, or less demanding technical systems. In rights-intensive digital environments, simplification can instead depend on a more sophisticated legal-technical architecture: precise duties, stable standards, reusable implementation artefacts, conformance testing, durable records, and supervisory guidance that move complexity away from repeated ad hoc graphical user interface design and into accountable infrastructure. Properly understood, simplification is therefore not the reduction of rights or obligations, but the institutional and technical organisation of those obligations so that they can be fulfilled more reliably at scale [5,21].

Rights Beyond Personal Data. Data protection law sits within a wider constitutional environment that includes dignity, autonomy, non-discrimination, freedom of expression and information, consumer protection, children's rights, accessibility, and democratic participation [9]. A rights-first infrastructure should make human agency and fundamental rights effective in use, not only visible in principle. A user agent that helps reject tracking may also reduce manipulation; a user-side record may support complaint, explanation, or contestation; and a privacy communication layer may become a template for other rights-relevant communications.

Children and Supported Agency. The shift from banners to user-side architecture is especially important for children and other users who need contextual, linguistic, cognitive, or collective support. Real users include children, older adults, disabled persons, neurodivergent persons, people with migrant backgrounds, people affected by poverty, people acting in unfamiliar languages, and people who rely on parents, guardians, civil society, accessibility tools, or professional intermediaries. A rights-first architecture should allow support without replacing the person: age-appropriate defaults, accessible explanations, refusal and withdrawal histories, and trusted assistance where appropriate [11,14,16].

Sustainability, Accessibility, and Economic Growth. A machine-readable privacy layer can support a more sustainable digital economy. The banner regime externalises costs onto users through attention loss and onto controllers through repeated, inconsistent, and fragile graphical user interface engineering. Standardised communication can reduce duplicated compliance work, create clearer expectations for lawful interaction, and support services around user-side assistance, audit, accessibility, and conformance [16,21]. Rights-first infrastructure is therefore compatible with responsible innovation and sustainable economic growth because it converts privacy-engineering knowledge, including privacy-enhancing technologies, into reusable, verifiable, and legally meaningful communication channels. A human-compatible, accessible, and trustworthy digital ecosystem is one condition for sustainable competitiveness [15].

Sovereignty, Digital Resilience, and Democratic Resilience. The same infrastructure has implications for EU digital sovereignty, digital resilience, and democratic resilience. If the main graphical user interfaces through which people exercise rights are controlled by a small number of platforms, browsers, operating systems, or advertising intermediaries, rights become dependent on private architectural choices. Open, interoperable, and legally anchored standards reduce that dependency. They also make democratic oversight more realistic because regulators, researchers, courts, journalists, and civil society can reason about structured signals and records more effectively than about millions of idiosyncratic banners [3,5,20]. This matters where profiling, political persuasion, discriminatory targeting, and manipulation affect not only individual privacy but also collective autonomy.

AI and Emerging Environments. The lesson also travels beyond ordinary web pages. Connected devices, IoT environments, mixed-reality systems, AI assistants, and automated user agents are increasingly becoming part of everyday life across domains such as communication, work, mobility, health, education, consumption, and public services. These technologies should not inherit the weaknesses of cookie banners; they should respect legally meaningful choices and machine-readable communications, expose records where needed, and remain accountable to users and supervisory institutions. ADPC-IoT work shows that the communication model can travel into connected-device environments, while research on human-compatible AI underlines that AI should support human needs and capacities rather than replace them [13,15,17].

Standardisation and Enforceability. Rights-first digital infrastructure requires more than good intentions. It requires an ambitious scope, open standards, conformance testing, accessible implementations, security review, supervisory guidance, meaningful remedies, and sanctions for non-compliance. Standardisation should be an inclusive public-interest process because the resulting protocol will structure how rights are exercised, remembered, delegated, and audited. It should be technology-neutral, future-improvable, and protective of open competition, and it should prevent standardisation capture, platform dependency, and new forms of domination. It should also cover browsers, browser extensions, operating systems, mobile and desktop applications, connected devices, AI-mediated user agents, and the controllers and third parties that receive and must honour machine-readable rights communications. A machine-readable choice that controllers may ignore is not a rights layer; it is only an unenforced preference.

From Data Protection Control to Digital Protection Control. In this broader horizon, *Advanced Data Protection Control* remains the immediate data-protection mechanism: a way to communicate requests, preferences, decisions, refusals, withdrawals, objections, and records. *Advanced Digital Protection Control* names the wider ambition: rights-supporting infrastructures through which digital systems can communicate, assist, document, and enforce legally and socially significant choices. The distinction matters. The privacy layer should not be diluted into an abstract slogan about digital rights. It should be built precisely, implemented reliably, and enforced seriously. If that is achieved, it can become the first mature component of a broader architecture for human-compatible digital protection.

9 Conclusion: Toward a Rights-First Architecture of Privacy Choice

The provision initially labelled Article 88b GDPR may be renumbered, revised, absorbed into another legal form, or not adopted. That uncertainty does not diminish the structural deficit made visible by the 2025 Digital Omnibus proposal. European privacy practice cannot continue to rely on controller-controlled banners as the main route for communicating consent, refusal, withdrawal, and objection. The problem is architectural.

DNT showed that technical signals without strong legal support do not shift market practice; GPC shows that legal recognition and enforcement can make a machine-readable signal matter. Yet GPC's binary opt-out model remains too narrow for a European framework centred on prior, specific, informed, and revocable consent. Among the mechanisms assessed here, ADPC is the most congruent candidate because it can carry richer legal acts as structured, configurable, assistive, and auditable communication [12,14,22]. Implemented well, such a layer could give *privacy by design* and *by default* the infrastructural complement they have long lacked: a durable, reviewable, and rights-respecting *architecture of privacy* choice.

Acknowledgement. This research was partially funded by *netidee*, the funding program of the Internet Foundation Austria (Internet Privatstiftung Austria), under the projects RESPECTeD (Project No. 4625), RESPECTeD-IoT (Project No. 5937), HALE–KIDS (Project No. 6442), and GUARDIAN (Project No. 6944). This research was also partially funded by Wirtschaftsagentur Wien, a fund of the City of Vienna, through the CHAnGE project under the Call Tech4People 2023 program. The author further acknowledges financial support from the Jubiläumsfonds der Stadt Wien für die WU Wien.

Declaration on the Use of Generative Artificial Intelligence (GAI). Generative Artificial Intelligence tools were used to support linguistic improvement, stylistic consistency, reference-management support, and LaTeX/BibTeX template adaptation.

Disclosure of Interests. The author has contributed to prior ADPC-related research cited in this paper.

References

1. Acquisti, A., Brandimarte, L., Loewenstein, G.: Privacy and human behavior in the age of information. Science **347**(6221), 509–514 (2015). https://doi.org/10.1126/science.aaa1465
2. Bravo-Lillo, C., Cranor, L., Komanduri, S., Schechter, S., Sleeper, M.: Harder to ignore? revisiting pop-up fatigue and approaches to prevent it. In: Proceedings of the 10th Symposium on Usable Privacy and Security (SOUPS), pp. 105–111 (2014). https://www.usenix.org/conference/soups2014/proceedings/presentation/bravo-lillo
3. Degeling, M., Human, S.: Internet privacy protocols. Zeitschrift für Medienwissenschaft **15**(28-1), 55–70 (2023). https://doi.org/10.14361/zfmw-2023-150107
4. European Commission: Proposal for a regulation of the European Parliament and of the Council amending regulations (EU) 2016/679, (EU) 2018/1724, (EU) 2018/1725, (EU) 2023/2854 and directives 2002/58/EC, (EU) 2022/2555 and (EU) 2022/2557 as regards the simplification of the digital legislative framework, and repealing regulations (EU) 2018/1807, (EU) 2019/1150, (EU) 2022/868, and directive (EU) 2019/1024 (Digital Omnibus). COM(2025) 837 final; Interinstitutional File 2025/0360 (COD) (Nov 2025), https://eur-lex.europa.eu/legal-content/EN/TXT/?uri=CELEX:52025PC0837

5. European Data Protection Board and European Data Protection Supervisor: EDPB-EDPS joint opinion 2/2026 on the proposal for a regulation as regards the simplification of the digital legislative framework (Digital Omnibus). Official joint opinion (2026). https://www.edpb.europa.eu/documents/legislative-opinion/edpb-edps-joint-opinion-22026-on-the-proposal-for-a-regulation-as_en
6. European Parliament: Simplification of the digital legislative framework – Digital Omnibus (Omnibus VII): Procedure 2025/0360(COD). Legislative Observatory procedure file (2026). https://oeil.europarl.europa.eu/oeil/en/procedure-file?reference=2025/0360(COD)
7. European Parliament and Council of the European Union: Directive 2002/58/EC concerning the processing of personal data and the protection of privacy in the electronic communications sector (ePrivacy Directive). Official Journal of the European Communities (2002). https://eur-lex.europa.eu/eli/dir/2002/58/oj/eng
8. European Parliament and Council of the European Union: Regulation (EU) 2016/679 of the European Parliament and of the Council of 27 April 2016 (GDPR). Official Journal of the European Union (2016). https://data.europa.eu/eli/reg/2016/679/oj
9. European Union: Charter of fundamental rights of the European Union. OJ C 202, 7.6.2016, pp. 389–405 (2016). https://eur-lex.europa.eu/legal-content/EN/TXT/?uri=CELEX:12016P/TXT
10. Gray, C.M., Santos, C., Bielova, N., Toth, M., Clifford, D.: Dark patterns and the legal requirements of consent banners: an interaction criticism perspective. In: Proceedings of the 2021 CHI Conference on Human Factors in Computing Systems, pp. 1–18 (2021). https://doi.org/10.1145/3411764.3445779
11. Gsenger, R., Human, S., Neumann, G.: End-user empowerment: an interdisciplinary perspective. In: Proceedings of the 53rd Hawaii International Conference on System Sciences, pp. 4102–4111 (2020). https://doi.org/10.24251/HICSS.2020.502
12. Human, S.: Advanced Data Protection Control (ADPC): an interdisciplinary overview. arXiv (2022). https://doi.org/10.48550/arXiv.2209.09724
13. Human, S.: ADPC-IoT/RESPECTeD-IoT: really enforceable solution to protect end-users consent and data protection decisions in IoT. In: Tech. rep. Sustainable Computing Reports and Specifications, WU Vienna University of Economics and Business, Wien (2024)
14. Human, S.: Humans [plural] in the loop: the forgotten collective aspects of privacy, consenting, controlling and digital protection. Front. Polit. Sci. **6**, 1391755 (2024). https://doi.org/10.3389/fpos.2024.1391755
15. Human, S.: Human-compatible digital protection: A cornerstone of sustainable digital transformation. In: Carroll, N. (ed.) Research Handbook on Digital Transformation and Responsibility. Edward Elgar Publishing (2026). https://doi.org/10.4337/9781035339884.00029
16. Human, S., Alt, R., Habibnia, H., Neumann, G.: Human-centric personal data protection and consenting assistant systems: towards a sustainable digital economy. In: Proceedings of the 55th Hawaii International Conference on System Sciences, pp. 4727–4736 (2022). https://doi.org/10.24251/HICSS.2022.576, https://hdl.handle.net/10125/79913
17. Human, S., Bernroider, E.: AI-assisted framework for sustainable human-compatible innovation and transformation. In: CENTERIS - International Conference on ENTERprise Information Systems (2024)

18. Human, S., Cech, F.: A human-centric perspective on digital consenting: the case of GAFAM. In: Zimmermann, A., Howlett, R.J., Jain, L.C. (eds.) Human Centred Intelligent Systems. SIST, vol. 189, pp. 139–159. Springer, Singapore (2021). https://doi.org/10.1007/978-981-15-5784-2_12
19. Human, S., Kazzazi, M.: Contextuality and intersectionality of E-Consent: a human-centric reflection on digital consenting in the emerging genetic data markets. In: 2021 IEEE European Symposium on Security and Privacy Workshops (EuroS&PW), pp. 307–311 (2021). https://doi.org/10.1109/EuroSPW54576.2021.00051
20. Human, S., Neumann, G., Peschl, M.F.: [how] can pluralist approaches to computational cognitive modeling of human needs and values save our democracies? Intellectica **70**, 165–180 (2019). https://doi.org/10.3406/intel.2019.1897
21. Human, S., et al.: Data protection and consenting communication mechanisms: Current open proposals and challenges. In: 2022 IEEE European Symposium on Security and Privacy Workshops (EuroS&PW), pp. 231–239 (2022). https://doi.org/10.1109/EuroSPW55150.2022.00029
22. Human, S., Schrems, M., Toner, A., Gerben, Wagner, B.: Advanced data protection control (ADPC). Tech. Rep. 2021/01, Sustainable Computing Reports and Specifications, Vienna University of Economics and Business (2021). https://doi.org/10.57938/149a03c3-2f39-4ca0-8ff7-be7f8ded61b8, https://research.wu.ac.at/en/publications/advanced-data-protection-control-adpc-7/
23. Lehtiniemi, T., Kortesniemi, Y.: Can the obstacles to privacy self-management be overcome? exploring the consent intermediary approach. Big Data Soc. **4**(2), 1–11 (2017). https://doi.org/10.1177/2053951717721935
24. Morel, V., Santos, C., Lintao, Y., Human, S.: Your consent is worth 75 euros a year – measurement and lawfulness of cookie paywalls. In: Proceedings of the 21st Workshop on Privacy in the Electronic Society, pp. 213–218 (2022). https://doi.org/10.1145/3559613.3563205
25. Nouwens, M., Liccardi, I., Veale, M., Karger, D., Kagal, L.: Dark patterns after the GDPR: scraping consent pop-ups and demonstrating their influence. Proceedings of the 2020 CHI Conference on Human Factors in Computing Systems, pp. 1–13 (2020). https://doi.org/10.1145/3313831.3376321
26. Obar, J.A., Oeldorf-Hirsch, A.: The biggest lie on the internet: ignoring the privacy policies and terms of service policies of social networking services. Inf. Commun. Soc. **23**(1), 128–147 (2020). https://doi.org/10.1080/1369118X.2018.1486870
27. Santos, C., Bielova, N., Matte, C.: Are cookie banners indeed compliant with the law? deciphering EU legal requirements on consent and technical means to verify compliance of cookie banners. Technology and Regulation pp. 91–135 (2020). https://doi.org/10.71265/g317tv72, https://techreg.org/article/view/10990
28. State of California Department of Justice: Attorney General Bonta announces joint investigative privacy sweep: CO, CT, and CA investigate businesses refusing to honor consumers' right to opt-out of the sale of their personal information. Official press release (2025). https://oag.ca.gov/news/press-releases/attorney-general-bonta-announces-joint-investigative-privacy-sweep%C2%A0co-ct-and-ca
29. State of California Department of Justice: Global Privacy Control (GPC). Official guidance page (2025). https://oag.ca.gov/privacy/ccpa/gpc
30. W3C: The platform for privacy preferences 1.0 (P3P1.0) specification. W3C Recommendation, 16 April 2002 (2002). https://www.w3.org/TR/P3P/, obsoleted by W3C on 30 August 2018
31. W3C Privacy Working Group: Global Privacy Control (GPC). W3C Working Draft, 11 June 2026 (2026). https://www.w3.org/TR/gpc/

32. W3C Tracking Protection Working Group: Tracking preference expression (DNT). W3C Working Group Note, 17 January 2019 (2019). https://www.w3.org/TR/tracking-dnt/
33. Zimmeck, S., Alicki, K.: Standardizing and implementing Do Not Sell. In: Proceedings of the 19th Workshop on Privacy in the Electronic Society, pp. 15–20 (2020). https://doi.org/10.1145/3411497.3420224
34. Zuboff, S.: Big other: surveillance capitalism and the prospects of an information civilization. J. Inf. Technol. **30**(1), 75–89 (2015). https://doi.org/10.1057/jit.2015.5

Informed Consent by Design: Developer-Oriented Privacy Best Practices for GDPR Compliant mHealth Applications

Ramona Adair[1(✉)], Harald Zwingelberg[2], Michael Friedewald[3], and Ina Schiering[1]

[1] Institute of Distributed Systems, Ostfalia University of Applied Sciences, Wolfenbüttel, Germany
{r.adair,i.schiering}@ostfalia.de

[2] Independent Centre for Privacy Protection Schleswig-Holstein, Kiel, Germany
hzwingelberg@datenschutzzentrum.de

[3] Fraunhofer Institute for Systems and Innovation Research ISI, Karlsruhe, Germany
michael.friedewald@isi.fraunhofer.de

Abstract. When developing applications that collect and process personal data, caution is needed due to the potential for significant harm to individuals' rights and freedoms. This risk is particularly pronounced in the domain of health applications, where data sensitivity is intensified by the intimate nature of health information and the potential for misuse, discrimination, or unauthorized access. Central to safeguarding these rights is the principle of informed consent, enabling individuals to make well-informed decisions about whether to share their data and under what circumstances. However, effective implementation of informed consent remains a persistent challenge in practice. While numerous theoretical models and design concepts for improving consent mechanisms have been proposed in the literature, their concrete implementation remains limited. A key barrier lies in the fact that software developers are expected to implement complex regulatory requirements, such as those outlined in the General Data Protection Regulation (GDPR), with limited legal expertise and without clear guidance on what specific technical or procedural measures are necessary for compliance. Interviews with software developers and product managers involved in healthcare applications highlighted a consistent gap in specific, actionable guidance for implementing data protection requirements. To this end, we have developed privacy best practices to support development teams in designing and implementing effective, transparent, and user-centric informed consent.

Keywords: Informed Consent · Transparency · Intervenability · General Data Protection Regulation · Best Practices

F. Pallas et al. (Eds.): APF 2026, LNCS 16847, pp. 226–252, 2026.
https://doi.org/10.1007/978-3-032-35899-8_11

1 Introduction

Privacy is part of everyone's life. It is a fundamental right, which is at least the base for data protection [43]. Just as we can decide for ourselves who we let in our home and who we don't, we should also be able to decide who knows what about us. It should be possible to assess the extent of information shared, the circumstances under which information shall be shared, and for what purpose. Furthermore, just as we can expel someone from our property again, we should be able to revoke further sharing of our personal data. In addition to ethical considerations, the General Data Protection Regulation (GDPR) lays the basis for transparency and intervenability. Informed consent plays a crucial role in the processing of personal data. Especially in the processing of special categories of personal data such as health data the effective implementation of informed consent is indispensable.

Although ethically and legally bound, many health applications lack compliance. Incomplete privacy policies, vague descriptions, and inconsistencies of data flows and the information provided undermine consent [1,13]. Although privacy policies have improved regarding completeness and references to data subject rights since the GDPR came into place, they still often lack understandability [46]. Furthermore, even when compliant, consent notices often place greater emphasis on meeting formal requirements than on providing genuine transparency or truly empowering users, even though a clear and reasonable permission request leads to a more positive cognitive assessment [6]. Inadequate informed consent not only undermines user trust but also increases the risk of data misuse, especially when handling sensitive health data. When users cannot meaningfully understand or influence how their data is used, they are less likely to engage with health technologies, potentially widening health disparities [48]. From the users' perspective, clear and concise information, along with even minimal configuration options, goes a long way towards reducing frustration caused by overly long privacy policies full of technical jargon, which are merely linked to [6].

However, the reasons why compliant and effective implementation of informed consent is often unsuccessful remain unclear. To identify the underlying issue, we conducted qualitative interview studies with developers and product managers of digital health applications. During these semi-structured interviews, it emerged that privacy patterns, privacy-enhancing technologies, and approaches to analyzing privacy risks were largely unknown. This highlighted the need for software development and product and project management to align existing privacy by design concepts and methods more closely to the needs of practitioners who have only limited knowledge on how to implement data protection requirements. In response, we propose pragmatic, actionable Privacy Best Practices (PBPs) that operationalize Privacy by Design principles and emphasize clarity, usability, and meaningful user control, bridging the gap between legal compliance and genuine user empowerment. PBPs enable precise guidance. Concrete, demonstrative examples further facilitate comprehensibility and the transfer to specific use cases.

2 Informed Consent

2.1 The General Data Protection Regulation

In Europe, the GDPR governs the processing of personal data, protecting the fundamental rights and freedoms of natural persons. Processing of personal data is prohibited unless it is based on one of the lawful grounds set out in Article 6 GDPR. One such basis is consent, as defined in Article 6(1)(a) GDPR, for one or more specific purposes. Consent is defined in Article 4(11) GDPR as "any freely given, specific, informed and unambiguous indication of the data subject's wishes by which he or she, by a statement or by a clear affirmative action, signifies agreement to the processing or personal data relating to him or her" [35]. This definition is further specified in Recital 32, which states that pre-selections and inactivity cannot constitute valid consent. The Court of Justice of the European Union (CJEU) confirmed this in the Planet49 judgment (C-673/17), holding that pre-ticked checkboxes for tracking cookies do not constitute a clear affirmative action and therefore cannot serve as valid consent. This interpretation ensures that consent is an active expression of will rather than the result of the user's passivity or "click fatigue".

Moreover, consent must be specific to clearly defined purposes and should, where appropriate, allow separate consent for different processing operations, rather than bundling unrelated purposes together. This helps to ensure that consent remains freely given, as emphasized in Recital 43, and avoids situations where data subjects are pressured into accepting multiple, unrelated processing activities in a single, bundled consent. Recital 43 GDPR and the European Data Protection Board ([11], para. 75) underline that such bundling and situations of power imbalance - for example, when access to a service is made conditional on unnecessary data processing - call into question whether consent can be regarded as "freely given".

Article 7 GDPR requires that consent can be demonstrated and the consent-text is presented in a manner that is clearly distinguishable from other matters, easily accessible, and expressed in clear and plain language. The data subject may withdraw consent at any time with effect for the future, and controllers should provide simple and effective means to do so without detriment to the data subject. In line with Recital 42, consent must reflect a genuine choice, with no adverse consequences for the data subject if consent is not given or is withdrawn. Furthermore, consent can only be considered informed if the data subject is clearly made aware of essential information including the identity of the controller and the specific purposes for which their personal data will be processed, along with other relevant information needed to understand the implications of the processing.

Regardless of the legal basis for processing, certain information must be provided to the data subject as set out in Articles 13 and 14 GDPR. According to Article 12 GDPR, the controller is obliged to take appropriate measures to ensure transparency. Such information must be concise, easily accessible, easy to understand, and where appropriate may be visualized. In addition data subjects should be made aware of risks, rules, safeguards and rights in relation to the processing of personal data and how to exercise their rights.

Special care must be taken when processing special categories of personal data as defined in Article 9 GDPR. These include, inter alia, health data, genetic data, and data concerning a natural person's sexual orientation or sex life. Where consent is the legal basis for processing special categories of data, explicit consent is required, meaning consent which, in addition to the usual requirements, includes an explicit verbal or written statement that clearly and specifically authorises the special category processing in question ([11], para. 93 et seq.). The CJEU interprets "data concerning health" broadly. In Bodil Lindqvist (C-101/01), it held that even a brief reference to a colleague's foot injury and part-time work on medical grounds constitutes data concerning health. Building on this, in Lindenapotheke (C-21/23) the Court reaffirmed this broad interpretation by classifying order data for non-prescription, pharmacy-only medicines in an online shop as health data, because linking a specific medicinal product and its therapeutic indications to an identifiable person can reveal information about that person's health status. Such categories of data are particularly prevalent in mobile health (mHealth) applications, which are becoming increasingly widespread.

Building on these legal requirements, a growing body of European work on data protection by design and by default has sought to translate Article 25 GDPR into engineering concepts, protection goals and technical building blocks, for example in the work of Hansen et al. on privacy engineering and protection goals [16], and in the analysis of Jasmontaite et al. on Article 25 as a concrete controller obligation [22].

2.2 Privacy by Design and Privacy Patterns

Privacy by Design (PbD) is a proactive approach to data protection that integrates privacy and data protection principles into the design from the very beginning, rather than adding them as an afterthought. Cavoukian [3] defined PbD by seven foundational principles. These include using proactive and preventative rather than reactive and remedial measures. Privacy should be embedded into the design, respecting user privacy while maintaining full functionality, emphasizing privacy as the default. Accountability and trust are to be achieved by visibility and transparency. Under the GDPR, these ideas are partly codified in the legal obligation of data protection by design and by default in Article 25, which requires controllers to embed data protection principles into systems and default settings.

PbD defines the company's approach to privacy and how it integrates this into all aspects of its operations. To support PbD throughout the full software development life cycle Hoepman introduced eight privacy design strategies: minimize, hide, separate, aggregate, inform, control, enforce, and demonstrate [17]. During the implementation phase privacy enhancing technologies (PETs) can be deployed. PETs are a set of tools, protocols, and techniques designed to protect personal data and ensure privacy in digital environments. Typical PETs within the context of consent are attributed-based, role-based, or policy-based access control as well as privacy policy visualization, user privacy preferences, and more [5]. ENISA's work on "Privacy and Data Protection by Design - from policy to engineering" [9] and "Privacy by design in big data" [8] develops this further by mapping data protection principles to concrete PETs and technical building blocks, including anonymisation, encrypted search, granular access control, policy enforcement and user-facing transparency tools.

Between principles, strategies, and technologies, privacy patterns describe common practices in standardized terminology [39]. Various privacy patterns have been collected in catalogs [7]. Patterns that are linked to informed consent are for example Informed Consent for Web-based Transactions, Layered Policy Design, Privacy Icons, Privacy Policy Display, Platform for Privacy Preferences and more. The research on privacy patterns is wide-ranging. Beside pattern proposals and pattern catalogs, pattern languages and pattern taxonomies are discussed [28]. Although patterns are powerful building blocks, in order to integrate them into a concrete application, developers and privacy engineers need to find the appropriate pattern, understand the abstract concept and adopt it to their specific context.

In conclusion, the precise implementation of informed consent within the framework of PbD, the concrete adoption of privacy patterns in relation to informed consent, and the implementation of PETs for informed consent in specific application contexts remain unclear. A significant gap persists between these abstract frameworks and their actual implementation in real life projects.

2.3 Informed Consent and Digital Health Applications

Europe has begun establishing frameworks that enable certain mHealth applications, known as digital therapeutics, to be prescribed by doctors. These frameworks were first implemented in Germany, Belgium, France and Austria [14]. In Germany, as a pioneer, mHealth apps can be registered as digital health applications (Digitale Gesundheits-Anwendungen, DiGA) in the DiGA directory. Doctors can then prescribe these applications to their patients so that the costs for using them are covered by health insurance. In order to be included in the DiGA directory, in addition to providing evidence of a positive healthcare effect, applications must meet requirements in security, quality, and data protection. This includes a GDPR-compliant, user-friendly, and effective implementation of informed consent [15].

In addition to the legal obligations, users of mHealth applications have expressed their demands to be able to control the disclosure of their personal data, including informed consent [49]. They may not want to share their data with specific parties like insurance companies, advertisers, or family members, and their privacy concerns and preferences differ depending on the type of information collected [34]. Kassam et al. [25] discovered that in most studies granular, informative, and transparent consent choices were preferred. Further, they noted that transparency and adequate information are of utmost importance. Interestingly, despite differing preferences for how information is presented, a common thread is that the amount of information in a consent notice matters less than the quality of that information. Issues such as unclear privacy policy statements [49] and complex privacy laws [34] hinder transparency and informed consent. However, most patients are willing to consent to sharing their data under the right circumstances. The willingness depends on the comprehension of consent notices; the implementation or lack of information and transparency; concerns and perceived sensitivity related to the collected data; and with whom their data is shared, as well as how and for what purposes the data is processed [25].

From the patient's perspective, it is important for informed consent that it is usable, expressive, intuitive, and transparent [34] as well as meaningful and customizable, fostering greater control and trust [25]. In an interview study by Schneider et al. [41], patients reported that they often gave their consent to data processing within mHealth apps without reading the documents thoroughly, as the technical and legal content is difficult to understand. They wished for clear, transparent and comprehensible privacy information, as well as alternative formats of presentation. Overall, it is important from both an ethical and a legal perspective that app developers address the issue of informed consent and ensure that it is effectively implemented.

3 Related Work

Although legally required and also relevant from a user perspective, studies examining app compliance have revealed significant shortcomings [1,4,13,31]. Even in the case of mHealth applications, where particular care is required due to the processing of special categories of data, widespread non-compliance was observed. This ranges from a complete lack of information or consent, data collection prior to consent, and other inconsistencies between data collection practices and the privacy policy, to incomplete information and obstacles such as language barriers [1,13]. The most common lack of information concerned the precise categories of data collected and processed, adoption of technical measures to protect personal data, and user rights to access, correct, or delete their data, as well as information about the consequences if a user decides not to share their personal data [4,13].

There can be a wide variety of reasons for the non-compliance observed. Horstmann et al. [19] conducted a study in which 30 software developers were asked to complete various programming tasks in compliance with data protection regulations during a five-hour session. The study was concluded with short follow-up interviews during which the participants were able to reflect on the tasks and their implementation. The participants reported significant challenges in implementing general data protection requirements. Over half of the participants were unsure whether their implementation was compliant with data protection regulations, and only three were actually confident about their implementation. In the end, the solutions of almost all participants were not GDPR-compliant. This shows that there is a great deal of uncertainty and a lack of awareness and necessary skills.

In addition, Horstmann et al. [18] had previously explored the communication process between development teams and privacy experts. They identified a gap between privacy experts and software developers based on the lack of understanding of development on the one hand and privacy laws on the other. In a third study, participants were tasked with identifying privacy issues and potential mitigation strategies in a fitness app scenario. Notably, rather than turning to traditional sources such as search engines or online forums, they increasingly relied on AI assistants to find information. As in earlier studies, participants struggled to recognize privacy risks and propose effective solutions [20].

On the other hand, Spiekermann et al. [42] conducted a survey on the perspectives of developers on security and privacy engineering. They noted that perceived responsibility is a key point in addressing these two values while many engineers showed limited responsibility. Time constraints and the lack of appropriate norms within organizations make this area even more challenging.

Whilst organizations lack concrete measures, the literature discusses many ways of implementing informed consent. Schmidt et al. [40] conducted a systematic review identifying key technical challenges in implementing informed consent, along with corresponding concepts, methods, and potential solutions proposed in the literature. However, the economic viability and practicality of the various proposals still need to be assessed. There remains a need for clear, comprehensive guidelines that do justice to the complexity of the subject matter and take account of the challenges within organizations.

4 Insights from Practitioners

4.1 Participants and Methodology of Interviews

To investigate the needs of software developers and product managers of digital health applications, we conducted five qualitative, semi-structured interview studies. In each study, the participants were interviewed for an average of one and a half hours. The first part covered privacy-related aspects such as the collection of personal data, data flows, risk assessments, consent, and data protection requirements, using an application from the participant's portfolio as a reference. The second part focused on company-related aspects of privacy and security, including processes, personnel, and competencies, as well as the technologies used, best practices, and guidelines. The final part addressed the participants' personal perspectives, concluding with questions about needs, available resources, and information sources. Find the interview guide in Appendix A.

Of the five participants, four identified as male and one as female. Most were in the age group 35 to 44 years old, with one participant in a younger (25–34) and another in an older group (55–64). Almost all of them held a university degree in computer science or a related field. One person was a lateral entrant and had completed vocational training. The length of professional experience varied, with two people having between 1 and 10 years, two people between 10 and 20 years, and one person with more than 20 years' professional experience in this field. Three of the participants work in software development, and two in project and product management. In two cases, the reference application was a registered DiGA.

The interviews revealed a variety of practices and challenges in how privacy and security are addressed throughout the development lifecycle of digital health applications. While participants demonstrated awareness of core data protection principles, the implementation of well-defined concepts was less evident, reflecting both competence and resource constraints. In the following, key findings from the analysis are presented.

4.2 Findings Concerning Privacy

For quality assurance, methods such as branching, testing, and multi-stage release processes, including internal releases, were identified. Testing was conducted using white-box testing, manual testing, and a test book. However, no specific methodologies for assessing data protection risks to individuals were identified. Risk management was largely reactive, relying on ongoing monitoring and internal coordination. Monitoring mechanisms included GDPR-triggers, customer feedback, stakeholder-reported bugs, and technical system monitoring. This is particularly interesting as organizations in the DiGA sector would have to carry out data protection impact assessments regularly.

Requirements for IT security and privacy are incorporated based on best practices from IT security and data protection principles, such as data minimization. These best practices are primarily adopted as processes rather than as concrete building blocks. Concepts such as privacy patterns were not mentioned. Data protection requirements are defined through privacy policies and typically clarified in advance by data protection officers or other individuals with legal expertise.

Only a limited number of team members within the companies had experience in IT security and privacy. Data protection officers were appointed as contact persons for privacy matters. In some cases, legal expertise was provided through cooperation with partners. Training opportunities in the area of IT security and privacy were scarce. Competence-building took place mainly through internal exchange, which was promoted by regular meetings and independent research.

Participants highlighted their need for practical approaches to obtaining informed consent and managing changes in applications. They sought insights to implementing new laws and regulations, data protection in the context of AI, accessibility, and digital transformation in healthcare. There was also a clear demand for practical guidance on integrating privacy into development processes.

Overall, there was a strong desire to enhance privacy expertise. Participants noted that many legal frameworks and white papers tend to use vague language. Therefore, there was a call for more concrete technical recommendations, best practices, and structured presentations and comparisons in order to better understand and evaluate the various options for implementing requirements. The sources of information mentioned included specialist portals, specific websites for the specialist context, newsletters, search engines, news sites, social networks such as Instagram, internet forums, offerings from specialist publishers such as Heise and Golem, as well as large language models such as ChatGPT and CoPilot. Participants also learned about new technologies and concepts through events, specialist working groups, conferences, trade fairs, workshops, courses and informal exchanges.

In summary, it appears that in all cases they lack a clear privacy culture. Although abstract concepts such as PbD were known, there is a lack of specific implementational components and guidance.

5 Informed Consent by Design

In an earlier literature review, we elaborated on five main challenges of informed consent [40] (see Fig. 1). Informed consent needs to be *obtained*. It needs to be *ensured*, that consent is obtained and valid, before collecting and processing any personal data that is based on consent. On the other hand, the data subject needs to be able to *manage* their consent in order to be able to exercise their rights. For example, to withdraw consent. In order to be able to obtain and manage informed consent, *information* needs to be provided, and the data subject needs to be able to inform themselves based on the provided information. Further, in order to prove that consent was given and for the data subject to retrace what processing activities they have consented to, *evidence* is needed.

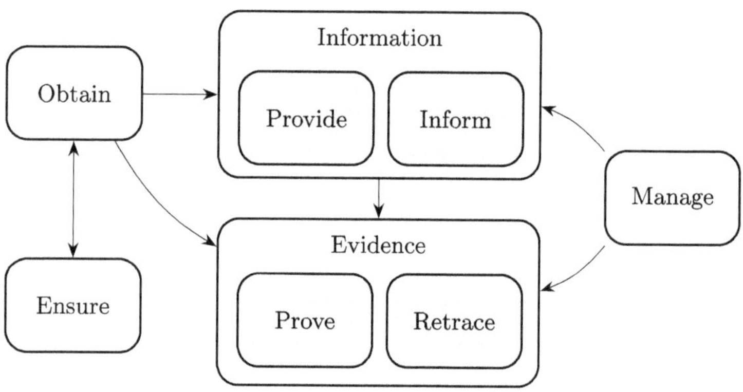

Fig. 1. Challenges of Informed Consent [40].

The interviews with practiciners showed that although many solutions exist for these challenges and privacy patterns may assist developers, the lack of privacy culture and therefore clear guidance hinders the effective implementation of privacy including informed consent. Often, they are not even aware of all the requirements and are unable to adapt them to their specific use case.

We propose an additional approach. Alongside abstract guidance such as PbD and privacy patterns, developers should be provided with simple and concise privacy best practices (PBPs). To overcome vague descriptions, developers should be given practical examples that show them how to interpret these practices, how to apply them to typical situations, and how they interrelate.

Based on the GDPR, we formulated PBPs, organized systematically around the five challenges of informed consent. Each practice is expressed in a concise manner, prioritizing simplicity to ensure relevance across diverse sectors and organization sizes. To support a deeper understanding, each practice is accompanied by a detailed description. Furthermore, to strengthen the legal basis of the recommendations, the relevant GDPR articles and clauses are referenced. The PBPs are further discussed in 5.2. The full collection of these PBPs can be found in Appendix B. In addition, the proposed PBPs were implemented as an example within a demonstrator application.

5.1 Demonstrator as a Tool

Although the PBPs are formulated with a focus on simplicity and applicability, they still need to be interpreted in terms of implementation. We therefore propose creating practical examples for conveying PBPs.

In order to create the most representative image of a generic mHealth application, twelve applications, most of which approved as DiGA (Cara Care Reizdarm, Doku4ME, Emendia, glucura: Typ 2 Diabetes Coach, Hellobetter: chronic pain, Hellobetter: diabetes and depression, Kaia COPD, Kalmeda, Mindable: Social Phobia, PINK! Coach, ProHerz, and Vivira) were examined in terms of their core functionalities and structures.

It was established that, in all cases, the app must first be activated, for example by using a code, and an account must be created. In each application, there were functions that did not require any further personal data, such as information about the medical condition or general exercises. In addition, each recorded some type of medical information such as vital signs or symptom diaries. A core functionality was the progress of this information. Beyond the decision to consent to the collection of medical information, the method of collection should also be clearly addressed. While most applications require users to actively enter their symptoms, some enable passive symptom tracking by automatically collecting vital signs.

Based on the observations our generic mHealth application demonstrator consists of a start page greeting the user, an information page presenting non-personalized content, an entry page for active symptom tracking, a progress page processing and presenting collected symptom data, and a profile and settings page including privacy functions. The application can be accessed via a login or, for first-time users, via an onboarding process. During the onboarding process, users are first informed of the controller's contact details and their data subject rights. Subsequently, information relevant to distinct data processing activities is progressively disclosed, with explicit consent requests when necessary.

The entire application is divided into two modes, which can be switched between at any time. Within the first mode developers can examine what the implementation of the best practices may look like (see Fig. 2a). The second mode adds notes and tooltips guiding developers through the various points of interest indicating specific best practices (see Fig. 2b).

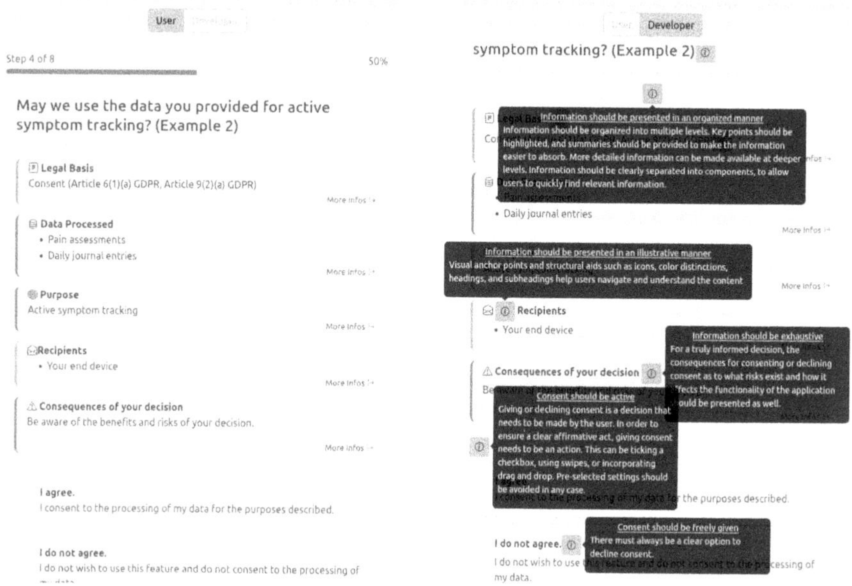

(a) Best Practices Viewable

(b) Best Practices Tooltips

Fig. 2. Conveying best practices through a demonstrator (here the onboarding).

5.2 Privacy Best Practices

In this section, we present developer-oriented PBPs in the context of informed consent. Before considering how consent should be implemented, it is essential to assess whether consent is indeed required in the given context. In accordance with the principle of data minimization, it must first be established that only the data strictly necessary for the specified purpose are processed and that such processing is limited to the minimum extent required. Additionally, a valid legal basis for processing must be identified. This depends on the context; for example, in some cases, processing is more appropriately grounded in contractual necessity or legal obligation than in consent.

When obtaining consent, it is important that separable processing activities for different purposes require separate independent consent requests. The consent must be informed, active, explicit, and freely given. Furthermore, the consent should be customizable and the consent process transparent. For further information on these PBPs for obtaining informed consent, see Appendix B.1. An example for a Privacy Best Practice can be seen in Fig. 3a.

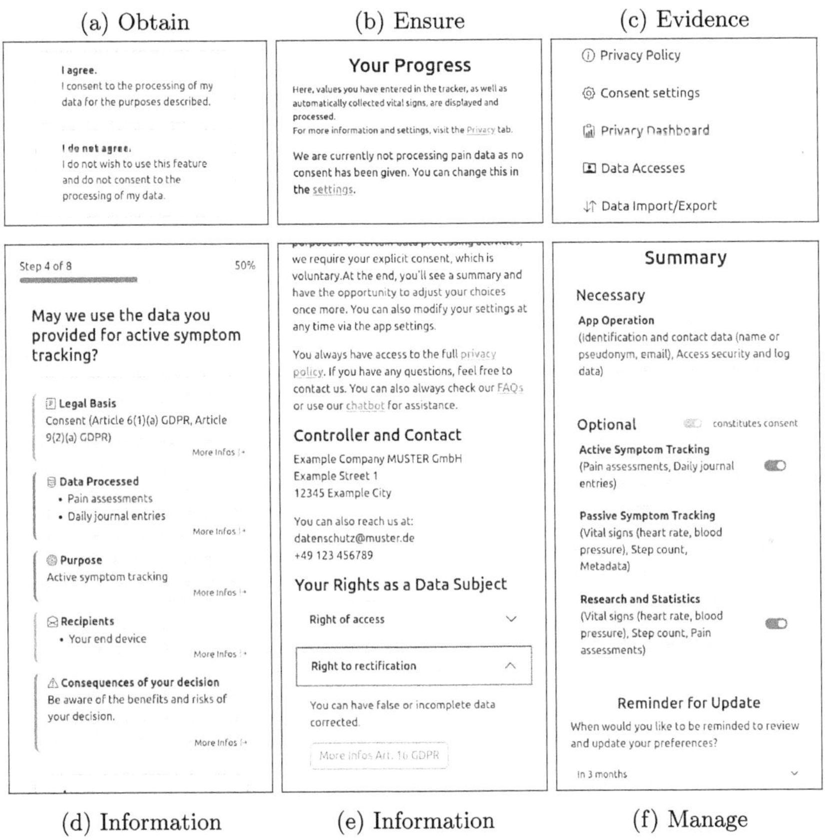

Fig. 3. Examples for Privacy Best Practices for Challenges of Informed Consent.

Giving or declining consent is a decision that needs to be made by the user. In order to ensure a clear affirmative act, giving consent needs to be an action such as ticking a checkbox. Pre-selected settings should be avoided in any case. Further, it must be clearly recognizable which action corresponds to consent. Therefore, clear text should be formulated next to the check-boxes, and color coded switches without explanations should be avoided (see this aspect also in Fig. 3f).

As previously mentioned, all relevant information must be provided to the user before obtaining consent. This information must be presented in a way that allows users to understand it well enough to make a well-informed decision (see PBPs in Appendix B.2). The information should be exhaustive and easily accessible. Texts should be comprehensible. To avoid overwhelming users with exhaustive information, it should be presented in an organized and illustrative manner. Finally, it is important to ensure that the entire process is barrier-free and that assistance is available if needed.

In addition to information related to the processing of personal data, the user needs to be informed in general about the controller and their rights as data subjects. Procedures should be made clear, assistance should be offered, and complex legal content explained in understandable terms (see Fig. 3e). Full texts can be made available in subsequent layers. In the same manner information concerning a specific consent request should be layered and supported with headlines, colors, and icons. For a truly informed decision, the consequences for consenting or declining consent as to what risks exist and how it affects the functionality of the application should be presented as well (see Fig. 3d).

To ensure that consent has been obtained, this must be enforced technically. By default, no data should be collected. Informed consent must be systematically incorporated into the testing workflow. Additionally, any data disclosed to third parties must continue to be governed by the initial consent agreement, preserving data subject rights and ethical integrity throughout the data lifecycle. Further information on these PBPs for ensuring consent can be found in Appendix B.3. If no consent is given, content should not be loaded. Instead, the user may be informed that a specific function is deactivated (see Fig. 3b).

Throughout the entire period of use, users must be given the means to manage their own consent. Informed consent should be customizable. It is important that giving and withdrawing consent are equally easy. Additionally, consent should be kept up to date and updated regularly. In order to do so, a reminder may be considered (see Fig. 3f). See these PBPs in Appendix B.4.

Finally, evidence of consent must be gathered and managed. Informed consent must always be traceable and verifiable. Likewise, data sharing with third parties should be traceable to enable the path of consent to be retraced and updated. Additionally, proof must be transparent. Like personal data itself, consent should be confidential and tamper-proof. Further information on these PBPs for evidence of consent can be found in Appendix B.5. Within the application, evidence and management of consent should be easily accessible. Clear settings to access the privacy policy, the consent settings, and observe collected data, data accesses, as well as the possibility for data import or export (see Fig. 3c).

Many of these PBPs recur throughout the entire application. The PBP *Information should be easily accessible* (Appendix B.2) can be found first within the onboarding process (Fig. 3e), second within common functionalities such as the progress page (Fig. 3b), and finally in the settings (Fig. 3c). The PBPs are closely linked to PbD [3] and the supplementing strategies [17]. The PBP *By default, no data should be collected* (Appendix B.3) is linked to the principle of Privacy as the Default. It concretizes to disable tracking tools and instead of making the display of loaded content dependent on consent, loading only that content for which consent is not required or has already been given. In this way developers can ensure a privacy-sensitive default.

In conclusion, PBPs simplify privacy requirements and abstract approaches, while demonstrators exemplify them, thereby addressing developers' need for practical guidance with clear language and actionable recommendations.

6 Limitations and Future Work

The aim of the interviews was to explore concrete needs of practitioners. Although the sample size of five is limited, the consistency of the needs expressed across all cases provides a compelling basis. Prior studies have identified developer uncertainty in controlled settings [18–20]. This study extends those findings by showing that such concerns are not confined to artificial tasks, but arise naturally in ongoing, real-world projects. While the findings offer valuable preliminary insights, they should be interpreted with caution. Future work should aim to validate these patterns through larger-scale studies across diverse development contexts and teams. It was not possible to derive how developers interact with privacy patterns and PETs in their projects. We could not make general assessments at which concrete points within the development life cycle further assistance is needed.

Further evaluations are also needed with regard to the concept of the PBPs. Upcoming workshops with users are intended to show whether the recommended practices actually reflect their wishes and needs. In addition, workshops should be held with developers to determine whether the concept is considered beneficial. The usability of a demonstrator and the comprehensibility of the practices, which have been simplified to the essentials, must be evaluated. A guide for developers on implementing informed consent incorporating the demonstrator, including PBPs is currently in progress.

The concept was applied in this case to strengthen the implementation of informed consent within digital health applications. It is also worth exploring how the concept can be applied to other domains, such as mobility, or other design challenges such as explainability in AI systems.

7 Conclusion

Although privacy and informed consent are fundamental rights, their implementation is often inadequate in concrete applications. Numerous concepts and approaches, including privacy patterns, have been proposed to improve the quality of informed consent. However, these approaches are rarely integrated into actual software development processes. Actual development processes are often characterized by uncertainty and a lack of privacy engineering expertise. Practitioners see a need for clear and concrete recommendations and well-structured guidance to overcome this problem.

To address this issue, we have proposed privacy best practices (PBPs) developed based on the GDPR and supported by recognized concepts from the literature on the implementation and enhancement of informed consent. These PBPs are intended to support development teams in designing and implementing applications that collect and process personal data, in particular sensitive data, thereby promoting compliance with privacy regulations and fostering ethical data handling.

Acknowledgments. This work was supported by the German Federal Ministry of Research, Technology and Space (BMFTR) under Grants 16KIS1884K and 16KIS1885.

Appendix A Interview Guide

The interviews were conducted in German. The interview guide is provided below in English.

A Context Which of your projects fits best within the healthcare context? Please tell us about this project:
- (1) What is the goal of the application?
- (2) Who are the users?
- (3) How have risks for the affected individuals been analyzed?
- (4) *Data*
  - (4.1) Please provide a brief sketch of the architecture to visualize data flows. Where are data collected, stored, and processed?
  - (4.2) What data or personal data are collected and for what purpose?
- (5) *Consent*
  - (5.1) How is user consent obtained? (Informed Consent)
  - (5.2) How are users informed about data processing? Are users also informed about consent during usage?
  - (5.3) How are users informed about data protection incidents?
  - (5.4) How can users exercise their data subject rights?
- (6) What concepts are used in the application to implement data protection requirements?
- (7) Have you already experienced an incident related to IT security and privacy? Please describe how the incident was discovered and the subsequent actions taken.

B Company-related
- (1) *Processes*
  - (1.1) Does the development process follow a reference model? Does your company hold certifications in this area?
  - (1.2) *Framework conditions:*
    - (1.2.1) Is development carried out exclusively in-house, or are freelancers / partner companies / service providers involved? Are they based in Germany, Europe, or offshore?
    - (1.2.2) Which software development methodology is used? (For example: Scrum)
  - (1.3) *Development process:*
    - (1.3.1) How frequently are new versions released?
    - (1.3.2) How is quality assurance carried out?
    - (1.3.3) How is risk management conducted?
    - (1.3.4) How are risks monitored?
    - (1.3.5) How are IT security and privacy requirements integrated into the development process?

(2) *People and Competencies*
  (2.1) Do you or any team member have experience with IT security and privacy? Please briefly describe this experience.
  (2.2) *Competencies:*
    (2.2.1) Are there training offerings in the areas of IT security and privacy?
    (2.2.2) How are competency development and professional exchange among team members generally supported in your company?
    (2.2.3) Are there initiatives such as pair programming?
  (2.3) Does your company have legal expertise in IT security and privacy?
  (2.4) Does your company have a data protection officer?
(3) *Technologies*
  (3.1) Which technologies are used in development? (Frameworks, cloud services, databases, programming languages, etc.)
  (3.2) Which technologies are used to implement IT security and privacy requirements?
  (3.3) Are there best practices from other projects that are being leveraged? (Libraries, individual code components for specific functions, etc.)
  (3.4) How do you implement informed consent and transparency for affected individuals?

C Personal

(1) What do IT security and privacy mean to you personally?
(2) Which aspects of IT security and privacy are personally important to you?
(3) How do you experience transparency when using digital services?
(4) In which areas related to IT security and privacy do you already build upon proven solutions? (Especially transparency and informed consent)
(5) Are there areas where you have questions or a need for information and guidance?
(6) What information sources and resources do you use to stay informed about new technologies and concepts? And what opportunities do you have to experiment with them?

Appendix B Privacy Best Practices

The following tables suggest best practices for implementing informed consent. Please note that consent is only one of several possible legal basis under Article 6(1) GDPR (for example, performance of a contract, compliance with a legal obligation or legitimate interests). Depending on the circumstances, a different legal basis may be more appropriate, or individual aspects of processing may have to rely on another legal basis because the processing is mandatory for the controller. In such cases, the following practices can sill provide useful guidance on how to present data protection information and, where applicable, consent requests to data subjects. In particular, processing that is required by law or strictly necessary for the provision of a service should not be presented as if it were optional and based on consent, in order to avoid creating misleading impression of choice.

B.1 Obtaining Informed Consent

Best Practice	Description	GDPR
Consent has to be informed.	Before obtaining consent and processing data, all relevant information must be provided to the user. To clarify information relevant to consent the information should be presented directly before obtaining consent and clearly distinguished from other information.	Articles 6(1)(a), 4(11), 12-14, Recitals 32, 60, 61
Separable processing for different purposes require separate consent.	Different purposes must be clearly distinguished. Separate consent options should be provided for each separable purpose, where appropriate, enabling data subjects to choose between them. If one purpose requires multiple processing activities, a single consent may cover all those activities, provided they are clearly described as serving that purpose. Where the same processing activity serves several purposes (e.g. one data set used for shipping a product and for marketing), the respective purposes must be clearly explained and consent should be granular per purpose.	Recitals 32
Consent should be customizable.	Model consent using dynamic consent [10,27]. This allows data subjects to make granular decisions about consent for different purposes and adjust them later. Broad consent should be avoided but may be appropriate in certain circumstances, such as for research purposes [12,21] where the exact processing is not foreseeable. Avoid all-or-nothing approaches and keep the option open to deselect individual functions. If possible, give the data subject the ability to formulate constraints under which consent is given such as time or access constraints [26]. Consent must be independent of other consent decisions for different purposes.	Recital 43, 33
Consent should be optional.	Consent is not considered freely given where access to a service or the performance of a contract is made conditional on consenting to personal data processing that is not necessary for performing that contract, or if separate consent cannot be given for different processing operations where this would be appropriate. Always have the option to decline consent.	Articles 4(11), 7(4), Recital 43

Continued on next page

Obtaining Informed Consent – continued from previous page

Best Practice	Description	GDPR
Consent should be active.	Giving or declining consent is a decision that needs to be made by the user. In order to ensure a clear affirmative act, giving consent needs to be an action. This can be ticking a checkbox, using swipes, or incorporating drag and drop [24]. Pre-ticked checkboxes should be avoided.	Recital 32
The default option should be to reject consent.	If a default is set, it must be to decline consent. Checkboxes and toggles must therefore be unticked or configured to reject consent.	Recital 32
Consent should be clear.	Regardless of which action is selected to give or refuse consent, it must be clearly recognizable which action corresponds to consent. Formulate clear text next to the checkboxes. Avoid color-coded switches without an explanation of which color and position corresponds to consent. It must also be clearly recognizable what is being consented to. To do this, clearly separate the information for the respective purposes. Present the most important information at the point where the decision regarding consent is made.	Recital 32
Be clear regarding the legal basis.	Clearly distinguish processing based on consent from processing based on other legal grounds. Clearly state the legal basis on which processing is based. Where processing is based on consent, the controller must be able to comply with a withdrawal of consent and may not switch to another legal basis later in order to continue the same processing ([11] paras. 121–123). Processing that is mandatory under Union or Member State law should be indicated as such, to avoid creating the false impression that the data subject has a choice. Avoid misleading representations, such as non-customizable checkboxes for data processing that is based on a legal ground other than consent.	Articles 5(1)(a), 5(2), 6(1), 7(1), 7(3), Recitals 42,43
Consent Process should be transparent.	A brief description of the process ensures transparency. More complex consent processes can be broken down into steps, with progress displayed throughout the process to prevent user privacy fatigue [6]. Indicating that settings can be easily adjusted at any time within the application can help reduce uncertainty.	Article 12, Recital 58

B.2 Information for Informed Consent

Best Practice	Description	GDPR
Information should be complete and appropriately detailed.	Information related to consent must contain: the identity and the contact details of the controller or its representative, contact details of the data protection officer, and information about the rights of the data subject, including the right to withdraw consent at any time. Additionally, for each separable consent, information must be provided concerning the legal basis, the data to be processed and its purposes, as well as the recipients of the data, any intention to transfer personal data to a third country, and the storage duration. For a truly informed decision, the consequences for consenting or declining consent as to what risks exist and how it affects the functionality of the application should be presented as well [32].	Articles 6(1)(a), 12-14, Recitals 32, 60
Information should always be accessible.	The processing-related information must be available and easily accessible before consent is obtained, while it is being obtained, and afterwards. Where the information is provided by another medium (for example via a link or QR code during a paper-based consent process), it must at least be offered and readily available in the same format as the consent at the time consent is obtained. In addition to information presented directly during consent collection, links to the full privacy policy must be clearly visible.	Article 12(1), Recitals 39, 58
Information and settings should be easily accessible.	To ensure availability, a dedicated tab at the highest level of the application settings can be provided. Long navigation paths should be avoided, and information must not be hidden under multiple tabs or within long texts.	Article 12(1), Recitals 39, 58
Links should be provided where relevant.	References to the information / privacy policy should be included at relevant points, for example whenever personal data is entered or displayed. Provide a link to the privacy settings so users can update their preferences as soon as they become aware of data processing.	Article 12(1), Recitals 39, 58
Text should be comprehensible.	Texts should be written in clear and simple language. Complex sentences, legal phrasing, and technical jargon should be kept to a minimum. If such terms cannot be avoided, they must be explained. Vague, unclear, and ambiguous expressions should also be avoided.	Article 12(1), Recitals 39, 58

Continued on next page

Information for Informed Consent – continued from previous page

Best Practice	Description	GDPR
Information should be presented in an organized manner.	Information should be organized into multiple levels [37]. Use headlines, highlight key points and relevant risks, and provide summaries to make the information easier to absorb. To avoid information fatigue, more detailed information may be made available at deeper levels ([2], para. 35-28). Information should be clearly separated into components, to allow users to quickly find relevant information.	Article 12(1), Recital 58
Information should be presented in an illustrative manner.	Visual anchor points and structural aids such as icons, color distinctions, headings, and subheadings help users navigate and understand the content [36,44]. Visualizations such as graphs, tables, or diagrams are suitable for complex structures and processes [36,38].	Article 12 (7), Recitals 58, 60
Information should be barrier-free.	Information must be accessible to all users. Common visual impairments, such as color blindness, should be taken into account. The format should be compatible with screen readers or allow voice-over capabilities [33]. If relevant to the user group, an additional plain language version should be provided.	Article 12(1), Recitals 39, 58
Assistance should be available.	To address any issues with clarity, guidance such as FAQs [38], chats [47], and similar [40] should be provided. Furthermore, it is important that your contact details are clearly visible in case there are any further questions.	Articles 12, 13

B.3 Ensure Informed Consent

Best Practice	Description	GDPR
Consent must be enforced technically.	Before collecting any data , the system should check whether consent is required and has been given as well as whether it is still valid. Systems should only be able to collect and store personal data when valid consent is present. Similarly, before any data is processed, it must be checked whether consent is required, has been given, and is still valid. Systems should only be able to process or forward personal data when valid consent is present.	Articles 24, 6(1)(a), 7

Continued on next page

Ensure Informed Consent – continued from previous page

Best Practice	Description	GDPR
By default, no unnecessary personal data should be collected.	To prevent personal data from being collected and processed before the data subject has been informed or without their consent, personal data should be completely avoided when starting an application. Tracking tools are disabled by default and must be actively enabled. Content that requires consent should only be loaded by the system once consent has been obtained or is available.	Articles 5, 6, 25, Recital 39
Informed consent should be tested.	Automatic tests should be in place. These tests should verify that personal data is only collected with consent. They should also verify that personal data is no longer collected if consent has been withdrawn or if conditions, such as a time limit, have expired. Before any processing of personal data takes place, it should be verified that valid consent exists, and processing should be prevented in the absence of valid consent.	Article 24
Data shared for processing with third parties is still bound to consent.	When personal data is shared with processors or other recipients on the basis of consent, it is important that the recipient party is obliged to only process the data in the manner to which consent was given [30]. Sticky policies can help to link data and processing requirements [45].	Article 28

B.4 Manage Informed Consent

Best Practice	Description	GDPR
Consent should be adjustable.	Throughout the use of the application, options to grant, withdraw or adjust consent settings should be available. This also includes adjustments to conditions to which consent may be subject, such as access authorizations for specific persons, specific periods or expiry dates, and other restrictions.	Article 7(3)
Giving and withdrawing consent should be equivalent.	Changes such as withdrawing consent must be as easy as giving consent. Specific settings and withdrawal options must be provided. Moreover, these features should be easy for users to find and use.	Article 7(3)

Continued on next page

Manage Informed Consent – continued from previous page

Best Practice	Description	GDPR
Informed consent should be kept up-to-date and updated regularly.	Changes in user needs or circumstances may affect the decision to give consent. Therefore, set up regular reminders to review and adjust privacy settings as necessary.	Articles 5, Art. 7(3)
Informed consent should be able to respond to changes.	Over time, processing procedures or purposes and the legal framework may change. Therefore, establish a way to inform users about these changes. Set up processes to keep users informed and obtain an updated consent if necessary.	Articles 6(1)(a), 5(1), 12, 13, 14(4)

B.5 Evidence of Informed Consent

Best Practice	Description	GDPR
Informed consent should be traceable.	Information on whether or not consent was given should be accessible at all times. Information available during the consent process should also be accessible afterwards if required. Likewise, the settings should be traceable in terms of time, for example via a timestamp showing the date of the last update.	Articles 7(1), 5(2), Recital 42
Informed consent should be verifiable.	For each consent decision, a record should be created. This record should document how the consent was obtained, what has been consented to (including the versions of the information provided and working of consent), which data may be processed for which purposes, and the period of validity. Include further the dates when consent was given, updated, expired or withdrawn.	Articles 7(1), 5(2), Recital 42
Proof should be transparent.	The record and, therefore the proof of consent and its circumstances should be communicable. Users should be able to obtain proof, for example by using consent receipts [23,29]. Changes such as the granting or revocation of consent should be confirmed to the user. Inform the user about changes to their consent status, for example, when it expires due to a time limit.	Articles 7(1), 12(1), Recital 42

Continued on next page

Evidence of Informed Consent – continued from previous page

Best Practice	Description	GDPR
Consent should be confidential and tamper-proof.	The decision to give or withhold consent is personal data in itself. Consent records must be stored in a way that preserves their confidentiality and integrity, so that they cannot be accessed or altered by unauthorized parties.	Articles 4(1), 5(1)(f), 32
Data-sharing with third parties should be retraceable.	Third parties processing shared data must be informed of any changes to the consent as well as any requests for rectification, erasure or restriction. Further, the data subject may request information about those recipients. To fulfill these obligations, sharing activities must be logged and documented.	Articles 19, 7(1), 5(2)

References

1. Alfawzan, N., Christen, M., Spitale, G., Biller-Andorno, N.: Privacy, data sharing, and data security policies of women's mhealth apps: scoping review and content analysis. JMIR Mhealth Uhealth **10**(5), e33735 (2022). https://doi.org/10.2196/33735
2. Article 29 Data Protection Working Party: Guidelines on Transparency under Regulation 2016/679. Working Paper 260 rev. 01, Brussels (2018). https://ec.europa.eu/newsroom/article29/items/622227
3. Cavoukian, A.: Privacy by design: The 7 foundational principles, Toronto (2009)
4. Cejas, O.A., Abualhaija, S., Sannier, N., Ceci, M., Bianculli, D.: GDPR compliance in privacy policies of mobile apps: an overview of the state-of-practice. In: 2025 IEEE 33rd International Requirements Engineering Conference (RE), pp. 320–331 (2025). https://doi.org/10.1109/RE63999.2025.00038
5. Cha, S.C., Hsu, T.Y., Xiang, Y., Yeh, K.H.: Privacy enhancing technologies in the internet of things: perspectives and challenges. IEEE Internet Things J. **6**(2), 2159–2187 (2019). https://doi.org/10.1109/JIOT.2018.2878658
6. Chen, M., Chen, M.: Trust, privacy fatigue, and the informed consent dilemma in mobile app privacy pop-ups: a grounded theory approach. J. Theor. Appl. Electron. Commerce Res. **20**(3) (2025). https://doi.org/10.3390/jtaer20030179
7. Colesky, M., et al.: privacypatterns.org. https://privacypatterns.org/ (2006). Accessed 27 Mar 2026
8. D'Acquisto, G., Domingo-Ferrer, J., Kikiras, P., Torra, V., de Montjoye, Y.A., Bourka, A.: Privacy by design in big data: an overview of privacy enhancing technologies in the era of big data analytics. Publications Office of the European Union, Luxembourg (2015). https://data.europa.eu/doi/10.2824/641480
9. Danezis, G., et al.: Privacy and Data Protection by Design: From Policy to Engineering. Publications Office of the European Union, Luxembourg (Dec 2014). https://doi.org/10.2824/38623

10. Dankar, F.K., Gergely, M., Malin, B., Badji, R., Dankar, S.K., Shuaib, K.: Dynamic-informed consent: a potential solution for ethical dilemmas in population sequencing initiatives. Comput. Struct. Biotechnol. J. **18**, 913–921 (2020). https://doi.org/10.1016/j.csbj.2020.03.027
11. European Data Protection Board: Guidelines 05/2020 on consent under Regulation 2016/679, version 1.1. Guidelines 05/2020, Brussels (2020). https://www.edpb.europa.eu/sites/default/files/files/file1/edpb_guidelines_202005_consent_en.pdf
12. European Data Protection Board: EDPB Document on response to the request from the European Commission for clarifications on the consistent application of the GDPR, focusing on health research, Brussels (2021)
13. Fan, M., et al.: An empirical evaluation of GDPR compliance violations in android mhealth apps. In: 2020 IEEE 31st International Symposium on Software Reliability Engineering (ISSRE), pp. 253–264 (2020). https://doi.org/10.1109/ISSRE5003.2020.00032
14. Fassbender, A., et al.: Adoption of digital therapeutics in Europe. Ther. Clin. Risk Manag. **20**, 939–954 (2024). https://doi.org/10.2147/TCRM.S489873
15. Giebel, G.D., et al.: Integration of digital health applications into the German healthcare system: Development of "The DiGA-Care Path". Front. Health Serv. **4** (2024). https://doi.org/10.3389/frhs.2024.1372522
16. Hansen, M., Jensen, M., Rost, M.: Protection goals for privacy engineering. In: 2015 IEEE Security and Privacy Workshops, pp. 159–166 (2015). https://doi.org/10.1109/SPW.2015.13
17. Hoepman, J.H.: Privacy design strategies. In: IFIP International Information Security Conference, pp. 446–459. Springer (2014). https://doi.org/10.48550/arXiv.1210.6621
18. Horstmann, S.A., et al.: "Those things are written by lawyers, and programmers are reading that." Mapping the Communication Gap Between Software Developers and Privacy Experts. Proc. Privacy Enhanc. Technol. **2024**(1), 151–170 (2024). https://doi.org/10.56553/popets-2024-0010
19. Horstmann, S.A., et al.: "Sorry for bugging you so much." exploring developers' behavior towards privacy-compliant implementation. In: 2025 IEEE Symposium on Security and Privacy (SP), pp. 1215–1233 (2025). https://doi.org/10.1109/SP61157.2025.00146
20. Horstmann, S.A., Hong, S., Niazian, M., Santos, C., Naiakshina, A.: "I need to learn better searching tactics for privacy policy laws." Investigating Software Developers' Behavior When Using Sources on Privacy Issues. In: 2026 IEEE/ACM 48th International Conference on Software Engineering (ICSE26) (2026). https://doi.org/10.1145/3744916.3773150
21. Hutchings, E., Loomes, M., Butow, P., Boyle, F.M.: A systematic literature review of attitudes towards secondary use and sharing of health administrative and clinical trial data: a focus on consent. Syst. Rev. **10**(1), 132 (2021). https://doi.org/10.1186/s13643-021-01663-z
22. Jasmontaite, L., Kamara, I., Zanfir-Fortuna, G., Leucci, S.: Data protection by design and by default: Framing guiding principles into legal obligations in the GDPR. European Data Protection Law Review **4**(2), 168–189 (2018). https://doi.org/10.21552/edpl/2018/2/7
23. Jesus, V., Pandit, H.J.: Consent receipts for a usable and auditable web of personal data. IEEE Access **10**, 28545–28563 (2022). https://doi.org/10.1109/ACCESS.2022.3157850

24. Karegar, F., Pettersson, J.S., Fischer-Hübner, S.: The dilemma of user engagement in privacy notices: effects of interaction modes and habituation on user attention. ACM Trans. Privacy Secur. **23**(1) (2020). https://doi.org/10.1145/3372296
25. Kassam, I., Ilkina, D., Kemp, J., Roble, H., Carter-Langford, A., Shen, N.: Patient perspectives and preferences for consent in the digital health context: state-of-the-art literature review. J. Med. Internet Res. **25**, e42507 (2023). https://doi.org/10.2196/42507
26. Konstantinidis, G., Holt, J., Chapman, A.: Enabling personal consent in databases. Proc. VLDB Endow. **15**(2), 375–387 (2021). https://doi.org/10.14778/3489496.3489516
27. Lee, H., Lee, U.: Toward dynamic consent for privacy-aware pervasive health and well-being: a scoping review and research directions. IEEE Pervasive Comput. **21**(4), 25–32 (2022). https://doi.org/10.1109/MPRV.2022.3210747
28. Lenhard, J., Fritsch, L., Herold, S.: A literature study on privacy patterns research. In: 2017 43rd Euromicro Conference on Software Engineering and Advanced Applications (SEAA), pp. 194–201 (2017). https://doi.org/10.1109/SEAA.2017.28
29. Lizar, M., Hodder, M.: Usable consents: tracking and managing use of personal data with a consent transaction receipt. In: Proceedings of the 2014 ACM International Joint Conference on Pervasive and Ubiquitous Computing: Adjunct Publication, pp. 647–652. ACM, New York, NY, USA (2014). https://doi.org/10.1145/2638728.2641681
30. Mbannaso, U., Sogbesan, A.: The conceptualisation of a configurable consent architecture for personal data release. In: 2022 IEEE Nigeria 4th International Conference on Disruptive Technologies for Sustainable Development (NIGERCON), pp. 1–5 (2022). https://doi.org/10.1109/NIGERCON54645.2022.9803088
31. Nguyen, T.T., Backes, M., Stock, B.: Freely given consent?: studying consent notice of third-party tracking and its violations of GDPR in android apps. In: Proceedings of the 2022 ACM SIGSAC Conference on Computer and Communications Security, pp. 2369–2383. ACM, Los Angeles CA USA (2022). https://doi.org/10.1145/3548606.3560564
32. Nusbaum, L., Douglas, B., Damus, K., Paasche-Orlow, M., Estrella-Luna, N.: Communicating risks and benefits in informed consent for research: a qualitative study. Global Qual. Nurs. Res. **4**, 2333393617732017 (2017). https://doi.org/10.1177/2333393617732017
33. O'Connor, Y., Rowan, W., Lynch, L., Heavin, C.: Privacy by design: informed consent and internet of things for smart health. Proc. Comput. Sci. **113**, 653–658 (2017). https://doi.org/10.1016/j.procs.2017.08.329
34. Prasad, A., Sorber, J., Stablein, T., Anthony, D., Kotz, D.: Exposing privacy concerns in mHealth. In: 2nd USENIX Workshop on Health Security and Privacy (HealthSec 11). USENIX Association,, San Francisco, CA (2011)
35. Regulation (EU) 2016/679 of the European Parliament and of the Council of 27 April 2016 on the protection of natural persons with regard to the processing of personal data and on the free movement of such data, and repealing Directive 95/46/EC (General Data Protection Regulation). OJ L **119** (2016)
36. Reinhardt, D., Borchard, J., Hurtienne, J.: Visual interactive privacy policy: The better choice? In: Proceedings of the 2021 CHI Conference on Human Factors in Computing Systems, pp. 1–12 (2021). https://doi.org/10.1145/3411764.3445465
37. Renaud, K., Shepherd, L.A.: How to make privacy policies both GDPR-compliant and usable. In: 2018 International Conference on Cyber Situational Awareness, Data Analytics And Assessment (Cyber SA), pp. 1–8 (2018). https://doi.org/10.1109/CyberSA.2018.8551442

38. Rossi, A., Lenzini, G.: Transparency by design in data-informed research: a collection of information design patterns. Comput. Law Security Rev. **37**, 105402 (2020). https://doi.org/10.1016/j.clsr.2020.105402
39. Schiering, I., Friedewald, M., Schmidt, R.: Datenschutz-design-patterns. Datenschutz und Datensicherheit - DuD **48**(9), 583–588 (2024). https://doi.org/10.1007/s11623-024-1979-x
40. Schmidt, R., Schiering, I., Zwingelberg, H., Friedewald, M.: Challenges and solutions in implementing informed consent in digital environments: a scoping review. IEEE Access **13**, 71965–71983 (2025). https://doi.org/10.1109/ACCESS.2025.3562773
41. Schneider, D., Koch, J., Schlüfter, C., Zwingelberg, H., Friedewald, M., Heyen, N.B.: Einwilligen, aber informiert: Die Perspektive von Patient:innen auf die informierte Einwilligung bei der Nutzung von Gesundheits-Apps. In: Friedewald, M., Roßnagel, A., Karaboga, M., Geminn, C. (eds.) Datenschutz und Digitalpolitik in krisenhaften Zeiten. Nomos (2026, forthcoming)
42. Spiekermann, S., Korunovska, J., Langheinrich, M.: Inside the organization: why privacy and security engineering as a challenge for engineers. Proc. IEEE **107**(3), 600–615 (2019). https://doi.org/10.1109/JPROC.2018.2866769
43. Tzanou, M.: Data protection as a fundamental right next to privacy? "Reconstructing" a not so new right. Int. Data Privacy Law **3**(2), 88–99 (2013). https://doi.org/10.1093/idpl/ipt004
44. Ugaya Mazza, L.: Exploring the use of pictograms in privacy agreements to facilitate communication between users and data collecting entities: randomized controlled trial. JMIR Hum. Factors **10**, e34855 (2023). https://doi.org/10.2196/34855
45. Ulbricht, M.R., Pallas, F.: CoMaFeDS: Consent management for federated data sources. In: 2016 IEEE International Conference on Cloud Engineering Workshop (IC2EW), pp. 106–111 (2016). https://doi.org/10.1109/IC2EW.2016.30
46. Wagner, I.: Privacy policies across the ages: content of privacy policies 1996–2021. ACM Trans. Privacy Security **26**(3), 1–32 (2023). https://doi.org/10.1145/3590152
47. Xiao, Z., Li, T.W., Karahalios, K., Sundaram, H.: Inform the uninformed: improving online informed consent reading with an AI-powered Chatbot. In: Proceedings of the 2023 CHI Conference on Human Factors in Computing Systems, pp. 1–17 (2023). https://doi.org/10.1145/3544548.3581252
48. Zhang, D., Lim, J., Zhou, L., Dahl, A.A.: Breaking the Data value-privacy paradox in mobile mental health systems through user-centered privacy protection: a web-based survey study. JMIR Mental Health **8**(12), e31633 (2021). https://doi.org/10.2196/31633
49. Zhou, L., Bao, J., Watzlaf, V., Parmanto, B.: Barriers to and facilitators of the use of mobile health apps from a security perspective: mixed-methods study. JMIR Mhealth Uhealth **7**(4), e11223 (2019). https://doi.org/10.2196/11223

Transparency and Intervenability in Privacy Engineering: From Research Gap to GDPR Challenge

Tanel Mällo[(✉)], Ainika Harro, and Liina Kamm

Cybernetica AS, Tallinn, Estonia
{tanel.mallo,ainika.harro,liina.kamm}@cyber.ee

Abstract. Privacy-enhancing technologies address personal data risks through three privacy protection goals from European privacy discourse: transparency, intervenability, and unlinkability. Despite legal frameworks like GDPR mandating transparency and intervenability alongside unlinkability, practical engineering implementations remain imbalanced. Through keyword frequency analysis of 2,920 articles from three major privacy venues (PoPETS, USENIX, SOUPS) spanning 2002–2023, we demonstrate that transparency and intervenability are significantly underrepresented as compared to unlinkability. This gap reflects a broader challenge: privacy engineering has focused on technical solutions for data protection (unlinkability) while practical tools and standardized methods for implementing transparency and intervenability remain scarce. Also, this highlights the most critical gap in the whole privacy discourse from research to engineering: maintaining the idea of individuals as passive data subjects protected by process owning organizations. Our analysis reveals a positive shift toward addressing these goals following GDPR adoption in 2016, alongside increased interdisciplinarity in privacy research. We identify specific engineering practice gaps and argue for balanced development of privacy engineering solutions that support all three privacy goals, enabling both regulatory compliance and meaningful user control.

Keywords: transparency · intervenability · unlinkability · privacy goals

1 Introduction

We live in an almost omnipresent data processing reality. While data-intensive technologies and services are convenient and efficient, they also pose acknowledged risks. Privacy risks are a major concern, potentially affecting personal well-being, freedom and agency. This has sparked a global wave of progressive privacy and data protection regulations, most notably the European Union's General Data Protection Regulation (GDPR), which established legally binding requirements for transparency, intervenability, and unlinkability in data processing systems. Privacy seems to be the keyword as central to the discourse on the

F. Pallas et al. (Eds.): APF 2026, LNCS 16847, pp. 253–266, 2026.
https://doi.org/10.1007/978-3-032-35899-8_12

health of the digital environment as sustainability is to the physical one. As Acquisti et al. observe: "If this is the age of information, then privacy is the issue of our times." [1].

As a solution to these tech-induced privacy concerns, a layer of technologies are implemented. Privacy-enhancing technologies (PETs) are implemented as integrated components of existing technologies and services. However, there is a fundamental problem that lies in the evasive nature of privacy itself. The continuously changing technologies (see, e.g. in [6]) and differences in cultural norms [28] make it difficult to define privacy in universal legal or technical terms, not to mention the highly vulnerable collective and individual norms of privacy [3].

Hence, privacy research is inherently interdisciplinary, integrating diverse conceptualizations and insights from technical fields like computer science and information technology, as well as from social sciences, law, ethics, and cultural studies. Achieving comprehensive privacy protection necessitates a harmonious blend of "soft measures" – including legal, ethical, and social considerations – along with robust technological solutions [1,4]. While both dimensions are crucial, some technological aspects have been underrepresented within privacy research [16]. While certain privacy goals may rely on softer means, such as fostering general transparency and user awareness, every privacy goal must be supported by effective technological solutions to ensure robust protection. This technological support is essential because modern data processing systems can often undermine privacy even when softer measures are in place [6]. Therefore, a comprehensive approach to privacy research - and privacy engineering - must not only emphasize the importance of interdisciplinary collaboration but also advocate for the development and implementation of technological solutions that reinforce privacy goals across the board.

With this ideal in mind, we herewith ask how the self-identified privacy engineering community distributes its attention across the different privacy goals, and what this reveals about which goals it treats as engineering problems. To answer this question, this paper makes the following contributions: (1) a quantitative analysis of 2,920 articles across three major privacy venues spanning 2002–2023, documenting the relative representation of all three privacy goals; (2) an analysis of trends correlated with GDPR adoption; and (3) an identification of specific engineering practice gaps, with recommendations for a more balanced research agenda.

1.1 Privacy Goals

The holistic privacy discourse of the European Union [4], codified in GDPR requirements, builds on the model of three security protection goals and three privacy protection goals originally proposed by Rost and Pfitzmann [21] – namely *integrity*, *availability*, *confidentiality*, *transparency*, *intervenability* and *unlinkability* (see also [9,10]). We focus on the privacy protection goals.

Transparency as a privacy goal aims to guarantee that stakeholders (e.g., individuals, data-processing entities, supervisory authorities) understand privacy-relevant data processing, fostering trust between data subjects, data processors and service providers [4]. Transparency is crucial because it enables individuals to evaluate, contest, and challenge flaws that may affect them [11]. GDPR Articles 13–15 mandate specific transparency requirements that data controllers must fulfill, including clear communication of identity of data controllers, purposes of data processing and rights of data subjects. These legal obligations necessitate practical engineering implementations of transparency mechanisms. Transparency-enhancing tools (TETs) provide users with insights into how their data is collected, processed, and shared [17,18]. This can be achieved e.g., through logging and reporting, documentation of data processing, and user notifications [10,11,23]. On the other hand, challenges related to user judgment and misdirection can undermine the intended benefits of transparency, rendering them less effective than anticipated [2]. In broader terms, transparency has been reported to remain under-researched in information and software systems development [19]. By ensuring that users are aware of their data processing rights and have means to exercise them, transparency fosters control and autonomy. This relationship underscores the necessity for organizations to provide actionable avenues for users to understand and respond to organizational data processing practices, with transparency serving as a precondition for intervenability.

Intervenability as a privacy goal is defined as the property that intervention is possible during ongoing or planned privacy-relevant data processing [4]. It enables control over one's data and how it is processed. Intervenability can be achieved by, e.g., implementing dedicated intervention services, defining break-glass procedures, and means to override automated decisions, as well as providing data subjects with options such as the ability to access and to review their personal data, to challenge the accuracy and completeness of their personal data, to withdraw consent, and to object to data processing [9,10,17]. Additional mechanisms include ensuring data subjects are informed about their rights and choices regarding their personal data, which is a crucial aspect of transparency that supports intervenability. Mapping intervenability notions in literature, the authors of [15] report giving or withdrawing consent as the most often discussed option.

Unlinkability as a privacy goal entails that privacy-relevant data should not be linked across domains constituted by a common purpose and context [4]. Hansen et al. [10] suggest a broader definition that includes processes and domains that should not be linkable. (1) Privacy of data in information systems and analytics includes applying privacy-enhancing technologies (PETs), such as differential privacy and secure multi-party computation, pseudonymization and anonymization. (2) Privacy of identity and authentication focuses on technologies like blind signatures and zero-knowledge proofs, which allow verification without revealing identity. (3) Privacy of communications and transactions includes secure messaging systems, mix networks, and onion routing, designed to obscure identity and content of communications. In this work we focus exclusively on privacy of data in information systems and analytics, because the use of solutions for the latter forms of unlinkability are an active choice by the users, not an external implementation for an otherwise passive data subject that is the focus of our current investigation. For instance, differential privacy allows organisations to analyse datasets while providing mathematical guarantees that individual privacy is protected [4]. In a similar fashion, secure multi-party computation enables multiple parties to compute functions while keeping inputs confidential, preventing data linking [31]. However, significant challenges exist in unlinkability, as e.g., traditional anonymisation techniques remain vulnerable to re-identification attacks. Furthermore, the application of unlinkability strategies must be context-sensitive, as the requirements for unlinkability may differ based on the specific use cases and regulatory environments [10].

1.2 Relevance of Privacy Goals to Different Stakeholders

Of these three privacy goals, transparency and intervenability are highly relevant for individuals, relating to their right of informational self-determination [7]. However, they are not motivating from the organizational perspective due to implementation costs and limited business benefits [10]. In comparison, unlinkability, if implemented properly, significantly reduces the risk of privacy breaches and possible costs for the organization. While benefits of unlinkability are similar for both individuals and data processing organizations (e.g. individual anonymity is retained and legal requirements are met), the implementation of transparency and intervenability brings the additional value of individual agency and control, but not necessarily visible business benefits that would compensate for the inevitable costs of adding the functionality. Related to this, the authors of [10] point out a crucial difference: while privacy takes the individual's perspective, data protection refers to the organizational perspective. For individuals, privacy is a broad personal matter [14], while for organizations, it is concrete liability emerging from strict regulations [31]. While there are good reasons to strive for privacy from both perspectives, differences in motivation and capabilities between individuals and organizations lead to an imbalance in actual methods applied, mirroring the broader power imbalances [11]. This often results in accountability and fair use of data being overlooked when focusing solely on data protection measures [24]. It promotes a research and engineering focus on unlinkability at the expense of transparency and intervenability. This gap persists despite GDPR's equal legal weighting of all three privacy goals, highlighting a disconnect between regulatory requirements and engineering practice.

2 Methods: A Keyword Analysis of Privacy Engineering Research

We hypothesise that, despite the growing endorsement of privacy-enhancing technologies (PETs) as essential tools for fostering ethical, legal, and responsible data practices [13,24,27], the current discourse and landscape of PET research and development exhibits a notable bias toward the goal of unlinkability compared to transparency and intervenability [12]. This imbalance could hinder a holistic realization of privacy objectives. The predominant focus on unlinkability aligns with organizational imperatives (compliance, risk mitigation) while sidelining the privacy goals most relevant to individual agency and control. To substantiate this claim, we conduct a comprehensive analysis of the research and development efforts surrounding PETs as published in the proceedings of (1) Privacy Enhancing Technologies Symposium[1] (PoPETS), (2) Symposium on Usable Privacy and Security[2] (SOUPS) and (3) USENIX Security Symposium[3] (USENIX), systematically examining the prevalence of keywords related to privacy-goals in these venues.

We deliberately selected venues that explicitly position themselves as privacy-focused rather than security-focused: PoPETS is dedicated to privacy-enhancing technologies, SOUPS to usable privacy and security, and USENIX Security represents the broader security community's engagement with privacy. This selection reflects our research question: not whether transparency and intervenability appear in the literature overall, but whether the self-identified privacy engineering community prioritizes them. If transparency and intervenability are delegated to adjacent communities rather than claimed by privacy engineering proper, this itself constitutes the gap we aim to document.

By scrutinizing the frequency of these keywords in the articles, we quantitatively assess the alignment of privacy technology efforts with foundational privacy goals, highlighting an important gap that has not been sufficiently addressed in prior studies. This investigation not only contributes to a deeper understanding of the current state of PETs but also aims to catalyze a more balanced discourse and innovation in PETs development, emphasizing the underrepresented goals of transparency and intervenability.

We performed full-text keyword analysis using Python version 3.9.12, with each article read and parsed with the aid of Python library PyPDF2. We included whole texts of articles in the analysis (excluding headers and footers) and counted the occurrences of each keyword per article.

As the three privacy goals are not necessarily mentioned under their specific terms in the published articles pertaining to those topics, we generated a set of possible synonyms and related keywords for each privacy goal based on domain expertise and materials provided in [4] and [5]. Our keyword selection strategy focused on terms representing either technical implementations (e.g., 'privacy dashboard,' 'consent management'), regulatory mechanisms (e.g., 'DPIA,' 'data subject access request'), or research concepts (e.g., 'explainability,' 'dark patterns') directly associated with each privacy goal in privacy engineering literature. Table 1 represents the final keyword sets used for analysis. If a keyword consisted of multiple words (e.g., "privacy label"), it was treated as a string to ensure accurate identification in the text. Some closely related keywords could not be used due to their general meanings in different contexts. For example, 'control,' 'inform,' 'fairness,' 'consent,' 'usability,' and 'policy' appear frequently

[1] https://petsymposium.org/popets/.
[2] https://www.usenix.org/conferences/byname/884.
[3] https://www.usenix.org/publications/proceedings.

in security and usability discussions unrelated to specific privacy goals, creating excessive false positives. We retained more specific compound terms (e.g., 'consent management,' 'privacy control(s)') that unambiguously indicate privacy engineering contexts.

To reduce noise from incidental keyword mentions, we set a threshold of four or more keyword occurrences per article to identify works substantively addressing each privacy goal. We determined this threshold through manual validation of articles with varying keyword frequencies, and we found that it provided the best balance between false positives and false negatives. We also manually validated whether keyword presence reliably indicated substantive engagement with the respective privacy goal.

Table 1. Synonyms and related keywords used for finding articles addressing transparency, intervenability and unlinkability.

Privacy goal	Representative keywords
Transparency	access tracking, consent form, dark patterns, data access request, data auditing, data processing opacity, data sharing practices, data subject access request, deceptive design, DPIA, explainability, parent* control app, privacy dashboard, privacy impact assessment, privacy interface, privacy label, privacy notice, privacy notification, privacy perception, privacy policy, privacy policy icons, privacy statement, self-sovereign, TET, transparency enhancing technologies, user perception
Intervenability	consent flow, consent management, disabling permission, opt-in, opt-out, PDS, PIMS, personal data store, privacy assistant, privacy control(s), privacy interface, privacy preferences, privacy settings, rectification, self-management, self-sovereign, usable privacy
Unlinkability	anonym*, data avoidance, data minimisation, data minimization, de-identification, differential privacy, identifiability, identifiable, minimise data, privacy preserving, privacy-preserving, private set intersection, pseudonym*, quasi-identifiers, re-identification, secure multi-party computation, unlinkable, untraceability, untraceable

3 Results

The analysis of keyword occurrences across the three venues reveals key trends in privacy goal representation. Table 2 presents our primary empirical findings: the annual percentages of articles with threshold-limited (≥ 4) occurrences of privacy goal-related keywords. This threshold-filtered analysis identifies articles with substantive engagement with each privacy goal, distinguishing them from those with only incidental keyword mentions. Because several venues publish relatively few articles per year, percentages should be read alongside the underlying counts shown in the table: at small n, a single article can correspond to a sizeable percentage (e.g., one paper among 15 is 6.7%). We therefore treat low percentages as indicative rather than precise, and base our claims on patterns sustained across multiple years rather than on individual values.

Table 2. Annual percentages of USENIX, SOUPS and PoPETS articles with threshold-limited ($n \geq 4$) occurrences of respective privacy goals related keywords within the article text. n - number of articles, U - Unlinkability, I - Intervenability, T - Transparency.

Year	USENIX				SOUPS				PoPETS			
	n	U	I	T	n	U	I	T	n	U	I	T
2023	423	7.8	0.2	0.7	24	12.5	8.3	4.2	123	50.4	4.9	2.4
2022	257	10.9	1.2	0.0	24	8.3	13.0	0.0	128	30.5	4.7	3.9
2021	247	10.5	1.6	0.8	24	0.0	12.5	8.3	81	34.6	4.9	2.5
2020	158	8.2	0.0	0.0	24	0.0	8.3	4.2	79	25.3	3.8	0.0
2019	114	7.9	0.9	0.0	24	8.3	12.5	4.2	66	22.7	3.0	0.0
2018	101	5.0	1.0	0.0	24	4.2	8.3	4.2	35	31.4	0.0	0.0
2017	86	8.1	0.0	0.0	24	4.2	4.2	0.0	52	32.7	0.0	0.0
2016	73	4.1	0.0	0.0	23	0.0	4.4	4.3	51	35.3	0.0	0.0
2015	68	7.4	0.0	0.0	22	0.0	4.5	4.5	23	30.0	4.3	0.0
2014	68	7.4	1.5	1.5	21	0.0	9.5	0.0	16	37.5	0.0	0.0
2013	45	8.9	0.0	0.0	15	6.7	6.7	0.0	13	38.5	0.0	0.0
2012	44	6.8	0.0	0.0	13	0.0	0.0	0.0	16	50.0	0.0	0.0
2011	36	11.1	0.0	0.0	15	6.7	6.7	0.0	15	40.0	0.0	0.0
2010					16	0.0	0.0	0.0	17	52.9	0.0	0.0
2009					15	0.0	6.7	0.0	14	64.3	0.0	7.1
2008					12	0.0	0.0	0.0	14	64.3	0.0	0.0
2007					13	7.7	0.0	0.0	16	43.8	6.3	0.0
2006					14	0.0	0.0	0.0	24	29.2	0.0	0.0
2005					10	0.0	0.0	0.0	17	47.1	0.0	0.0
2004									22	36.4	0.0	0.0
2003									14	35.7	0.0	0.0
2002									17	52.9	5.9	0.0

For PoPETS, transparency- and intervenability-themed articles began to appear at a rate higher than one per year only from 2015 and 2016, respectively. It is only in recent years, starting from 2019, that nine or more articles addressing these topics were published annually, raising their proportions beyond 10% of the increasingly large pool of published works. The types of articles classified under transparency and intervenability categories varied broadly, falling into at least two major categories, where the specific privacy goal (transparency/intervenability) was either the main topic of the article, or a significant side issue. The occurrence of unlinkability-related articles corresponding to our criteria has steadily decreased over the past decade, likely reflecting the maturation of specific techniques, replacing the general term.

For USENIX, unlinkability-themed articles consistently remained below 12% annually, with a peak of 11.1% in 2011. Transparency articles were almost negligible, rarely exceeding 1% annually, while intervenability-themed works were practically absent throughout. This limited focus on privacy goals likely reflects the broader technical scope of USENIX and its emphasis on general systems security over specific privacy themes.

At SOUPS, transparency-themed articles emerged more prominently than in the other conferences, reaching their highest proportion of 8.3% in 2021. Transparency at SOUPS has seen a modest yet relatively stable representation over the years, contrasting with the sharper increases observed in PoPETS post-2015. Intervenability in SOUPS appeared slightly more frequently than in USENIX, with years like 2023 reaching 8.3%, but it remains a niche topic also for this venue. Unlinkability, as in USENIX, showed consistently low and fluctuating representation.

Across all three conferences, the prevalence of unlinkability-related articles displays a varying pattern, reflecting the growing maturity and variations in popularity of the various aspects of the concept across years.

Among transparency-themed work, some addresses the goal directly – for example, studies of the usability of app privacy labels [29] and of privacy interface design [20] – while in others it appears as a significant side issue, such as assessments of privacy perceptions [25] or of dark patterns in consent management [26].

Intervenability, by contrast, is rarely the technical focus: the few relevant works address the consequences of intervention [22] or describe contexts where it is hard to tell whether a solution delivers intervenability or unlinkability [8]. The near-absence of articles proposing concrete intervenability mechanisms is itself a finding, underscoring the limited attention this privacy goal has received in the broader research landscape.

4 Discussion

4.1 Evidence from Privacy Research Venues

Our analysis comparing PoPETS, USENIX, and SOUPS highlights key similarities and differences in their treatment of privacy goals. Unlinkability remains steadily the most popular privacy goal across venues. Historically, when the PETS conference started in 2002, its participants mainly came from the anonymous communication and information secrecy research community, being very much focused on the tech/crypto/network traffic algorithms discussion. Hence, the roots and birth date of PETS influenced how its central terms were conceptualized, as historically privacy was more concerned with confidentiality and data minimisation, and less perceived as data protection that has the data subject more in focus. USENIX exhibits consistently lower focus on privacy goals overall. Despite its broader scope and high article output, its attention to transparency and unlinkability is sparse. Intervenability remains absent from USENIX. SOUPS presents a different picture. Transparency and intervenability are more prevalent in SOUPS compared to other venues, reflecting its emphasis on user-centered design. This aligns with SOUPS's focus on human interaction rather than system-level technical guarantees.

Across the analyzed time period, PoPETS and SOUPS show increase in transparency mentions in recent years, correlating with GDPR implementation. This shift is concurrent with the adoption of the GDPR in 2016 (in full effect since 2018). This regional legislation marked a significant global advancement in empowering individuals by providing a robust legal framework for the control and protection of their personal data and privacy. It has effectively caused research from extended disciplines reaching computer science venues, while also motivating computer scientists to move into the domain of privacy protection. A similar, albeit transitory, effect of GDPR has been reported in [19], who identified four transparency-focused papers in their systematic literature review for 2016, up from one per year in 2014, before returning to the same level by 2020.

4.2 Privacy Engineering Practice Gaps

Our analysis demonstrates that transparency and intervenability – privacy goals enabling individual control – have received meager attention in PETs research. Of the 2920 articles published at three privacy research venues over 22 years (2002–2023), only a handful addressed transparency and intervenability until 2016. This attention gap is not inferred from publication volume alone, because unlinkability draws on substantially larger and more mature research fields than transparency and intervenability. Rather, the identified gap is one of delegation rather than volume: transparency and intervenability are largely addressed within adjacent communities (usable privacy, human-computer interaction, law, etc.), rather than claimed as engineering problems by the self-identified privacy engineering community whose venues we analyse.

Several factors help explain this delegation. Transparency and intervenability fall rather to the more soft categories of engineering, usable privacy, user experience (UX) and social studies, and are more focused on human-computer interaction and questions like whether users really understand the transparency information, which controls do users apply, how to implement features that allow users to have control and know how their data is processed. As such, they have not been perceived to yield good research questions, as their solutions have not needed many technologies (at least not novel, research-worthy ones), while most of the PETS community are computer scientists who tend to focus on the problems they know how to solve. As a result, these topics have not been traditionally prioritized in the computer science-driven PETS community, an effect previously demonstrated by [30] with no significant change visible over the five years after their study. The focus of the community has largely been on technical privacy solutions like anonymity and encryption, with less attention given to the challenges of enabling individual control over personal data. Beyond these disciplinary factors, the gap also reflects a lack of societal demand and research/business interest in these goals, and the considerable complexity of implementing intervenability in particular, which helps to explain why the challenge is seldom accepted in research and practice. This is visible in the market as well: privacy icons and privacy dashboards illustrate the gap, as despite repeated research proposals and design efforts, neither has converged on a widely adopted standard, leaving each deployment to reinvent its own approach.

The same logic applies across venue types. Goals tied to data subject rights of access, rectification and erasure tend to surface where law and human-centered design set their agenda, rather than in the technically oriented venues that the privacy engineering community treats as its own. The fact that these goals are more present in adjacent fora is not a counterargument to the gap we describe, but rather its clearest expression.

The distinction between technical and organizational measures is important in this context. While GDPR refers to "technical and organizational measures,' privacy engineering research has focused predominantly on purely technical solutions. Transparency and intervenability inherently require integration of organizational processes with technical implementations, such as handling data subject access requests, propagating consent preferences through multi-service architectures, and integrating transparency mechanisms into existing workflows.

Privacy is commonly perceived as something passively guaranteed to data subjects. The same effect is evident in the broadly circulated PET overviews that focus on unlinkability [13,24,27], defining a norm that privacy protection is something happening far away from the reach of individuals behind said protection. This highlights the most critical gap in the whole privacy discourse from research to engineering: maintaining the idea of individuals as passive data subjects protected by unlinkability by process owning organizations. This is the result of powerful organizations (private and public), and not data subjects, determining the rules of how the data is accessed and analyzed, mostly to focus on legally clear areas to avoid GDPR fines.

4.3 Limitations

Our analysis has several limitations that should be acknowledged. First, keyword frequency analysis is a shallow proxy for research content: articles may address a privacy goal substantively without using our specific keywords, and conversely, keyword matches may be incidental. We mitigated this through a threshold of ≥ 4 occurrences and manual spot-validation of borderline cases, but false positives and negatives remain possible. However, based on manual validation, we determined, that the ratio is low and the percentages are not greatly affected by the false classifications. Second, our venue selection covers three conferences and excludes journals, workshops, and gray literature. This means we measure the priorities of the academic conference community, not privacy engineering practice at large – a distinction that likely understates the practical adoption of transparency and intervenability mechanisms, which are more often documented in standards, regulatory guidance, and industry reports. Third, the venues selected have historically emphasized technical privacy, which may inflate the apparent dominance of unlinkability. Our argument, however, is precisely that the self-identified privacy research community has underinvested in transparency and intervenability – and the venue selection reflects that community's self-definition. We did not, however, empirically test how venues of differing orientation would compare. Venues with a stronger legal or interdisciplinary focus (including APF itself), where these goals have featured in the past programmes, would likely show greater representation of transparency and intervenability topics. A systematic cross-venue comparison incorporating such fora remains valuable future work.

5 Conclusions and Recommendations

We have highlighted the need for a more balanced approach in PET development that would equally address transparency and intervenability alongside unlinkability. Our analysis demonstrates that these privacy goals have historically been underrepresented in PETs research, with unlinkability receiving the most attention. Transparency and intervenability are viewed as less central to the computer science-driven community, which traditionally prioritizes technical solutions like anonymization and encryption. The recent increase in research addressing transparency and intervenability in response to GDPR and evolving societal expectations shows that there is now a greater recognition of the need for these goals in the context of privacy protection. We recognize that transparency and intervenability are not silver bullets, and broader reconceptualization of privacy is needed. As noted, increased transparency does not automatically produce fairness if structural power imbalances remain, and intervenability with limited or deceptively designed options may entrench rather than challenge those imbalances. The shift from a passive to an active data subject would bring about greater fairness in the digital landscape, but it is not a sufficient condition for meaningful privacy. What engineering can contribute is expanding the space of what is technically possible – making genuine control implementable – while acknowledging that social, legal, and organizational conditions determine whether that control becomes real.

Our findings celebrate the slight shift in PETs research over past several years towards considering transparency and intervenability as problems with technical solutions. Privacy as a domain is also becoming more interdisciplinary. This calls for stakeholders to explore further the potential of these privacy goals in their solutions:

Privacy Engineers in Practice: Develop privacy solutions that go beyond traditional, technical approaches, focusing also on transparency, individual agency and a more user-centered model of privacy. This includes designing solutions that empower individuals, align with legal frameworks, and consider the interdisciplinary nature of privacy protection.

Privacy Engineering Practitioners and Tool Developers: Prioritize developing production-ready, standardized implementations for transparency and intervenability mechanisms that complement existing unlinkability technologies.

Researchers and Programme Committees: We need furthering conceptualizations, multidisciplinary research and development efforts of transparency- and intervenability-enhancing tools to identify and solve the obstacles to their implementation, and take steps towards a holistic notion of privacy, enabling both meaningful regulatory compliance and user empowerment.

Regulators and Enforcement Authorities: Enforcement actions focused specifically on inadequate transparency and intervenability implementations would signal to the engineering community that these goals carry real consequences – comparable to those already associated with data breach and unlinkability failures.

Acknowledgements. This work was supported by the Estonian Research Council (PRG2177 and PSG1228). The views expressed are those of the authors only, not of the funding agencies.

References

1. Acquisti, A., Brandimarte, L., Loewenstein, G.: Privacy and human behavior in the age of information. Science **347**(6221), 509–514 (2015). https://doi.org/10.1126/science.aaa1465
2. Adjerid, I., Acquisti, A., Brandimarte, L., Loewenstein, G.: Sleights of privacy: framing, disclosures, and the limits of transparency. SSRN Electron. J. (2013). https://doi.org/10.2139/ssrn.2186530
3. Cichy, P., Salge, T.O.: The evolution of privacy norms: Mapping 35 years of technology-related privacy discourse, 1980-2014. In: International Conference on Information Systems (Dec 2015). https://publications.rwth-aachen.de/record/568149
4. Danezis, G., et al.: Privacy and data protection by design – from policy to engineering. arXiv preprint arXiv:1501.03726 (2015). http://arxiv.org/abs/1501.03726
5. Deng, M., Wuyts, K., Scandariato, R., Preneel, B., Joosen, W.: A privacy threat analysis framework: Supporting the elicitation and fulfillment of privacy requirements. Requirements Eng. **16**, 3–32 (2011). https://doi.org/10.1007/s00766-010-0115-7
6. Finn, R.L., Wright, D., Friedewald, M.: Seven Types of Privacy, pp. 3–32. Springer Netherlands (2013). https://doi.org/10.1007/978-94-007-5170-5_1
7. Fischer-Hübner, S., Angulo, J., Pulls, T.: How can cloud users be supported in deciding on, tracking and controlling how their data are used? In: Hansen, M., Hoepman, J.H., Leenes, R., Whitehouse, D. (eds.) Privacy and Identity Management for Emerging Services and Technologies, pp. 77–92. Springer, Berlin Heidelberg (2014)

8. Gao, C., Fawaz, K., Sur, S., Banerjee, S.: Privacy protection for audio sensing against multi-microphone adversaries. Proc. Privacy Enhanc. Technol. **2022**(2), 146–165 (2022). https://doi.org/10.2478/popets-2019-0024
9. Hansen, M.: Top 10 mistakes in system design from a privacy perspective and privacy protection goals. In: Camenisch, J., Crispo, B., Fischer-Hübner, S., Leenes, R., Russello, G. (eds.) Privacy and Identity Management for Life, pp. 14–31. Springer, Berlin Heidelberg (2012)
10. Hansen, M., Jensen, M., Rost, M.: Protection goals for privacy engineering. In: IEEE Security and Privacy Workshops, pp. 159–166 (2015). https://doi.org/10.1109/SPW.2015.13
11. Hicks, A.: Design and Usage of Transparency Enhancing Technologies. UCL (University College London) (Dec, Doctoral (2023)
12. Hubaux, J.P., Juels, A.: Privacy Is Dead, Long Live Privacy. Communications of the ACM (Jun 2016). https://cacm.acm.org/opinion/privacy-is-dead-long-live-privacy/
13. Information Commissioner's Office: Chapter 5: Privacy-enhancing technologies (PETs). draft anonymisation, pseudonymisation and privacy enhancing technologies guidance (2022). https://ico.org.uk/media/about-the-ico/consultations/4021464/chapter-5-anonymisation-pets.pdf
14. Kitkowska, A., Wästlund, E., Meyer, J., Martucci, L.A.: Is it harmful? re-examining privacy concerns (2018). https://doi.org/10.5281/zenodo.1297340
15. Meis, R., Heisel, M.: Computer-aided identification and validation of intervenability requirements. Information **8**(1), 30 (2017). https://doi.org/10.3390/info8010030
16. Meis, R., Wirtz, R., Heisel, M.: A taxonomy of requirements for the privacy goal transparency. In: International Conference on Trust, Privacy and Security in Digital Business, pp. 209–223 (Sep 2015). https://doi.org/10.1007/978-3-319-22906-5_15
17. Murmann, P., Fischer-Hübner, S.: Tools for achieving usable ex post transparency: a survey. IEEE Access **5**, 22965–22991 (2017). https://doi.org/10.1109/ACCESS.2017.2765539
18. Murmann, P., Karegar, F.: From design requirements to effective privacy notifications: empowering users of online services to make informed decisions. Int. J. Human-Comput. Interact. **37**(19), 1823–1848 (2021). https://doi.org/10.1080/10447318.2021.1913859
19. Ofem, P., Isong, B., Lugayizi, F.: On the concept of transparency: a systematic literature review. IEEE Access **10**, 89887–89914 (2022). https://doi.org/10.1109/ACCESS.2022.3200487
20. Patrick, A.S., Kenny, S.: From privacy legislation to interface design: Implementing information privacy in human-computer interactions. In: Dingledine, R. (ed.) Privacy Enhancing Technologies Symposium, pp. 107–124. Springer, Berlin Heidelberg (2003)
21. Rost, M., Pfitzmann, A.: Datenschutz-schutzziele - revisited. Datenschutz und Datensicherheit **33**(6), 353–358 (2009)
22. Smith, M., Snyder, P., Haller, M., Livshits, B., Stefan, D., Haddadi, H.: Blocked or broken? automatically detecting when privacy interventions break websites. Proc. Privacy Enhanc. Technol. **2022**(4), 6–23 (2022). https://doi.org/10.56553/popets-2022-0096
23. Spagnuelo, D., Ferreira, A., Lenzini, G.: Accomplishing transparency within the general data protection regulation. In: International Conference on Information Systems Security and Privacy, pp. 114–125. SCITEPRESS (2019). https://doi.org/10.5220/0007366501140125

24. The Royal Society: From privacy to partnership: The role of privacy enhancing technologies in data governance and collaborative analysis (2023). https://royalsociety.org/-/media/policy/projects/privacy-enhancing-technologies/From-Privacy-to-Partnership.pdf
25. Tolsdorf, J., Reinhardt, D., Iacono, L.L.: Employees' privacy perceptions: exploring the dimensionality and antecedents of personal data sensitivity and willingness to disclose. Proc. Privacy Enhanc. Technol. **2022**(2), 68–94 (2022). https://doi.org/10.2478/popets-2022-0036
26. Toth, M., Bielova, N., Roca, V.: On dark patterns and manipulation of website publishers by CMPs. Proc. Privacy Enhanc. Technol. **2022**(3), 478–497 (2022). https://doi.org/10.56553/popets-2022-0082
27. United Nations Committee of Experts on Big Data and Data Science for Official Statistics: United nations guide on privacy-enhancing technologies for official statistics (2023). https://unstats.un.org/bigdata/task-teams/privacy/guide/2023_UN%20PET%20Guide.pdf
28. Whitman, J.Q.: The two western cultures of privacy: Dignity versus liberty. Yale Law J. **113**(6), 1151–1221 (2004). http://www.jstor.org/stable/4135723
29. Zhang, S., Feng, Y., Yao, Y., Cranor, L.F., Sadeh, N.: How usable are iOS app privacy labels? Proc. Privacy Enhanc. Technol. **2022**(4), 204–228 (2022). https://doi.org/10.56553/popets-2022-0106
30. Zibuschka, J., Kurowski, S., Roßnagel, H., Schunck, C.H., Zimmermann, C.: Anonymization Is Dead - Long Live Privacy. Lecture Notes in Informatics, (2019). Open Identity Summit
31. Zwingelberg, H., Hansen, M.: Privacy protection goals and their implications for eID systems. In: Privacy and Identity Management for Life, pp. 245–260. Springer, Berlin, Heidelberg (2012). https://doi.org/10.1007/978-3-642-31668-5_19

Author Index

F. Pallas et al. (Eds.): APF 2026, LNCS 16847, pp. 267–268, 2026.
https://doi.org/10.1007/978-3-032-35899-8

GPSR Compliance
The European Union's (EU) General Product Safety Regulation (GPSR) is a set of rules that requires consumer products to be safe and our obligations to ensure this.

If you have any concerns about our products, you can contact us on

ProductSafety@springernature.com

In case Publisher is established outside the EU, the EU authorized representative is:

Springer Nature Customer Service Center GmbH
Europaplatz 3
69115 Heidelberg, Germany

www.ingramcontent.com/pod-product-compliance
Ingram Content Group UK Ltd.
Pitfield, Milton Keynes, MK11 3LW, UK
UKHW022109180926
475695UK00001B/64

* 9 7 8 3 0 3 2 3 5 8 9 8 1 *